Obscure in the Shade of the Giants

Publishing Lives Volume II

Books by Jerome Gold

Fiction

Sergeant Dickinson (originally titled
The Negligence of Death)
The Prisoner's Son
The Inquisitor
Of Great Spaces (with Les Galloway)

Poetry/Fiction

Prisoners

Nonfiction

Obscure in the Shade of the Giants:
Publishing Lives Volume II
Publishing Lives: Interviews with Independent Book
Publishers in the Pacific Northwest and British Columbia
Hurricanes (editor)

Obscure in the Shade of the Giants

Publishing Lives Volume II

For Nancy,
Jerome Gold

Jerome Gold

Black Heron Press
Post Office Box 95676
Seattle, Washington 98145
www.blackheronpress.com

FOR DAVID, JACK, AND LEAH

ISBN 0-930773-61-6

Grateful acknowledgment is made to the following for the photographs used in this book: Kari Ryder for the photo of Pearl Kilbride; Dee and Chuck Robinson for the photo of themselves; Karen Bodeen for the photo of Jim Bodeen; Kevin White for the photo of Fiona McCrae; Jim Adams for the photo of Vito Perillo; Tom Sweeney and the Minneapolis *Star Tribune* for the photo of Marianne Nora and Lane Stiles; Fran Funk and the *Willimantic Chronicle* for the photo of Alexander Taylor and Judith Doyle; Gail Kump for the photo of Eric Kampmann; Miriam Berkley for the photo of Daniel Simon; Astrid Myers for the photo of Barney Rosset; Clare Smith for the photo of Harry Smith; Mario Luna for the photo of Peter Rosset; Mary Randlett for the photo of Judith Roche; Barbara Martinelli for the photo of Charlie Winton; Milkweed Editions for the photo of Emilie Buchwald; Coffee House Press for the photo of Allan Kornblum; Carin Kuoni for the photo of John Oakes; Joan Harrison for the photo of Bob Harrison.

Black Heron Press
Post Office Box 95676
Seattle, Washington 98145
www.blackheronpress.com

Contents

(Photographs follow page 215)

Introduction

This book came about because I did another, *Publishing Lives: Interviews with Independent Book Publishers in the Pacific Northwest and British Columbia.* The idea for that book came when I found myself caught up in the stories my publishing peers were telling me of their lives, and I decided to abandon the article based on a statistical study that I had originally intended to do. My idea for a statistical study arose when I grew curious about what it was I was doing as a publisher, and what it might mean, and where independent publishing fit in the larger scheme of things.

I spent four years interviewing, transcribing, and editing the interviews that appeared in *Publishing Lives.* Toward the end of this time a friend told me that I had fallen in love with every one of the publishers I had interviewed. But whether it was love or only fascination, I did experience something like a grief reaction, a sense of loss, when the book was finally done.

The subjects of conversation with other publishers included freedom of expression, the roles of the writer and the publisher in society, the risks inherent in publishing imaginative literature (by which I mean fiction, poetry, drama, and essays that use language in uncommon ways) in the United States, the state of corporate publishing, author-publisher relations, and a host of other topics that fall into that area between how-the-world-should-be and how-the-world-is. That four-year period was one of the most stimulating of my life, and when it was over, I wanted to do it again. Instead, I did this book. As indicated by its subtitle, I consider it to be Volume II of *Publishing Lives.* Like Volume I, it concentrates on what brought independent publishers into publishing.

In the first volume, I was concerned with the range of publishing in the Pacific Northwest, the region in which I live. I should point out that although all of the publishers I interviewed for that book resided and had their offices in the Northwest or southwestern Canada, only seven may be considered "regional" in that they did not have wholesaling or distribution arrangements that carried their titles to other parts of North America. With one exception, these publishers were among those operating the smallest presses, in terms of number of titles published per year.

All of the others—the publishers of twenty-four presses—saw their books available throughout their respective countries. A few also had European distribution. Except for the smallest literary presses and those who limit their marketing to a particular geographical area, there are no regional presses.

In Volume I, I included an interview with Tim Lander, a poet-publisher who slept under a bridge most days of the week and who gave away much of his work. I also interviewed Scott McIntyre of Douglas and McIntyre, the largest independent publisher on the West Coast of North America. I interviewed niche publishers, those who publish books appealing to a specific, well-defined segment of the book-buying public. Such books might include ethnic cook books, tabletop books of outdoor photography, or books about women's issues. I interviewed general trade publishers, publishers who produce and sell books in several genres; for example, literary fiction, travel books, books on drug-and-alcohol abuse. And I interviewed publishers, nonprofit and for-profit, who produce literary work—imaginative literature—exclusively.

In *Obscure in the Shade of the Giants*, I have focused primarily on general trade publishers and secondarily on literary and niche publishers. I have restricted the compass of interviews in order to compare publishing across geographic regions. Thus, I interviewed publishers of similar lists in New York, the Twin Cities, and the West. I have deviated from this plan where I found a publisher who distributed or otherwise sold his books in an unusual way.

I did not interview Canadian publishers for this volume. I wanted to explore the variety of ways by which publishers deal with similar problems, and Canadian publishing is different enough from publishing in the United States (owing to the relative ease by which Canadian publishers are able to obtain government funding, and their lack of opportunity to sell subsidiary rights; see the interviews with Canadian publishers in Gold 1996) as to fall outside the boundaries I set for this book.

But of the thirty-five people interviewed in this book, only twenty-six are publishers. In addition, I have included interviews with a novelist and a poet, a sales representative, a wholesaler, three distributors, and the owners of a bookstore. My idea has been to follow the track of a book, through interviews with literary gatekeepers, from its author to its readers. (I did not include electronic publishers or booksellers in this volume; that would take a book in itself.)

It was while transcribing the Barney Rosset interview that I looked at my old Grove Press editions of *Waiting for Godot* and *Endgame* and considered not only how fragile is life, but how perishable is literature. And so I have also tried to elicit some of the ways by which a book may be prevented from reaching its public. It may be the most wonderful book, but it may not be published because the author gets discouraged after a number of rejections, or because he or she cannot find the right publisher for it, or because there is no publisher for it. A book may be printed but trapped in a wholesaler's or distributor's inventory when it files for bankruptcy. A book may not be presented to bookstore buyers, or it may be presented but buyers may not be impressed with it. Buyers may accept a copy or two, but not reorder because it sells too slowly or because they forget. A book may not be promoted by its publisher. It may not sell enough copies, or sell so slowly as not to justify keeping it in print. Or, with a great deal of luck, and an author who promotes himself or herself shamelessly, and a publisher who is passionate about his or her work, it may thrive.

As with the first volume, I have interviewed only independents. That is, I did not interview publishers whose presses are owned by a parent corporation or bookstore owners whose store is one of a chain. There were two exceptions: AK Press, an offshoot of AK Distribution, and Food First, a part of a larger nonprofit corporation. I have included these interviews because of their atypical distribution or marketing arrangements. Another benefit to having interviewed Food First's Peter Rosset was Peter's openness about some of his father's influence on him. Peter is the son of Barney Rosset who is perhaps best known as the man who established Grove Press and thereby was able to bring Samuel Beckett's work to American audiences and get Tropic of Cancer before the Supreme Court. Possibly a third exception is Confluence Press, an independent, but one apparently influenced in its operation by its close association with a college. I included this interview in order to show a type of dependence not seen in presses unconnected to colleges or universities.

SUCCESSION. In Volume I, almost all of the publishers I interviewed were the founders of the presses they ran. For the present volume, I interviewed several publishers who were not founders but who took over presses that were ongoing operations, or, in the case of Grove Press, was moribund when Barney Rosset bought it. More than in the first volume, I have been concerned with the problem of succession. Some of the founders are approaching the age when they want to consider retirement. The question, then, is how to manage the transition. Curbstone Press' Sandy Taylor and Judy Doyle attempted to identify their own successor, with the idea of grooming him or her for the job, but ultimately decided to leave the problem to their board of directors to solve. Milkweed Editions' Emilie Buchwald, on the other hand, is relying on people within Milkweed to take over her roles of business manager and acquisitions editor as she phases herself out. Bruce McPherson intends to sell McPherson and Company. Confluence Press' passage from its founders to James Hepworth and Tanya Gonzalez appears to have gone smoothly, but years after Scott Walker's departure from Graywolf, the press he founded and ran for twenty years, Fiona McCrae, his successor, who had nothing to do with his ouster, still lived in his shadow. (As with independent publishers, succession is a concern of the owners of independent bookstores. See the interview with Chuck and Dee Robinson of Village Books in this volume.)

The fact that publishers are thinking about succession implies that their presses have achieved a certain level of maturity. All of the publishers interviewed for this volume have survived years or decades of running independent presses, and many were seeking to expand or otherwise improve their operations. Simply hanging on was not an issue. Of the twenty-nine presses whose publishers I interviewed for Volume I, seven have since folded or reduced their operations to producing only the occasional book.

DISTRIBUTION. *Obscure in the Shade of the Giants* explores distribution more than Volume I does. As I noted earlier, interviews with the CEOs of three major distributors—Publishers Group West, Consortium, Midpoint Trade Books—and one wholesaler—Pacific Pipeline—are included here (see the glossary for the distinctions between distributors and wholesalers). Most of the publishers I talked with have or have had a distribution arrangement with one or more of these distributors. Other publishers have no distributor at all. Blue Begonia Press relies on the poets it publishes to sell their books at readings and on its own displays at book fairs and trade shows. Malachi McCormick of Stone Street Press sells at book fairs and through his mailing lists. Harry Smith deals directly with wholesalers and uses mailing lists he's compiled over the years. Soho Press distributes its books through a larger company, Farrar Straus Giroux.

Different publishers may make different choices insofar as those choices are available. Juris Jurjevics of Soho, which has a strong fiction list, sought a distribution arrangement with a publisher noted for its own fiction. Emilie Buchwald, on the other hand, chose a distributor among whose clients Milkweed Editions would stand out as different.

Toward the end of my interview with Randall Beek, CEO of Consortium, I commented that if we "look at the different functions of production, marketing, promotion and sales, then what [Random House did in the 1940s and '50s] is what the modern independent press plus its distributor do now.... [W]hat we call the publisher is really the publisher and the distributor together." What I was trying to get at is the nature of the relationship that exists between independent presses and their distributors. Distributors are essentially sales organizations, selling a product (books) that they do not manufacture, but acting as intermediaries between the manufacturers (publishers) and the buyers (bookstores, libraries, wholesalers). "Distributors mimic 'a big publisher with lots of different imprints,'" John Hummell, then of Access Publishers Network, a major distributor, says in a *Publishers Weekly* article. "'[S]mall presses become part of a cohesive presentation'" made to store buyers (Angel 1997: 33). Bob Harrison, a commission sales rep interviewed in this volume, regards Consortium as a publisher because it is his client, just as The Mountaineers and Globe Pequot are. Harrison points out that bookstore buyers define the publisher as the source of the books they buy. If a buyer orders a Graywolf Press title, Harrison passes the order on to Consortium, not to Graywolf.

Eric Kampmann of Midpoint Trade Books sees the role of the independent publisher vis à vis his or her distributor as basically editorial: establishing and maintaining author-editor relationships, coordinating manuscript development, preparing the manuscript for production as a book, and marketing and promoting the book. Sales are the job of the distributor, but in order to facilitate sales, publishers must adhere to industry norms, especially in the areas of jacket and cover design, and here the distributor can advise them. Both Randall Beek and Charlie Winton of PGW see the distributor as being active in decisions on jacket and cover design as well as marketing and promotion. Winton also describes working with some publishers on developing the book's content.

Blurring the line even more between the functions of publisher and distributor is the increasing tendency of distributors to buy small publishing houses. In August 1998, National Book Network, another major distributor, acquired five publishing companies, and by late February 2000, Avalon Publishing Group owned all or part of at least ten companies (see the Charlie Winton interview in this volume; also Milliot 1998, Kinsella 2000a, and Reid 2000).

SUBSIDIARY RIGHTS. In conducting the interviews for this volume, I asked about subsidiary rights sales, specifically the sale or lease of reprint and translation rights. I began with the hypothesis that the closer, geographically, a publisher is to the big houses that buy paperback reprint rights, the more likely one is to sell those rights. I think now that this is not quite true. It seems not to make a difference whether one is in Minneapolis or Seattle; it does pay to be located in or near New York where the largest corporate publishers and other mass media are centered. The sale of translation rights to foreign publishers seems not to depend on where in the United States a publisher is located, despite the fact that most scouts for European firms, at least, are located in New York.

REGIONALISM/NONPROFITS AND FOR-PROFITS. To do the interviews that would go to make up *Obscure in the Shade of the Giants* I traveled to New York, the Twin Cities, and the Bay Area. I conducted all but one interview face to face. The interview with Sandy Taylor and Judy Doyle was done over the telephone.

There is a kind of regional sensibility, even if books are not usually oriented toward a specific region. Landscape and climate aside, each locale comprises its own web of social, commercial, professional, and historical relationships. But these webs are finite, and whom a colleague does not know or has not heard of can be surprising. Names of publishers and others in the industry arose during the interviews. If they were located in the West, I had probably heard of them, but someone in

New York might not have: Bruce McPherson didn't know who Charlie Winton is. If in the East, I might have heard of the press, but not its publisher: I was aware of Station Hill Press, but not of George Quasha.

But, in another way, comparing one region with another presents artificial boundaries. A perusal of Consortium's catalogue, for example, shows that literary, feminist, gay and lesbian presses and others are found throughout the United States. Often enough, publishers of each genre publish the same authors.

The larger—in terms of income—nonprofit publishers are aware of each other regardless of distance separating one from another. Because most of the publishers of nonprofits I interviewed for this volume are located in Minneapolis, the reader may have the sense that they define their region. In a way, they do, because their number is so concentrated. But comparing these interviews with those of the publishers of nonprofit presses in the Northwest (see Gold 1996) or with that of Sandy Taylor and Judy Doyle, it is apparent that in at least one of their major concerns, the nonprofits have more in common with each other, whether they are located in the Northwest, the Midwest, or the East, than they do with other presses. The crucial concern they share is that of obtaining grant money. Donations not only enable a press to continue its operations, but seem also to validate that press' very idea of itself as a publisher of superior work. Grants and individual donations may account for forty percent or more of a nonprofit press' annual income.

The publishers I interviewed in New York all run for-profit presses. They distinguish between themselves and the corporate houses that we in other parts of the country refer to as "New York." The Manhattan independents publish commercial work so that they can finance more significant work. This is what the largest houses did before they took on the corporate ethos, then afterward did it less, then dropped most serious literature, though they insisted that the lighter work they were publishing was important, then gave up the pretense altogether. The nonprofits do not have to publish commercial books. But I think this freedom, if it is that, puts them in a somewhat rarefied atmosphere similar to the one academicians breathe.

If the nonprofits are free to publish noncommercial work, they still may choose to publish what will please their funding agencies. Fiona McCrae, who went from Faber and Faber to Graywolf, compares "having to plead with the marketing department" of Faber, though one of the finest houses in the world in terms of the literary merit of the books it puts out, and the effect this has on acquisitions, with the temptation in a nonprofit to acquire titles that will assure funding. This temptation, and surrendering to it, have been the objects of criticism by publishers of other noncommercial, but non-nonprofit presses (see, for example, the interview with Harald Wyndham in Gold 1996).

(If I raise doubts about nonprofits' dependence on their funders, it is not because I think that serious fiction and poetry can sustain themselves without help. I am convinced that, in the United States, a publisher who puts out only imaginative literature cannot turn a profit. Such a publisher must either find patronage or subsidize his or her own press, as Harald Wyndham of Blue Scarab Press and Harry Smith of The Smith do, and as Anna Johnson of Open Hand Publishing has [Gold 1996]. But few others can afford to do this or are passionate enough about publishing to want to do it.)

Among the New York independents there is a sense of immediacy, a preeminent interest in what is current. At the same time, there is an acute awareness that today's small independent publishers are part of an American publishing tradition extending back two and a half centuries. Their living hero is Barney Rosset. Rosset has shown tremendous personal courage in publishing unconventional works that have challenged the mores and institutions of the country. This, we would like to think, is what great literature has always done, and what great publishers have always helped it to do. Rosset, a model for those who would persevere, remains an unrepentant progressive concerned with the individual's relationship to power, and vice versa.

In the Northwest, two names regularly arose among publishers: Dan Levant of Madrona Publishers and Scott Walker of Graywolf Press which was originally located in Port Townsend, Washington (Gold 1996). Neither has been especially political but both are noted for encouraging other, less experienced publishers. In the Twin Cities, no model or mentor was mentioned by more than a single publisher. Several, as have a few in the Northwest, have been given generous financial assistance and organizational advice by the Lannan Foundation, the National Endowment for the Arts, the Lila Wallace-Readers Digest Foundation, the Andrew W. Mellon Foundation, or by a number of these together, and

18

acknowledge their debt to these institutions. I interviewed only two publishers in California, not enough for me to attempt a generalization about heroes or mentors.

PUBLISHERS AND THEIR PRESSES. In Volume I, I noted the personal identification of independent publishers with their presses. By and large, this holds true for the publishers I interviewed for *Obscure in the Shade of the Giants*. Malachi McCormick says of his relationship with his press: "I am Stone Street. Stone Street is me." Reminiscent of Dan Levant's interchanging the words "Madrona" and "me" (Gold 1996) is Sandy Taylor's expression, "most small presses like ourselves."

As with the first volume, I was struck by the interconnectedness and commonalties of the publishers I interviewed. There is a relationship with Latin America that several publishers enjoy: Bill Truesdale with Mexico via Margaret Randall of El Corno Emplumado, Jim Bodeen with Chile, Sandy Taylor and Judy Doyle with Nicaragua particularly and Central America generally, and Peter Rosset with Mexico, Nicaragua, and Costa Rica. (Indeed, Latin America has significance for some of the publishers interviewed in Volume I also; see the interviews with Margarita Donnelly of Calyx and Catherine Hillenbrand of Real Comet Press.)

Barney Rosset and James Hepworth each named one of their companies Blue Moon, though they have not published the same kinds of books.

Hepworth published books by prisoners through his Blue Moon Press. Jim Bodeen has had a connection with prisons for juvenile offenders through his teaching in an alternative high school in Washington state. Also in Washington, Judith Roche and Robert Gordon have taught in both adult and juvenile prisons, and Tamara Menteer, who interviewed them, has been a counselor in a prison for juveniles and a parole officer and ombudsman in the adult system.

Confluence Press and New Rivers Press are committed to publishing authors' first books. Confluence, Mid-List, and Ruminator Books publish books by midlist writers who, fifteen years ago, would have been published by the major houses. In fact, these three presses plus Curbstone, The Smith, and Milkweed Editions all were started up or, in the case of Milkweed, began a new book division, in response to larger houses' no longer publishing, or publishing fewer of the kinds of books the smaller publishers consider important.

Some presses represent their publishers' social or ideological concerns: in this volume, see the interviews with the AK Press collective, Sandy Taylor and Judy Doyle, Barney Rosset, and Peter Rosset. In Volume I, see those with Margarita Donnelly, Ruth Gundle, Anna Johnson, Brian Lam, Rolf Maurer, Karl Siegler, and Barbara Wilson.

Three of the publishers interviewed for the present volume are writers who have been published by their own presses, but also by other presses. Five were writers who stopped writing, capitulating to the demands of publishing. Seven continue to write despite the demands of publishing.

Five publishers came to book publishing from magazine publishing. Two edited medical journals.

Four came from corporate book publishing. Three of the four currently run for-profit presses.

Six came from letterpress operations. Five of these now operate nonprofit presses.

Three publishers saw military service.

Five of the thirty-five people interviewed in this volume—three publishers, a distributor, and a wholesaler—graduated from Brown University. No other university or college is represented here more than twice.

Five publishers earned Ph.D.s, none from Brown.

THE INTERVIEWS. Except for the interviews with Robert Gordon and Judith Roche, which were done earlier, the interviews in this book were conducted between August 1996 and April 1999. The interviews with Gordon and Roche were intended to be published individually as chapbooks by Black Heron Press. While Roche's was in fact published, the series was abandoned before the Gordon interview could be printed.

I do not vouch for the objective truth of anything said during the interviews. As in the first collection, sentiment and opinion are interwoven with cognition. All conclusions are tentative.

I asked the same questions of every publisher I interviewed, adapting them for suitability with the sales rep, the wholesaler, the distributors, and the booksellers. With the latter categories, I asked additional questions pertaining to the nature of their work. The questions

Judith Roche and Robert Gordon were asked were designed to illuminate the relationship between their personal lives and their writing.

I encouraged interviewees to run with the questions, as Ms. Menteer did with Roche and Gordon. The questions provided a framework, sometimes only a way to get started; the flesh of the interview came from the person interviewed. But often enough I got caught up in the conversation, and there is perhaps more of myself in this book than I might have preferred.

I do not know if I fell in love with anybody I interviewed, but I was fascinated by every one. Doing this book brought its own rewards. There was the discovery with Jim Bodeen, and then with Juris Jurjevics, that we'd been in the army in Viet Nam at around the same time, and in the same part of the country. I enjoyed watching Dan Simon think, and appreciated his thoroughness as he turned his thoughts around and around. I appreciated, too, both his and Jurjevics' insights. I enjoyed joking with John Oakes and with Jim Hepworth and Tanya Gonzalez, and Harry Smith's nostalgia, and Allan Kornblum's, and Sandy Taylor's and Judy Doyle's expression of their quest for social justice, and Bruce McPherson's pronouncements on literature. Listening to Barney Rosset's tales of publishing way back when, I was struck by the obvious pleasure he has taken from his work. At least in retrospect, publishing, for him, appears to have been fun.

In Volume I, I quoted Barbara Wilson to the effect that independent publishers get addicted to the "risk factor" in publishing, and noted both her and Dan Levant's appreciation of the power inherent in it. Perhaps these more than anything else are what make independent publishing so attractive that once you are a part of it, you cannot easily walk away from it. I, at least, cannot imagine any of my peers—those who have survived the book industry's economic volatility or their personal disappointments— leaving it short of death or retirement I thank them all, the seventy-plus people interviewed in both volumes, for their hospitality and for the generosity with which they gave of their time and opened their lives to my view.

NOVELIST AND POET

Robert Ellis Gordon

"I was reckless enough in my twenties to simply go for it; to live without knowing where the next month's rent was coming from. I was able to put up with that then. I was very driven. Absolutely driven."

Robert Gordon was born on May 25, 1954—"Raymond Carver's birthday," he notes—and grew up in Newton, Massachusetts. His father was a salesman, his mother a teacher. His novel, When Bobby Kennedy Was a Moving Man, *won a regional award, the King County Arts Commission Publication Award for Fiction, and was published in 1993. It received laudatory reviews from the* New York Times Book Review, Publishers Weekly, Kirkus Reviews, Booklist, *and the* Philadelphia Inquirer. *Since 1989, Gordon has taught fiction workshops in Washington State prisons. Shortly after this interview was completed, he began teaching at several of Washington's juvenile facilities, as well. He recently completely a collection of nonfiction prison stories. In 1999, having grown dissatisfied with his novel, he asked his publisher to withdraw* When Bobby Kennedy Was a Moving Man *from the market. The book was declared out of print in the latter half of that year.*

The interview was conducted by Tamara Menteer on June 19, 1994 at Gordon's apartment in Seattle's Mountlake district. Ms. Menteer has worked as a parole officer and as a counselor in one of Washington's juvenile facilities. She was later appointed an ombudsman for a civil commitment unit in an adult prison.

So when did you decide you were going to be a writer?

Not until my senior year of college. Which was a year later than it should have been, anyway. I was taking some time off from work with politics. I had written articles, and knew I enjoyed writing, but I was a U.S. history major and sensed I would go into law or public service. I really didn't have a passion in life. I worked as a moving man in college for The Harvard Student Agencies, and as a speech writer for a politician. Then I took this one course in creative writing. And the first story I wrote—the process of writing, well, it just mesmerized me, absolutely mesmerized me. That first story, needless to say, was horrible. But in the six weeks it took to write it, the decision to become a writer was made.

Did your family influence your having political or public service aspirations?

Certainly there was a lot of talk about politics. There still is. I don't know what congressional district Newton belongs to now, but it used to be in the Fourth Congressional District. That was a very interesting district. Father Drinan came out of there. He was a Jesuit priest and an antiwar activist and the former dean of the Boston College law school. But he was enough of an agitator for the pope to ultimately issue an edict telling all priests to get out of politics. Then Drinan was replaced by Barney Frank, who is highly visible today. Michael Dukakis comes from that district. And, of course, it's next door to Tip O'Neil's district, and Tip O'Neil's seat was previously held by Jack Kennedy. There's nothing to compare to it in the state of Washington. The level of political awareness back there is so much higher. It was in the air. The region is very rich with it.

You made a move that was pretty dramatic then.

Yeah, yeah, it was. I think if I'd moved to journalism or towards a more conventional career, with financial security to go with it, that wouldn't have been so dramatic. And certainly I had easier options. At the age of twenty-two I could have become press secretary for the Massachusetts Secretary of State, who appeared, at the time, to be headed for the governorship. And, if I'd stayed in Boston, I would never have had an excuse for not having a job. I was too well connected back there. But I chose a different route. Living in rooming houses, installing mobile homes, working construction, and so forth and so on. Anything that would at least give me the illusion that I wasn't committed to any full-time work, so I could write.

Right. And enjoy constant rejection.

After a while you get inured to it. I was reckless enough in my twenties to simply go for it, to live without knowing where the next month's rent was coming from. I was able to put up with that then. I was very driven. Absolutely driven.

Sounds like you would have been driven in just about any field you would have chosen.

Provided that the emotional commitment was there. I think my own drive is not always healthy. It's an attribute that can be overdeveloped. A sense of obligation isn't simply a matter of virtue; you can hide behind it easily enough. I pay a high emotional price for that. I just turned forty in May, and I think, I hope, I'm reaching a point where I'm going to be a little less driven and a little less single-minded. A little less lopsided. For me, the writing was a mission. And it's been my sole mission for many years. Then I stumbled into the prison teaching in '88.

Let's back up before you talk further about the prisons project. You said that you decided to make a change as a senior in college?

Yeah.

Where were you attending?

I was at Harvard.

Then somehow you ended up at the Iowa Writer's Workshop?

I was frightened of just going off on my own to be a writer. I didn't...I hadn't been literary. I didn't know what it meant to be with literary people. And I wasn't very good. I didn't have much control of the language, or of anything, really. I just knew I wanted to do this. This mesmerizing work. So I thought it would be very nice to be in a graduate program where I would not feel so isolated. And I applied to about six schools. And happily got into only the state schools, since those were the only ones I could afford. And I went to Iowa. Which was good. Not so much because of the teachers. Iowa was still preeminent then and attracted any number of famous writers. Some of them were good teachers. Some of them were not. There's no real correlation between the ability to wield the language and the ability to teach it. The caliber of students was very high. And they were also, but not always, quite humble about their work. Most of them knew quite well how incredibly difficult this path was and how unlikely it would be that they would be able to make a career of it. And so they were far more humble than the few writers I encountered at Harvard [laughs]...who were perhaps born arrogant. But to get back to the Iowa students, they're the ones who take you seriously. Those are the people you'd sit around the bars with, and sit around the cafes with—the ones who take your work seriously. Whereas the famous writers, who are there for six months simply to do their job, teach. But most don't take you that seriously, and maybe they shouldn't. That may not be appropriate. We were very much their apprentices.

So I went to Iowa for two years, I lived in a rooming house, I worked as a piano mover, and I worked the final summer for a speed framer named Chainsaw Hanson. He'd sight down a wall, and if a stud was out of line, he'd knock it out with a chainsaw. And I should have known something was up when I learned he hired only ex-convicts—and me. It was, I see now, a portent. Then I bought my first car, which was a '63 Chevy Impala with three on the tree, and I had to beg to get out of the state. You see, the way they got rid of old cars in Iowa was to refuse to permit old junkers to pass inspection. So there was my junker at the inspection station, and they were refusing to pass it. And I just promised them that if they would only give me a passing mark, I would leave the state immediately. Which I did. And I drove out here. [Laughs.]

How did you pick Washington? Did you have a purpose here, or was it just the end of the land mass?
Not really. I knew a few people around the country. I knew I did not want to go back to the cocoon. It was more than a cocoon. There was a lot of family pathology that I had not even begun.... I'd been reacting to it for a long time, but I couldn't acknowledge that I wasn't ready to deal with it. But my instincts said, "It's perilous. Don't go back there." In 1980, Weyerhaeuser ran very lovely ads of the Pacific Northwest. And they always showed pictures of mountains and the ocean, and I thought, "Mountains and ocean, how nice." There was no teacher I wanted to be with.

How old were you then?
Oh, I must have been twenty-four.

And you moved to Seattle?
Yeah. I moved into a rooming house in Seattle. I worked con-

struction. I had spent one summer here. I'd taken a semester off from graduate school here, so I guess I did know a few people and had liked it here. So I did my graduate work in two and a half years, then came back. And I worked construction and did odd jobs, just to survive. It's just the classic writer's story. For many years I did that. But very much on the margin. And I played soccer for a team that was sponsored by a moving company, and I got a job with that company and I still work for them. The people I started with now own a couple of companies, actually. And during the '80s I moved to Port Townsend, twice. I went back and forth. So I spent about half the '80s in Port Townsend. Got married in '90 and divorced March '92.

Any kids?
No. Then I came back here when I left my wife. I came back August 1992. It was a very short marriage. A couple of bruised adults.

Magnetically drawn to each other.
We fell in love right after I had this pneumonia that really scared me. It frightened me. I had been too isolated and much too work-oriented. Here was this chance to be with this kind, stable person who felt safe.

You seem reluctant to talk about your marriage. Is divorce a source of shame in your family? Are you Catholic?
No, I'm Jewish, so I'm forever guilty.

Was your family against divorce? Some families say they're against divorce, but everyone in the family is divorced.
No. Actually, I think I'm the only one who has been divorced.

So that would be wrong in your family.
Right. In my family we get married and stay married. [Laughs.] Sometimes we wonder why. Not always.

In your college years and in your youth, retrospectively, how do you think you were influenced by other writers?
I would tend to fall in love with an author. I'll tell you a nice story. When I was twelve, somebody introduced me to Tolkien. I was walking

along the beach carrying *The Fellowship of the Ring*, and this big guy came running up, and I didn't know why, and I was frightened. He said, "Is that the first time you've read that book?" And I said, "Yes," and he said, "I envy you." I envy you. It was a lovely thing to say. Through the years, I've encountered different authors who speak to me at a certain time, like music. I will read them over and over, like I will listen to music over and over. And I've stayed constant with them. It's a very eclectic collection. People like Grace Paley, Raymond Carver, for a period. I haven't looked at him for many years. Michael Herr. Tolkien I go back to. I'm trying to think of people who really gave me direction. Lynda Barry is a wonderful storyteller. A very important storyteller. More important than she is given credit for being now, but ultimately she will be. I have been told I am an Americanist, and I guess that's true. I think the people I fall in love with tend to have really strong voices. Grace Paley, Isaac Bashevis Singer. During the great minimalist period of the '70s and '80s I stopped reading *The New Yorker*. I really was looking for an infusion of the tale teller's stories. And when I encountered a writer who was a tale teller, I would prick up my ears. I'd listen to the stories. That's when I really paid attention. One of the problems I've had with contemporary American literature has been my sense that the storyteller is so detached. So much of writing has become a very dry, intellectual endeavor.

In your book, there's a really strong voice that parallels what you're saying. Well, there are actually two: the author's voice and—
The rogue, Stanley V. Higgins. I had a student at Twin Rivers [a penitentiary in Washington state] who was on loan from Colorado. This was back when Washington had too much cell space. He was a very, very intense fellow. A good writer. He was transferred or shipped back to Colorado and managed to publish an article about the difficulty of writing in prison, and told me, "I'm going to pay for this." And then I got a letter saying he was going to be transferred to a psychiatric facility where he would not have access to pencils or paper, writing implements. This was his passion. And I've never heard from him again. So I made my narrator Stanley V. Higgins. I have no idea what became of him. None. Zero. He was doing hard time and long time, and I don't think he's ever going to get out. I don't know what he was in for, but certainly something

heinous. I remember that on only my second day of teaching in the prisons, I asked Stan, this intense guy, "How do you survive?" And he said, "Well, I used to survive by planning my next escape, but now I do it by writing." And he brought that same intensity to his work. They took that from him; his work. So that's why I named my narrator Stanley V. Higgins.

That's a good story.
It's a sad story.

In your book, you make reference to family dynamics. How does that play into your life?
That's true. When I embarked on the book, about a third of the way through, I thought, "At last I've emancipated myself from autobiographically based writing." And about halfway through, I began to look at some of the emerging patterns and realized I had simply found a metaphorical vehicle—the Kennedys. Certainly there was a fractured relationship, in Bobby's case, between father and son—in the sense that he could never meet his father's expectations. There was...oh boy. Could you ask a more specific question?

How was your relationship with your dad?
Uncomfortable sometimes, but loving. Maybe I'd better get back to the Kennedys. I think there was a lot of love there, and a lot of pressure there, and there was a lot of anger. Rose Kennedy was long-suffering, obviously, but made some kind of a deal, because she put up with it. And the children were able to, apparently, frequently work stuff out in surprisingly positive ways. Which is to say, through active engagement. Bobby Kennedy, to me, is the most attractive of the lot, because he was clearly the most anguished. And of the males, he was clearly the most decent. At the end of his life, especially, he seemed to have the best sense of who he was, and understood, among other things, that he wasn't ever going to be able, personally, to put it all together, to be fully integrated, as they say nowadays. He wasn't destined to be happy. He had his demons. And those demons drove him relentlessly. He made his brother president. He was one determined, driven, fellow. He tried to live up to his father's expectations, he tried everything possible. He reinvented himself, became a tough guy, when apparently he was really the sweetest, nicest of the male

Kennedy children.

And then, the final six years of his life, I believe his spiritual life was very much on the ascendant. He knew what to do with it, which was not to indulge it. Not to play with it, but to put it to service. For others. And I think something, much of this, really, came through publicly, in brief moments. The day of the California primary, he also won in South Dakota. All the Indians on the reservations came out to vote for him. He was delighted by that. That day, in California, he had a ninety-percent turnout among Chicano populations in L.A. It's never happened before or since. He was the second choice of the McCarthy voters, he was the second choice of the George Wallace voters. He was the most transcendant political figure of our time. Absolutely. And something was coming through besides policy. It wasn't simply because of the policies he espoused. Yes, he was competent; he was extremely competent. But something visceral was coming through to people. Something about his vulnerability, his ability to be both vulnerable and tough. All of that.

How this ties to my family, I'm not sure [laughs]. Certainly I revere the memory of Bobby Kennedy; he became a very attractive figure to me. I know, it's a hell of a thing I did to him in this book, but I revere his memory. I've yet to encounter his likeness in public life, at least not among national figures. We encounter people all the time who carry their pain with them and who bring many gifts from their families, and many demons from their families, and somehow put them all to work. Turning back to my family, I was given many gifts, certainly much in the way of privilege—I went to Harvard, for Christ's sake [laughs softly]...

Was that paid for? A scholarship?
The first two years were paid for.

Mm. That's a gift.
Yeah, that's a gift. The next two years I paid off with the Iowa loan. The Iowa loan I paid off with construction work. Whatever it was, it didn't cost so much back then. But, yeah, it was a gift. And there was music; there were piano lessons, we never missed a meal, we never wanted for anything. There were certain emphases on education. From the outside, what you would expect from a solid, upper-middle-class Jewish family in the Boston area. And that's a lot. In the prisons, I work with

the autobiographically based story. People survive incredible battles. And I had a cushion, there's no doubt about it. That's the good stuff. But it was a complex family. Alcohol abuse exacerbated the situation. Regardless of the specifics, you don't get to the bottom of this stuff. Ever. And a lot of it feeds our work, too. You draw from it.

Is that why you enjoy the prisons program? There is certainly some therapeutic aspect to it.

For me, yes, certainly. But I don't know why. There are just some things you don't question, like why you write, why you fall in love, why you go teach a class in a prison. It's the same when I'm writing a book. I don't sit down and say, "I'm going to write about conflicts and family history." I just write the story. And then think about it later. Maybe. Or let others do the thinking. In prison, I feel very, very safe when the classroom door closes and I am alone with my students. It is emotionally the safest place I know. I don't know why. I'm not safe when I'm dealing with the bureaucrats. I feel uncomfortable; I don't like it. When I'm alone with my students, it's just fine. It's just wonderful. It's very gratifying, teaching them.

How did you get involved with that?

Stumbled into it. I had done a bit of teaching here and there. Jim Heynen brought me to Centrum in '86. In '87 I got into the Artists-in-Residence program, and I stayed. At that point, they had vast sums of money. You'd get paid a hundred dollars per day, plus a per diem which at that time was thirty-five dollars. It was a vast sum of money compared to what I'd been making. And then I was asked to teach at Twin Rivers. And I was petrified. Curious, but petrified. But I couldn't turn down work at that time. I taught, and I loved it. It took me about three days to settle in. Maybe just two. I keep it in mind, whenever I have guests in the classroom, to find the most mature, the most trustworthy student to be their escort. It's a big memory, the terror I felt, coming into that institution for the first time. It's actually a very, very safe place. Obviously the streets of Seattle are much more dangerous for us than the prisons. And then I went on to do many, many residencies all over the state. Between March and June of this year, I spent two and a half months inside. That's a lot. Four to six hours a day in class, five days a week, over the course of six months. All with the same students.

Oh, that's wonderful. I'd love four to six hours of daily class time.
It's very, very intense.

So you're really establishing solid relationships there.
Oh, yeah. By the second week, we're on a different planet. People come to visit, but they can't fathom where we are.

It must have been really intimidating to try to develop a course plan that was going to cover four to six hours.
Easy. Easy. Because once you get going, the students' writing is the course. As is the case with any graduate-level workshop. The students look at one another's work and the teacher facilitates the discussion. And that is the substance of the course. I may bring in an author here and an author there, to read from. A trick of the trade here, a trick of the trade there. But basically the course is the students' own stories, which makes it more intense yet. They go home every night with a big stack of stories to read, and then discuss them the next day. And it's pretty amazing, the amount of ground they cover.

Is that the same format you're going to use for the juvenile facilities?
I would if they'd give me time, but they're not going to. They're breaking it up into smaller classes, so I can't.

It'd be harder, with their attention spans.
Yeah. Actually, for the first time in a while, I'm pedagogically insecure. Which is probably—

Wise [laughs].
Probably not a bad thing. But everybody has the age group that they have a hard time with. Now I have no problems with adult felons. Sometimes it's just wonderful to go on an outward-bound of the soul with people who maybe just sold drugs or maybe did something quite heinous. Regardless, they've made a decision, just by coming to the workshop, to at least look at a different way to be. And it's nice to be there when they're

34

thirty or thirty-five and deciding to change.

Is that the general age you work with?

I'd say twenty-five to thirty-five. I'm not getting the twenty-two-year-olds.

It's kind of a rule of thumb that when they get close to forty, they burn out.

Yeah, I've come to figure that out intuitively. I'll hear about someone's infractions early in his sentence, but by the time I see him he's just an angel in class. And not only in class: He seems to emanate grace at all times. And someone says, "Well, you should have seen him when he was twenty." I respond, "Well, I didn't see him when he was twenty, I see him now." The transformation is extraordinary. But I find the most depressing group to be very troubled adolescents, because it's my sense that, in most cases, they're going to do what they're going to do. And there's very little in the way of interventions that is going to stop them. That makes it harder for me.

That's interesting, because that's just the opposite of how I feel. Having worked with both age groups, it seems to me that the adults are the ones that are the more entrenched, whereas the juveniles still see hope and light at the end of the tunnel. They're still looking, they're still ripe for something to happen.

I hope you're right. I guess I got that sense from teaching at a couple of alternative schools where they just—

And the other issue is what it triggers in you. It may be so uncomfortable because of your own history. How did you get involved in the juvenile program?

They'd heard about my prison work, and there's a big NEA [National Endowment for the Arts] grant involving a writer, a visual artist, and a musician...several artists, anyway.

So they solicited you.

They solicited me, yeah. It is flattering and I was quite reluctant.

I have two more questions. Did you have a hero as a child?

Bobby Kennedy.

How old were you when you chose him?

Fourteen. When he was assassinated. "Hero" doesn't do it justice. He haunted my memories. From the time he was assassinated to the
day I put that manuscript in the mail to an agent, I would have these big
mythic dreams. I've had very few since the book came out. I don't even
know if hero is the right word. Icon. I think one of the advantages of
growing up in a culture where, for most of us, there is no cohesive spiritual
system is that we get to choose our icons. That is not a conscious decision.
It may be Ken Griffey, Jr., or Mother Teresa. It can be anyone, because
when gods and goddesses aren't here for us, humans can take on those
attributes, assume mythic proportions. That's what happened. When I was
fourteen, in 1968, the country was falling apart. And my own family was
falling apart, and my own neighborhood was falling apart, and my community was falling apart. From a writer's perspective, that's a wonderful
juxtaposition—is that the right word? Where the interior world and the
exterior, political world intersect. Yeah. The floor falls out. All over. And
this was during my adolescence, of course. I went to a very rough and tough
junior high on the wrong side of the tracks, I was the wrong religion, and
so forth and so on. It was fine, I survived, but it made those years extremely
piercing—maybe this gets back to your question about working with
adolescents. Those were extremely painful years for me. But I was alive.
I was alive like I've rarely been since. And out of this—Bobby Kennedy.

How about now? Do you have heroes now?

There are people I admire, and they aren't usually very famous.
There's a poet in Yakima named Jim Bodeen, who was losing about
twenty-five percent of his kids every year. He teaches at Davis High
School. It's a very tough school on the wrong side of the tracks in
Yakima, and the kids he was losing were working in the fields. So he
went out and spent three years working in the asparagus fields on weekends, and he and these kids came out with this wonderful book called *The
Asparagus.* Terrific poems. But it's not just that, not just that he did a
good deed. Sometimes people do good deeds and they're real jerks. In
fact, they're insufferable. This is not the case with Bodeen, and I don't
know him that well, but I look at him and I feel, well, he teaches. He says

without saying, by example, without insisting that this is the way to be, and this is what's important, and this isn't what's important. He inspires without trying, just by being himself.

The writer, David Lee, is very important to me. I only met him once. But he gave me an answer to a question about how he got started, and I could see so much integrity [in him]. Then Ernie Brown at Twin Rivers taught me a lot about how to be. And many of my students—I look at them, and.... I wasn't in Viet Nam; this is as close as I'm ever going to come to seeing people in the worst of situations, the most difficult of circumstances, which don't end. And those who emanate grace are very, very good. They teach me constantly. They keep me humble.

And then different people teach different things. Judith Roche has been one of my teachers. When you really know someone well, and you're really close friends, it's hard to look at them and say, "You're my hero," but they teach. In some way. Sharon Doubiago is a very important teacher. Linda Waterfall. If there's a quality that each one of these people possesses, it seems to be integrity. About the way they work, and about the way they live. It is wonderful, humbling, to be around such people.

Judith Roche

"Another language beyond the words... I think it's what I'm getting at. It's close to the archetypal ideal about an ur-language, that is no language, the universal language beyond all languages. To me, it's the language that is coming through the language I am using... Something you can't really say. And you can't do it on purpose. You work so hard, and you work so long at it, and something starts to happen, it starts to fall into place. It's like this other music that is beyond the melody that is coming through."

Judith Roche has published two books of poetry, Myrrh/My Life as a Screamer *and* Ghosts. *Her poems have appeared in such journals and anthologies as* Yellow Silk, Gathering of Poets, Central American Women's Poetry for Peace, Dalmo'ma Anthology, The American Voice, Willow Springs, Poets. Painters. Composers., Backbone, Contact II, Permafrost, *and others. She has taught in the University of Washington Extension Program and at Antioch Seattle and participates in the Washington State Artists in Residence Program in prisons and schools. Grants and awards have come from the King County Arts Commission, the Seattle Arts Commission, PEN, the Allied Arts Foundation, and Artist Trust. She has collaborated on two public art installations, with visual artists Claudia Fitch and Maggie Smith. She has been the Literary Arts Director for Bumbershoot in Seattle since 1986. In 1999 she and co-editor Meg McHutchison won the American Book Award for their anthology* First Fish: Salmon Tales of the North Pacific.

Tamara Menteer interviewed Roche at her home in Seattle's Leschi district on a soft, rainy Saturday afternoon in early October 1995.

Could you give me some background as to where you were born, et cetera?

Sure. I was born in Detroit and grew up in Detroit. Didn't leave until I went to college, and then I didn't go very far away. I went to Eastern Michigan University, which is in the shadow of Ann Arbor, so in the shadow of the University of Michigan. I studied literature. I became a high school teacher with the idea of teaching poetry, with the idea of talking about poetry to kids, because I didn't know what else to do then [laughs softly]. But I wrote constantly, and since it seemed presumptuous that I would be a poet, I thought I should *teach* poems. But eventually poetry took over my life.

When you went to college you got a Bachelor's Degree?
Yeah. I got a B.A. in lit. and a teaching certificate. I was married. I had my daughter by that time. It took me a couple of years longer to get through those four years because I had a baby. So I started teaching in a suburb of Detroit. Then we moved out here, to Anacortes, Washington. I wrote up and down the coast for a teaching job. It was 1968, the world was getting wild. And I ended up in Anacortes and taught high school English there, which I really did enjoy.

It's a beautiful town.
It was really beautiful. I was really young and extremely passionate about literature. The kids just loved me, because I was young and passionate, as were they.

You were still married when you came out here and got this job?
Yeah. He came and got a job as an airline pilot. His dream job. But then the marriage started to get bad. I went to Reed College for the summer, and it got really bad. The short of it is, we limped along for another few years and had Robin at a time when we should have broken up instead, and Robin was kind of broken and we couldn't fix him, so we didn't separate for another two years.

When did the transition take place between teaching full time and defining yourself as a poet?
After the divorce, I came to Seattle with my two kids. One of the reasons being—well, first, I wanted to be in the city, but primarily I needed more educational opportunities for Robin.

Robin is here. He's at the table doing some writing work.
Right. Banging his papers on the table [laughs].

I have a roommate who has a two-year-old with Down's Syndrome.

Oh! How lovely! How fortunate. Oh, how wonderful!

Yeah. She's just a doll. So sweet.

Oh, God. Down's parents are so gifted. They don't always know it, but it is such a gift. Such a teacher to us.

So you moved.

It was a dramatic thing when I came to owning who I was, and who I am. In the mid-70s I had an Alaska boyfriend who helped me work on this house. He suggested I come up to Alaska and work on the pipeline. So I arranged that the kids stay with their father, and I went. I'd go up and spend several months doing that. I'd been substitute teaching here in Seattle because there was a big teacher glut and I couldn't get a teaching job. I was trying to take care of both kids on very spotty work. It was kind of grim. And trying to get a proper educational program for Robin, and for Tari who was an extremely bright young girl. So anyway, I went to Alaska and I'd stay for a few months and work, then I'd come home and do my kids intensively for a few months, then I'd go back for three or four months. Once I stayed five months, which was a huge amount of time away from my kids. That went on for a couple of years.

What did you do up there?

I worked on the pipeline. I built pipelines. I was a union laborer. I got tons of money for that short time and had incredible life experiences. It was a true American boom story. Boomtown America. It was historical. You felt like you were part of some kind of moving force of history. An incredible experience for me, basically a middle-class white girl, just to be working in that environment, all those people. It was an amazing, exciting time for me. I really loved it. When I came home, I couldn't teach anymore. I just couldn't go back into the kind of structure that teaching is. The ordered, regulated life of it. And also when I came back, I knew I was a poet. I knew that that was an extreme priority for me.

Do you think working a job that forced you to push yourself physically beyond the limits that you knew was an influence?

That was part of it. The other part was that the land just broke me open.

Oh! And that is so clear in your poetry!

Yeah. The land—it had this capacity to just break me open, and once I was broken open, it was a different me. And, I like to think, the truer me. And it freed me. Well, you know, once you're free, there are different responsibilities. I still had to provide a home for my children, all those things. I couldn't go back to a regular job, so I continued being a union laborer. Here in Seattle. It was wonderful. I loved the physicality of it, and I loved the seasonal work. I could work three months, get laid off, there would be enough money, I could write. Do my kids. Write. Study. It was very freeing for a while.

That's great. A great story of you. What kind of labor were you doing?

I helped build Denny Creek Bridge on top of Snoqualmie Pass. I managed to crawl through most of the storm sewer pipes of Mercer Island at one time or another.

[Laughs.] The true underground tour of Seattle.

Yeah, I kept trying to write sewer poems [both women are laughing] but they didn't come, so I determined they really weren't in me. Yeah, it was thirty-six-inch pipe and it was a new storm-sewer system and we were sealing leaks. I found I wasn't particularly claustrophobic. So I did that for a while and it paid for this house. It took care of my living and kept me really physically active. And that is a good thing for writing. When your other work is extremely physical, then you can be cerebral in the writing. It frees you in a certain way. So I guess a whole lot of what I've done is to try and search out ways to free myself so I can write. And part of that has been doing nontraditional work for a woman. Especially an educated woman. Just that I'm doing something unexpected is freeing. There's an adventuresome quality to it. That's freeing. That was pretty necessary for me, for all the little wild heart poems that come and go.

It sounds like you were very young when you fell in love with literature.

Oh, I was. Yeah. I was completely in love with literature when I was really young. The stories my grandmother read to us. My mother read to us all the time too, but my grandmother read to us more. She had more time. From the time I could write, I wrote little stories, little poems. My mother says my first poem, when I was three, was about a little girl living on the railroad tracks. I don't know where that came from. When I started to read, I read everything. Mostly I read poems, nineteenth-century poets. Because that's what we had around. I got deeply immersed in Longfellow and those long narrative story-poems. It was so romantic. Poe. Poe and all those dead girls! [Laughs.] So romantic. Keats. Shelley. We had the classics in the house.

Were your parents influential at all?

Oh, yeah, yeah, yeah. My parents were old-style leftists. Socialists. They were really active in politics and the union movement in Detroit. I grew up marching in picket lines and such things. Both parents abandoned that later when they got busy with three girls—I'm the oldest of the three—but that was a legacy I took to heart. And though I've tried a lot of political poems, my poems don't seem to be specifically political. But I think there is an underlying deep structure that comes from that influence of my parents.

My father was a court clerk and bailiff. My mother had various jobs, but she didn't have a real career. She worked for the county doing taxes and various kinds of accounting things. She was a serious reader though. I think it was she who gave me the love of literature. And the stories that were part of my family and part of my whole life. Myth and story. The books my grandmother read me were important, but the myth material my mother told me, as if the characters were real people, family members, was probably more important, really.

In her introduction to Myrrh, *Sharon Doubiago says that a person's soul hears its name and plays out the story heard in the sound.*
I love that.

How do you think it applies to Judith? When you talk about myth and the little girl you were, I think of you somehow getting the message

42

that you lived in Camelot.

Uh huh. I lived in my imagination a lot. I was an extremely romantic child. I was always playing out these stories to myself and with myself. Judith—I like that story, but I've never written anything about it. Judith, of course, is the heroine, the Jewish heroine who slays the evil leader of the army that is oppressing the people. She does it wonderfully, by seducing him. She gets him drunk, takes him to bed, and in his post-coital slumber, cuts off his head.

I like that story, too!
Yeah. Comes out holding his head by the long hair.

Kind of the Sharon Stone of the Jewish mythological world.
Yeah, I like it a lot. But I've not closely identified with it. Sometimes I've had that Judith in me, but it has not been one of my major myths by any means. I'm steeped in Western myth. My myth, internal structure, is not terribly multicultural. Celtic myth. I come from Celtic people. Rhiannon, the horse goddess, the Arthurian stories, Greek myth, of course. And Myrrah is another one I have an uneasy connection to.

Why uneasy?
Myrrah took me over in some way. But I came to *Myrrh* through H.D. Myrrh is a major symbol in H.D.'s trilogy. I went to graduate school after *Ghosts*, by the way. After *Ghosts*, I figured I was going to write another *Ghosts* or I was going to do something to up the ante, push me further. Put me in a different place. So I went to graduate school, late. And went to San Francisco, and did all that. I looked around and thought to myself: Who is the most important poet to me? I was doing this late in life and figured I'd better get what I want. And Diane DiPrima had been the most influential contemporary person alive to me at that point. So I searched out Diane and found out she was teaching with Robert Duncan, which was too much, the two of them together. So I went to New College and studied with Diane and Robert. I'm still closely connected to Robert Duncan's work, as well as to Diane's. By this time, Tari is in college and Robin can live with his father. So it worked out. I did happen to be married at the time, and that was a little more difficult.

What happened to that relationship?

It ended. When I published a shortened version of my thesis on H.D.—which was still eighty pages—in *Line Magazine* out of Simon Frazer University, I remember telling somebody, "I paid a perfectly good marriage for this piece." It was a culmination of two years of work and three years of serious immersion into H.D. I recommend that, by the way, a serious immersion into one poet. It's not that I write like H.D. now. I don't. But a serious immersion in one person, I think, is extremely valuable in terms of knowing who you are and structuring your own work.

Why is that?

I think some of it is similar to what I said about physical work and creative work, in that immersing yourself in another person's work is so different from your own, even though you've chosen someone whose work is similar to your own. You get to the differences and you get more to who you are, just swimming in something deep. I think it's a good thing for us creatively and intellectually. And also, I think, writing critical work, doing literary criticism, is really good intellectually. It teaches us how to think in a different way.

Did you do that in your Master's program, literary criticism?

Oh, of course. You can't escape it then. But to go back later and search it out, and seriously go into somebody else, that took knowing where I wanted to go. And some of those important decisions that you make, and I think this one was absolutely the right one—they come about intuitively. You just feel like, Oh, that's where I need to go. It is an intuitive thing, and one thing leads to another, and there you are.

But there are huge bridges to cross when you take those steps. Perhaps you didn't think you were walking away from a marriage when you went to grad school, but at some level there was a risk.

Oh, yeah. And when you take a risk, you don't always win. But, actually, I think I did win. I think I got what I needed. What I needed from work as well as personally.

Your work, for me, is so subliminal. There is such an undercur-

rent of expression hitting me that is not the language itself. There is another language, almost, beyond words.

I like that. Another language beyond the words. Because I think it's what I'm getting at. It's close to the archetypal ideal about an ur-language that is no language, the universal language beyond all languages. To me, it's the language that is coming through the language I am using. The language that I'm using is the language I've been given. We're working in English here and so we're manipulating the words and the phonemes and the sounds, but it's like something else is coming through. Something you can't really say. And you can't do it on purpose. You work so hard and you work so long at it, and something starts to happen, it starts to fall into place. It's like this other music that is beyond the melody that is coming through. Pound says, "Follow the tone leading of vowels." And nobody knows what that means, but I try to do it. So it's working with sounds, trying to tease this other thing to come out, allow it to come out, to set it up so the sound—it's almost making magic. I mean, you're using sounds, sounds. To say the right chant. And something magical happens.

I've read the book [Myrrh/My Life as a Screamer] *several times. I read it again before this interview. The writing hits me much deeper than intellectually. I wanted to tell you that there is a deep movement that goes on for me when I read your work.*

That's what I hope for. Thank you. Good.

I was also intrigued to hear you read [a few weeks before the interview]. It is always so different to hear an author's work, rather than read it. One thing that struck me were the silences. The pieces of silence that you fit into the work. I don't know if this is true, but I conjectured that maybe there was some connection to Robin in that.

That's an interesting thought, but one that's not conscious. Silence, along with sound, is what makes the melody of what we do, and what makes the *melos*. That's interesting. Twenty-four years with a very, very loved, adored child who can neither hear nor speak has got to affect me. It has got to affect my work. I've not written about it consciously, except in two poems. I guess I don't want to write about it very much. But it's interesting. I'm not sure how it affects me, but I know it must. And silence has got to be part of it. And the silence, too, is part of the magic, part of the connection of sounds, vowel and consonant sounds, that we put together. And silence is the something else that allows the other thing to speak through.

Now I wonder, too, about the effect of sign language on my poems, since that's my strongest other language. And I want to lead back to that—the language of the body. I feel like writing is a whole body activity.

I think you connect words in a way that is perhaps done in signing more often than in spoken language.

I don't know about that, but I think I'm going to explore that.

One of the things I identify with in the poetry is, of course, being a woman.

They're very female, aren't they?

They are very female. And I was trying to figure it out: Why are these more female than anything else I've read? I think that what I tie into is this unconscious display of courage in the poetry. There's this understanding of being the underdog, or at least... Some of these words are so political nowadays, you can't...but there is some level of victimization, and yet this willingness to keep trying.

Yeah, or trying differently. Doing something a little different. Yeah. A defiance. Fuck you, I'm doing it anyway, I'll do it a little differently.

And your mother, you had a reference to your mother: "The sound I learned from my mother's song..."

That's my mother, and the sea mother, and the great goddess mother. It's layer upon layer of the great motherness.

"Go for the wildest blue, whether ocean or air..." It's so idealistic.

Well, yeah. And I love the theme in that poem. The persona in that poem says, "I heard each word behind..." That's like the secret message I received from my mother. And I did get that from my mother. It was the secret message. The message beyond the words, which were probably more like "Behave well. Get a good education..."

46

[Laughs.] "Be careful."

Yeah, but there was a wildness in my mother. A wildness and a courage and a great deal of feistiness. And that's what I heard from my mother—"Go for the wildest blue...." Though she didn't mean to pass it on to me the way she did. As I talk to my sisters, of course, I realize we all three got different messages from my mother. We all took what we needed. And the message I got from my mother was very different from the ones my sisters got.

What messages did you get from your dad?

The message I got from my father was that men are delightful and fun to play with, but if you want anything else, such as intellectual conversation, or anything you can count on, go to a woman. My father was charming and delightful and a very good guy and a good husband and an okay father. But I did not get what I wanted. I doubt I ever had a serious conversation with him. But he was great to play with. He played with us while we were young. Once we got older, he didn't know what to do with us. When girls get older, men get a little afraid of them. It was a very female household. Which my father reacted to by being absent a lot. Going out with the guys.

Which is a recurrent theme in your work. There's a lot of leaving.

Yeah, there's a lot of leaving. Lot of leaving.

I think that is a feminine experience.

Lots of guys leaving, lots of women staying.

Exactly. And the encumbrance of what's left over—the houses, the children.

Um hm. But still insisting on freedom within. Taking care of the responsibilities and still having that freedom and adventure. Taking life as an adventure.

The screamer—that experience of just becoming free in the glory of who you are. Overall, I didn't pick up a sense of defiance or a "Fuck you" attitude in the collection.

47

That's not my personality. I'm very nonconfrontational. I'll be like water—find another way. I'm not a confrontational person, so it's not that way in the poems.

I think women prioritize relationship much higher than men do, and so, as a result, even when they're confronting, what they're doing is making an effort to save this high-priority item. What I experience in the implications of the poems is that relationship is an experience of entrapment. Does that ring true for you?

I think it might. I think it's both. Both an entrapment and a thing we want most. What we work so hard to make, we want to *make* love. And making love is making something. It's making *love.* And that's what we want. But there is the entrapment in it, too. It's always that double-edged sword. And so there is this feeling of danger, but then the danger is that you are walking a high wall. It's exhilarating. You could fall either way. The exhilaration is in walking this high wall and not falling into this entrapment of dependence. Entrapment: someone subverting your freedom; dependence: you're subverting your own freedom. And so to walk that wall, that's the exhilarating and freeing thing, and I think there's a lot of edge walking. And that's the emotional place you have to put yourself in. It's that willingness to put yourself in high-risk situations. But the high-risk situation is going to get you something higher. Something wonderful. The other thing about relationship—it is the thing we grow through personally. The thing of working out problems, becoming your better self, through this meshing and pulling with somebody else. Mystics do that with the gods. It's the deep involvement that makes us become our higher selves, and teaches us. And you don't do that without emotional risk.

The other thing I think about with poems you mentioned is the "Desire" poem. The one about living in a state of desire. It's not the fulfillment of desire, it's the desire.

Do you see that impulse to move towards desirability to be a more masculine or more feminine trait?

Well, I'm talking about being in a state of desire. I'm cautious of what's male and what's female. I don't want to be simplistic about this, and I think we've tended to become simplistic about it in the last twenty,

48

thirty years. But I think it is probably more of a feminine trait to want to live in that state of tension.

Do you feel that everything is autobiographical in your poetry?

No, no, no. It's beyond the story of my life. I don't think anyone is interested in that. I'm not particularly interested in telling it. But good writing touches on real emotions, and the real emotions come from your life. The real passion comes from your life, then it moves beyond that and becomes something else. It is something deeper than the story of your life. I'm very bored with the kind of poetry that just assumes that everybody wants to know what my father did and what my mother did. And I also find it, really, not poetry. It has to move beyond that to be a poem.

You said that when you were in Alaska the exposure to the land broke things open for you. When I went through your work last night, I wrote a list of words that are repeated throughout your poetry: mountain, trail, bones, earth, trees, boat, bird, wind, sea, forest, blood, moss, waves, salmon, rock.

It sounds like I'm a Northwest girl! Yeah, it's a deep experience with this material. I've done a lot of salmon fishing. These are all earth things. I've spent a lot of time hiking and living on the earth, really. And I've spent a lot of time on boats. It feeds me. I need to ground myself with the earth and water. That's the angel in me I have to have. And that's the wildness, too. And yet I'm not a Northwest nature poet.

Not at all. In fact, when I'm reading it, I don't get images of the Northwest. The experience I get from it is that I'm pulled down into that earthiness. Earthly experiences are so much of what womanhood is about. Having that strong connection with earth.

Yes, that groundedness.

I guess what we haven't discussed is where you're going next.

Wherever the muse takes me. I don't know. I know there's been a switch again, after *Myrrh*. The voice that is emerging is a little different from the *Myrrh* voice. It's a little more playful and yet there's an awful lot of hard stuff. A little more wry, but also touching deep. It's about grief. And yet the voice has found a little more playful place to touch that grief.

It's part of maturity, I think. So I feel the work is maturing. I like what is happening to the poems. I'm not a prolific writer. I write slowly and I rewrite and rewrite a lot. I don't think I ever said, until thirty seconds ago, that it's all about grief. But there has been a lot of grief. So we'll see what it does.

It's necessary to not get discouraged. To believe the poems are there and they will come in their own time. They tend to come slowly to me. The good pieces do. The real poems don't come very often. But I keep writing, and they come. They come. Robin's and Tari's father, who was sick a long time, died recently. I'd been working on a poem for months. I had the beginning, which was, "At the end, someone will come and tell you a story so beautiful, you will rise out of yourself and go into it. It will be your own story, told true..."

We knew he was dying, and I had that beginning for a long time and I couldn't get anywhere with it. It just wouldn't happen. Then he died September 7th, and the 8th I sat down and wrote it out. It just came. I'm so pleased with that poem, and it's probably the poem I'm proudest of now, and probably the most deeply felt. So there's a little story of how I write. It really wouldn't come until it was ready.

PUBLISHERS

Jim Bodeen
Blue Begonia Press

"Poetry is what it's about. The press is in the service of poetry. It's great to be part of this press, but it only exists for the poem."

I talked with Jim Bodeen in mid-afternoon of the last Saturday of August 1996. We sat on a brick planter just west of Seattle Center's Exhibition Hall. It was Labor Day weekend, which meant it was the weekend of Bumbershoot, Seattle's annual arts festival. We were taking a break from manning our tables at the small press fair inside the hall. Outside it was cloudy and the air was a little cool and I, at least, began to feel refreshed.

Bodeen was born on April 9, 1945, what he calls a "swing date." It was the day the United States dropped the atomic bomb on Nagasaki, three days after dropping it on Hiroshima. He spent his first ten years in Bowbells, North Dakota, a small town on the Canadian border where his father operated a grain elevator, then moved to Seattle. He graduated in history from Central Washington University in Ellensburg, took a master's degree in English there, and then another master's in religious education from Seattle University. As a part of the latter program, he and his wife Karen lived in a community of Catholic priests and nuns for three summers in the early '70s. He and Karen now live in Yakima, Washington.

I know you're very religious.
Yeah. It's more of a...I'm kind of a spiritual cross-dresser.

[Laughing:] What does that mean?
Well, it's Christ-centered, but in the Christian tradition of—I was raised in the country, in the Lutheran church in North Dakota. I got trained in Vatican II Catholicism. And so I don't fit in the Lutheran church, I don't fit in the Catholic church, and it seems to me that my day-to-day living is sort of a Buddhist kind of practice. We're living in

a time when you have access to different ways to tap into spirituality.

You said you were born on a swing date? Isn't that what you said?

Yeah. I think Margaret Mead said somewhere that anyone born after the nuclear bomb is born into a new time. And I was born on that day. I'm one of those guys.

When you were living with the priests and nuns—did you enjoy that?

It was amazing, yeah. It took all of the handles away from my Christianity.

The "handles"?

Yeah. It freed me. Left me radically free. But it was too big, you know. I didn't have a community of like believers after I left there. So it went arrogant on me, and—

You became arrogant?

Yeah, arrogant in my beliefs. So I ran into some trouble later on.

Have you had many crises in your life? You sound like you're talking about a personal crisis.

Yeah. Yeah, yeah. I've had a lot of gifts, and probably.... When I was ten years old we had to leave North Dakota, so we were part of that early exile. There were family times in North Dakota that were tough, but when we left in 1956, and I was ten years old and was leaving, looking out the rear window at my grandma's face, that was the big one. Yeah.

Even before we left North Dakota, I had read poetry. And I felt called—you know, I knew there was something in the poem. In reading poems. In reading out loud. I remember I had Dr. Seuss books, in Bowbells, in the early '50s. But poetry had a hold on me early.

Where did that come from? Your mom, or your dad, or—?

Well, I think it came from books. But then when I was in the seventh grade I had a teacher, Mr. Case. He taught us "The Chambered Nautilus", and he taught us Blake's lamb and Blake's tiger. You know, I was still trying to figure out why I wasn't in North Dakota with grandma.

So you left North Dakota at ten and you went to—?
Seattle. Actually, I worked at the World's Fair at Seattle Center when I was in high school. Tried college, took some English courses. Ended up in the army, in the Medical Service Corps. Ended up in Viet Nam in an evac hospital.

Where was this?
Qui Nhon. In between—

I've been there.
Yeah. So you know where it is on the South China Sea. Beautiful place.

When were you there?
'Sixty-seven, '68.

I was there a year before you.
We took all of the casualties from the north during the battle of Hue, and Phu Bai, and An Khe. In a surgical hospital.

Were you a medic?
I was the Medevac NCO. I was in charge of getting the diagnosis and the wounded soldier and the right hospital together. It was real important work for me. It was real intense and it was real good. Yeah.

So you came back, out of the army. You had been to college—
Yeah, I had like two years. I took a couple of poetry courses in the Canal Zone in Panama when I was down there—

I was stationed in Panama before I went to Viet Nam!
I was at Gorgas Heights. I worked at the hospital there in the Canal Zone.

Right. I was at Fort Gulick. I was there for fifteen months.
Oh. Isn't that something?

55

Yeah. Nobody ever talks about Panama. Panama was a great experience. A really interesting experience.

Yeah. I was too young, really. I couldn't handle all that freedom. When I left Panama before I went to Viet Nam, we drove back. We drove through Central America. Drove the Panamerican Highway. I was with an older guy who went to Viet Nam with me. Sergeant Tommy Pendergrass. He was a literary guy. He was a west Texas, Irish Baptist. And he'd read Hemingway and talked Hemingway with me. We read *The Ginger Man* together. And then we also read *The Magus* together.

God, I remember those books. I read those books and loved them.
Yeah.

That was a great era for English literature.
Yeah. And so this older guy who was with me—before we went to Viet Nam he flew up to Seattle to kind of be with me, be sort of my spiritual father as we went to Viet Nam.

You were together all the time you were in Viet Nam?
No, we weren't together. We actually met in Australia a month before I came home. Went on an R-and-R together there.

That's great. It's great to have a mentor.
Yeah, I had an older man, really, take me to war. Yeah. Yeah, right on.

Okay, you left Viet Nam—
Yeah. Got married. A marriage of twenty-seven years. Got a son, twenty-five, and twin daughters, twenty-two. And taught in public schools. This'll be my twenty-sixth year.

Where did you start teaching?
In Yakima. Started teaching in an alternative high school. Then when the city high school turned into the alternative high school, I went to the city school. So I've been teaching there.

How is it in Yakima?

Well, the school I worked with, the alternative school, was connected with the parole system. I toured all of the juvenile institutions the month I started teaching. So I visited the diagnostic center in Tacoma, and the learning centers in Tacoma, and visited Echo Glen Children's Center.

This would have been in the early '70s?

Yeah, in the early '70s.

Things are a lot worse now.

Yeah. Yeah. So I worked with those kids. And so our lives crossed there, too.

Yeah. Were you into publishing before you started Blue Begonia Press?

Barry Grimes and I started a magazine called *Yakima*. But all along the idea was to find our own poems, and find our own voices, and learn how to write. The great thing in my relationship with Barry is that we knew we had to do this thing. We've had a twenty-year conversation over poetry. It's been a daily conversation. And it's been one of the most incredible conversations that people have ever had. Barry was just back from the Iowa Writers program, and he ended up teaching in the public schools, too. And we were odd guys. We didn't fit and we did fit. But we found each other and we created a school of poetry. In some ways it's not about the press, it's about the Yakima school of poetry. We had William Carlos Williams and we taught each other from his books. And nobody knew about this conversation. Nobody knew about this school. And it's been an incredible run of talking to each other and writing poems and sharing those poems with each other. And gradually we brought other people into it. That conversation with Barry Grimes has really been more important to me than what I've learned from the press.

What's he doing now?

Barry teaches at the same school I do. Yeah, we teach together.

You have a gift for loyalty and friendship, don't you?

Well, yeah, I've had very good friends. But I've found people

I've needed to find in my life. Today I'm finding women who are—I'm finding that women are leading the spiritual journey. They are mapping the inner world. And I've been lucky to find some guides along the way that.... Six years ago, Jerry, I had a seizure. And I was blind in one eye and paralyzed on one side of my body. And the journey to understand what happened then has led from the shaman in Chilean Mapuche villages to dreamwork in the last year and a half.

Did you go down to Chile?
Yeah. I was lucky to be on a Fulbright. Six months. Five months after the seizure. So I was in my initial recovery period before I knew what had happened. I was in a Mapuche village, in a hut where the shaman had his fires going and was talking to us about mapping the inner journey and how not to get lost. And I was getting about sixty percent of his Spanish and filling in the rest with answers that I needed for my own map.

And this led to dreamwork a year and a half ago?
Well, that earlier experience with the *machi*—that's the Mapuche word for shaman—and in the last year and a half I've been doing some dreamwork with a Jungian analyst, and that's been leading to an incredible writing experience. Poems as the dream. Dreams from the evening are mixing in with the dreams of the day.

Is Barry Grimes associated with Blue Begonia also?
He's done several broadsides and a chapbook and a trade book. And we have the conversation. Actually, right now Karen and I are doing the books together. Karen's turned out to be an incredibly gifted book designer. So that's been an interesting part of my life, to watch her develop as a book designer. So Karen and I have the press, and we do one trade book a year. Right now we're trying to commit ourselves to doing a book by a woman each year.

In addition to the trade book, or—
No. That's going to be the way we go, because we're getting these manuscripts that deal with all sorts of issues. It's not a political agenda, but there are all of these incredible manuscripts, incredible

58

poems, coming from these inner worlds. And so our little contribution will be to select from this deep pool of good writers.

You do exclusively poetry, right?
Yeah.

You don't do essays or—?
No, we're only about the poem. Yeah. We're only about the poem.

So you do one trade book a year plus broadsides and—how many chapbooks?
Actually, we're going to develop a new series of chapbooks. We've just started them. We're going to select about ten poets and we're going to have these people working in pairs. And we're going to have each pair edit and design their own chapbooks. And then we're going to have a simultaneous publication in the spring. So it's going to be a cooperative effort of poets, using the techniques of the handmade book combined with computer technology. We're excited about it.

This chapbook will be by one person or by two people?
One person.

But you'll have two people helping each other with both books.
Yeah. Hopefully we'll end up with ten books edited and designed and crafted uniquely and individually, but within the same kind of spiritual framework. We're real excited about it. We don't know what we'll get.

Paul Hunter was telling me that doing letterpress—well, you do both. You do letterpress and offset, don't you?
Yeah, I have.

Well, he was saying that doing letterpress has affected his style, that now he goes for a simplicity of style that he could not find before he started doing letterpress. Do you think that works?
Well, all kinds of things happen, working letterpress. I was trained by Tree Swenson at Copper Canyon.

Oh, I didn't know that.

Yeah. So when we put the press together in this little garage—there's like two halves to it. There's a library and writing space, and then there's a place for the press work. Press work is very physical and very dirty and very labor-intensive, and it makes a different thing, and different things happen out there. And it slows us way down. For us, I would say that the letterpress, the press work, is where we've created the community. I know Tree and Sam [Hamill] in the early days used to talk about when you set the type by hand, you find out how many words you don't need. And all that stuff is true. But for us, the actual letterpress, that great big, Blue Begonia piece of steel is a place that draws people together. That's where the community was formed.

Is it in your home?

It was a one-car garage, yeah. And now it has these beautiful walls, white walls and a high ceiling—

Same building? You just made it into a—?

Yeah. Same building, and one poster of Blake and a great big picture of Whitman and the work that we've done on the walls, and it's a very sacred place. I spent some time right before Bumbershoot, sitting at the press, thinking about it.

Forming your community through involvement with the press, you and other people—It's right off your house, so it's also a location for getting together.

Yeah. During the time when we were printing a series of broadsides called "sHADOWmARKS" anybody who stopped by had to write their own business card. And their business card had to have a title and two lines and their name. And we published those in an envelope [labeled] "sHADOWmARK business cards: literature that means business". And they went in and out of print and they were never for sale. And they were great fun.

How do you sell your books? How do you get them to readers? Let's say chapbooks: How do you get them to readers?

I don't think it really matters. The poem has to be so intimate, it almost has to be an eye-to-eye deal. So we do it at readings. With chapbooks there's no problem, because we're talking about editions that go from as small as twenty-three to large editions of two hundred or three hundred. But we learned as much about poetry and the poem from small editions as from large editions. When we went to the trade edition, nobody believed we were legitimate poets. And so we had to work the readings harder.

Do you have any regrets about going into trade editions?
You know, in some ways we've had to leave some things behind. It's like the trade editions are following us into a larger world.

Those are offset, right?
Yeah, where we print a thousand copies of a book. One of the things we've done to stabilize ourselves—this sounds pretentious, but we planted a poetry pole in our garden this spring. It's a cedar pole, and we've got Tibetan prayer flags over the pole. We have access on Bell Avenue to the street, and anyone who wants to can put a poem there, and read the poems. It's just off the side of our house there, in the rose garden where the path of the mailman intersects the path of the butterflies and hummingbirds. At the same time the pole gives us direction, it's not a regional pole. It has something to do with the larger world, and we're just finding out what that is.

When you were doing only broadsides and chapbooks, you would sell them at readings?
Yeah. It's pretty much the poets' responsibility to take his book/ her book into the world and exchange it for money. Looking back at the work we put into those—all the letterpress work is volunteer work, it's labor for poetry.

Who's volunteering? Do you mean you and Karen and—
Yeah, whoever works. What we do is try to pay for materials. So the work on the press really honors poetry. When people talk about getting the book, well, my experience is if you're going to have a life in poetry, you've got to give to poetry. So it's more than just having a book.

So if somebody comes to you and wants to do a chapbook, and you decide it's good and you want to do it, do you get them involved in the actual manufacture of it as well?

At some point that person has to be involved in the working or the distribution of the work, yeah. I have to be careful here, but university poets who write books for university presses, they have to be very careful not to become involved in a world that gives nothing to poetry itself.

I'm not following what you're saying. University—

Well, I think...well, I don't know enough about it, so I don't want to go down that road. But the poet who doesn't work for poetry is going to end up finding something wonderful missing.

Now the trade books—how long have you been doing trade books?
Six years.

How do you sell those; how do you distribute them?

Well, you know, I'm learning from you, Jerry. [I laugh.] Well, we've become a school of readers. Last year we had five of the Blue Begonia poets in Port Angeles at one bookstore, and they gave one reading.

You also have some on consignment with Bookpeople, right?

Yeah. But we haven't really gotten that connection to work for us yet. We'll be at the Pacific Northwest Booksellers [trade show] in Eugene next month. And Judy Skillman will be there and she's got a book-signing, so we'll give forty, fifty books away to bookstores, and—

Why? To introduce it, or—?

Yeah. That's sort of our way of advertising. Theoretically, we can get back our costs for this book. But all of the gas and all of the time and labor is donated. Karen and I want to do one book a year for the next five years, until I'm retired from public schools, and then we'll see if there's a different road for the press, and we'll see if this work that we've been doing for the last five years has been nurturing the press for another kind of mission. We take the gift exchange, or the book exchange, or the marketing of each book very seriously.

You live in Yakima, so aside from your seeing buyers at trade shows, have you established relationships with bookstores outside of Yakima?

Yeah. You know, once people meet our poets, it makes a difference. Our poets are mature people. We're coming into our maturity as individuals. We have impact. And it makes a difference. It makes a difference in people's lives to hear poems read.

Is everybody you publish from this area generally?

Yeah. We're regional in this sense. Pablo Neruda, in his Nobel acceptance speech, said, you know, I'm the most local poet of poets anywhere in the world. So we're local poets, but are we regional? What interests me more about Blue Begonia poets is not are we local or regional, but what rivers have we crossed in our lives. I'm interested in a poet whose poems show that they are on a journey and that they're dealing with that journey. So I am interested in story telling and I'm interested in how a story is told.

And you feel now that women are more advanced along that journey, or their journeys are more interesting, or—

Well, all of that. I've read some...all of that stuff, yeah. I think the women are mapping the heart world, and are no longer afraid of a poem that charts the emotional journey. They're not afraid of their emotions. The women are not afraid of their poems turning into sentimentality, which used to be one of the big romantic sins. We're finding that the poem doesn't dissipate, the poem doesn't decay in the emotional journey. The psychological journey. The spiritual journey.

Do you think men tend to avoid emotional risk?

Well, I know that the manuscripts from men that I've seen in the last few years haven't been strong and haven't been as interesting. I've learned about poetry from men. So it's not as though men have no place in poetry.

I asked about regionalism earlier. What I was trying to get at is this: If you publish a poet who is from, say, Michigan, and lives in

63

Michigan, that poet still has to get out there, in Michigan at least, and get himself or herself known to the bookstores and get the book sold.

Yeah. We've been talking about women, but, actually, we're doing a chapbook by a Jewish man who lives in Teaneck, New Jersey and teaches in the Bronx. That book is *Al Het* and it's by Zev Shanken. We're going to have two hundred copies of this little book, so we're going to see if it works. We don't know.

Is he the first one—?

Yeah. It all seems foolish when we look at it from a rational point of view, this venture. But it seems to be devotional work, something that we feel. I don't know if we believe [in] what we do, but we feel it.

I get the impression that for you and Karen and maybe for Barry Grimes, the press is a vehicle for development of some kind.

Poetry is the vehicle. Poetry is what it's about. The press is in the service of poetry. It's great to be part of this press, but it only exists for the poem. Yeah. Yeah.

James Hepworth & Tanya Gonzalez
Blue Moon Press; Confluence Press

"[Y]ou start doing that too much in academic politics, they send you to mental health counseling. You can't escape it if you're a press in residence... That kind of conflict seems to be inherent in the nature of any press that has anything to do with an academic institution."

Jim Hepworth was born at the end of December 1948 in Ontario, Oregon on the bank of the Snake River near Boise, Idaho. He grew up "all over the Northwest. I was a child of an itinerant coach and teacher. When my dad would decide to get ambitious or get fired, we would go somewhere else. I grew up a lot in southern Idaho, on a reservation in eastern Washington—the Colville Reservation—at a little, tiny place called Inchelium, and then just...lots of places." He earned his MFA in creative writing at the University of Arizona, then went into the doctoral program in English, ultimately getting his Ph.D.

Tanya Gonzalez was born on the first day of October 1956 in Santa Fe, New Mexico and raised in Santa Fe. Several years after finishing high school she went to work for the Forest Service in Washington, D.C. Later she decided to go on to college and in 1980 she entered the University of Arizona, majoring in English and earning her B.A. She and Hepworth met in 1981 when both were working for Charles Davis, the director of composition at the university. They are married and have three children. At the time of this interview Gonzalez was working on her M.A. at the University of Idaho.

We talked on September 1, the third day of Bumbershoot 1996. We sat outside the Exhibition Hall, where the book fair was located, in the same spot where I had interviewed Jim Bodeen the day before (see Bodeen interview, this volume). It was a warm, sunny afternoon with hardly a cloud in the sky.

What is it you're studying?
Tanya Gonzalez: I'm doing an M.A. in English with an emphasis

65

in American literature, and my topic is a guy named Cabeza de Baca.

James Hepworth: Why don't you tell him who Cabeza de Baca is? Just briefly. That's important.

TG: I know. I was going to. I was waiting for you to ask.

Who is this person?

TG [laughs]: Cabeza de Baca was an explorer who shipwrecked in Florida in 1528. He shipwrecked with four hundred men on the west coast by Tampa Bay, I believe. And then, through a series of mishaps—they tried to make barges and things—they ended up in Galveston. He and three others.

They crossed the Gulf of Mexico?

TG: They survived eight years. They were slaves and then faith healers.

They were slaves of the Nachez?

TG: They were slaves of the Indians of the region, whoever they were.

They were swapped and sold?

TG: Yes. And then he was also a merchant. He became a merchant too. Because he was an Indian ward, he was allowed to roam. And then he wrote a report about it. And my thesis is that this report should be looked at as literature. Not just anthropologically valid or valuable, or geographically, but as literature as well.

Why should it?

TG: Because it's an adventure. It's a captivity narrative, it has—

Marco Polo's adventures are considered literature, aren't they?

JH: Sort of. But Marco Polo didn't leave as good a record. Cabeza de Baca's record is remarkable because it really is the paradigm out of which American literature grows, in some ways. For instance, race is a big issue.

Really.

JH: And, unlike other explorers, Cabeza de Baca has to become American. He has to live, he has to speak the languages, he has to trade, he has to conduct business not as a foreigner, but as a member of these cultures. And his report is also interesting structurally, I think—at least, this is what I've learned from Tanya—in that it reads like a novel. A lot of the stuff, for instance, that Gary Snyder is doing now, that the Green writers are doing, really comes out of that tradition.

Have you read Vargas Llosa's The Storyteller?
TG: I haven't read that.

As you were talking about his having to learn different languages and different cultures and being an intermediary, I was reminded of it. That's Vargas Llosa's theme, is that that's what holds a culture together. He's got a foreigner, a Peruvian rather than an Indian, going among the remnants of the tribes and spreading gossip, really, and telling stories. Making them up. But if they all know the same stories, then that holds them together.
TG: That sounds like a great story.

It is a wonderful book. Okay. That was fun. Publishing. [Gonzalez laughs.] Now you were writing before you were publishing. No? Yeah?
JH: Yeah. I wrote. But I started publishing when I went back to Inchelium to teach. On the reservation where I'd kind of gone to school and grown up a little bit. And founded Blue Moon Press [not to be confused with Blue Moon Books. See the Barney Rosset interview, this volume]. There's a bar in Seattle where, when I came over, I would drink with Joan Swift, who doesn't drink. And Roethke and some other people hung out there. And a blue moon only happens once in a while. You know what I mean? It's a very rare occurence, but it is a geophysical phenomenon. And I didn't want to be stuck with a schedule. So that's how the name of that press originated. And I also wanted to just do occasional things.

And then when I got to Arizona I had retirement money from teaching, because I'd only been in the system a little while and wasn't vested. So I went through that really quick. I went through it, like, within a month. And then I had to borrow money to go to school, in addition to teaching. I didn't realize that my teaching would be able to provide me with subsistence. So with the money that I borrowed I decided to keep doing Blue Moon. And did a couple of books. And to my utter horror and shock, the books got ordered. You know, I would send them out and money would come back in the mail.

How did people hear of them to order them?
JH: Well, I just printed up little—you know, did a direct mail kind of thing. And the campus itself was thirty thousand or something. And I was only doing two hundred copies. So that was pretty much Blue Moon.

And then Tanya and I moved to Idaho where I had a job at Lewis and Clark State College, where I teach now. And they didn't want me to keep publishing Blue Moon, which I think was a mistake on their part. They saw it as a conflict of interest.

What kinds of books did you do as Blue Moon?
JH: We did chapbooks. Two prison anthologies.

By prisoners?
JH: By prisoners, yeah. Kind of remarkable books in the sense that Michael Hogan, for instance, the editor of one anthology, won an NEA [National Endowment for the Arts] fellowship. That was pretty controversial. Michael was eventually released from prison and is now in Mexico. He's a very fine poet, a very fine writer. But that was a little bit problematic. But we had the help of the Arizona Commission on the Arts, too. And Dick Shelton, who has probably run the most successful prison writing program, in terms of recidivism. I mean I don't think—Dick would have to tell you, but I don't think any of those guys who got out ever went back. I mean they might have had a drug problem or they might have gotten in trouble with parole, but they never went back to prison. So the recidivism rate for Dick Shelton's prison writing workshop is remarkable, and even the government couldn't argue against it effectively. And that program is still going. I don't know how much Dick is doing.

That's out of the U of A?
JH: Yeah. Well...yeah. It's Dick. It's not so much the university. It's Dick himself. I mean you go inside those walls—those were hard-core guys. But I don't know, that's one of the great things about writing. There

68

is some therapy. And we still sell those books. They're in their second printing, third printing. That was the sort of thing I was into at Blue Moon.

So you got hired by the English department at Lewis and Clark?
JH: Yeah. So then I took over—Confluence was founded by Keith and Shirley Browning in 1976. And Keith and Shirley pretty much started in their house. But because they were connected to the college, the college eventually took the press under its wing, in the sense that they decided that they could have an office and retain their legal identity, right? And so Confluence Press was founded as a not-for-profit, 501(c)(3) organization. It still is.

I think I skipped something.
JH: That's okay.

You went from high school to graduate work. What happened between high school and graduate work? [Hepworth and Gonzalez laugh.]
JH: Well, I went to grade school and junior high all over. And then we landed in southern Idaho for three years, which allowed me to get kicked out of high school but readmitted to high school, and I actually graduated in southern Idaho. And then I went to play basketball for Eddie Sutton at a junior college in Twin Falls. Eddie's now been to the NCAA more than any other coach. But I kind of quit playing basketball and had a little revolution. You know, some young teachers took can openers to my mind. So then I went to Luther, which is a private liberal arts school, because at Berkeley I'd gotten my head bashed in and decided I really wasn't going to live in Berkeley happily ever after.

You're talking about college now.
JH: Yeah.

Where is Luther?
JH: Luther is in Decorah, Iowa, in a little river valley.

When did you get your head bashed at Berkeley? 'Sixty-eight?
JH: 'Sixty-eight and '69. I'd go and then I'd leave. I was never an official—I got admitted but I never paid to go to class. And People's

Park—I mean Berkeley was just overwhelming to a rural guy, you know? I mean it was just too much for me. You went there, didn't you?

No, I got my B.A. and master's degree at the University of Montana.
JH: Really.

And then I came to the University of Washington, and that was a terrible transition for me. I don't think I ever really made it. Missoula had thirty thousand people—I think once you get above fifty thousand people, something kicks in and it becomes very impersonal and institutionalized. I'm talking about the community. Fifty thousand is an arbitrary number, but there's some point at which it just kicks in. And when you have half a million people it's obviously there already.
JH: Yeah.

Okay. Tanya. Hi.
TG: Hi, Jerry.

We left you studying English. Do you write?
TG: I was writing before I went to college, and then I quit writing after that. I realized how poorly I wrote. That was back when, you know, before I got my degree. But college was great for me. I had a great time. I still do. I'm not finished yet.

Do you think you'll go on for a doctorate?
TG: I'm thinking about it. I didn't think I wanted to, and I may not. But it's an option that I have.

You got into publishing with Confluence Press? Or had you done any publishing before?
TG: With Jim, no. When I met Jim he was doing Blue Moon. I helped him fill orders, basically. When he started at Confluence, that's when I started. Not right away.

You've got Confluence physically located at the college. Is the college proprietary about it?

70

JH: The college provides us with editorial offices. Some warehouse space. Some part-time help. In exchange for internships. And with some money for—I don't know. She—Linda Vacura—was a receptionist, bookkeeper, accountant, you know. Really, she functioned as the one solitary paid employee of the press. She usually comes here [to Bumbershoot].

TG: Really what happened was Jim established a position for her and he got the college to pay for half of it and the commission on the arts to pay for the other half.

JH: Yeah. See, I wasn't too keen on having the college pay for half of it. Because I knew there would come a day—like now. But they wanted to do that. They wanted to sort of have a stronger marriage between the press and the college. So they said, "We'll pay for half of you having a full-time employee. Then gradually we'll pick up the other half." That was the part that interested me. They would pick up the other half, freeing up, see, money that I could be spending on first and second books and, you know, helping people break into print.

But that day never came. You know, every year I would go and say, "How about this year?" They would say, "No, this is not a good year." Or I would say, "Well, how about some computers?" And they'd say, "No, this is not such a good year." Then, last year, I think we came to a day of reckoning where we're going to have to figure out what the relationship is going to be from here on out. Because they did away with their half of the employee.

The employee would also supervise students. In bookkeeping, that sort of thing. We didn't just do internships in publishing, we did them in accounting and business, too. You could, if you were a student, come and learn bookkeeping, say, double-entry or whatever you were interested in. And the same was going to be true in marketing, but we didn't get there. 'Cause the press has its own market. [Laughs.] You know, we're not really ready to teach anybody how to market books. That's for sure.

You said the college saw your publishing Blue Moon books as a conflict of interest. Why would there be a conflict of interest?

JH: I could never figure it out. I think it was because they wanted all the emphasis on Confluence Press.

71

Had the Brownings already left?

JH: The Brownings had retired from teaching. They're still supportive, I'd say. I don't know. What was the conflict of interest?

TG: I think you're right. I think they wanted you to focus your energies on Confluence Press and not on Blue Moon. 'Cause you also had to teach. The other thing you didn't mention was that Blue Moon won two Western States [Arts Federation] book awards.

Oh. No, you didn't mention that.

TG: That's important, I think, because it was such a small press. Didn't you win those the same year?

JH: Yeah, we won the first two, and then...Nancy Mairs won in poetry.

TG: *In All the Rooms of the Yellow House* was the name of the book.

JH: Alberto—Tito—Rios won for short fiction. And then Nancy got a citation of excellence, I think, for her essays. But that was the first year of the awards. 'Eighty-two, wasn't it?

But still.

TG: But still.

JH: Well, I don't know. I felt good. Robert Penn Warren was one of the jurors, and I think he was very fair. Nancy—Harper picked her up and then Beacon Press has really been great for her, I think. She's gone on to establish a real presence. So has Alberto. Alberto is now, what? Regents Professor at Arizona State? I mean I was looking through Norton's *Anthology of Modern Poetry* the other day, and there's Tito.

Let's go back to Confluence now, if we can. When did you go to Idaho, to Confluence?

JH: In the fall—when, Tanya?

TG: It was '84.

How much does Confluence publish? Has it been consistent?

TG: I think it's consistent in terms of—it publishes something every year. But the number of books—I think it's done a lot, hasn't it? We've had better years, I suppose, but now we do at least four titles a year.

72

JH: Four titles, and then we still do the equivalent of Blue Moon, which is James R. Hepworth Books. Like last year we did an interview with Wilma Mankiller, a woman chief of the Cherokees, and did, oh, several little tiny projects. I like to do letterpress when I can. I still do that. Trade titles, we try to do four or more a year. But we probably never did more than eight.

That's quite a bit for—
JH: For me it's a lot, and for Tanya it's a lot. For doing it part time, it's a lot.

It is. I do four a year. It kills me.
JH: Right.

You also have another full-time job, as I do. Confluence is kind of a half-literary, half-scholarly press, isn't it? Or am I typifying it wrong?
JH: I don't think there's anything very scholarly about it. The most scholarly books we publish are probably the American authors series. What we try and do is get some of the writers' work, then interviews with the writer, and photographs. And then there's usually a section where we do invite scholars. But because of the state of literary criticism, the condition where, in my opinion, literary critics can no longer effectively communicate with the public, with the possible exception of reviewers—I mean, everything is based on theory—we mostly ask other writers to comment on the work of the writer who's the subject. We're doing a volume on Gary Snyder. We hope to do one on Joan Didion.

Great. She's one of the few American writers I follow. I follow only about half a dozen. She's one of them.
JH: Yeah. She's great. I agree wholeheartedly. So that's, I guess, pseudo-scholarly. But the emphasis, really, is still on first and second books. As Tanya and I get more interested and learn more about science—for instance, we're doing a geological history of Hell's Canyon which is much more dynamic geologically than the Grand Canyon. But nobody knows—where is Hell's Canyon?

We've got a book coming on Nez Perce treaties, because the Nez

Perce are right next door to us. Nobody seems to be doing that. We can't find the treaties—I mean they're all scattered. Then the language of the treaties makes a difference which treaty version you're reading. So we've asked a constitutional lawyer to put the treaties together, give us some historical context for those things as well as some analysis and interpretation.

We're doing autobiography, or whatever you want to call it. It's really different in the sense that it's oral tradition, because not too many people are going to sit down and write their autobiography, because it's outside their tradition. They'll tell you, you know, but usually the emphasis is on dreams, healing, and the things in their life that they think are of cultural importance, but not so much a life story. I guess what I'm saying is that, for instance, Tanya's book is really important. I'd love to publish Tanya's book. I think it's just a breakthrough book.

Is this the Cabeza de Baca?

JH: Yes. Because Tanya is probably the heart and soul of the press. And she's very modest. It's like you asked her a minute ago if you write, and she was not saying anything. Yeah, she writes. She's a good writer. But because she's at the press, probably her book will come out somewhere else. And that's a goddamn shame. [Gonzalez laughs.] I mean that's one of the things we do that I'm not so sure is smart. That's why I like *Publishing Lives*. It's because it looks to me like your thumb prints are all over it, from the design to—I mean that kind of control, that single-minded vision—it's not that you can't have it with two people, but they've got to be close. And that kind of control really makes the best books, I think.

I don't think we do much scholarly publishing, really. We don't do novels. Very, very, very, very, very, very seldom do we do novels. That doesn't mean we don't think that somebody shouldn't be doing novels. In fact, I would say just the opposite. Somebody ought to be devoting a press just to the publication of fiction. We do short fiction.

Collections of short stories?

JH: Yeah. And we've been okay there. They don't make us a big reputation, I don't think. But I think the books we've done are pretty important books.

If you don't do novels, why do you do short fiction? Short fiction is harder to sell.

JH: That's why we do it. Because short fiction is a tougher fucking market. It's a lot harder—I mean look at—Jesus, even the success stories like—who would be a success story for the short story? Well, I guess Carver. Eudora Welty. But look at Eudora Welty. You would think, "Oh, well, she's Eudora Welty." I don't think she's very wealthy for being Eudora Welty. You know what I mean? And the short story is an American form. It's a form people need to pay attention to. It's not a dead form. It's very much alive. And with the novel, I think too, there's a real opportunity. It's just that we haven't done that. You can't do everything.

With your letterpress work—do you actually do hands-on letter- press, the two of you?

JH: We want to. But I cannot. This is, again, a college problem. As an academic person, I can't go in to the vo-tech part of our school and print on the letterpress. I can't do that.

Why not?

JH: Well, because I am an academic faculty member and the vo- tech part is funded differently. I think it's basically because I am such a pain in the ass that they don't want me in the shop. So what we're going to do, probably, is buy our own.

You do have letterpress work done, though?

JH: Yeah. And we sew the books, bind the books. But we can't, at this point, print the books. And so what we're doing right now is making a deal with a local printer who will either print for us or allow us to use his shop. 'Cause we can't seem to quit.

You say "we." When I say "we" I mean me. But when you say "we" you mean you and Tanya.

JH: Yep.

Yeah? Do you look at it that way too?

JH: Well, Tanya—

TG: Yeah.

JH: —just doesn't talk much. [Gonzalez and I laugh.]

TG: I think that's true. Jim also has a lot of students who are interested. It goes in spurts, but he gets a lot of students who just excel in this kind of environment. They can do whatever they want to do. Because when they have an idea, he says "Okay, do it." There are students who just thrive. When he says "we" I know that he means those students as well. They're always changing, but there are always those students who come through and, you know, make their mark and go off to graduate school or something.

JH: That's a really interesting question, I think. Maybe it's not a question, but that's one of the things that the founder—Keith Browning—and I really disagree about. Because he wants to say that Confluence Press is Jim Hepworth, and I think Confluence Press is much more than Jim Hepworth. I mean Paul Pintarich wrote some article a while back in the *Oregonian*. And he said something like "Jim Hepworth's Confluence Press." Now I do imprint books sometimes. A James R. Hepworth Book. If I acquire it, if I have a lot of ego involvement, it's about my only way to get a credit. [Laughs.] You know what I mean? So I'll say "A James R. Hepworth Book."

But the only reason I started doing that was because—I don't even want to say the names of the authors, but when I first got to Confluence, the college had such a bad reputation for paying its printing bills that no printer would give me credit and no writer that I wanted to sign would do it, because there had been no contracts with authors that anybody could find. And so one of the authors that I wanted said, "Well, if you will personally put your name on the cover, and if you will personally guarantee that the things you told me are really true, I'll do it." And I said, "Okay." And then once I started doing A James R. Hepworth Book, Mary Ann Waters, a very fine poet—I will never forget doing her book—she said, "How come your name isn't on this?" And I said, "Well, because it's just something I did, you know, to get a book." And she said, "Well, I want this to be A James R. Hepworth Book." So I did it. And then you're stuck. But I think there are many, many independent presses where when they're saying "we" they mean "me," you know? But I don't think we're one of them. And the main reason is Tanya.

It's all your fault, huh?

JH: She is involved, whether she wants to be or not.

TG: Oh, I'm involved, but, you know....

JH: She designs the books, she types up the books, she edits the books, she—

TG: And I like the press. The work. I love to do that.

You edit?

TG: I have edited.

JH: See, here's what happened, Jerry. The college didn't want me to pay her to do anything. I can pay everybody else, but they didn't want me to pay her. So I said, "This is bullshit. She's working for maybe three cents an hour as it is, and...." Anyway, she's not editing now.

Do you find yourself, as a publisher whose physical plant is at the college, under any kind of pressure from the college to do certain things or not to do certain things?

JH: Yeah. You have someone who's on your board, and he comes up to you and says, "I want to do this project. I want to—" And my response to that is to treat him just like everybody else, and say "Well, that's fine, but you don't get any royalties. Your royalties go into the scholarship fund for Native American—whatever." Well, you start doing that too much in academic politics, they send you to mental health counseling. You can't escape it if you're a press in residence. You've got to be good to your neighbors. That kind of conflict seems to be inherent in the nature of any press that has anything to do with an academic institution.

Which is leading me to think that maybe, you know, maybe that's a bad idea. Or at least maybe a bad idea for me. Maybe Confluence should just go back to being a quiet little chapbook kind of limited-edition press or something. There are enough conflicts in publishing as it is. I mean, the whole problem with me is the one where the author and the publisher, by nature, have an adversarial relationship. And it can't be that way. It's got to be a marriage. It's got to be a friendship. You're in it together. But because we're human, we're going to always have some sort—but you understand what I mean. I like the marriage metaphor a lot. It's like getting an agent or anything else. You're doing something important together. You're making something from nothing, man. Jesus

Christ, I feel like I'm on a soap box! Let's go preaching!

TG: Yeah!

I love it when the person I'm interviewing gets passionate about something. What about your own writing? Are you doing it? [Hepworth does not answer.] Are you able to do it in addition to everything else? [Hepworth still does not answer.] Should we go on to something else? [Gonzalez and I laugh.]

JH: Tanya should answer that question.

TG: He's starting to really focus on his own writing.

Just recently?

TG: Yeah. Before, he would just say, "Well, I can't really work on my stuff now because I've got this book," you know, whatever it was. Now it seems to me that he's saying, "I have to work on my stuff." Which is good. I think it's kind of, you know, it's a good thing to happen because the press is changing so much. We don't know where it's going to go. So I think it's good.

JH: I want to write books with Tanya. And I also have some people now coming and saying, you know, "Why don't you—I saw your piece in *Outside Magazine*—why don't you write that into a book." You know what I mean? One hand kind of washes the other after a while. I do think that it's a continual conflict, internally, for anybody who writes seriously and who publishes. I think that's always going to be there. On the other hand, as I move towards fifty and I look at my kids and I see that I haven't left the kind of record I want, that's becoming more important to me. And I think you've probably—I think anybody who publishes—you have to put the author first. To some degree, your stuff has to stay on hold while you do the other. Now that may just be a cycle that is subject to change. But I can really see it in Tanya. I can see the way she's suppressed her own writing, right? And I don't think it can always be that way. I think she's got some things to write that she's just going to have to do. Somehow. Now how you prioritize all that, I have no....

It's interesting. I ask you about your writing, you want Tanya to answer for you. And now you're answering for her. [Gonzalez and Hepworth laugh.]

TG: That's true.

JH: Ye-e-ah. Well, it's easier.

Yeah. I asked Rob McDowell a similar question [see Gold 1996].
Story Line Press?

JH: Yeah.

He says that he tries to just turn it off at night. Turn off the press
at night. He says it's difficult, but he does his best to concentrate on his
own stuff at night. That's his full-time work, is the press. He gets grants.
Sam Hamill says that his editing and his writing inform each other, and
he doesn't see a conflict between the two [Gold 1996]. So, assuming
that they're both exaggerating a little bit [Hepworth and I laugh],...

JH: Yeah. Yeah, they probably both are.

Yeah. How do you sell your books? How do you get them to the
person who may want to pick one up to read it? We're talking about sales
and distribution now.

JH: God, that is the question of the hour. Here we sit, doing an
interview, while people are at our booths. [All three of us laugh.] So I
guess the answer is, try and get them to steal the books. What a great thing
that would be. I mean, if people were stealing books instead of
submachine guns. I can tell you how we try. But I think we're—you know,
our biggest selling title is like just under ten thousand copies.

You've done three times better than I have then. I've never sold
more than three thousand copies of a book.

JH: Well, on some books that may be the right number. But with
the trade books, we have what I call tier-one distribution, which is the
major accounts in the United States. Everybody from Ingram to Barnes
and Noble. I mean not just stores, but, you know, big accounts. Those
are sold for us by Eric Kampmann [of Midpoint Trade Books]. And
Midpoint takes, you know, that's their action, too. But I would say they go
down to tier two. And then we have a group of really dedicated, hard-
working, honest people who are a family. The Stuart Group. Well, Joyce
Abdill is not a Stuart, but she might as well be. And they represent our
books in the West. So, in theory, that's the structure.

And then we do direct mail to the five thousand largest libraries [and to] individuals. We try to go to Bumbershoot and at least let people know we're still here. The PNBA [Pacific Northwest Booksellers Association trade show], the ABA [American Booksellers Association trade show, now the BEA—Book Expo America] in Chicago. I don't know how long we can do that.

The thing that's going to be interesting to me is to see how things like electronic publishing, the Internet, various alternative means of distribution—yesterday Tanya and I were talking about an idea we've had for a long time, which is to set a returns policy that we could live with. Instead of you being able to return a book—you're a bookstore—for credit, we just say, "If you want this book, you buy it. There's no returns." Now Dover does this, and they've been doing it for a long time. And we were wondering, well, is this going to kill us? You know, nobody will buy a book from us ever again. But individuals would buy. Then along came—who was it, Tan, came by the booth? Oh, Alan Stark. Alan Stark came by and said, "Yeah, that's a good idea, but have you thought about net?" I said, "Yeah, I have. I have, but I can't make it work." He said, "Well, this is what's going to happen—"

And Alan's idea is that in the future we're going to see a book priced at net. You're going to set a price—four dollars and fifty-seven cents—and you're going to sell to any individual who wants that book at that price. But you're going to do the same thing with bookstores. Now they might jack up the price, but you're going to sell it to them at that price. Another way we try to get around that problem of how you price the book, how you discount the book, is to give a deep discount even to, especially to, independent booksellers. Right? Not forty percent, but forty-seven across the board. And the reason we do that is to try and get low returns. Because we continually get—when a book like John Rember's *Cheerleaders from Gomorrah* is reviewed by the *New York Times*, and then is out of stock in our little three-thousand-copy edition before it's in print, we have a big cash-flow problem. We can't...we're not big enough...we don't borrow money. We don't—we're out of debt. We could, I suppose, try and borrow money.

So I don't know how we get books to readers. We give a lot of books away. That's another thing. If somebody came up to the table and said, "I don't have enough money for this," we'd want them to have the book. So I think we're horrible at it. I don't know what the answer is.

At the publishers' meeting yesterday morning and this morning [prior to the start of the book fair], one of the things we talked about is approaching independent booksellers' organizations and trying to get them to accept a no-returns policy in exchange for deep discounts. The thing that concerns me is—I asked a couple of bookstore managers and owners—I may give them a fifty-percent discount, say, so they don't return the book to me, but they can return it to my wholesaler who will then return it to me. That's happened. I've been burned like that. And it's been done by otherwise decent people.

JH: Yeah. This isn't something somebody's out there trying to, you know....

[A distributor] told me about this publisher who printed a thousand copies of a novel but had to buy back twelve hundred. It didn't sell well, he remaindered them, and then they found their way back into the wholesale system and came back to him again.

JH: Yeah.

I don't see a control for that. There are going to be some abuses. If you could get the stores to go for a no-returns discount, the question then is: Can we tolerate the abuses of that?

JH: Then there's the rep, for us. Like, if we went to a no-returns policy, how the hell would they sell the book? And if we went to a net policy, then we've got to be sure and figure their money in there too.

Yeah, the reps would have to be consulted.

JH: Yeah, they'd have to be consulted, and on the net policy you'd have to build them into it if you wanted them to represent you.

Well, on the net policy, if you sell a book for, say, five dollars to an individual, and you sell the same book for five dollars to a bookstore, what you're really saying is you don't want to sell books to bookstores. Because they have to raise the price.

JH: That's right. That's what I mean. That thing really has to be thought through. The thing I like about selling to bookstores is the booksellers make some money, the reps make some money, authors make some money—I should start with authors, because I think the authors really—the first person you should pay is the writer. You're not ever going to pay the writer who spends ten years on a novel a decent wage immediately. But the hope is subsidiary sales, something, mass paper, I don't know—you know, there's more potential there than with a book of poems. Usually. And over the course of time maybe the author would go from there. That's another thing. Everybody deserves to be paid in the currency of the dominant culture. If that's money, then that's what it is. If that's books, fine.

That's another struggle we've had, because when Tanya and I got there the authors weren't paid. It was assumed that if you were doing a poetry book, you were just going to get books, and not necessarily very many books. You might be able to buy them at a discount and sell them and make a little money that way. But I think, especially in the case of fiction, especially in the case of poetry, that there has to be some way to recognize the work of the person without whom there wouldn't be the book. And that has to be a meaningful exchange in terms of what the culture values. Or whosever values we're talking about. The author's values, right? And money is important.

Now how you do that when you take away all the subsidy for poetry, all the—I don't know. You see, I still don't get it. Because you can subsidize wheat, you can subsidize tobacco, you can subsidize anything that grows, but you can't—there aren't going to be any more art subsidies, apparently. Now maybe that's a really, really good thing. I don't know. But what I do know is that it's hard to break into print. Especially if you're sixty years old and you're writing your first book. It's hard enough if you're twenty-five years old. I think the commercial publishers really have a legitimate place. But because they're luckier to have the credit line, they're also more obligated to do something where they give back.

I don't think they recognize that system of morality. It's a moral system you're talking about, and I think they operate under a different system. I think they're honest to their own system, but it's not this one. Those people are corporate people. It's a different world.

JH: Yeah.

TG: Maybe.

82

JH: I just.... While I think commercial publishing can be a big whorehouse and a sham, I also respect and admire lots of books that are published commercially. I think they make tremendous changes in the culture. Books are still the agent of change for our culture. Without books our civilization would perish. Now maybe the book is going to go away. My students keep telling me that. The librarians, some of them, tell me that. I don't know. I don't think so. If it is, I'm going to keep my books.

A few years ago I had dinner with a Palestinian poet who lived in Syria. He was able to support himself by writing for television. He said he was one of half a dozen writers in Syria who could do that, but that his true love was poetry. He was in the United States on a State Department fellowship which allowed him to tour the country and talk to people. Kind of a Fulbright in reverse, I suppose. He was very anti-U.S. because of our Mideast policies. But his library, his personal library, was in English. And his son, whom he was devoted to, he was going to send to study in England because he wanted him to become fluent in English. Even though he didn't like the English either. He liked the French. But he wanted his son to be fluent in English because he wanted him to be able to read his library. To me, that's a fascinating story. To devote your child to your library.

JH: Yeah. See, I think that's another place where Tanya's really essential. Because the more we look at our family—for instance, the language question. We don't speak enough Spanish at home for our kids to be fluent in it. But I really like that story because the father is devoted to the kid in a total sense. Looking after his mind. If I had a wish it would be that the kids could read Tanya's library. [To Gonzalez:] Because your library is really important to them.

TG: We have a pretty good library, both of us.

JH: Yeah.

TG: They've read a lot of good stories.

JH: Not as many in Spanish.

TG: Well....

I have no more questions. Is there anything else either of you would like to say?

JH: Let's end...let's end...war. [Gonzalez laughs.]

Ramsey Kanaan, Michael Rejniak, Paul Dalton, Craig O'Hara, Craig Gilmore, Bill Mithalski
AK Press; AK Distribution

"One of the great strengths in having our own distribution system is the ability to move books into alternative or little known distribution channels."

I visited the AK collective at its warehouse and offices in San Francisco's Mission District in mid-May 1998 on a rainy morning complete with thunder and power outages. As I had met him years earlier in an anarchist bookstore in Seattle, I felt that I already had an introduction to Ramsey Kanaan and I anticipated talking with him alone, as the publisher of AK Press, but in the last of a series of telephone calls made to arrange the interview he informed me that I would be interviewing all of the collective together. This may have been fine from the point of view of AK, but it proved difficult to elicit personal insights or anything that might have resulted from introspection, probably because, talking with so many at once, I was not able to establish the kind of rapport necessary to have them confide in me in the presence of the other members. It was only after the interview, when I was packing my cassette recorder and notebooks to leave, and most of the collective had already resumed their day's work, that Michael Rejniak talked a little about his father and Craig Gilmore talked more fully about his experience in sales and distribution.

During the interview itself, while I was running the tape, most responses to my questions were brief, even skeletal; the more personal parts of their lives leaked out primarily in relation to the theme of anarchism. It was like interviewing a being with six heads: there was some diversity of thought, but still, it was a single being. We sat in a sort of half-moon configuration in the center of their work space, I facing them arc-ed before me, open space between us, computers arrayed at their backs. Someone said this was how they met each morning to start the day.

Once before, I had interviewed several members of a small publishing company (i.e., Copper Canyon Press; see Gold 1996). It had been a hard interview for a number of reasons, but, seated around a conference table, every person's voice carried clearly onto the tape. The interview with AK, too, was not easy, issues of rapport aside. One reason was the spaciousness of the room in which we were seated; words seemed sometimes to evaporate even as they were spoken. Another was the apparent reluctance of Ramsey Kanaan to reveal himself. Though he sat closer to the recorder than anyone else, he spoke so softly that the microphone sometimes did not pick him up. Only about halfway through the interview, when we were talking about the possibility of implementing anarchism, did his voice acquire potency enough to become consistently audible.

Those I talked with were Kanaan, then thirty-two years old; Michael Rejniak, twenty-five; Paul Dalton, thirty; Craig O'Hara, twenty-seven; Craig Gilmore, forty-seven; and Bill Mithalski, thirty-three. Kanaan hails from England by way of Scotland, the others from East (Paul Dalton, Connecticut; Bill Mithalski, Minnesota) and West (Michael Rejniak, Craig O'Hara, and Craig Gilmore all from California, though O'Hara was raised in Pennsylvania).

All have some college, Kanaan having the most formal education, with an M.A. in modern history. His answer was not audible when I asked where he went to university; he might have said Edinburgh. (I sent a copy of the unedited transcript to AK for comment and clarification, but received no response.) Others attended Fullerton Junior College (Rejniak—majored in journalism, did not graduate), Syracuse University (Dalton—American history and secondary education, dropped out), Boston University (O'Hara—majored in philosophy; his answer to the question of graduation was not audible), Claremont Men's College (Gilmore—philosophy and politics, graduated), and Louisiana State University (Mithalski—photography and graphic design, graduated).

Was anybody here in the military?
Bill Mithalski: No.

That was a resounding no.

Craig Gilmore: Some of us have fought against the military.

Before you got involved in the book industry, how did you make a living? Ramsey? Or were you always involved in the book industry?
Ramsey Kanaan: The only paid job I've ever had, other than AK, was with Polygram.
Michael Rejniak: Office.

What brought you here?
MR: Politics.

There are other anarchist groups though.
MR: There are other anarchist groups, but none of them publish books or seemed successful enough in business practice. So....

Paul?
Paul Dalton: My last paid job—I was on disability for five years before coming here, but before that I worked for the Berkeley Free Clinic, doing a lot of different things.

Could I ask what you were on disability for?
PD: Yeah. I have AIDS.

Karl Siegler of Talon Books up in Vancouver—the reason I asked is that it was his disability also that led him, indirectly, into publishing. Craig?
Craig O'Hara: I worked at a warehouse for a catering company.

How did you get from there to here?
CO: Well, besides being friends with the fellows who work here, I've always had a great deal of interest in political writings, and, in particular, anarchist books and literature.
Craig Gilmore: He's one of our best-selling authors.
CO: Yeah, I also wrote a book that was published by AK Press.

What's the title of your book?
CO: It's called *The Philosophy of Punk*. I don't know if that

helped me get the job or not, but.... [Laughter from several of the collective, including O'Hara.]

Craig?
CG: I've been in various parts of the book business since I got out of college.

You were a sales rep for Inland.
CG: Before that I was in retail bookselling.

Oh. Which store?
CG: Originally Huntley Bookstore in Claremont. A college store at Claremont College. But it wasn't only there. I had this desire as a youth, you know, once I was old enough to catch the bus and leave home, I would haunt the great bookstores of Fresno. I lived in Fresno for a while in my teenage years. I would take the bus downtown to this bookstore, and I loved it. I had this idiotic, romantic notion of working in a bookstore—smoking, reading books, and, like, meeting cute girls who would be impressed that I smoked and read all these books. My idea of a career when I was thirteen and fourteen was to work in a bookstore.
MR: And smoking.
CG: And smoking. [Laughter.] So, you know, I got a job in a bookstore and here I am.

You went from a bookstore to being a sales rep to here?
CG: Yeah. More or less.

Bill?
BM: Immediately before I started working here I was unemployed and volunteering with AK, which is how I came to be employed here. Before that I was a paper buyer for a printing company, a maintenance man, and before that I worked in photography labs. Started off cleaning toilets when I was sixteen.

Maybe I should ask you the positions you have here. Is there a publisher and a managing editor and a—?
CG: No.

So how do you decide who does what? You just kind of gravitate toward what you do best, or what you like to do?

CG: We meet every morning and discuss what we're doing. Although each of us has areas of responsibility.

BM: When it comes to publishing, usually someone brings an idea in and then it gets kind of developed and goes from there, people being in charge of different aspects of different projects. We haven't been six people for very long. For the majority of what gets published, Ramsey is the main person who decides.

CG: As far as our structure goes, we have this new—because we haven't been six people for very long—we have this new kind of project coordinator, a situation where one person is in charge or will see the project all the way through. But any one of us can do...or someone will be assigned or volunteer to coordinate the project.

BM: Maybe ninety-nine percent of what we do is distribution.

CG: Right.

BM: Time spent on publishing is minor. Precious. And we try to divide it up as much as we can so no one person is too overburdened with it. There's so much day-to-day stuff to do.

How many books per year do you publish?

BM: It's gone down at the moment, but I'd say it was around a dozen. This year we'll probably do more like eight or ten.

How is a book acquired? Your book was published here, right?

CO: Sure.

Okay. How was it acquired?

CO: Well, there seems to be two ways for things to be acquired. There's either the submission of manuscripts, which is more or less how I did mine. They liked it enough to publish it. Or else we can contact an author and say we're interested in having you write us something. So it's done either through a submission or contact.

PD: Most of the things we've published, we've asked for them.

So at one of your morning meetings somebody brings up the idea of asking so-and-so for such-and-such?

PD: Yeah.

CO: The meetings tend to be divided into subject matter. One day we do publishing, for example.

What led you all into—I'm speaking to you collectively, but I hope to get individual answers—what led you all into anarchism as opposed to...anything else? Nobody wants to answer.

BM: Really, there's not much of a choice. I was led to anarchism probably as.... It's kind of an odd question. I'm not sure how to answer it.

MR: My introduction to anarchism came from punk music. So it was kind of very early on, age thirteen, fourteen, getting ideas and starting to read up on it.

PD: That's probably a common strain for almost everybody here, that punk rock has played a part in it. For me, though, like I came to it through anti-nuclear politics. I was involved in anti-nuclear politics and met anarchists through that.

Now you wrote a book on punk, right? [Laughter.] What's funny?

CO: Yeah, the book is sort of—I wouldn't say it's a running joke, but it's not the most serious book ever written, that's for sure. Not nearly. It's a great book. [Laughter.] As far as weighty issues, it's on the lighter side of the scale. Getting to anarchism—not necessarily through punk rock, but the politics that punk rock criticized so frequently, and finding myself agreeing with those criticisms whether it be against environmental destruction, racism, nuclear politics—all of these seemed to coincide in the fact that they were being caused by a hierarchical, governmental, political economic system which was at the root of all these things. And being an anarchist, whether it meant leaving these establishments behind or destroying them, tended to be the only option. That's my next book: post-punk anarchism. [Laughter.]

In the '60s and '70s, when the different -isms were being bandied about—including anarchism, both right and left forms—judging from the conversations I recall from those days, people thought it was just impractical; it could not be implemented. What do you think? Can it be implemented?

89

BM: That's what we're trying to prove, that it can be. I think that's why all of us are here, doing this now, to try to show that, you know, business or publishing, whatever it might be, can function within capitalist society but in an anti-capitalist way. If we can show that it can, other people will try and do it too. It'll spread.

CG: I think we also think that it's not that anarchism is impossible—I mean anarchism hasn't had a chance to grow, to flourish. And I think our position is that the alternatives to anarchism have proven themselves to be impossible. You know, we've seen what capitalism's done, and it's clearly not a sustainable, not a humane system. We've seen that the authoritarian left has failed. I mean, it seems to me that anarchism is the only—I would, I guess, turn the question around.

Well, I don't want to be in the position of defending something that—

CG: I didn't mean turn it around on you. Turn it inside out, I meant. Rather than say, "Do we think it's really possible?" we think nothing else is possible.

Do you think it's possible to implement? Well, okay, here you are—

CG: I think it's essential to implement it.

But that's not my question.

RK: If I didn't think it was possible I wouldn't be doing this, or have been involved in other forms of political activism over the last twenty years.

Twenty years?

RK: Nineteen years. Since I was thirteen. If I didn't think it was possible, and very possible, very plausible, I'd be wasting my time.

At the age of thirteen how did you get involved with, or into...thinking the way you do?

RK: My parents always encouraged me to read. That's the only thing I can really point to, since by the time I was thirteen I'd decided that—I knew about anarchism and decided that that was a good idea. I

90

never went through any other leftist parties or authoritarian groups. I participated in some anti-nuclear stuff in Britain. But by then I was already calling myself an anarchist and had a fairly sophisticated view, as much as a thirteen-year-old can, of what anarchism was about, though I didn't read anarchist books. I'd read *Homage to Catalonia* by George Orwell. My parents always encouraged me to read it and the other classics. When I decided I was an anarchist, I then pursued more actively ...[inaudible].

What do your parents do for a living?
RK: My father was a doctor.

Do you all come from middle-class parentage?
MR: My dad is a pipefitter, and my mom's a telephone operator.
PD: ...[Inaudible] and my mom is his secretary.
CO: My mother and father both had various odd jobs working for the state government in Pennsylvania.
CG: My father worked for a bank, and then in a little law firm, and then he was in prison, and then worked for accountants.

Bill.
BM: My dad was a chemical engineer and my mom for a long time was just a housewife and then she worked in a drugstore and she's worked in mental institutions and...I think she just like sits with dying people and hangs out with them while their family goes out to see a movie once in a while.

She's a hospice worker?
BM: I guess that's what you call it. It's very informal. She kind of has contracts with people she just knows. I think it's like through a church and stuff.

My generation and Craig Gilmore's generation—it's been said that our antiauthoritarianism is a result of rebelling against our fathers. Were you or have you been in rebellion against your fathers, or parents?
CG: I was. Hasn't everyone?
MR: I think real rebellion begins in your head.

PD: My dad was not the authority in my household. I mean my politics have nothing to do with rebelling against my parents. I didn't rebel against my parents' politics. Both my parents...my dad is pretty leftist, so.... He was involved with SDS [Students for a Democratic Society]. I did rebel against my parents, but not around politics. More around other...like leaving the church. They are Catholic.

I don't think the argument goes that you're in rebellion against your parents' politics; it's that you're in rebellion against your parents, and politics is a way for it to express itself.
RK: I think that's a very immature theory.

Why is it an immature theory?
RK: It takes no concept of anything else.

All things have to start somewhere. The idea is that a person's first relationships are with the family he's born into. And there's a dynamic there. And then that dynamic gets transformed later in life into other things. But that doesn't mean that the other things are not important. That would be the logic. You don't agree?
RK: It may be a factor. But beyond that....

Craig, what do you think?
CG: My experience—I mean while the specifics might be different than Paul's, I would echo some of what Paul just said. My parents and I clashed about political issues. But I think it would be reductive to suggest that my interest in activities and political issues as a teenager were ways to get at my parents. It's rather that sometimes they disagreed with my politics, sometimes they were concerned that I was going to be arrested—showing maybe overly protective, parental...and that caused clashes with my parents. It wasn't that my politics came out of conflict with my parents. It's rather that my politics sometimes caused the conflict. So I would say—maybe this is part of what Ramsey was saying—for me it would be very misleading to suggest that the parental relationship was the cause of, or the seed from which the politics grew. Indeed, it was their somewhat conservative and Christian-based teachings of, you know, right and wrong and standing up for what you believe

in that sort of pushed me over when I saw police and National Guard beating up black people in the South who were trying to get a seat at a lunch counter.

You saw this on TV, you mean, or were you—?
CG: I saw it on TV.

PD: In my experience, lots and lots of people were in rebellion against their parents and most of them didn't become political. Almost everyone I went to school with was in some form of rebellion against their parents, and most of them are corporate lawyers now. I think it's a feature of most people's lives. I mean I have a child—she's in conflict with me already. She's five. She rebels against me. I don't know what her politics will be when she's old enough to have them. But I think it's a common feature of life to be in conflict with your parents. But I don't think that translates into having it determine your politics. At least that's not been my experience. If everyone who is in conflict with their parents became an anarchist, we would have won generations ago.

Yeah. Okay. [To Kanaan:] But you weren't in conflict with your parents at all. Or am I wrong? Is this an American thing?
RK: I have no idea if it's an American thing or not. I had a very secure background when my father died shortly after my anarchism. My parents were pretty much apolitical. My father was an immigrant.

Your father died shortly after your anarchism, you said?
RK: My father died when I was sixteen. So, shortly after.

Shortly after you became an anarchist?
RK: Yeah.

You were born in England, you have a connection with Edinburgh.
RK: [Inaudible]

Your father grew up in Lebanon and then came to England?
RK: Yeah.

93

How did the press get founded? Was that you? You and others?

RK: It was started by me. Then it was just me until it became a workers' cooperative. It was the first time AK was a legal entity, as far as the state was concerned.

This is still in Scotland?

RK: Yeah.

Then what? When I met you years ago, I think you had just come to San Francisco. When would that have been?

RK: I first came here in '89.

You had a distribution company, AK Distribution, in Edinburgh.

RK: There's never been any distinction as such between—most of what we do is distribute other small presses and independent concerns, but [also] our own published titles. AK Press is just a publishing arm. AK started off as a distribution thing and was involved with publishing a few things that came out of the workers' cooperative—

When you say workers' coop, do you mean in the informal sense or in the legal sense?

RK: Both. A workers' cooperative is an actual British legal structure. Which is one of the peculiarities of British history: there's actually a legal thing.

So what is it in America? Are you incorporated here?

BM: A California corporation.

Okay. AK is a press. The press is an arm of a larger entity which is basically wholesaling. And you have a relationship with Inbook.

BM: For the publishing we do. They distribute the titles we publish. We also wholesale a lot of the publishers they distribute.

It must be an interesting contract.

RK: Inbook or LPC [Login Publishers Consortium: Inbook's parent corporation] are our primary distributor for AK Press-published titles. Where we distribute our own titles, we use a wide variety of other wholesalers. While LPC are our primary distributor, they're not exclusive. Well, our contract with LPC states that they are our exclusive primary distributor to the book trade with as many exceptions as we want. But in terms of quantities, we sell more of our titles than LPC does.

Because their strength is general trade stores and you have a niche? Or why would that be?

CG: I think it's because we sell books outside—I mean, as you know, the independent trade stores are struggling, have been struggling virtually since the time AK Press started publishing books. One of the great strengths in having our own distribution system is the ability to move books into alternative or little known distribution channels.

I had assumed that you had your own network of anarchist stores, like Left Bank.

BM: That's part of it.

CG: That's part of it, yeah.

So what other types of stores—what?

BM: There's like three anarchist bookstores in the world.

RK: Well, there's a couple in Canada. There's three in the U.S. and a couple in Canada. In the whole world there are probably no more than ten anarchist-identified bookstores.

CG: To give you an example of one of the things that we do: We just published an animal-rights novel. And we have various animal-rights activist groups who table at various animal-rights demonstrations, selling books. So they're getting the book out to what would be our target audience. Traditional bookstores that LPC—I mean it's not a criticism of LPC, but the structure of getting books out into the trade stores and out to the other wholesalers, to the chains, would never reach those readers. But we know the readers are out there. We're selling them books.

Right. Of course, that's the problem with all of publishing, whether you're large or small—it's hard to get to the readers that you know are out there. What about the San Francisco Book Fair in the fall? Do you go to that?

BM: Oh, yeah. We do really well at that. Ramsey's part of

Bound Together Bookstore Collective which organizes a—it's one of the three anarchist bookstores in the country. But they have an annual anarchist book fair in Golden Gate Park, which is another way of selling directly to the public.

You say you do really well at the book fairs: What proportion of your sales would come from book fair sales?

BM: Proportion of sales over a year? For two days in the year—there's two big book fairs. One percent or less. Which I think is pretty good.

Yeah, it is.

CG: But also whenever we table we take a stack of catalogues. And one of the things it's hard to measure is how much business we get as a result of the catalogue.

Blue Heron Publishing up in Hillsboro, Oregon, when they go to book fairs that is how they measure their success. They bring so many hundreds of catalogues, and they figure the more catalogues they get rid of, the more successful they are. Nobody knows how that translates into sales, but that's how they do it. Open Hand in Seattle does the same thing [see Gold 1996]. Subsidiary rights. Do you try to sell subsidiary rights? Foreign rights? You're smiling.

RK: We're recently trying—

BM: We contracted with an agent through the Industrial Workers of the World—a former union member—who's going to try to sell foreign rights for us in Frankfurt [i.e., the annual international book fair in Frankfurt, Germany].

RK: The last couple months is the first time we ever tried to sell foreign rights. The first time we've ever tried systematically. We made a couple of tentative efforts occasionally over the years, which came to nothing.

BM: There have a been a few editions of AK books in other languages, but there was no money exchanged. But we've got a guy who's going to the Frankfurt Book Fair, representing us, his own press, and two or three other presses. He does a lot of New Agey kind of stuff. But, interestingly, the way we actually found out about each other was he approached us at a book fair and basically hooked us up with an animal-rights novel we published. I met him like two or three years ago. He was the author's agent.

Did he go to the last Frankfurt Book Fair?
BM: This will be his first time.

I went to the last one. The first time I'd been. Have you been to one?
RK: No.

Let me tell you, it's an experience. I could give you statistics on it, but it doesn't convey the experience. But the fair itself, where you have more than a quarter of a million people speaking over a hundred languages, and in various national dress, was really kind of...awesome. Everybody should go there at least once. Everybody should go there. That's the world, all meeting at one place.
PD: The literate world.

Well, not necessarily. I was talking with somebody from [a certain magazine], and I mentioned a couple of authors. I mentioned Beckett. And James Joyce. And she didn't know who they were. And I said, "Well, one won the Nobel Prize and the other is one of the greats of twentieth-century literature and the mentor of the first." And she said, "Well, I'm in marketing." So they're not all literate. Um. Now you're actually wholesalers rather than—you don't hire sales reps, do you? For AK Distribution, that is. You send out your catalogue and wait for a response? Is that essentially it?
CG: We try to be a little more active than that. We call stores. In the retail world, our two principle markets are relatively local bookstores, and then left bookstores across the country. Anarchist-identified stores. We're probably the best—our specialization in terms of having anarchist and other left-wing books makes us an important resource for Hungry Mind Bookstore—

Stores that buy directly from you: Would you say that they want anarchist materials, or you just happen to be carrying certain titles that—?

PD: It's a mix. Like we get a lot of single-title orders from chain stores like Barnes and Noble and Borders. And those are almost exclusively special orders. That is, customers want books that we carry. And through their central office they know that we carry them and they fax us the orders, or whatever. But then we also get stores that want to stock anarchists, or that have an anarchist section. Like Cody's Books in Berkeley; they have a couple shelves of anarchist books they get mostly from us.

BM: Powell's in Portland.

RK: Certainly it's also a case of presuming that the buyers of whatever stores have no antipathy towards anarchism. They simply see it as another salable item. Insofar as AK's objective, we're selling our more supposedly salable items as a way to get into a store. And then, once they trust us and we've built a relationship, we can tie on our backlist.

Are stores carrying backlist titles? My experience is that frontlist is important to the stores. My backlist is selling on the internet, not in stores. Are you on the internet?
BM: Yes.

Do you have a web site?
BM: Yes.

Is that working for you? Do you get orders from it?
PD: Yeah. It's most of our retail mail-order channel, as well.

Retail mail-order channel?
PD: Yeah, we sell retail mail order as well.

BM: A pretty big chunk of our business, actually, is direct to, you know, people in Alaska or who live nowhere where there's a bookstore.

Oh, to individuals.
PD: Right. That's a big part of our business.

You send out catalogues to individuals? The cost of sending them out, and the sales that result from that—is it cost-effective?
PD: We believe so. It's the best thing we have so far.

CG: One of the major subjects of yesterday morning's meeting was the fact that we have such a huge backlog of requests for catalogues. We've got a stack like this—we're that far behind in just sending catalogues out to people who've written in.

CO: Every day in the morning mail we have a big stack like this, people saying, "I've heard about you. Please send me a catalogue." Then they get the catalogue, they go to the back page and send in an order. Hopefully it's cost-effective.

How would they have heard of you?

CO: AK Press gets a lot of publicity in the underground rock 'n roll world. I've personally done, and a lot of people have done, tabling at, say, punk rock or rock-'n-roll concerts. And that's where you meet a lot of young people who are sympathetic to these kinds of ideas. And they certainly see a lot of things. Ramsey and I went on tour with the bands, selling the merchandise as well as the political books and what not. The bigger these bands get, they spread the word for AK Press as well. These kids buy a new record from whatever; I sell some books at whoever's rock concert.

Can you tell if your books appeal to any particular age group?

RK: Well, it depends what books we do. I'd say that the more overt the politics are, the less the book sales. That's not to say that there's no politics in our animal-rights novels.

Are you 501 (c) (3), or for-profit?
CG: We'd like to be.
BM: We're all for it; we just don't necessarily achieve it.

Have you thought about going nonprofit?

BM: Yes. Other than just kind of talking about it as an idea, we haven't formally talked about it. We have to look at our options. One idea we had is to formally incorporate the publishing arm as a nonprofit and keep the distribution as it is, so we can get tax-deductible donations and grants and things for publishing, because that is really where— Distribution pretty much sustains itself. What little profit we can glean from distribution goes into publishing. One of the other ways to raise money for publishing would be to go nonprofit.

PD: It's a very involved process, nonprofit status.

BM: Yeah.

CG: One of the things that we're able to do that helps put the publishing— We're able to go out and do a lot of events which, if we were just a publisher, we wouldn't have enough books to sustain it. That is, we can sell a lot of Craig's books at music shows, but we don't do enough other music books to make it worth our while to take the table and spend the money to do it. But our wholesale company allows us to take books from different publishers, sell a lot more of AK Press books, get a lot more people on our mailing list, and that kind of synergy between the distribution side and the publishing side works really well for us.

Peter Rosset
Food First Books

"For us, publishing is social activism. There's no doubt about that."

I interviewed Peter Rosset on a warm, sunny Thursday in May 1998 at the Institute for Food and Development Policy, located in a large corner house in a residential area of north Oakland, California. Rosset is tall, slender, reddish-haired. I looked for a resemblance to his father, Barney Rosset, whom I had interviewed in New York a year earlier, and decided it was in the evenness of the smile and the shape of the nose at the bridge.

Peter was born and raised in Manhattan. He went to Brown University, as did Harry Smith, Bruce McPherson, Eric Kampmann, and Vito Perillo, all interviewed in this volume. ("Brown! Brown University keeps coming up. You're the fifth person of twenty that I've interviewed—!") At Brown he majored in ecology, later earning his Ph.D., also in ecology, from the University of Michigan at Ann Arbor.

I was there from '78 or '79 to '86. But most of the time I was enrolled as a graduate student I was actually living and working in Central America and doing my dissertation on the side.

You're not in academia, I take it.
Well, I teach a course once a year at Stanford in Latin American Studies, and about once every three years at Berkeley, so I have connections with academia. I worked at Stanford for two years, actually, before coming here. I was teaching there.

Did you like working in academia?
I loved teaching. I didn't like Stanford very much. It was too much of a conservative, closed-minded atmosphere. Berkeley I like much better, although you can get lost in the vastness of it.

How did you get interested in ecology?

I think it was the contrast between New York City and outside of New York City where I had the opportunity to go sometimes on weekends, to Long Island, and sometimes in summers to various places. Something about the contrast between countryside and city, I think, gave me the interest.

A friend of mine spent several years in India, and when she moved back to the United States she lived on Long Island. She used to go through the woods picking up good things to eat. [Both of us laugh.] She did that for years.

Great. Good for her.

So you went directly from Brown to the University of Michigan?

No, I went from Brown to the University of London where I did a master's degree, and I went from there to the U.S. Department of Agriculture, which I hated. So that drove me back to graduate school for a Ph.D. as a way of escaping that career route. And that brought me to Central America where I spent most of the next dozen years until, basically, taking this job. Even when I was at Stanford I was actually running a research center that they have in southern Mexico. Chiapas, where the Zapatistas are.

Originally I was going to do my doctoral research in anthropology there.

Oh, really? What university were you in?

I was at the University of Washington.

Uh huh. The joke in Chiapas is that the typical family unit is mother, father, five kids and an anthropologist. A lot of anthropologists there.

There's a similar joke in New Guineau.

Oh, really? [Laughs.]

And that's primarily the reason I didn't go there.

Yeah. There was that whole Harvard project there for about

forty years. There are generations of faculty members all over the country now who did their dissertations on Chiapas. None of them predicted the rebellion, so so much for all of that.

Well, I used to go down to northern Mexico and the problem, from an outsider's point of view, was that it seemed as though there should be a rebellion any moment.
Right.

But it had seemed like that for sixty years.
B. Traven wrote the great book about Chiapas. What was it called—*Rebellion of the Hanged* or something? I can't remember if that's the exact title—in which he described a rebellion in Chiapas almost exactly like the Zapatista rebellion.

I haven't read that one. I read March to the Montería *which was also set in Chiapas.*
He wrote a whole series of five or seven books about Chiapas.

Were you living on grants down there, or—?
I was partially living on grants, but I worked for a number of organizations. I worked for a regional organization based in Costa Rica that does agricultural development. I worked for them for two years in Costa Rica and two years in Nicaragua. I had money for a couple of years from the Organization of American States, a grant from the National Science Foundation, a Fulbright visiting professorship at the university there for one of the years that I was in Nicaragua, and two years at Stanford had me in Chiapas, so one way or another I managed to piece it together.

How long have you been back now?
I've been back full time, living in the U.S., since December 15th, 1993. But for the two years before that I was part-time in the U.S. and part-time in Chiapas. With the Stanford job I was in both places.

I'm surprised you know the exact date.
Well, mainly it's because it was two weeks before January 1st, 1994, which is the date of the Zapatista rebellion and NAFTA [North

American Free Trade Agreement] being signed into law. Which, to me, was pretty amazing. Moving out of Chiapas on December 15th, everything seeming completely normal, and then two weeks later we arrive at our house in San Francisco and there's a message on the answering machine from a friend in San Cristobal de las Casas saying that the guerrillas have just taken the city. We thought, This must be April Fool's Day. There's absolutely no way that could be possible. Then we turned on CNN and saw Marcos in the ski mask in front of the municipal palace.

NAFTA was signed on the same day the Chiapas rebellion began?
Actually, it wasn't signed then; it was the day it went into effect. That was one of the things they mentioned in their declaration of war. They said that that was the final nail in the coffin for Mexico's indigenous people.

I remember that. So how long has Food First been in existence?
Twenty-three years. It was founded by Frances Moore Lappé after the success of her book, *Diet for a Small Planet*, which sold about four million copies in the U.S. and was translated into twenty-two languages and was a best-seller in many countries. That was the book that made the first connection for a popular audience between our high-consumption life styles in countries in the north and poverty, hunger, and environmental problems in countries in the south where our ecological footprint is. Basically, it suggested that people could start to make a difference by thinking about the food they eat and changing their diet as a way of changing their impact, and that that would be a step towards broader social activism.

After that book was so successful, she felt there was a need for an organization that would carry out alternative analyses of our food system and hunger on an ongoing basis. And she met a gentleman named Joseph Collins, and together they founded Food First. Our real name is the Institute for Food and Development Policy, but Food First is our nickname. It came from the first book that they did together, called *Food First: Beyond the Myth of Scarcity*, which was also a pretty big seller. Ballantine did both *Diet for a Small Planet* and *Food First*. So most people know us as Food First.

That book [*Diet for a Small Planet*]—a whole generation of

activists came from that book.

Was the title Food First *a play on Earth First!?*

No. Food First was around before the Earth First! people. They stole our name. [Laughs.] Now there's Earth First!, Fish First, all these different something-first organizations. Food First is the first one, as far as I know.

I began thinking about food in a different context when I was in Samoa, because it's so important there—so consciously important. As a gift. To solidify relationships. To establish relationships. If you deny food, then you're denying a relationship.

Well, I think that says a lot about our U.S. culture, because we're not conscious about food. Kids who grow up in a city may think that tomatoes come out of a factory in styrofoam and plastic. There's a real separation between production and consumption. What Frances Moore Lappé really highlighted and what led to the success of *Food First* was the realization that food is both personal and political. And if you can get people to think about what their food means, both to them and their own health as well as to the world and other people and the planet's environment, then it's a very good way to make that connection between personal and political. We like to say that you have to think about what you're eating. For example, if you eat a cantaloupe that comes from El Salvador, you could think about different aspects of that. Like, how much fossil fuel was expended in flying the refrigerated plane? Who grew it? What food crop was displaced by deciding to grow melons for export? What small farmers lost their land? How much pesticide was doused on what farm worker? Of the dollar that you pay for that melon, how much goes to the farmer? How much goes to the farm worker? It turns out that less than two cents goes to the farmers and the farm workers. How much goes to the shipping company? to the fruit broker? to the packager? to the advertiser? to Safeway? Who gets to eat and who doesn't, as a result of producing that melon?

Food is a window into any society. Just looking at who eats and who doesn't, who produces food and who consumes it, tells you a lot about things as diverse as democracy, economics, the organization of society, compassion—really, it's a window into different cultures.

105

Is the Institute for Food and Development Policy an educational institute, in part?

Yes. We do research, analysis, what we call education for action, advocacy. Basically, our goal is to explode the myths about the real causes of hunger and poverty, what you might call popular misconceptions that block real change, because as long as we don't understand the true causes our solutions are going to be misdirected. We feel that sometimes the myths immobilize people, give them a sense of despair, and don't show people that we really do have the power to change things. So we try to do what we call "mobilizing works"—books that take what was maybe originally academic research but put it into popular language, make it accessible as a way of empowering people with information about true causes and alternative solutions.

How do you get books to people that you want to have them?

One of the main ways that we've had impact over the years is through undergraduate course adoptions. That's probably our single largest market. There are generations of activists around food and hunger issues who had their lives changed by reading a Food First book they were assigned in an introductory course. That's a big market as well as a big way that we have impact, and a big way that we get our message to people whose lives then are dedicated to effecting the kind of change— really, the largest audience, sales, market, and impact is through that. Secondary ones would be through influencing academics, policy makers, nonprofit organizations, activists. A lot of church activists will use our books, will have discussion groups about them. But in terms of volume, course adoptions is by far the biggest. We're trying to build our books for general public sales.

In course adoptions, do you go after particular professors to let them know—?

Yeah, we do targeted mailings to professional associations or lists of professors who buy books on particular topics. Really, I would say that we almost have a brand-name recognition in that there's a small but loyal contingent of faculty members across America, who may number several hundred, who love to use Food First books in their courses and always want to have the latest Food First book and the latest edition as a course adoption. It's hard to tell how effective we are in terms of our efforts to sell books because there's a certain suspicion that we would sell almost as many books no matter what, because of that loyal market. It's unclear how many additional books we're selling because of our actual efforts to sell them. So it's a little bit of a dilemma in terms of evaluating the impact of our sales efforts. It's good to have that loyal market but it also makes it unclear how effective we are in selling to anybody else.

In selling to the college market, do you do your own fulfillment, or does Subterranean [Food First's distributor]—?
Subco [i.e., The Subterranean Company] does the fulfillment.

Can you tell from your statements how much is going there and how much goes elsewhere?
Only by interpolation. But I would say that probably seventy percent goes to the college market.

You were doing your own fulfillment before you went to Subco?
Yes. It was a nightmare. When I took over as executive director the entire basement was filled with books and the entire staff was almost incapable of doing any of their other work because the 800 phone would ring every five minutes and whichever staff member was nearby would take the call, take the order, write up the bill, go downstairs and pack the books and ship them. It was a nightmare. So the very first thing I did when I came—in fact, on the advice of my father, the long-time, experienced publisher, who said, "Get the books out of the building." And it's been such an alleviation of both space problems and personnel problems to get them out of here, it's just been miraculous.

We're not substantially better off [with a distributor] in terms of money. And, because our publishing operation is merged into a larger nonprofit who does a lot of things that aren't publishing related, it's difficult for me to tell: Are we running a profit or a loss on our book operations? I would say that we're probably breaking even. We ought to be making money on them.

How many titles a year do you publish?

Two to six.

How big a print run do you do on the first printing?

Anywhere from two to five thousand, pretty much because of our brand-name recognition. This doesn't sound like very much, maybe, for a trade publisher, but it's a lot for an academic publisher. We'll automatically sell three thousand copies of any title that comes out with our name on it. Which really means that—if that were, say, our average sales figure; our average might be higher than that—if we had enough titles we could be profitable, but we don't have enough titles at that level of sales to be profitable. So we either need more sales or more titles, or both. That's the dilemma that we're in right now. The difficult thing about more titles is cash flow. We don't have the capital to bring out the ten or twelve titles a year that we would need to be profitable at that level of sales.

That's the classic dilemma for a small company.

Exactly. Yeah, we're in that classic dilemma. It hasn't brought us to a crisis because the overall organization is large enough that in a bad year in book sales it's subsidized out of our larger budget, which hurts but doesn't drive the publishing operation out of business. I guess that's allowed us to be a little lax about taking more decisive action in terms of the economics of the publishing operation, although I think we're starting to move towards the point of acting, though I don't know what direction we'll go.

What has allowed you to be lax?

The fact that we're not sinking or swimming, or living as an organization, on whether or not the books are profitable. If we were, we would either be gone or we would have decisively changed the organization, and therefore the economics, of our publishing a long time ago.

How many people work for Food First Books?

The institute has seven full-time employees. Publishing is usually one full-time person plus parts of some other people. In other words, my dedication, when we have a managing editor—right now our managing editor position is vacant—might only be fifteen percent to Food First Books as the publisher. The managing editor would be a hundred percent

108

dedication, or eighty percent, because we have some other activities. But right now, in the absence of a managing editor, much more of my time as well as the time of another person here is devoted to publishing. We also rely a lot on volunteers for our overall operations, so in addition to the seven paid employees, we usually have ten or fifteen interns and volunteers. Only a small proportion of their time would be devoted to the book publishing.

Do they come from the universities?
Universities, yeah. Around the world, actually.

You can't do anything for them financially?
No, but a lot of them are able to get some kind of scholarship from their college, or from a church group. Or a lot of them will work here two days a week and get a part-time job for four days a week, and make it work. You know, share an apartment with a bunch of other kids.

You're the executive director of the Institute for Food and Development Policy?
And, therefore, automatically I'm the publisher of Food First Books.

So one goes with the other.
Yeah. For the time being. One of the options we're considering is spinning off Food First Books into a for-profit company owned by the nonprofit.

Why would you do that?
Well, it's difficult for a nonprofit to raise capital. If we were to decide that the analysis I just gave you is the correct one—i.e., we need to have more capital to bring out more titles and then we'll almost automatically be profitable—how would we raise that capital? Usually banks are loathe to give small business loans to a nonprofit. We couldn't sell twenty percent of it to an investor, or something like that. But if we had a for-profit subsidiary, then there would be a variety of ways that we could capitalize the company in order to bump up the number of titles. I only say that as something that we're considering; no decisions have been

made. But there are a number of ways we could go. We're continually being encouraged to associate ourselves with a larger commercial company.

Any particular one?
Well, because we sometimes have more titles to bring out in a given year than we have capital to publish them, almost every year or every other year we do one or two titles with outside publishers. We've done titles with Ballantine, HarperCollins, Grove/Atlantic, Zed, Pluto, and probably a couple of others that I can't remember, and we have yet to find what I would call a satisfactory relationship. We definitely, definitely, definitely make more money on a title we publish ourselves than on any that we co-publish, so it doesn't feel like a full association is the right way out, although sometimes it seems like it's the only way out.

Let's say you do a book with Ballantine. Who does the distribution on that?
They do. On all of our outside-published books, they're the nonexclusive, main distributor. We take some stock and leave it at Subco for people who order from our 800 number. That's usually a trivial amount of the total sales, although it's important to us to serve [those of] our membership who like to buy that way.

We don't have to go into this if you don't want to, but is it a fifty-fifty deal with Zed or Pluto or Ballantine or—?
Well, we've tried the classic co-publishing, which would be to split costs and profits. I'm not going to mention the names of any publishers, but that has never worked because we've always ended up having a dispute over what the real costs are. I've yet to find the outside publisher who will be completely transparent on that. It's very annoying when the per-copy costs seem to be much higher than when we do them ourselves.

Even with the smaller publishers?
I would say more or less across the board, but I don't want to name names. Then when we've done other [co-publishing arrangements], we've been the equivalent of the author. And that's even more depress-

110

ing, because of the small royalty we get compared to what we get when we publish the book ourselves, although the costs are lower. The income just pales in comparison. We could sell a quarter as many copies and make twice as much money. So, from a financial point of view, it's frustrating either way.

Now I should point out that we don't publish books to make money. We publish books because our mission is to have an impact on the world. So there's a little bit of a trade-off. With Ballantine, just to use a name, we're going to sell more copies, so we're going to have more impact. On the other hand, we can't continue to have impact unless we don't have too many losses, because then the organization will disappear. So it's a kind of balance of the short-term/long-term issue in terms of making clear decisions about how we should go in our publishing.

It seems to me that to the extent you associated Food First with HarperCollins or Ballantine, you would lose a proportionate amount of control.

Right. Exactly. That's one of the things that would argue against doing that. Although presumably they would be able to move many more titles. And since the goal here is to have an impact, and we can only have that by people reading the books, there's an argument in favor of that. I'm not saying it's the argument to trump the others, but it's definitely something that has to be balanced in the analysis.

So we're getting back to the idea of co-publishing where you probably weren't losing money—

No, we weren't losing money, but sometimes we end up having to put up almost as much money because it miraculously and mysteriously costs more for them to produce a book than it does us. So even though we're paying half, we're not paying half of a hundred percent, we're paying half of a hundred and eighty percent. So how much are we saving in exchange for only half of the profits? It's been frustrating. My best description of co-publishing is it's been frustrating. Then arguing about other things, like will it come out only in hardcover or will it also come out in paperback? Will it be affordable to the audience we want to read it, or will it cost, as in one case, forty-two dollars a copy? So those are the losing-control issues, as well as not being compensated in terms of a good

111

financial arrangement. It's been frustrating.

The books that Food First does itself—can you tell if they get to people who ordinarily cannot afford other books?

I don't think they do, because the economics of publishing is such that there really is a bottom line in terms of pricing the books, and that makes them pretty expensive. You're not going to get a trade paperback for much less than twelve-ninety-five these days. And for people who truly have a low income, that's a lot of money. In fact, I don't buy a lot of books because that's a lot money for me.

Regarding nonprofit status, one of the publishers I interviewed in Minneapolis said, as I recall, that forty percent of their income is earned; the rest of it is grant money. That's fairly common, I think.

As an organization, the proportion of our total budget that comes from book sales is well under twenty percent. However, the proportion of our total expenses that go to book production is also under twenty percent. That's why I say that the publishing operation, Food First Books, is pretty much a break-even operation, although I can't nail it down exactly because there are so many shared costs that it's hard to assign them with absolute certainly.

What I was getting at is your saying earlier that it's hard to get grant money.

Actually, we have not made a concerted effort to fund our publishing specifically through grants. Part of the reason we haven't done it is, in looking at the foundation world, it hasn't seemed like it would be very easy. We are able to get grants for other things, and it feels like we should go with the things that we're pretty sure we'll going to get a grant for, rather than investing in writing proposals for something that doesn't seem like it's going to have a high chance of success. Very little of our publishing is grant financed, although as an organization we're probably thirty-five or forty percent grant financed.

You mentioned before I turned on the tape that you have eight thousand members. What's a member?

Some organizations might call them donors, but they're people who believe in the mission of Food First and who support us by—a typical person might contribute thirty-five dollars a year. In exchange for that they get a quarterly newsletter and what we call "backgrounders," which would be like briefings on different issues, and then they get a twenty-percent discount on all the books we publish in-house. We can't afford that discount on the co-published titles. But, really, that's the legacy of Frances Moore Lappé and *Diet for a Small Planet* and those kinds of books that influenced people when they were college students. And there are a lot of seniors and church organizations who believe in the organization and who support our work.

You might say that we are a think tank. And as a think tank, we're the only one that has that kind of independent member support for finances. They provide about half of our income. Not compared so much to publishing companies, but compared to think tanks, that makes us very independent, because we are less dependent on foundation support. We don't get any corporate support, don't get government support, so we're more insulated from the kind of fashions that come and go in that kind of a funding community. Yes, it affects us, but much less than other policy think tanks.

What about subsidiary rights sales? Do you try to sell translation rights or foreign rights?

We have had translations of our books in, I think, twenty-two or twenty-eight languages, something like that, over the years. However, the vast bulk of those are kind of like solidarity rights. We're writing about a lot of activist issues, and so some activist coalition in the Philippines wants to re-do one of our books but they don't have any money and would we just give them the rights. So a substantial proportion of our overseas rights is donated. We do have some income from subsidiary rights, but not that much.

Have you gone to the Frankfurt Book Fair or sent anybody to the Frankfurt Book Fair?

There are some small-press-representation companies who go there and set up a booth and then talk to people about rights. We have done that at Frankfurt and we usually get from five to seven nibbles which turn into zero or one sale. And that costs us several hundred dollars, so it's kind of an iffy proposition. We used to go to the ABA every year, but that doesn't really seem to be worth the expense, and it's even more expensive to go to Frankfurt. So the short answer is no, not really.

Grove/Atlantic is doing a book with us right now, and for some reason that I really don't understand, when we were doing the contract, they said, "We'll just take U.S. English language rights. You can keep the outside deals." So we immediately turned around and sold it to a British publisher, Earthscan, who's doing a nice print run. That was actually very nice for us. I'm not sure they realized what they were giving up.

How did you find this job?

How did I find this job? Well, I'm one of the people who was very affected by reading Food First books when I was a college student. And I'd been a very big fan, and I'd managed to meet and become friends with the founders, Frances Moore Lappé and Joseph Collins. They were actually doing research on Nicaragua when I lived there and they used to stay in my house when they came to visit.

This is a convoluted tale. But at that time my father, Barney Rosset, was still the publisher at Grove Press. And Food First Books had decided that they wanted to have an outside publisher do all of their books. And I said, "Well, I can set you up with my father because it seems like you have similar interests." So I hooked them up and Grove Press started to do all the Food First books shortly before my father was sacked by the Gettys. [See the Barney Rosset interview in this volume.] Which didn't help Food First very much because then there was nobody there with any personal interest in the books. And Food First in subsequent years was not happy with the relationship and ended up going back to in-house publishing long before I got here.

But I always used to think about working here someday. Actually, my real fantasy was founding an organization like Food First that I would be the executive director of. It never occurred to me, being the executive director of Food First, until I was teaching at Stanford and part time in Chiapas. And I got an e-mail—this is very convoluted—Food First was advertising for a new executive director. Somehow that got e-mailed to a friend of mine in Nicaragua who e-mailed it to me in Chiapas from where, based on my long-term affection for the organization, I applied for the job. And here I am.

114

You know, publishing is very much in my blood. I grew up with publishing. I used to work all of my summers at Grove Press and saw all the operations from the inside and heard about it at dinner and, you know, really was involved with it, but never thought that I would actually end up in publishing. And then, miraculously, January 1st, 1994, I became a publisher. So, it's one of those things.

Could we go back to your childhood?
Sure.

I'd like to talk about what Grove Press, or your father's involvement with Grove, meant to you.
You mean both. Grove Press was the family business. Everybody lent a hand in the family business.

When you say family, do you mean father and mother and children, or extended family?
Extended family.

Your father told me—
He's been married several times. And my mother, even after divorcing him, continued to be a freelance editor for Grove Press. She was very knowledgeable about Eastern philosophy and Eastern religion, so for decades, I believe, she edited their Eastern philosophy and Eastern religion series, which was always a big seller for them—all their stuff on Buddhism—even though they were divorced. At the same time my father was working there, my stepmother was working there, I was working there—you know, anybody with any connection to the family would somehow be roped in. A classic family business.

Really, it was a family business in the sense that a baker loves making bread, and it's like an art or a pleasure or a joy or a craft, as opposed to the kind of corporate, faceless thing that big publishing has become since then. So I grew up in publishing, not with the transnational, megaconglomerate publishing, but with the small-press family business, the love of the art of publishing, the crafting-books kind of experience.

And personal relations with all of the authors. All of the Grove Press authors would stay at our house. Many Nobel Prize winners—

Samuel Beckett, Norman Mailer would be in the house. All the vast stable of bizarre characters we published would be hanging out and hanging around and almost be part of the extended family. I don't think that most of the authors at Random House, for example, are spending the night at the CEO's house and getting to know his family. Maybe with Bennett Cerf, but not currently.

Publishing should probably have remained a cottage industry.
I think so.

Kurt Wolff, in his memoir, said he didn't think publishers should publish more than a hundred titles a year. Beyond that it isn't publishing [Wolff 1991:5].
Right. It's like making cars on an assembly line. Not only did I grow up with authors in my father's company, but also publishers. My father was friends with many small, alternative publishers from around the world. They would also be around, all kinds of folks. So that was quite an experience. As well, Grove Press was almost like a school for publishers; many of the editors went on either to found their own houses or to become high-level executives at other houses. So it gave me a sort of connection with the publishing industry, at least one part of the publishing industry—the more alternative, more cottage-industry part of it.

Your father's activism and your activism—do you see similarities? Obviously your sympathies are similar.
Right.

Yet you're part of something and he's more entrepreneurial.
Yeah, I think he's more of an entrepreneur and a rugged individualist, and I'm more of a being-part-of-a-movement, being-part-of-an-organization, institution-building kind of person, although certainly the sympathies and the basic world view are the same.

Your interest is in trying to promote food activism.
That's right. And broader social activism about social justice issues in general. This organization has given birth to other organizations that started as programs. Just to give you an idea: The Pesticide Action

Network which is active, obviously, around pesticide issues, started as a project here. An organization called Global Exchange which does reality tours to Cuba, Viet Nam, Haiti, places like that, started as a project here. An organization in Vermont called the Center for the Art of Democracy was started by folks here. A number of other activist organizations have been direct spin-offs. We work with environmental organizations, farm-worker organizations, welfare rights, homeless, you name it. Both in the U.S. and internationally. Alternative, grass-roots, development organizations.

What is it you do?

Well, we ourselves are not an activist organization. We don't do canvassing or go out and knock on doors. We don't do direct aid. We don't send money for development projects or those kinds of things that other organizations do. We don't do political lobbying. But we support organizations who do those kinds of things by providing them with analysis, with written materials that help them in their work, either by educating them or that they use to educate their target audiences.

This is the Institute you're talking about.

The Institute, right. That's our relationship to a lot of other organizations. Much of our work is in larger coalitions of more activist organizations. We're kind of like the education/research part in a larger division of labor. For us, publishing is social activism. There's no doubt about that.

I don't have any more questions. Is there anything you would like to talk about.

I think the dilemma of being a small publisher in a nonprofit [organization] is what has to be resolved. Do we go the direction of The New Press and try to get grant funding directly for our publishing? Do we go the way of handing over our publishing program to a commercial publisher, as has been tried earlier here at Food First? Those are the questions that are in my mind right now, at least. What do we do about distribution? What do we do about sales and marketing? How will the internet influence our business and future direction?

At the sales conferences, how do the sales reps respond when you're describing your books?

Very positively. But that's not translated into sales. [Laughing.] I have good relationships with them because, actually, a number of them have been sales reps for my father over the years. So it's like old times. When I worked on-again, off-again for Grove Press during my young adult years, I often used to go to the ABA to help staff the booth, and therefore I went to the old Grove Press sales conferences. So I got to know a lot of their commission sales reps, and some of them are Subco reps now. It's a small world.

Before we went to Subco one of biggest problems was collections. Probably thirty percent of our accounts we were never able to collect from, and many others would be twelve months, eighteen months past due when we got paid. So, basically, the bookstore industry as a whole was stiffing us on a routine basis. I'm not necessarily talking about the smaller independents either. That alone was making our publishing operation unprofitable. So even if our distributor didn't boost sales, getting paid for all of them, and only three months later, has been a real pleasure. It's really stemmed some of the hemorrhaging.

Malachi McCormick
Stone Street Press

"They'll have none of the important books, or it'll be hit and miss whether they have the important books. They'll have somebody in charge of it who has no idea of what they're doing. I went looking for *Ars Poetica* at Barnes and Noble recently. 'Can you spell that?' I spelled it out for them. 'Author's name?' Horace. 'First name?' Too awful. It's ridiculous. Horace."

On the Friday evening preceding Labor Day weekend 1996, after the small press fair at Bumbershoot had closed for the day, Malachi McCormick and I went for coffee at a food kiosk in Seattle Center and I turned on the cassette recorder.

McCormick was born in 1937 in Cobh in County Cork, Ireland. He lives now, and has his press, a letterpress operation, in Staten Island, New York.

You come out here almost every year.

Well, I think I've been here every year since I started. But when I started was, I think, I guess, about five years, possibly six years ago. I'm not sure.

Is it financially feasible for you?

Well, it's getting marginal. Last year I thought it was really not worth my while to come, when I thought of the airfare and all of that. One big factor which I could measure was the fact that the outside of the building [Seattle Center's Exhibition Hall, where the fair was held] was under construction. I thought I might give it another crack this year, but I was really unsure. And at the same time, I had realized that I had to find, very quickly, more book fairs to do. I'm losing independent bookstores. I'm losing some of my customers. Some have gone out of business, and others, even though they're still in business, they seem to feel they have to compete more directly with the chains. My idea would be that they emphasize what the differences are, which, of course, is to feature, not in a huge way, but to feature, in a way, small press stuff. But there is something that is happening, and I realize I can do—

It's hard to predict how many books you'll sell at any kind of book fair, but if it's above a certain level, then I tend to think it's worth my while in terms of books sold, in terms of— If it's reasonably good, it's a pleasure, the unpredictable conversations you have, the people you meet. You expand your mailing list, and if you can cover your costs, that's very good. And if you can do more than that, that's very good, too. I would like to do more than that. As I say, last year I got into the zone of thinking it might be better for me to find a local fair in New York. And I'm discovering this odd fact about my end of the book business, being hand-made books and being very much crafted, I would say, much more than the average book. It's a curious thing to find that people at craft fairs are more aware of what's gone into making the object, which happens to be a book, than often a book person is. There's obviously a gap in education there.

I remember being at an ABA. I go to the ABA every year. And that's a sad story, too. That's a decreasing market for me. I now look at it almost like, not to get orders, but.... It's like another fair, you know? So it's still worth my while to do it. And I pick up some orders, and I see some of my independent bookstore buyers. Often when I'm making a new book, I'll still be working on it at the fair. Somebody who had been selling my books for a number of years in her store came along to put an order in—it was about three or four, five years ago at the ABA—she came along to put in an order, and I was sewing, doing something, and she says, "You don't make all of these...?" She'd been selling them for years. She says, "You don't make all of these things by hand, do you?" It's just a very curious thing. It shows you there's a certain—I don't know how wide the demographic is, but it shows that some people just are not aware. To some people it's very important, as you know. And some people, it might only be content, it doesn't matter what the book is like.

But at craft fairs people are attuned to thinking that craft means somebody has put some work into this. So they're more prepared, I suppose, to see.... So I'm looking for a fair in New York to replace Bumbershoot. And I found one, but it's next weekend, so I thought I'd just come to Bumbershoot and give it a shot.

120

Let's go back and get the biographical data out of the way, okay?
Okay.

High school graduate? College graduate?
Actually, I left school at the age of seventeen. My father died and we all went out to work, to earn some money. My interest at that time was chemistry, and I had been something of a chemistry whiz at school. My oldest brother was a chemist, an industrial chemist. I thought I'd do that and discovered that industrial chemistry is not the chemistry that I loved. I was more an alchemist than a chemist.

So I left that and went to school to get a degree in science at night while I was doing this work, then got the opportunity to train as what they called an industrial engineer. The whole idea was to look at these operations, ways of working, and make them more efficient. How to produce more, done with less people. And I trained—there was a company near where I lived in Ireland, Irish Dunlop Company, and I worked with them for a while. And then I went to London when I was about twenty, with another training program with a larger English company. That was about 1957 I went to London. And I worked with them and was reasonably successful for some eight, nine years or so. Which brings us into the middle of the '60s. And at that point I found it somewhat depressing that I could see myself doing this for another forty years. That was a somewhat depressing thought. I didn't have a strong interest in what I was—I was very good at what I did, but it just wasn't good.

And there was an underlying thing also, which rather made me uncomfortable. Which was my father had managed the local labor exchange in Ireland, he was very involved with trying to find work for people, and I seemed to be getting people out of work. In the climate of the '60s, it seemed to be not a good thing. I would look at work and find a way that it could be done with, say, a gang of four people as opposed to six. Or I would put up production in some way. I would study quite precisely your methods of working. It didn't matter what field; manufacturing, even. I did a lot of work once with sales representatives. How many sales representatives do you need to cover England, you know. What do you want them to do when they get there, and all this. So I did that. But this all seemed to end up as a tool for management, and I worked for years to make them more efficient. And often that means you've got fewer people, or you simplify the work so it doesn't take such a high-paid operator. This was not really in my head at the time, but I think that underneath all that, I felt a little uncomfortable.

I was very interested in psychology. It was a difficult thing to actually get a grasp on, but I was very interested in reading psychology in the early '60s. This was when psychology was being written about. At the same time a number of friends were interested, and we began to have an interesting kind of social life. It was a way to be interested in the arts. I remember one time sharing an apartment with four friends of mine who were well versed in the arts, in movies, all that sort of thing. It was a cultural thing. Designers. Two guys were architects.

I mention it because there was a time one of these friends, an architect, with two friends of his, had tried to start a community, and had put a lot of energy into it and then found out the chemistry wasn't right. And then a couple of years later he went back in. In the meantime, I had found him somebody very interesting to talk with. And when he got back involved with this group—they were having a second run at making this thing work—I also became very interested, and at that time got very involved in a—this was a group with high energy and interesting, mostly well-educated people with relatively privileged backgrounds, and we started to make it. We had to start off with a lot of psychological interests.

So far as it pertains to what I do now, we did some publishing there, and put out a magazine. I remember once, the group—there was a lot of energy, and it was somewhat confused in terms of what it wanted to do. Did it want to be a separate community, separate from everybody else, or would it be involved in doing.... Did we want to be in the city and be an open door, or be more reclusive? We did both of those versions at different times. It was a very involved, very committed group of people.

About 1966, I got very involved in that. We once wanted to leave London, go buy an island somewhere. It's not that we had vast amounts—some people had a lot of money, I suppose, and we did everything in a communal way. So we lived in the Yucatán for several months and became more together as a group and went back to London and had our house, which we made an open house. We did various cultural things and liberalized the community. And started doing a magazine. I remember at one stage being, oh, on the periphery of that, actually. But I remember looking at a number of the magazine and saying, "What do we want to do with this magazine? What is this for?" And wrote a very—there were two people, a husband and wife who were the motive force and, in fact, they were people who developed—they were married but probably would not have been together if they didn't want to run this community, one of those situations.

But I wrote this critical letter to the head guru, the upshot of it being that they said, "You're right. Do it yourself." You know. So over the years, even though we did enjoy it, we didn't. At some periods we were more active in publishing than others, but we always had something going, and I always, for close on a decade, was very involved in doing a magazine, conceiving of it, although from time to time I would be interrupted; you're interfered with. Sometimes I would have great freedom. Then they would go through a cycle, and they would want to control. But I enjoyed a lot of involvement in the conceiving of the magazine. I worked very closely with designers who were really terrific, terrific designers. We had some really excellent people, and very experimental.

It was not tied to any particular time. At some times we tried to be quarterly, and other times it didn't quite go that way. We did have our monthly sort of newsletter, which was more elaborate than the normal newsletter. And of that I also was editor. So I was always writing, always conceiving, getting a lot of feedback from people, a lot of involvement. It was a very nice aspect of—and when I eventually...drew apart from the idea, I'd done a lot of work on that thing.

We started out in the '60s and in one form or another, I was doing publishing, and supervising the publishing, being a kind of chief editor of the publishing house, for about a decade. Started in London, did it in different parts of Europe. This was all within the community. We lived and worked in this community, and the magazine was produced by our community.

We were successful because, as I say, it was energetic and it seemed to be—there was a time when what we were saying seemed to be very important. And then when the '60s finally became the '70s, quite a different thing started. We began to develop internal—not "we," but the husband-and-wife team that I mentioned—their problems became rather accelerated at that point. And so we went through a lot of contortions. Just basically, you know, because of them.

And I suppose I always maintained that position of being the one in charge of the publishing. And when I eventually thought I had to leave, it was in New York in the late '70s and I was not sure what I would do. Whether I would go into publishing, what exactly I would do, I didn't know. When I left them, there was no golden parachute, so they said.

I had no resources at that point. And a couple of friends of mine had invited me—they did work with designers and artists, and happened to say—they must have been tuned in to my situation—"Look, we have a house and a studio and maybe, if you wanted to, you could take some time and be there, you know. You'd be very welcome." So I thought I would do that for a couple of months to get myself sorted out about what I wanted to do. And the oddest thing happened. I went back to Ireland at one stage—this was a vacation just around this time—and came across a book which I thought, "Eh, it's an interesting book, but they've really done a terrible job on it. In some respects, it's devalued by the way they've done the job."

The "job," meaning the production of it?

Yes, the production of it. And something in me that I never had thought of, something made me respond, "I could do much better than that," without knowing how I would go about it. And just at that time somebody who made books happened to move next door, just across the way, and she was involved at a place called the Center for Book Arts, in New York. And she was working for Richard Minsky who was the founder and director of the Center for Book Arts. He's still the president of the Center for Book Arts. And he had an economics degree from Brown and was wondering what he was going to do in the early '70s. He had books somewhat in his background.

Now I could get involved in this Center for Book Arts, all of these things, all these arts and crafts and bookmaking. So we set that up and I worked with Pam, my friend who moved in next door. One night when she came over and I said this was a project that I thought I could do better than the one I had seen, she said, "Why don't you do it yourself?" And it was really an outrageous suggestion. I had never thought about—"Gee, you mean a book?" "Oh, yeah, somebody made that book." It never had occurred to me. And I—it was rather intriguing. I would probably not have done it had she not lived next door, and I would have her kind of overseeing it and answering all my questions and directing me on to the next stage and all that.

And, of course, as it turned out, she never was available. I would catch her running from one place to another, from her apartment to her car, and she'd say, "Oh, you just do...." And then I wouldn't understand what it was, and I'd have to go back and try and invent what she said. But I ended up making my first book. Which is—I don't know if you saw the various proverb collections that I have, the Irish proverbs I did [A Collection of Irish Proverbs]. I think it's a nice book. I enjoyed doing the book very much.

I remember going to my first book fair, the small press fair at NYU Center. Loeb Center down on Washington Square. Nineteen eighty-one, I think it was. And I'd just brought out my first book. I had about twelve copies. I was forlorn about some of these large tables. I was much more interested in trying to see all the other presses. There were some names that I knew very well. Now that I was into bookmaking, I wanted to see how to do it. And this woman came up to my table, looked at the books rather closely and went off, and then came back at the end of the day and gave me an order. Six copies. First book. First book fair. First order. And she knew enough to know that if she took the six copies, then I probably wouldn't have much chance of doing any business.

Maggie Du Priest was her name. I forget now the name of her store. It was on Hudson Street in the West Village. Lovely old store. Just a plain, open space, shelves around it. And then in the center of it, a long, glass case with the more special books. And she was just a very nice character. And I give her the books and she gives me a check, and she opened the glass case and put in my books. It was just...really wonderful. And I could not believe that. I said, "I'm just amazed, I can't believe it. I feel terribly complimented. Are you really sure—?" And she told me that mine were the only books that she ordered at the small press fair. And she put them next to all the really great names. There was Barry Moser. That was a great compliment.

And it actually just occurred to me: When I think of what energy I derived from that compliment, it shows me how important it is, if you see something nice, to say that to somebody. It's a very important element in all of this.

I think, in all of life, there's no substitute for the personal touch.
Absolutely. Absolutely. Very powerful. I found that personal touch very much at the beginning. But I find it's not there that much now.

That may explain why there aren't that many young people going into this thing. They're not getting proper encouragement.

I suppose one of the things—in my neck of the woods, it's hard to compete with me. My stuff is translations of old Irish poetry. Not many people are competing with me. It may be that if I were doing something more like the mainstream, not that there is really a mainstream, but my market is quite—there's something definite there. There are many aspects of my market, but it's never entered my head, "Oh, if I tell them this, they'll be competing with me." It never seems to be that way.

How do you define your market?

Well, it's difficult to define. It's Irish material. It's old Irish material. It's Celtic. Irish and Celtic are not quite the same. And there's the craft people. And librophiles. Bibliophiles. It's rather curious. It's, um.... I think I'm protected by how marginal the whole thing is, you know. You have to really like to do it. I think a huge factor is the independence of— I had, on my previous swing of the pendulum, been in a very interdependent—even though I had a certain independence, I was in an interdependent community where ultimately I didn't have the last word. I would have it, then I wouldn't. You never knew that you had it, so you might as well not have it. So it became very important to me to be master of my own ship. It's a great luxury to know I might do this book, or I might not, I might do something else. It's a great freedom.

Do you have other income?

No. This is my income. And it is marginal. I have low overhead, but not that low. It is marginal. I sold three books to Random House, and that's gone rather well. In the next few months I'll have another couple of proposals. That will be nice to do, because that's an income which I wouldn't get any other way.

You sold three books to Random House? Are those books that you did that they took over?

They're books I did first as hand-made books that they later did.

They're not handmade.

No, no. Not handmade. That's an interesting element, too, if you want to go into a discussion of a relationship with a large publishing company and all that can mean.

Yeah, I would like to.

I feel I can always get an idea, you know. I have hundreds of ideas, and...there's no situation in which I can't have a better idea, you know, to do it. That's an optimism I have. A competent, interesting version of something. That's something I enjoy very much. I've never.... Like my friends who are—"How about this? Do you have that same feeling?" Is that something that worries them, upsets them that they have, or would like to have? I've never talked about that, but it seems to me the best thing, in a sense, is to have that optimism. Some optimism can be blind.

Can we talk a little bit about your relationship with Random House, or Stone Street's relationship with Random House?

Well, I am Stone Street. Stone Street is me. I do actually have—in the last, oh, how long? maybe six years? seven years?—have had an apprentice helping me, maybe one day, two days a week. And that, too—I've had really high-quality people. Even though they work for very little, they're actually getting more than I get. That's another interesting element.

At one stage—I just had started baking, and I had never thought about making it, but when I got to making bread, I thought of doing a book of Irish bread recipes. Then, later on, I did another book with another aspect of Irish food. It's restricted, in terms of—the range of Irish food is not excessive. When I had three books done relating to food, I put three books in a slip case. When you do very slim books—booklets, pamphlets really, is a more accurate, technical description; there's no spine and no spine label—a way to have a spine label would be to put three in a slip case and have the slip case have a spine label, so it could be in a bookstore. Often I've found that because they like the look of the books, they display them in a special way, which is very good. But some of them just want them on book shelves. If I did that, I would have a spine label.

So I did my three Irish books about food in a slip case, and then thought, "This I'll sell at a certain rate and I'll generate more sales." I didn't want to do this. I had reviewed books when I ran my magazine, and I published reviews of one twentieth of the books that had been sent to me for review. I didn't like the idea of my book languishing unopened on somebody's shelf, and I put a lot of thought into "Now how would it be if I was to send out just a dozen for review? Where should I send them?"

And I had a great idea, I think. It worked, certainly. When it comes up to Saint Patrick's Day, every food editor feels they want to write something about Irish food. And I said, "If I send out twelve books to twelve food editors in twelve cities with a notable Irish population—Boston, Chicago; I mean, really, every city now has got a sizable Irish population—I had a good chance of being successful. In fact, I think I got eight reviews out of the twelve, all of which were terrific. And a couple of them—they couldn't say enough about this book, you know. It was the most beautiful thing they'd ever seen—I mean really. And I'd also found a way—because I wasn't distributed; I've never been distributed, except for one small distributor. I did it all myself. And I found a way—you know, it's one thing to get a good review, but then how do you get them to put my name and address into that? I offered to send anybody who wanted the book—they could look in their local bookstore, or contact me if they couldn't find it—and if they wanted me to, I would be happy to inscribe the book. So a number of them did publish my name and address.

And I got so busy, that I really began to feel—you know, success, that kind of success, can change your operation. I realized the things I like are doing new work. When I'd start on something new, I'd research it, I would...well, the various things that are aspects of that cycle. But now I was becoming like a machine. You try and make three books per minute and send them out. And I realized that it was not very appealing to me. I'll do it within the bigger cycle, but not at the expense of the rest of the elements of the cycle. And I knew enough—one book fair I do every year is the Fifth Avenue book fair, "New York is Book Country." It's the third Sunday in September. It's been my busiest—it's a six-hour fair, eleven to five, and it's the busiest six hours of my year. And people always mob my booth, people are always around, they're looking at the books, they're asking questions. And somebody was opening a bookstore. How well do you know New York?

Not at all.

Well, for a number of years there was a very famous independent bookstore called Endicott Books, on Columbus Avenue and Eighty-first. It was run by a couple of people—one person had the expertise, the other had the money, and they went into business together. And the one who had the expertise and whose family I understood had been in—she knew publishing backwards and forwards. And she found my books and talked about what they were doing in this new store. Sold a lot of them. Whenever I'd bring an order—I would deliver stuff on my bicycle; I would drive my bike onto the Staten Island ferry, cycle up to the west side and go to her store and we would sit and talk. Became quite good friends.

And once, after two or three years, I got a little notice in the mail—she was now an agent. And it was just at the time it occurred to me, "Gee, wouldn't it be nice to shop the book around?" I didn't want to do it, but it would be nice to take its success and do something with it. So I gave her the book. She thought it was a good idea. And in a very short space of time had two offers, one from Random House. Actually, it was Clarkson Potter. They were very old, independent, were very highly thought of. I'd never really heard of them, but at that stage they were operating on their own. And I did the first book. Then they were taken over by Random House and I did a second book with them.

The other offer was from David Godine, from Boston. Does beautiful books, but didn't pay that much. So we went with the bigger offer. And they were very intrigued with my presentation, how it was three books in a slip case. I think I was selling it for sixteen ninety-five at the time. It's now twenty-two dollars.

In any event, they liked my work, but if they put something like that in their production, it would be fifty dollars, while I was charging seventeen dollars. So it's another interesting piece of information to have, what that work was worth in their eyes. That was too expensive.

Too expensive for their market?

For their list. To sell it for fifty, it probably wouldn't have done as well. The book is nice, but it's not an attractive book.

They did a cloth-bound edition?

Yes. Hard-cover, yeah.

Offset printing?

Offset, I suppose, yes. And it sold. Got paid back my advance and got some royalties out of it. So they were interested in a collection of cat folk tales that I had, and.... Something I learned—I've learned a lot from my relationship with these folks. The thing I learned—I defer to them. The way they designed it—they knew much better than I did, you know.

That's Random House?

Yeah. Random House. I would not have done the second book the way they did it, but I didn't say anything. Thinking these people—this is the biggest publishing company in the world, they know their stuff, you know. Much better than I did. But when it came to the third book, which is the tea book, *How to Make a Decent Cup of Tea*, which to me is like a tiny thing of about sixteen pages— I remember when I was writing the book, I'd been back to Ireland and somehow I was talking about tea, about how hard it was to get a decent cup of tea in New York, and she was saying how difficult it was in Ireland to get one, which is the home of good tea. And she'd been on the train from Cork to Dublin and asked for tea, and she was given this hot liquid and she said, "Is this tea or coffee?" That's how bad it had got. So we had a lot of fun with that idea. And I said, "It'll be a couple paragraphs in my book, *How to Make a Decent Cup of Tea*."

Then I was at the ABA and somebody who was running the retail store at the new museum in L.A., the LAMOCA [Los Angeles Museum of Contemporary Art]—I've not been there, but it's a huge new museum in L.A.; this was the middle '80s, late '80s—she always would stop at my books. I think she came from the Dutton Bookstore people in California. Do you know Dutton?

Yes.

She was one of that family and was running the retail store at the museum and loved my books and wanted to have them. She was looking for a way to have my books. And they were opening the museum and she happened to mention they were having a show of teapots. And I said, "Oh, I could make a little book, you know, out of this. It would be a couple of pages." And I made an edition of five hundred. And they were sold in three days. Sold out. At the museum. Just at one store in the museum.

Later on I returned to Random House—it was Clarkson Potter within Random House and the head of the Clarkson Potter aspect, Carol Southern is her name, she said, "Now we really want this to look like one of your books." And she said it in sort of a we-wanted-to-do-the-other-ones-but-it-hadn't-worked-out-but-now-we-really-want-this-this-is-going-to-be-important way. And as well as giving me an advance, they also gave me a fee to work with their design guy. So we worked together. So that was interesting. I had to say to myself, "How do I make a book look like one of my books?" Mostly it was materials. Everything I found—I found very suitable stuff—they always found a reason not to use it. "Oh, it won't fit in the machine." They always found a reason not to use it.

Other than that, we ended up with a very nice looking book. We won, actually, a special trade award. The New York Bookbinders Guild, or whatever their name is, did a special award for the book. It was really nicely done. But it was not—I suppose in their terms it was much nearer looking like one of my books, but in my terms it was not. It was interesting to see what was unique about—here were people with unlimited resources who could not make it look like one of my books.

They've done very well with that book. Actually, I think I've earned more out of that book than any of the other books I've done with them.

You sell to a diverse market. How did you make contact with the bibliophiles? Or how did they find you? Did they find you at book fairs?

Oh, I think it was that I found them and they found me. I suppose the reviews were a good way. People would read the reviews. There were, of course, the eight reviews I got that produced—and the *New York Times* does it, comes around. Actually, we sent them a review copy of the Random House version of my booklet. And they didn't do anything about it. I got a lot of raves from NPR [National Public Radio]. All Things Considered did a piece. Just terrific. And made it sound very interesting. That was after the Random House came out.

Had you had such a diverse market before the Random House books came out?

Well, I really was growing. I would go to book fairs. Nineteen eighty-four was the first ABA I did. At that stage I was expanding my number of books to bookstores across the country. Never a lot, you know, but I might come away with very good ideas. I got about twenty-five, thirty orders out of it, you know. One year I got the biggest single order I ever got, from the Art Institute in Chicago. It was like ten thousand dollars, which was a huge order for me.

So they would find me. I would start wandering around, and.... You never know the people you don't see, but the people who do find you are a very diverse— But in the same way as I know I'm going to find something, I suppose they're the sort of people who will find something too. If you're running a bookstore, and you are in charge of how the bookstore looks, you know, I think there is something about a hand-made booklet that stands out, something extra that draws people. And often, though I like my books, I have so many times seen, for all that I like them, when somebody who really likes them gets them, I can't match them. Because the book fills that thing in their life, or their vision, or their fantasy, which I can't know. I see it in their expression. They'll show it.

And my own response—I know that I'll walk around the fair tomorrow and I'll see something that excites me, that I think is very wonderful. I think that's a very nice thing to be a part of. I forget now what—

I was asking how you find people.

Oh, yes. So I got more stores, got more reviews, also the mailing list, you know, like people here today— Maybe people don't have the money, or maybe there's no real reason to buy now, but when they're looking for gifts around Christmas time, then if I remind them at that time, it's quite likely that they will order. It's a nice business to be doing, and then of course it runs right through the year. Nothing vast, but it's all very nice to have. So I have a mailing list that I've built up. People will see me at a retail craft fair. They'll find me from one of my books in a bookstore, and I'll always invite them to write for my list, so that's a way of getting out there too.

A month or two before Christmas, once a year, I do a mailing. I write a letter about what things came up this year. One year I went to Frankfurt to the book fair to see would that be an advantage for me, doing that. That was a very interesting trip. It was the year of the reunification of Germany. I had an interesting, very emotional walk around Berlin that I wrote about. My mother died, and she had actually met some people— some of my customers had been to Ireland and met her. And there were lots of references to her in my thoughts, in one way or another. So that was also something I wrote about.

Last year I wrote about the state of the book business. And it was run in the *Daily News* in New York as an op-ed piece.

Could you talk a little bit about that?

Yes. I had a very interesting experience at the ABA about four or five years ago. I was sitting at my booth, by my books, and this person comes around, a woman, she's looking at my books, and I notice that she's wearing an author's badge. And it's E. Annie Proulx. I don't know if you've heard of her. It was the year she won the Pulitzer Prize for *The Shipping News*. So I told her congratulations on having won. And she was not that impressed with the prize. She'd been writing for twenty years, so what was the big deal about this one, you know? And I discovered that the interesting thing about somebody who is a significant writer—there are many, you know; there are many we don't know, we've never heard of—and the relationship that she, as a writer, had with small presses—nobody had wanted her work; now they wanted it because she'd won the Pulitzer Prize. But before that they hadn't wanted it, and the small presses had published her. And independent bookstores would sell her, stocking only three copies. Independent bookstores—"I'll get one for Jerry, and I'll get one for...."—they'll order one customer by customer. They know who will buy them. They have this relationship. This never happens in a chain bookstore. Actually, it's a very tightly knit relationship—writer, press, and store.

And it occurred to me—maybe I told you this story today, of going into the Barnes and Noble bookstore in New York on Union Square North. Huge building. Five, six floors. A hundred and fifty thousand titles. And I sit down, have a cup of coffee in their...coffee place. I'm sitting there and I'm looking at this pretty mural, a kind of dark green, black-and-white mural of famous writers. Joyce, Shaw, Nabokov, Whitman—

They have that mural in a lot of their stores.

I think so. And I'm looking at all of these guys. And these were people who would be published by small presses. If they were around today, they wouldn't be—here they are, trading off this image, the respectability, the literariness of the whole thing.

Ulysses For four hundred and fifty coppers, the first edition of *Ulysses*. Sylvia Beach. None of these books would be in the dark places

133

of Barnes and Noble. We will have no writers because they will not support new, upcoming writers. Independent bookstores are disappearing. How will they be encouraged to do this? The tributaries of literate culture are being cut off. I know that a hundred and fifty thousand titles sounds like an awful lot of books. But I know from sheer experience, if I'm looking to research something of any unusualness, if they'll have anything on that subject, it'll just be garbage. They'll have none of the important books, or it'll be hit or miss whether they have the important books. They'll have somebody in charge of it who has no idea of what they're doing. I went looking for *Ars Poetica* at Barnes and Noble recently. "Can you spell that?" I spelled it out for them. "Author's name?" Horace. "First name?" Too awful. It's ridiculous. Horace.

Another very interesting thing. Somebody who went in, a young woman who had her degree at Harvard in English, working for Barnes and Noble, called me up. I was advertising for an apprentice. I'm paying her more than she was earning at Barnes and Noble. She was a book clerk at Barnes and Noble for like five dollars twenty-five cents an hour. So you know where this thing is going. We know that the general direction is a very bad one. It's tough to know how to deal with it. Is this inevitable oblivion? Inevitable winding down? It's hard to say.

A friend of mine who's been very supportive, he's bought my books and he's in the book business himself and he's always wanted to help me. And even when he changed his job and went to work in California, he found some bookstores and he carried this kind of introductory package of my books, and it worked pretty well. He told me there's a bookstore in Ireland, in Galway, it's called Kennys. Somehow they sold him the idea—they pay like a hundred dollars, or a hundred pounds a quarter and he tells them the areas he's interested in, and they'll send him from Ireland books in those areas of interest. I'm wondering if at some point that might be one way to sell books.

Well, I want to thank you, Malachi.
Oh, you're very welcome.

Alexander Taylor and Judith Doyle
Curbstone Press

"I think the real issue here is a right-wing assault on the arts and on reading in general, to be honest about it. Pornography, I think, is really a red herring. I don't think they want people to think. And I don't think they want an alternative voice in the society... It's really a national shame that a country this wealthy neglects the arts in such an incredibly stingy fashion."

Alexander (Sandy) Taylor and Judith (Judy) Doyle have been running Curbstone Press for a quarter of a century. They first met through their involvement in the antiwar and civil rights movements in the late '60s. Both were students at the University of Connecticut, Doyle an undergraduate in English literature, Taylor working on his doctorate in English. Each eventually went off into another life, then in 1975 began working together on Curbstone Press. "It was through working together that our relationship became more than a friendship," Doyle says.

Judy Doyle was born and raised in Franklin, Connecticut, and raised there. After college, she worked in various jobs in photography and did some freelancing. For a while she worked for a gravura printing company in the Philadelphia area. Later, with some friends, she started a gallery in Hartford where they also taught classes in photography.

Sandy Taylor was born on July 8, 1931 in Rumford, Maine and grew up in Glens Falls, New York. He went to Connecticut after working for a few years as a salesman for a paper mill. After he took his final degree, he taught at E.O. Smith High School, then went on to Eastern Connecticut State University. "That was a great experience. It's a great school, great people there. It was a teaching institution where the focus was on the students, not a school where you had to write more and teach less, which I guess is now the universal state. My interest was in teaching, not research."

He was teaching at the college and Doyle was at the gravura printing operation when they started Curbstone. She left to work full time at Curbstone. "By [1979] we realized one of us had to be here on a full-time basis." The printing company "was a job, and it was income, but it wasn't something I cared deeply about. So I started spending all my time on Curbstone."

I talked with them on the morning of March 14, 1997.

Why go into publishing? How did your activism lead into publishing as opposed to any other direction?

Sandy Taylor: Well, you know, that's a good question really. I had been formerly involved in doing a little magazine while I was either working or teaching. I had a magazine—*Patterns*—while I was working in the paper mill. Then I founded *Wormwood Review* with two other people, Jim Scully and Morton Felix, and later on ran it with Marvin Malone.

When did you do Patterns?
Judy Doyle: It was in the '50s.
ST: Late '50s. No, mid-'50s, that's right.

And Wormwood Review *was—?*
ST: In the '60s. Both were poetry journals. *Wormwood* was taken over by Marvin Malone who took it out to the West Coast. He died just last year, unfortunately. But he did a wonderful job with it. He kept it going beautifully for, God, thirty years, right?
JD: More. He was working with you—
ST: Yeah, he was working with me in the—
JD: Wasn't he a pharmacist?
ST: He was a pharmacologist. He was a very well-known pharmacologist.
JD: I love the combination.
ST: He was a researcher in pharmacology.

When you started Wormwood, *you were—*
JD: You were at UConn [the University of Connecticut].
ST: When I was at UConn. But those were really, you know, kind of—they came out when we were ready—erratic and occasional publications. But there is a history there, if you're interested. We printed some of the early copies of *Wormwood* on an old letterpress in a barn in the

136

winter with no heat. We stayed warm with martinis. But then we were also involved in the political stuff, the human rights stuff, so when Jim Scully came back from his residency in Chile, we got hooked on book publishing. He got there just after the Pinochet dictatorship took over. He had intended to go down and experience what it was like under the first elected socialist government in Chile. But while they were learning Spanish, the coup d'etat took place. That was the trigger that got us going on the book publication, because his book was a powerful book exposing the human rights violations in Pinochet's Chile. It's called *Santiago Poems*. You know, it's one of those things, like you've been thinking about doing something for a while and suddenly the urgency hits you, because we were pretty sure that this would not be of interest to major publishers. And so we just decided we had to start a press to get this book going.

JD: Right. And it was really—when we're asked that question, the thing that always flashes in my mind about beginnings was perhaps it's true for a lot of people who started in publishing back in the '70s. Certainly it's very different today, when there's so much more information that is available and is easily shared. Back then it wasn't something planned for. It was something that sort of evolved out of what was happening. You know, nobody sat down and said, "Gee, let's start a publishing house." As Sandy said, there was that book, and that needed to be published. There wasn't "Okay, now what groundwork are we laying for developing a real press?" It was a response to a specific situation.

And the next few books were the same. So there was this book that wasn't going to get published somewhere else, and it could be done on this basis. So the original—I mean the press needed to get established as a press after *Santiago* was published. And all the paperwork was filed with the state, and the effort to become nonprofit was initiated. That took a while.

When did you go nonprofit?

JD: We finally got it in...I think it was '78 or '79. We started going after it in '76, and it took a while.

ST: They made it very difficult, yeah.

They made it difficult?

JD: Yeah. There's a lot more precedent now, and IRS doesn't challenge it so much. But back in the '70s they were having a little trouble dealing with a nonprofit press. Everybody was having some trouble then. There wasn't the kind of precedent there is today. Today you don't get challenged that way. We had to get a lawyer involved, because we just kept going back and forth with all this paperwork, and they kept saying, "Well, I don't see how you're nonprofit."

Do you think, as far as the IRS was concerned, it may have been the nature of the work you were publishing?

ST: No, I really don't think so. I mean, we're as paranoid as the next, but I think they just couldn't understand it. Since we were paying royalties, why wasn't that a business?

JD: And since we were selling books.

ST: And since we were selling books. I recall it was a very long process. We finally got a lawyer and they came to an agreement.

You have interns, right? Volunteers?
ST: Yeah.

About how many do you have at any one time?
ST: We have between three and six at any one time.

That's interns and volunteers together?

JD: Yeah, that's combining interns and volunteers. We also see community service students, stuff like that. The colleges around here require the students to put in a certain number of hours per year at community service, so we get a couple of them.

ST: There's of couple of people we have who put in more. We love it when some students get drunk so we can get them for thirty or forty hours. [All three of us laugh.]

A friend of mine—Ed Varney, who has had a couple of presses up in Vancouver, British Columbia—said that small literary presses could not make it were it not for voluntary labor.

ST: I think that's absolutely right—I think most of them that didn't have money to begin with developed on real sweat equity.

138

JD: Certainly it was true for us for the first fifteen years—there was no payment to either of us. That was all volunteer.

ST: You know, you'd come home from work and go to work, in a sense. For the first seventeen years, really, we had to have other jobs, most of the time.

Do you regret missing out on anything in those seventeen years?

ST: No. I think I was right where—I was just where I wanted to be. We met the greatest people. Living here was like having a continual graduate school. Writers would come—Miguel Mármol and Claribel Alegría and Daisy Zamora—who could ask for more?

Do you have children?

ST: Judy always says the press is our child.

JD: Yes. That actually is something that we seriously thought about, and realized that the press was requiring the kind of energy, as well as financial support, that a child would need, and that we couldn't accommodate both and we felt a commitment to this. Sandy has children and grandchildren through his first marriage. So there's plenty of kids.

Yeah. My press is my wife.

JD: Oh, I like that. Can it cook?

No, but I can't either, so that's okay. [We laugh.] Getting back to business here, can you define the mission of Curbstone?

ST: I think we could define the roots of where we come from. Maybe that would be useful for people to understand, because we look back to the people who influenced us. It would be people like Richard Wright, Ralph Ellison, Berthold Brecht, you know, people who felt that literature had a social content, and could look outward into the community as well as inward on the self. In the beginning—do you have the book *Poetry Like Bread*?

Yes.

ST: In the beginning Galeano has a statement which is wonderful. He said it would be naïve to think that literature could change the world; it would be just as naïve to think that it has no effect. So the real focus for our press is to publish imaginative literature that deals with real issues, social issues, whether it's issues of racism or issues of human rights or issues of autonomy for independent third world nations.

JD: All issues. Sexism. You know, those issues that affect—

ST: That—to make us more human. We have a stress on intercultural understanding. Books that contribute to intercultural understanding and books that contribute to human rights. Books that contribute to building a better society.

Has Curbstone always had this stress on intercultural understanding?

JD: Yes. From the beginning that was—those issues that Sandy just said were a very big part of—

ST: They were central to us. Because they came out of our own experience in the way we were working against racial discrimination at the university.

Have you found that there is kind of an ebb and flow in people's interests in these issues, or has it been pretty consistent?

ST: In general, we can say that there's a consistent, and even growing interest. I think what's hard is that in our culture you have the mainstream culture police, right?

Uh huh.

ST: I like to call them the "culture police," after Roque Dalton's phrase. You know, it's hard to get these books reviewed because people look on them as not literature. I think Carol Bly somewhere has a wonderful essay which—you know, what's more imortant in your life, whether you're going to send your kids to the war, or whether you have an affair with a teenie bopper? You know, all these books that came out with college professors—

Right.

ST: —writing about academia. So I think there's a big art-for-art's-sake—you see it now with language poetry—as though there's no outside reality. It's like abstract expressionism in words. And we think that poetry, literature, does make things happen. It can make—it can raise

140

consciousness. We're not saying that the other aesthetic is wrong or not valuable or anything, but that we are, in a sense, more inclusive in our tastes because we recognize the value of work that has a social content.

You mentioned an essay by Carol Bly.

ST: She wrote an essay—and I don't remember where I read it, actually—in which she argued for a literature that was tougher, a literature that dealt with more of the realities of daily life. She was reacting to the kind of comment that "If it's political it's not poetry," or "That's political, that's not literature." You know that kind of thing.

I remember very clearly, there used to be a magazine called *Poetry Now* in California that was publishing a lot of my poems when I was writing poems. And it just struck me as really astounding, because in the course of—I had published five or six things and then I sent them a poem that had to deal with the war, you know, and he wrote back, saying "I don't like political poetry. I don't want to use these." And I said, "Well, how could anyone say that? It's like saying, 'Well, I don't like love poetry,' or 'I don't like Holocaust literature.'" I don't know what that means, you know. I don't like bad political poetry. Or agitprop. And I don't like bad love poetry, either. So it struck me as peculiar that he would just decide that a whole realm of human experience wasn't worth writing about.

JD: One of the things we have noticed in the past ten years or so is that this attitude has been changing. It used to be we would frequently hear that the words politics and poetry did not belong together in any regard. And we have noticed that there is a real change.

ST: I didn't notice it in the *New York Times*.

JD: Well—[Taylor laughs]—they disregard poetry, not just political poetry.

ST: No, they just reviewed a right-wing poem, an epic poem on the Alamo, last week. Fortunately, they didn't like it, but I don't know why they would review a right-wing doggerel poem with a quarter of a page and absolutely ignore Roque Dalton, who is a world-class poet.

JD: And a lot of other poetry books out there.

ST: And a lot of other poetry books out there, too. So I don't think they even understand what's going on.

ST: They do review more aesthetic literature. They review a lot of the Dalkey Archive books, which are very good books, but they tend to stay away from anything that's hard-edged politically.

I was responding to your question about whether the attitude is diminishing, and Judy's response was yeah, but we think more people are—I think she's right. But it's hard to really tell, if nobody will review it. One of our best-selling books of poetry right now is *Song of the Simple Truth* by Julia de Burgos, a very political book. She was an *independentista*. Puerto Rican. She died in the '50s in New York. A very feminist book, too. But that's because—I believe this deeply—in the *latino* culture you have more respect for poetry. It's been selling mainly, I think, to the *latino* audience.

Is it bilingual?
ST: Bilingual, yeah.

Did the funding cutbacks owing to the restructuring of the NEA hurt you?
JD: Not noticeably at this point. I mean, yes, last year there was a reduction in the amount of the grant we got—we were very pleased we still got one. It's too soon to tell, really, how that's all going to shake out. One thing that I was spending a fair amount of time on in '95, and a little bit last year, was the organization that calls itself Lit-Net that was very involved in arranging for not only getting information out on a grassroots basis to a broad range of people, but also arranging for lobbyists on the hill and for a lot of high-powered writers to come and speak to people in Congress. I do believe the group was very effective.

ST: I think the real issue here is a right-wing assault on the arts and on reading in general, to be honest about it. Pornography, I think, is really a red herring. I don't think they want people to think. And I don't think they want an alternative voice in the society. So they're trying to destroy the NEA, saying that it's spending all this money on "elitist" art when in fact we only spend about sixty-four cents per year per person in this country on all the arts together. It's really a national shame that a country this wealthy neglects the arts in such an incredibly stingy fashion.

JD: Yeah. Countries that our country is usually aligned with on other issues are way ahead of us when it comes to supporting the arts.

ST: Someone told me—I'd have to check it for sure—that the city of Dresden spends more money on their annual arts fair than our country spends on all literature. Think of Dresden spending more money on the arts than the United States. So I think it really behooves us all to put on political pressure as a counterforce to this attempt to destroy—

JD: People have to realize, too, that it never really goes away. You know, we gained a victory a year ago or so, but it keeps coming up again. And it will continue to be brought up again by those who want to oppose NEA support to the arts. You know, we all have to keep up our communication to our congresspeople and everyone else that we possibly can.

You've been involved with publishing for forty years. This right-wing assault on the arts isn't new. Or do you regard it as new?

ST: I think it's intensified. I think it's people like Jesse Helms and Dick Armey. We know where their alliances are. These are the people who were supporting the contras in Nicaragua. You know what Somoza said. Our big friend Somoza, when he was in Colombia—they were showing him a school—he said, "I don't want people who can read. I want cattle."

Well, it's true that if people don't have a vision of what a society can be, they can never make it change. Literature provides a vision. I really believe that a lot of right-wingers don't want people to read anything but the bible, and especially those portions of the bible that say there'll be pie in the sky by and by, when you die. Right? So you get your reward in Heaven. Meanwhile, the public relations people in corporations are frantically trying to explain why somebody deserves twelve million dollars a year, salary, plus benefits. The whole thing comes together in a pattern, you know, in the sense of the redistribution of wealth—I mean we are fast moving toward becoming a third-world country.

Uh huh. Most of us anyway.

ST: Most of us are already there. But even the middle class is getting hit now. The distribution of wealth hasn't been as skewed as it is now since the '20s. Of course you don't want people to think about those things. You just want them to go ahead and be cattle. Yeah, I think part of that assault on the alternative press is very political indeed.

I agree with you entirely, including your analysis of the relationship of our becoming a two-class society and the assault on not only literature, but literacy.

ST: Right. Taking away the benefits from families that are on Aid to Dependent Children [i.e., Aid to Families with Dependent Children: AFDC], that kind of thing, I think is going to be terrible.

Yeah, I did my master's thesis on the War Against Poverty, and I wrote a novel about it, and—

ST: Yeah. Wouldn't you say it's worse now than it was ten years, twenty years ago?

Oh, yeah!

ST: And getting to an explosive point.

Well, I think gang life, kids killing each other, relieves that sort of pressure. And I don't think it's an accident that it's happening that way.

ST: That's right. Like Fanon's psychology of the oppressed, you know, you can't do anything else, you turn on each other. And, of course, it's all so—as Luis Rodriguez says in *Always Running*, this is the only family that some of these kids have.

But I would say there's a light shining on the horizon. For example, Roque Dalton's *Small Hours of the Night* was reviewed in the *Boston Globe*. They called it "a gift to American poetry." Also in the *Minneapolis Star-Tribune*, and, of course, *The Nation*. So I think it's more possible now, even with the polarization going on—in some ways, I think it's easier to get a poet like Dalton reviewed at this moment than it was ten years ago. I don't know what that means, except that—it could mean two things: We're becoming more liberal, which I'm a little skeptical about, or it could mean that, well, we've already gotten away with that crime so now we can talk about it. You know what I mean?

Yeah.

ST: Like [the movie] *Missing* didn't come out till it was all over, you see. You weren't any threat to the existing policy.

Right. Do you usually get your poetry reviewed in Publishers

144

Weekly *or* Library Journal?

ST: Yeah, *Publishers Weekly* and *Library Journal* and *Booklist* have been very, very receptive. It's wonderful to have those journals for libraries. It's the strongest way to get librarians aware of these books. The whole thing about distribution is interesting. I think most small presses like ourselves go through a kind of growth. In the beginning it's extremely difficult because you're trying to market these books to individual bookstores, and of course you get nowhere, except for a few very courageous independents. But we could see a shift take place when we began to get distributors. We were first with Talman, and then with Inbook, and we're now with Consortium. So you have sales people going into the stores and representing your stuff for you. And, of course, the big deal there is the advantage for individual bookstores—they don't have to order from individual publishers. They can group their orders. So we saw an enormous leap in sales when we went with distributors.

Say you publish a book of poetry by somebody who isn't well known: How many do you think you can sell in two years?

ST: I think of it more on an annual basis. It depends a lot on the poet, even when they're unknown. I mean, if a poet is out there and is hustling in bookstores, giving readings and so forth— We have a couple of books that sold about five hundred copies the first year—new poets. And we have another one that sold a thousand the first year. But that's, I think, a reflection sometimes of what's "in." You know, multicultural stuff is really in now.

JD: And how active they are.

ST: How active they are.

The poets, you mean?

JD: Yeah.

ST: Uh huh. If the poet sits back and just waits for the world to come to him, he's going to be alone for a long time.

Yeah. I publish mostly fiction. I find that's true of literary fiction as well.

ST: Literary fiction is tough, too. Not as tough as poetry, but it's tough. And in some cases—we've had cases where books of poetry outsold some of the fiction.

JD: I was just going to turn it back on you. With an unknown writer with a new book of fiction, what kind of sales do you tend to see?

I changed distribution about a year ago, and the distributor I have now deals almost exclusively with the national accounts, meaning the chain stores and the major wholesalers and some of the larger literary bookstores. But they don't go to the smaller stores or smaller wholesalers. I deal with some of them directly. So it's a little different from your distribution. We presell, say, five hundred copies of a novel, and then over a year's period we'll sell another two or three hundred.

ST: So you're looking at under a thousand for the first year.

Yeah.

ST: And in three years, or two years?

Well, I haven't had this distribution arrangement that long yet, so I don't know. But for two years before that I had The Subterranean Company, which used some of the same sales reps as Consortium.

ST: Oh, I didn't realize that.

But they went down to...they were only preselling like a hundred and fifty copies of a novel.

JD: Oooh.

ST: That's terrible. You know, I think one of the mistakes made by a lot of publishers is to think that a distributor is going to sell your books for you. They can place them in the marketplace, but it's really up to the press to sell them. They can get them on the shelves. It's up to us to get them off the shelves into the hands of customers. We spend an awful lot of time with reviewers. We can see it reflected in the sales. When we get a lot of reviews we get a lot of sales; when we don't get reviews— We have this book, *They Forged the Signature of God*—it is not doing very well; it didn't get reviewed very well. Roque Dalton, as a matter of fact, is selling better than that because it's been reviewed. It just came out in *Z*, and it was reviewed in those places I've already mentioned, *Poetry Flash* and so forth. So I think it's a matter, again, of letting people know what it is.

146

Yeah. If you can get it reviewed. I've had some books that they just wouldn't touch.

ST: That's right.

JD: And the other side of it is that often we have seen a review come out so late that the books have already been returned, so nobody can find it in a store.

ST: That doesn't help much. Right. It seems to me that for most of us—I think most of us in the independent press world came out of literary, came out of English backgrounds, not business backgrounds. And I think we really had to learn a lot. We had to really go through training programs, continuous training programs, to try to get the books into the hands of readers.

The first book I did [Gold 1996], I interviewed the publishers of thirty-one presses, and only one couple came from a business background. Everybody had to learn as they did it.

JD: Right.

ST: That's right. Pain is a great teacher, isn't it?

JD: This is part of what I was referring to when I said that today new publishers have a lot of information available to them. And, of course, other presses that are willing to provide them with support in terms of knowledge. But all of us—one reason that I think we developed very, very slowly as presses was because we had so much to learn, and we were learning as we went.

ST: Yeah. We were, in some ways, constructing the paradigms.

JD: Right. And it's not just the marketing side of the business. It's knowing how to run a business, and how to set up your accounting, and analyze the numbers—

ST: The organization issues, too, with the board of directors, and—

JD: And hiring well.

ST: You talk to people and they say, "Oh, blah," because now with the people in the Mellon group—we say, "Jesus, remember in the old days when our board of directors was our two daughters and a cousin?" Yeah, you know, we just didn't have the experience. I think one of the things that has strengthened our press very, very much is the gradually acquired, very extraordinary board of directors. We didn't do the usual pattern of going to people because they have money. We went to people because they have knowledge.

JD: Skills and knowledge. I mean we don't expect them to come to the office and work, but we consult with them all the time.

ST: Yeah, they work real hard.

JD: We started building this type of a board back around '83 or so, and it's been a long, slow process. But we're very, very pleased with our board.

Have you thought about who's going to run this—
ST: Succession.

JD: Yes, we have.

ST: We thought about it for a long time and then we stopped thinking about it.

JD: Well, it was not that we stopped thinking about it. For a while we were looking at trying to set things up in the sense of hiring somebody who would eventually become the person that ran the press after Sandy and I no longer are. We began to realize that that was not the way to go about it. Perhaps along the way we will end up with a staff member that becomes a likely successor. But the focus now is on making sure that we have a good organization. And, of course, part of it is having a good board. The next step is that all the systems are in very good shape and that it's not an awesome task for somebody to figure out what's going on here and how to run it.

ST: We stopped worrying about it. We're no long worried about creating a Pygmalion, but we want to create an institution that is so strong that somebody wants it. And we know that the board will find the right person.

JD: Last spring I spent a week and a half in the Midwest meeting with different small presses, asking about this issue and how they were dealing with it. And I also made a point of talking with Fiona McCrae at Graywolf who went through the process of coming in to take over a press. I was very interested in finding out from her what made it work well and what made it difficult. Because those are the things that we wanted to be looking at—what concerns we should be addressing that make it difficult for a person who is not familiar with the press to come in and start to run it. And, you know, different presses are approaching it differently. And

148

some aren't yet really addressing the issue. With some, they and their boards are talking about it, and we and our board have been talking about it for two or three years now. And it was partly out of those meetings that—it just confirmed what we had already begun to believe, that what we need to do is make sure that the organization is set up in such a way that coming in and taking over is not so awesome.

Okay. I was going to ask you about course adoptions. How successful—?

ST: I think that's a very fruitful area for independents. A very difficult area to market in, because your distributors don't normally handle that. Most distributors for independents don't really have the expertise to do that, and many large publishers don't do it very well. We spend an enormous amount of time—and luckily we have interns to do some of this work—and what we found was most successful was actually writing off for the college catalogues from major universities and going through the catalogues and locating courses and teachers who would have interest in our books. We've got over two hundred universities using our books from time to time. And we're continually working on that. Right now we're working on researching holocaust courses and English courses.

We have a large focus on *latino* and Latin American literature, so that's the first one we did. In fact, in April I'll be going to the Latin American Studies Conference in Guadalajara. We exhibit at those conferences. We talk to teachers. We have, in fact, Teaching Friends of Curbstone, a group of people who like what we're doing, and we give those people special discounts and, sometimes, free books. And they provide us with information. For example, we had a Teaching Friend at Duke University who went to the library and made sure they ordered all our books. So you have kind of "Curbstonistas" nation-wide. And we're trying to network that way with people with similar interests so that we can build support groups in different universities. We have great contacts. People will call us and tell us what's going on, and how the books are doing.

We also did one course-adoption catalogue, and we're in the process of doing another one in which we quote teachers rather than reviewers so that teachers can see that other people are using them, and how successful they are. And then in *Curbstone Ink*, our little newsletter, we often will run articles by teachers about how they've used our books in courses. For example, one teacher wrote about how he used *Miguel Marmol* in the same course as Tom Anderson's *Matanza*, so he used the history and the literature of the same period together. Those go out to about ten thousand people, those newsletters. They go to our entire—

JD: —mailing list that we developed, and people—

ST: About six thousand of those are teachers, I believe. It's very hard to sell even one book, as people know. If you can sell one book to a course adoption, then that is likely to be a repeat sale. We've had some books of poetry, for example, that we've had individual orders of two hundred copies for a university.

I'd say getting the information is difficult, and nobody's list is as good as your own. Because you're finding the people who are in your patterns of thought, in your interest arena. When you buy a list from a list broker, the results are extremely poor. But if you can build what we would call a targeted list, as expensive as that is to do, it's kind of like future building. You're working toward...it becomes almost like an endowment; you can count on those sales every year. Or at least for four or five years in a row.

You said, Sandy, that you used to write poetry.

ST: Yeah. I had three books published. But, you know, I don't have any regrets. I still write when I feel compelled to. I think that at a certain point you have to make choices. So I don't consider myself a poet, but rather an editor who sometimes likes to write poetry.

Did you publish any of your own, or did you send them out?

ST: I don't send out anything anymore. Some of the ones that went out years ago are turning up here and there. You know how it is in publishing.

JD: Curbstone didn't publish any of Sandy's poetry.

ST: That was another thing. I didn't feel that we should ever publish any of the people working at the press. It didn't seem to be.... I don't want to criticize those who do it, but it just seemed to me that it's very difficult to be a judge of your own work. When some of the board members wanted me to publish my own work, I just said, "No, I can't do

150

it." If any of it's good enough, it'll get published somewhere. So...I don't have time to do it anymore. I do hear people complain about, oh, they don't have time to do their own writing. Well, you know, you have to make choices, and I think that you shouldn't complain about the choices you make.

The impression I get from your newsletter is that you're very much community-oriented. Locally as well as—

JD: Yes. Especially in the last two years. We've always done what we could in terms of bringing authors into this community. But the past two years in particular, it's intensified. A year ago we got together a group of individuals and organizations and institutions in the community and we formed a partnership over a program that's called the Windham Area Poetry Project. We hope it will become an ongoing program here. We're developing programs that bring poetry—in the form of readings and workshops—bring poetry into organizations that normally did not have access to this before. Organizations that focus on the elderly, social service organizations that—oh, some are rehab centers, some are teenage mothers, high schools, many high schools in the area. We had some programs at the Spanish-language church. There are a variety of different organizations and institutions in the community.

ST: Yeah, it's the community. What we want is to be visible in the community. I want to backtrack a minute, because we always did this but we didn't have the money to do it in any organized fashion. What we were doing was, if a poet was on tour and the university was paying their airfare, then the poet would donate time to a high school. I was with Claribel Alegría at Cardozo High School in D.C., which has a large Salvadoran population. We could not have done that on our own. We don't have funds for that. You don't sell enough books of poetry to pay for a plane ticket. Actually, that was the Smithsonian Institute that had her. So they brought her in and it was just beautiful. I mean the kids are absolutely—you should see this high school—the tiles are peeling off the wall, they don't have money for paper—

JD: They can't even Xerox anything.

ST: They can't even Xerox anything. It's a total mess, you know, in our grand capitol. So she did two readings. She did one in Spanish and one in English. And the kids, after the Spanish reading, clustered

151

around—they didn't have money for books, so they were copying her poems, in Spanish, out of Claribel's book into little, tiny notebooks. It reminded me of Nicaragua because they were using every bit of space on those pages. I mean it was probably the first time these kids had someone reading to them in their own language from their own country. It was really amazing. And the kids were just mesmerized. And then she did one in English for the other kids, and they were also mesmerized, and had great questions for her. So that we could provide to that high school free. But that was always just hit and miss. We couldn't do that in an organized fashion. This program that Judy's talking about is funded by the Connecticut Humanities Council.

JD: And the Connecticut Commission on the Arts.

ST: It's allowed us to not just do it in a hit-and-miss fashion, what we used to call "guerrilla-marketing" fashion, but allows us to develop a program so that—during National Poetry Month in April, for example, there'll be a poet every week in the Windham high schools. You know, we live in a community that's terribly poor. This is one of the two most economically depressed areas in the state, and they just don't have money for that stuff.

But what is amazing to me is that these programs have demonstrated the concept of the empowerment of the word, how words can empower people. Do you remember in Richard Wright—*Black Boy*—when he was in the library he had to borrow somebody else's card, pretend he was picking up books for a white person? He read Mencken, he said, "Wow! I can see words can be weapons!" This really becomes clearer and clearer to me on very specific occasions. When Luis Rodriguez was reading and talking about gang life at Windham High School a couple years ago, and we went and sat in the cafeteria with the kids, and the kids were clustered around him and one kid told him, "You know, Mr. Rodriguez, I was gonna join a gang this Friday, but now I'm not gonna do it." So, to go back to Galeano, literature can't change the world overnight, but little things happening all have an effect.

One problem is that we don't know what the effect will be.

ST: Yeah. One effect will be that they'll become independently minded, and that's not what everybody wants. They'll build confidence in themselves and they'll make their own decisions. That's not really what most people want to have happen.

Most people are afraid. I was talking with a guy in the record industry recently about Americans being so suspicious now of the imagination.

ST: Yeah. Exactly. Yeah, going back to the whole attack on the arts. It's like Plato's *Republic*: the intent of the artist is subversive in some way. That's at least how it's looked upon in our culture, I think.

Well, we are.

ST: We're subversive, but for the development of the human being. But to our society, I suppose, yeah, we are subversive, actually. We're subversive in the way Tom Paine was subversive, and George Washington was subversive, and in the way that Thomas Jefferson was subversive.

I have no more questions. Is there anything either of you would like to add?

ST: No. I think we've covered the essential.

Thank you very much, both of you.

Harry Smith
The Smith

"On a given book I might make money, but in the total scheme of things I don't. I always thought I'd prefer to make my money some other way than to publish the things that I know would make money. I've recommended many books to the major houses which have been accepted and which were successful. I've said, "Well, you don't need me. Simon and Schuster, I'm sure, would publish this.""

I arrived early at Harry Smith's house in Brooklyn Heights and no one was home. It was a sunny day, though cold, and I sat on the steps and waited for someone to arrive. Soon a tall man with hair like the mane of a white lion came trudging with a large old dog up the hill leading to the house. His beard, white as snow, reminded me of Christmas, and his wide smile also bespoke gladness and cheer. He had only just returned from the London Book Fair and a trip to Wales following, and he had given himself up to a cold. We talked on the afternoon of March 24, 1997 in the house he shares with his wife Clare, and Chris, his dog. Sixty-one years old, he had lived in this house for half his life.

This is called a town house?

Yeah, it's a row house. It's very much like parts of London and parts of Cambridge. It's an 1840s house. The houses are older as you're closer to the water. You go another block and you see grander town houses with twenty-foot ceilings and really big parlors from a decade later. So as you go farther away from the water, and further into Victorian times, they get more elegant. This house was—I researched it once—owned by a tea merchant named Brown. As you see, it's narrow. It's about twenty-one feet wide, but it's four stories; a cellar is beneath us.

Are you from the city?

Yeah. I was born in Queens. My parents were living there at the time. They previously lived in Brooklyn, the Greenpoint section of

Brooklyn. That's where, in more recent times, Marianne Moore lived.

What did your folks do?

Well, working backwards, my father was a banker—the Lincoln Savings Bank of Brooklyn—and he hated it. It was run by German-American bankers and industrialists. These were guys who went to Hitler's Germany and liked it. And I remember from when I was about four years old, or three even, I was allowed to sit with my father and his best friend, whose name was Al Jones, in the basement of the house in Queens, which was like a bar, dating back to Prohibition times. And his uncle, my great uncle, was a master carpenter, so it was a beautiful mahogany bar and all that, and a back room and even an old-fashioned wooden telephone booth. There'd be a pitcher of beer and a big bowl of pretzels. I was allowed to sit there, listen to them talk about the state of the world, how Hitler was a madman and so on. My father, though he was working for the bank and was a reasonably high executive—he was in charge of the main branch of the bank—he was secretly a Jack London socialist. He did some writing himself, which was mostly light verse, and he kept a lot of journals. So one of my early memories, about anything intellectual, at least, is to hear him talk about how Hitler was a madman and about how the people at the bank were a bunch of Nazis.

I enjoyed it. I was allowed to have what they called a "pony glass." It looked like a real beer glass, but much, much smaller. So I got one glass of beer and ate pretzels and I was supposed to keep my mouth shut and I did, although sometimes I agitated for a second beer. Once in a while I got one.

So, yeah, I'm really from the city. I spent a lot of time outside the city. When my father died and I was still only four years old—perhaps why I remember so many things from earlier, because the only way I could have a father was to be able to remember. I grew up after that in a town then semi-rural, about forty-five miles from New York City—North Bellmore. It was then about twenty-five hundred people, with a lot of truck gardens, small farms—very fertile land. My father's cousin—his age, so I called him Uncle Charlie though he wasn't really my uncle—had peach orchards on the adjacent property, and a big greenhouse set-up. He was a very successful florist who had plantations for bulbs down in Louisiana and Florida, and from early times flew the lilies all over the world. I remember one of my jobs when I worked part time for him was wrapping lilies in wet newspapers for shipping. Then when the temperatures would go down below freezing on the airplane the warmth from the ice freezing would keep the lilies at the right temperature.

There were woods behind, really brush, scrub oak for the most part. Quail, pheasants, rabbits. It was a town close to the Long Island Railroad where about half the people commuted to work in New York City. It became one of the first big suburban developments after the Second World War. It was a tremendous transition. All the farmland turned into housing developments. It was really great farmland, too. It's a shame. We'd had about six acres out there, and during the war my mother leased about three acres to a local farmer who grew a variety of crops. I also got to pick string beans, stuff like that.

Was your mother intellectual also?

No, she had a fifth-grade education. She was certainly very intelligent, I would say "shrewd," although suspicious of everyone. I think I have a kind of skepticism, which isn't as sharp or pervasive, but is related to my mother's attitude toward the world. She would be very suspicious about people's motives.

Had your family recently immigrated?

No, but it had been poor. Her father had been on whaling ships from the age of fourteen. He was shanghaied. He was first a cabin boy, and then a cook on the whaling ships. He was shipwrecked, not for the first time, but certainly the worst and final time, in the South Seas where it was very cold. I don't know how many weeks he was adrift in a life boat, with a lot of frost bite. Only he and one other man survived. He was in a hospital in San Francisco for many months afterwards. He lost parts of his feet. He was never entirely healthy again. He frequently had small restaurants, one at Roosevelt Field in the early days of flying. He met a lot of the famous aviators; I heard some of those stories. But he never made a lot money.

My mother went to work after the fifth grade as a sales girl and within a couple of years she was making more money than her father. She married relatively young—seventeen, eighteen years old. She would read. Of course, in those days, a fifth grade education meant you could

156

do your arithmetic and you could read and you could write, and she could. She would make some mistakes in sentence structure, perhaps. She would read best-sellers, that sort of thing, but she was not intellectual, whereas my father had a house full of books and I started to read, indiscriminately, when I was a child. I remember one time when I was maybe twelve years old and reading *Lady Chatterly's Lover* in bed. My mother walked into the room, asked what I was reading, and I told her. She asked—well, she was afraid it would affect my morals. I said, "Well, it's only a book, mom," and that seemed to satisfy her.

Had she read it?

I'm not sure of that. I think perhaps she had heard some discussion about it from my father. It was an expurgated edition but one could still get the idea quite well.

Did you go to college?

Yeah, I went to Brown. Got kicked out at the end of my junior year for—well, the official reason was very vague. To my surprise, after the school year ended I got a letter saying that I had been "unconditionally expelled for failure to abide by university regulations"—exact quote—and "extremely erratic academic performance"—again an exact quote. What happened is that I wrote a couple of things which were controversial. I didn't see why they should be so controversial. One was about the obsession, you know, at that time, 1956, with mammary glands, which were in fashion. This went on to be a discussion of how women were just considered decorative objects. Girls who didn't have big breasts felt they had to wear falsies. Women in the work place, no matter how slim they were, were considered to be radical, and certainly improper, if they did not wear girdles. Girls at college at that time were allowed to wear knee socks and Bermuda shorts; however, while they were outdoors, they had to wear raincoats. They couldn't show their knees; that was actually a university regulation at the time. So I went on to, I think, a humorous discussion about the injustice committed against women. You know, these were the days of the sweater girl, the plunging neckline, television personalities such as Dagmar, and so on, and I made fun of all of that. But of course this was before—

You were a premature feminist.

Yeah, that's right. Actually I'm listed as a feminist, and I might have been maybe the first man to list himself as a feminist, in the *Poets and Writers Directory*. A friend said, "You can't do that. That's illegal." But I did it. Of course, a couple of generations before, H.G. Wells was calling himself a feminist. So there was nothing new about it.

Was this a paper for a class? Or did you publish this paper?

It was in the newspaper, along with some other things. But the precipitating thing was that I caused a lot of people to sign a petition, chiefly the people in my dormitory, whereby we seceded from the governing structure of the university because of taxation without representation. I pointed out that at many medieval universities the students had selected the teachers. We had absolutely no say about that or anything else. We didn't have a say about the curriculum, certainly not about the hiring of faculty members or the rating of them, and we had very little to say about the rules by which we lived. They were paternally imposed on us, and student government was a joke. It was just to decide whether or not to have a dance or raise money to put a television set in the lounge, or something like that. So that was the gist of my complaint.

One of the deans called every signer, saving me for last. Everyone else said that they had nothing more to do with it or me, and the dean said to me, "It's a good joke, Smith, but it's gone far enough." I said, "I'm glad you appreciated the humor, sir, but it does have a serious intention." Of course I had no plans; it was more of a creative act than the beginning of a campaign to overthrow the governing system of the university. However, apparently they saw it differently. So anyhow, I said, "Like Joan of Arc, I will not abjure." The thing was, I was surprised when they threw me out, but I never questioned their right to do that; I never went through any process of appeal or complaint. I did return later and I very eventually got a degree. When I left again I was one course short because I'd been given an F, which is worse than failing; it means you're barred from ever taking the course again. It was a graduate school course I was taking with S. Foster Damon, the Blake scholar and poet, in allegory and symbolism.

It's a funny story, but I think relevant to everything else I did.

I seem to have been in a constant condition of rebellion, in which I was encouraged by some people who were there at the same time. There was a young professor, David Krause, the O'Casey scholar. Of course, O'Casey's dictum had been "Embarrass your elders," and Krause encouraged me mightily in all of that, and this is what I tended to do. I distrusted authority. So I was taking Damon's course and, it's true, I turned in some papers late. It was a seminar, the class didn't have the full benefit of him, but I wrote a movie review for the college paper, proving that *The Lone Ranger*—the movie—was a work as great as *Moby Dick* or *Paradise Lost*. What Damon did, and what other scholars did at that time—there was a vogue of symbol hunting. In *Paradise Lost*, for instance, chaos is the id. And it all works after a fashion. He won some fame as a scholar, doing that to Blake. And yet, if the symbolism is what makes a work great, well, hell, there's just as much in *The Lone Ranger*—the masked man, silver bullets, the relationship between the Lone Ranger and Tonto, the men and the horses, and so on. I proved it. It was actually used in a philosophy of literature course for years. A guy who was chairman of the philosophy department congratulated me, and it certainly had a negative effect on what happened in that course with Damon. At the end, he said, "Young man, there's no disputing the brilliance of your work, but, young man, you have demons in you!" That's funny, from a guy named Damon. "Demons in you, and you must cast them out!"

So I left one course short. A couple of years later I took a course at Long Island University for the credit. I didn't even bother to send it in for a while, but eventually I got my Brown degree. It wasn't easy, and I'm not sure it was worth it. Meanwhile I just went out and lied. I said I graduated from Brown when I hadn't, when I applied for my first jobs.

Henry Miller used to say he had a Ph.D. from Columbia.
Yeah. It seemed like the easiest thing to do, and there was some justice in it. I had gotten the highest distinction on the comprehensive exams in my major. At the same time, I wasn't allowed to graduate because of the fiasco with Damon.

Your major was...?
English literature. They had just started an honors program—

159

one of the first; it already existed, I believe, at Iowa—an honors program in creative writing in the years I was there. I think the year I left the first people graduated with an honors degree in writing. I tried to take a couple of the writing courses, and I found that it just didn't suit me to be doing one kind of exercise one week, and—if I disciplined myself, I'm sure I could have learned something, but I think that what I learned in, say, a course on medieval art was more relevant to what I would do later as a writer than anything I would have learned in the writing courses. Anyhow, I was impatient with them, and I didn't opt for that.

Your university experience, aside from being kicked out, is still very important to you, isn't it? I mean the intellectual experience of the university.

Yeah. It is. I look back with considerable nostalgia and realize that some people with whom I argued at the time, and perhaps even ridiculed, said things that were wise and important. They became more important in retrospect. In a couple of cases, with a couple of people, friendships developed at a later time. I'd taken a course with a poet, Charles Philbrick, and didn't get along with him that well, but I later published him in my magazine, and we became friends. We didn't always agree. We argued about things in letters, too. He didn't like something by James T. Farrell I'd published, and I told him why it was good, and so on. So we would still have disagreements. I published some of his poetry in the magazine, and I published his last book of poetry. It was then a posthumous work.

When you say "magazine," you mean The Generalist Papers?

The old *Smith.* Back in 1964. It was the first issue, spring 1964. I'd gotten the idea along about November of '63, sent out some letters to people whose work I'd seen and admired in other magazines, such as Menke Katz, whom I'd never met, and a bunch of other people. John Tagliabue. He must be in his seventies now, but I think he was in the very first issue. I had a lot of my own stuff in the issue, under pseudonyms; I didn't want to seem as though I'd created the magazine just to publish myself.

What were some of the pseudonyms?

160

Well...Hershel Kovacs. He wrote a series of essays called "Eros Underground." Actually, I got into a lot of trouble for that. *Saturday Review*, for instance, wouldn't accept my advertising. I was trying to place a little classified ad for the magazine—they had an acceptability, a review, committee, and they decided that even though it was just a fraction of the contents—and this was just before the big obscenity cases in the '60s. It was within a year that someone, maybe Grove Press, published something called "Eros Denied," which was much more sociological about sex. But this was all about sex. You know, I didn't...well, maybe it did have some content which would be obscene by the standards of the times, but not compared to Henry Miller, say, or Lawrence.

But it was only a couple of years after that that someone published the unexpurgated *Lady Chatterly's Lover*. I think it was Putnam that did *Fanny Hill*, and there were all these big obscenity cases, but I was a bit before that with this thing. Ironically, and at the same time, the advertising for books from Lyle Stuart, which would be—well, I satirized one in a fake ad that I did in the old Smith. I called it "A Golden Treasury of Atrocities." I mean he was publishing these books with color pictures of the atrocities in the concentration camps, and not for the right motives, I would say. *Saturday Review* wasn't the only place where I ran into trouble. I just used that as an example.

Was The Smith *your first magazine?*
Yeah, that was the first magazine.

That was several years after you graduated from college.
Oh, yeah, I'd been doing other things. My first job after college was as a newspaper reporter—a small daily newspaper in central Massachusetts, the *Southbridge News*. Then I worked at the *Worcester Telegram*, also as a reporter. Then I came to New York and worked on trade publications. I was news editor of a magazine for the Alcoholic Beverage Industry. And then just before I started *The Smith* I was editor of a newspaper for lawyers. And I was doing various kinds of freelance journalism at the time.

Also, there were some things that, without any great reflection, nauseated me. Sartre has a novel called *Nausea* which I think in some ways is an apt description of some of the things which were happening to me. The day would come, the opportunity would be there, but I would not want to do the publicity work for the Veterans of Foreign Wars, say. I worked for its state organization, and the lawyer who ran it was one of my clients. So, one by one, I gave those things up, just because I didn't want to do it anymore. I rejected a lot of jobs which would have seemed good to some people. I had an opportunity to work for *Newsweek*, but that would have been on the business side. I could have worked for the *Wall Street Journal*. I didn't want to work on the desk, otherwise I might have been able to work in New York. But the openings for reporters were in Dallas and Atlanta, and I didn't want to leave New York City. I was offered a job as the editor of a fashion industry magazine, which would have been very little work, very good pay, and I would have been supervising a staff of attractive young women for a job I could have done better than it was being done all by myself in a day or two a week. It was a big magazine; it consisted mostly of pictures and press releases and advertising. But I decided that was unworthy, and I didn't really want to do it.

That was sort of the state I was in before I started *The Smith*. It was a kind of Quixotic quest to find a job which, of course, didn't exist unless you created it for yourself. I didn't know what I was doing. I even went to see a psychiatrist who said, in short, "Well, you're a poet, you're a writer, you're not supposed to make a lot of money. You don't have a problem. If other people have a problem with it, it's their problem." I said, "That's right. Everyone else is crazy." It was the world's shortest psychotherapy. [Coughs.] Excuse me, I shouldn't smoke, and I do have a bad cold. It was worth it. I had a great time in London.

The Smith—*it sounds provocative. That's what you wanted to do, was provoke. That's what you wanted to do in college, too, with those papers you wrote, right?*

Yeah. That's true, but a lot of that was spontaneous and—yeah, I wanted to be a writer. I wasn't encouraged very much for my poetry when I was in college, but I was encouraged enormously for my satire, which was admired by various professors, like Krause, for instance. I think Philbrick never cared for the poetry I was writing at that time, but I had written some satiric things which he admired. And some people encouraged me in a literary career from the beginning. I started as a

162

chemistry major but I switched over after only a semester. I did decide it was a lot more fun to be a writer.

Do you still write?

Yeah, I do. It's always been a balancing act, a search for equilibrium, to find enough time to do all the other things I'm doing and a reasonable amount of writing. In recent years I've done the greatest amount of writing in Maine. [Smith has a summer cottage there.] I'm working on something which has some resemblance to a novel, but it also has...well, it merges with the epic. It doesn't really have a novelistic structure. It's something I'd begun around 1970, and I didn't know what to do with it. I set it aside. Some of the techniques I'd evolved in the parts that I'd written I used and extended in a work like *Trinity* which is a long poem, a book by itself. And I recently returned to this other work.

The working title is *Gawaine Greene*. You know, in some ways Gawaine and the Green Knight are the same character. They're really both champions of the goddess, that sort of thing. It's partly based on my own experiences. It's partly based on myth. It's been going fairly well. I finished the first book. There are five parts, but as I see it now, the fifth part is kind of small. I'm well into the second. I don't even have all of the first into my computer; I only computerized in the midst of doing this, so I have a lot of sections still in handwriting, which is the way I formerly wrote.

Now that I've gotten used to computers, seeing things on the screen and the ease in going back to revise something, I decided I like it. I can compose directly on the computer. So I'm still writing, but I continually find ways to distract myself. I think they're all productive. The rationalization is if I hadn't been in publishing and related activities, I wouldn't be together with you now. You meet so many people—not just stimulating, but often inspiring people. You know, being an editor and seeing what other people are doing—in that respect, what I like to think is that what I would be capable of would be less, more limited, if I hadn't spent so many years engaged in the little magazine and small press scene.

I've thought quite a lot about what you're talking about because I'm in a similar boat.

163

Yeah, I'll bet you are.

On the one hand, I'm an intellectual. I spent a lot of time in university life, and I was involved, both academically and politically. On the other hand I've written creatively all my life. But I came to the conclusion that as painful as it was for me to leave university life, it was the best thing that could have happened. Because it is so structured now— all corporate life is so structured, whether it's the university or the military—they demand to own you. I wouldn't be able to do something that the other side of my brain might tell me to do.

Well, I think maybe things got looser for a while, but I was looking into various job possibilities after college. One job, for instance, would have been editing the house organ of Mobil Oil. Well, those jobs paid a lot better than just being a reporter someplace. The trade magazines paid so much better than being a reporter; that's why I moved over to them when I came to New York City. But, yeah, you'd be asked stuff like "Why do you want to work for Mobil Oil Corporation?" And I'd say, "Well, I don't. But I can do the job better than anyone else. You want to send me into the next room to do something? I'll do it. But I don't give a damn about Mobil Oil. But I do care very much about the craft of the job. I like to do a good job." Well, of course, most places, you tell them something like that—right out the door.

And they'd be giving me these weird personality tests, and all of that. Even at the *Worcester Telegram*, when I first went there, you were supposed to check off all of these things—first you're supposed to go through and check what you thought applied to yourself: whether you're a coward or whether you're brave. I checked all of them. I'm a coward, I'm brave. And then you were supposed to go through again and check what you thought other people thought about you. And again.... The problem was that you couldn't analyze it. It was pretty complicated. A lot of times I was ashamed that I didn't do better in a particular situation; other times I think I did very well and stood up for what I believed in, or managed despite some difficulty, or I would be helpful to somebody who was in danger.

Routinely they would ask you questions like whether you owned your own house or not. You know, these were the big corporations in New York. How much did your house cost? What rent do you pay on your apartment? I remember submitting one application, I remember writing "None of your damn business," "None of your damn business," "None of your damn business," and so on. And then a few months later—I didn't take the job, but I enjoyed it so I called the office and they said, "That was a hell of an application." And the editor of one place actually liked it; it didn't always count against me.

I was offered a job once at *Esquire*, just reading the over-the-transome fiction, again when I was quite young, because I had the shortest resumé the editor-in-chief, Arnold Gingrich, had ever seen. I'd done a fair amount by then, but all I put down was "Reporter-Photographer, *Southbridge News*," nothing more. No elaborate description of what I did. I mean any damn fool ought to know what a reporter does and what a photographer does. Even with the college stuff in there, and some stuff from the other jobs I'd had: "It's the shortest resumé I've ever seen." So he loved it, but of course it went over like a lead balloon in a lot of other places. But, yeah, the corporate world—the big corporate world—was obviously out. They seemed to be making claims, as you suggested, far beyond what would be involved in the job itself. Loyalty. Attitude. No way.

I had been encouraged while at Brown, by Charles Philbrick and others, to stay around, to go to graduate school, get a Ph.D. Philbrick said, "Where else would you have this much creative time. I teach"—I forget how many hours a week he said—"ten hours a week. I have my long summers, my cottage at Wellfleet on Cape Cod. Where else would you have as much time to write? You want to be a poet?" I said, "Well, you know, I've been in constant trouble as a student. I can't see how it's likely to be different on the faculty." I mean it's fine as long as you don't get involved in anything—about the direction the university is going, say. I could imagine I would be in a lot of trouble all of the time. So it didn't seem a valid option.

But I had some romantic idea about—of course, you can't make a living as a poet—I had some romantic idea that, like Stephen Crane, like Hemingway, the newspaper experience would be good for me. But it's so totally ruled by events that I didn't get much writing done. But I think, in retrospect, I did learn quite a bit. I did come in contact with so many different kinds of people, so many different kinds of situations. And I think I learned quite a bit about economy—not using a big word when a small one will do, not having all sorts of unnecessary introductory clauses, whatever. I had a tough editor in my first job who was very good; I think I learned a lot from the guy, even though, as I say, while I was doing it I was very much ruled by events. Sometimes there would be some serendipitous circumstance where I could do something creative. I could do an interview and really get in touch with someone's dreams and values, you know, the whole life purpose, and manage to convey that in a feature story. But maybe that happened six or seven times when I was working on newspapers, a little bit more often when I was doing the newsletter. In addition to the old *Smith*, in 1969 I started doing a newsletter called *The Newsletter on the State of the Culture*, which was quite broad, though probably not as broad as the title implies. It was mostly about publishing.

Who did you send it to?

Well, it was read chiefly by the top editors and publishers in the established houses. This was at a time when *Publishers Weekly* had a lot less reporting than it has now. In fact, they even for a time, later on when they had a change of editors, had a newsletter section which was, to some extent, I think, shaped by or reacting to my format. I never had a circulation of more than eight or nine hundred, but it had tremendous influence. If I would report on some peculiar things happening at the *New York Times*, say, they'd change their way of doing things. It would be noticed; they knew their colleagues would be reading about their—

Just one trivial example that comes to mind: the *New York Times* owned a reprint company called Arno Reprint which was in competition with some others like Johnson Reprint, and so on. Johnson Reprint was later taken over by the Kraus-Thomson Publishing Company. This was Lord Thomson of Fleet. Well, there had been a favorable review in the *New York Times Book Review*. And, of course, routinely a publisher gets permission to either quote from the review or reprint the review and pass out copies. They had denied that permission to a competitor, but this was a decision made somewhere on the middle level of management. You know, once the higher-ups found out about it—but they only found out about it in my newsletter or when I called them up about it—they said, "Well, this is a case of the right hand not knowing what the left hand is doing. Of course we shouldn't do that. We'll stop it immedi-

166

ately." That's a trivial example. There are certainly more important effects of doing that. In reporting for the newsletter, I did some things which I think I could be more proud of. And it was good writing at the same time. It was good reporting, but of course, reporting, for the most part, is just a trend. There are various formulae, and you have to do it fast.

The Smith *began in '64. How long did it last?*

The Smith lasted until the late '70s and then it continued as *Pulpsmith*. It just had a metamorphosis. I have an issue somewhere that has a funny picture of me growing wings, or something like that. It was published like clockwork, quarterly, for about seven years. I gave it up. I'm proud of all of them to an extent. It was an attempt to escape the literary ghetto, to get out on the newsstands with the magazines that people associate with entertainment. I was out there with *Ellery Queen* and *Fantasy and Science Fiction*, you know, publications like that.

How did you get on the news stands? I remember seeing Pulpsmith.

Well, not very well. We had Metropolitan in the area of news-stand distribution, a magazine distributor, and the rest was catch-as-catch-can. We never did get very good national distribution, partly, I think, because of our own inefficiency, not going at it the right way. We did advertise it on jazz programs on the radio. Jazzbo Collins was a fan of *Pulpsmith*. He called me up to interview me in the middle of his jazz show sometimes. And we placed ads on his radio station. I forget which one it was.

In *Pulpsmith* we had a lot of the writers who would have been called "underground" in the '60s. People like Hugh Fox and John Bennett, along with people who were well-known writers in one genre or another. Mystery writers, science fiction writers, fantasy writers. It was very popular with writers.

But what we discovered is that the science fiction fans want all science fiction. They don't want a mix; they're not eclectic as readers the way I was when I was a kid, or still am. Maybe if I had a heavy concentration of science fiction and an interview with Theodore Sturgeon, I could get science fiction fans to buy it. And the same in the fantasy realm, if I had Frank Belknap Long and people like that. But actually the writers loved it. Sturgeon said it was weird and wonderful and so on. So we had this really curious mix of the underground and the established genre writers.

You did Pulpsmith *for seven years.*

Eight, actually. The last issue was just a giant annual, but it was about three hundred and eighty-four pages, and it was a kind of grand summation. I had a lot of the writers I liked best, and it was atypical in that at least half of it was the work of writers I had published before. Whereas the emphasis always had been in the old *Smith* and in *Pulpsmith* on discovery. I would say that seventy-five percent or more of any given issue were things from writers I hadn't published before. They were new to me and quite a few of them hadn't been published anywhere or much of anywhere. Others had been, of course, published in other little magazines, but not by me, so it wasn't presenting the work of the same people over and over. The last issue of *Pulpsmith* is the only issue where I ever made special invitations to writers whose work I especially valued; for instance, John Bennett. I published a hundred-page novella by him in that issue called "Flying to Cambodia". Within a year someone had a popular book with the title *Swimming to Cambodia*.

Spalding Gray.

Yeah. That happens. Leon Uris came out with something called *Trinity* about a year after I published my epic poem by that name.

The Generalist Papers. *I actually haven't seen that.*

It's just a good-looking newsletter, well-designed, sometimes with a fair amount of art work, although unhappily I don't always get that together. I don't do a stretch to include artwork. For instance, we did one, an essay by Marshall Brooks called "The [James T.] Farrell Underground". He'd found various books by James T. Farrell that people had made elaborate notes in, and he was commenting on the readers' notes that he'd found in these used books. And illustrations of the books themselves accompanied the essay. Likewise, when the same writer did a little essay on the literary history of the old Kenmore Hotel in New York City—people like Dashiell Hammett who'd been living there, and so on; some places like the Chelsea are famous, but there were other places, too, and this was one—we had a lot of old pictures which were

168

included.

So some of it was just good essays that were about something. Other issues could be classified as literary criticism. We've had some which were publishing history. We've had other, more general essays on the state of the arts. A guy named Matthew Paris wrote something called—I think it was "The Hell of the American Arts," something like that. We've had a number of essays on linguistics. There was one written by my son, who's a clinical psychologist, on Chomsky's theories, and then another issue that consisted largely of debate about that essay along with an essay called "Yiddish Dies Again" which is a debate among Jews as to whether or not Yiddish is a dying language. So that gives you some idea of the range.

The range seems fairly broad.

Yeah, that's why I called it *The Generalist Papers*. When I started *The Smith* I called it "the most general magazine." I thought that other people publishing at the time were just promoting a particular group of writers in their little magazines. I also thought that the bigger literary magazines such as the *Partisan Review*, the *Massachusetts Review*, the *Sewanee Review* had so many of the same writers, you could change the covers and no one would know the difference. You know, if you said that a particular issue of the *Massachusetts Review* was really the *Kenyon Review*, I don't know if anybody would have suspected a difference. They were all doing very much the same thing, and I thought there was probably a lack of receptivity to new writing, or to writers where there hadn't been a laying-on of hands in some ritual passage into publication at those places.

Others, I thought, were too narrow. Like Robert Bly, the *Deep Image* and all of that. Well, I thought there was a lot more to poetry and everything else than the *Deep Image*. Bly and I were favorably disposed toward each other personally, and had a fair amount of argumentative correspondence back in the '60s. He was in search of the deep image à la Neruda or something like that. A lot of it was just inadvertently ridiculous to the ear. You know, Bly would say things like "The thieves are crying out in the wild asparagus," and stuff like that. I felt it was an insufficient recognition or attention or appreciation for the role of music in poetry. And it was also true, in a different way, I thought, of *The*

Outsider where everything had to be free verse and all of that. And they were looking for the avant garde and of course they found it in Bukowski.

I was after something broader and I called it "the most general magazine" because I didn't want to set any way of doing things, any particular school, certainly not the promotion of any particular group of writers, ahead of the experience of the writing itself. "The value," I think Santayana said, "is in the experience." So how much does it affect you? Do you find yourself thinking about it a day later, or three days later? There are things that failed, yet seemed very important. They were after something important. So I published a lot of the failures, and I rejected a lot of people who were more accomplished. I can make a more impressive list, I think, of the people I rejected—you know, writers who were well known or who became very well known. Not so very many of the writers I published became famous.

When did you start publishing books?

Nineteen sixty-seven. Of course, that was a direct outgrowth of publishing the magazine. I'd been publishing some poetry and, again, it was a kind of reaching out on the basis of something I'd seen somewhere else. I sent a letter to a guy named George Abbe. I don't even know if he's still alive; he'd be pretty high in years by now. I've been doing this for more than thirty years, and he was then, I think, past fifty. He was an excellent lyric poet. He also, as quite a young man, had a novel; he was featured along with three other young writers on the cover of *Saturday Review*. Back in the '40s, with Norman Cousins editing, it was an influential publication. Abbe had another novel, which was flawed in various respects. I published his poetry and I published an essay from a book called *The Nonconformist* which was published elsewhere. He was politically radical. Of course, I identified with that; I was the one and only nonconformist at Brown. People I scarcely knew in my time [at Brown] remember me because I was the only one. There were no others—I mean in the area of ideas; there were people who went around with weird costumes or who performed intricate pranks. I was the only one doing things like The Declaration of Independence, or whatever.

Anyhow, it could have been a magnificent novel, but it would go haywire anytime they would start talking about anything political. The characters would just become mouthpieces for the ideas. So I wrote him

170

a series of letters. I accepted it, and though he always agreed with the things I said about what needed to be revised, it didn't turn into a great novel or even a well-organized novel. It has beautiful narrative sections in it. When it came out, a critic, August Derleth, wrote that it could be used in writing courses as a textbook example of how novels can go wrong.

Then a couple or three years later a book was published consisting of an exchange of letters between William Rose Benet and George Abbe. And twenty years before, William Rose Benet had said all the same things to Abbe about his fiction that I'd been saying. He had just been unable to act on the criticism, even though he had agreed with it. I always found later that the easiest people to work with were the truly great writers like [James T.] Farrell. If you'd say to Farrell, "I think you could just skip that paragraph. You did something a few pages earlier that made the same point, but better," he'd say, "I'll think about it." That, or immediately he'd say, "You're right. Let's do it." Yet there's another kind of writer, as you've probably discovered, who just can't see criticism. Even if they can take it, they can't act on it. Of course, the writers who achieve the most become fine critics of themselves, but they're quite willing to take criticism from any direction, and to act on it in order to make it better.

So that was the first book.
That was the very first book.

When you began publishing books—say, in the first five years—how many did you publish?
I kind of lost track of the numbers.

What I'm getting at is your rate of production.
Yeah. Not that many. Like a book a year, something like that. I started to get more ambitious in the '70s. And there was one year when I had seventeen titles, although quite a few of them were chapbooks. The '70s were a relatively high rate of production. Let's say it averaged six or seven books a year. Then *The Smith* magazine became kind of indifferent; years would go by between issues sometimes. I published it when I wanted to. But then when I was doing *Pulpsmith*, it started out as

a hundred-and-ninety-two-page format—it always had a lot of pages. I was doing it in quite an ambitious way, and getting an incredible number of manuscripts from everywhere. Book production slowed down considerably in that period also; I was just doing one or two books a year. I think in each of the last few years I've done about five books a year—since stopping *Pulpsmith*, which ended around 1990, I believe.

When did you start being able to make a living? I assume you're making a living now.

No. It's under the aegis of a literary foundation. No, all I do is lose money—on publishing.

Is The Smith *a 501 (c) (3) corporation?*

Yes, it is. But I only did that in 1974. I'd been publishing for ten years first, but privately, at my own expense. On a given book I might make money, but in the total scheme of things I don't. I always thought I'd prefer to make my money some other way than to publish the things that I know would make money. I've recommended many books to the major houses which have been accepted and which were very successful. I've said, "Well, you don't need me. Simon and Schuster, I'm sure, would publish this." And I've had, in recent years, absolutely no grant support. So it's an entirely individual activity.

The foundation though, that's aside from grant support?

Yeah. That receives some private contributions from people who like what I'm doing. Once upon a time, when things were somewhat more open, I did get some grants for special projects from the National Endowment to pay writers. When I was doing the magazine I had some grants which were just to pay writers more. I was paying something. I mean, a hundred dollars for a story is not a lot, but I'd be paying them. In a typical book that I publish, the author gets five hundred or seven hundred and fifty dollars in advance, that sort of thing, even if I know I'm going to lose money on the book. A lot of the books I published were poetry by people who weren't going to give a lot of readings and didn't have any particular recognition. The same is true for the fiction. I'm fortunate enough to have had sufficient income from investments to do that. Yeah, if I hadn't done all of this I suppose I could have had a big sailboat or something. But I'm really not rich.

I interviewed Sandy Taylor and Judy Doyle from Curbstone Press a few weeks ago. And I remember saying that I concluded that regardless of where the money comes from, a literary press in the United States can't make it without some sort of subsidy. It could be personal, it could be...in my case, for example, it's personal. In the case of a nonprofit, it's from public or foundation monies.

Right. I never could play that game well. But the foundation actually served to fund many other things. Like the original New York Book Fair, started by Jackie Eubanks. It was a very big event and very important in changing the consciousness of the public about small presses. As many as fifteen or twenty thousand people would come to it on a three-day weekend. Across from the Coliseum there used to be something called the Huntington-Hartford Museum where the first New York Book Fair was held, and there were lines about four blocks long to get into it. The building couldn't accommodate that many people at one time. We did things like have it in a big circus tent behind the main public library by Bryant Park. That was one of my favorite book fairs. It was at Lincoln Center a couple of years. It moved to Madison Square Garden in the '80s. It was quite a big event; it served its purpose in its time. And funding for those activities, which [was obtained by] just loosely organized committees—you know, we had a steering committee, which I was always on, and when he was in New York, Bill Truesdale of New Rivers, and Bob Hershon of *Hanging Loose Magazine* here in Brooklyn. Those are just a couple of names that come to mind, people who.... Joe Barbato now does a lot of writing for *Publishers Weekly*. He always did the publicity for the fair, was on the steering committee, and he used to have, when he lived in New York, a little magazine called *Remington Review*. And, you know, we'd just get together for a few planning sessions.

A lot of the funding for stuff like that went through The Generalist Association, which was the foundation I created. Other things, like there used to be a COSMEP prison project—there was a lot of funding for stuff like that. The New England Small Press Association. Even the ridiculous COSMEP van project came through The Generalist. I figured it was better than making bombs, so I didn't care if we

spent money on a truck that didn't work [that we sent] down south—
Appalachia or Lynchburg, Virginia, wherever they were—to try to
bring about consciousness about small press stuff. It's a long list of
activities which were rendered possible, using The Generalist as a con-
duit, as they say in the CIA, for those public monies.

As I say, the only things I used it for were special projects. One
of the reasons is that I was doing a lot of reporting on the inequities in
the grant system when I was publishing the newsletter on the state of
the culture. So in the early period I applied for no grants. It wasn't until
after I stopped publishing the newsletter that I ever applied for a grant. I
didn't think it was right to be reporting on that sort of thing, and
commenting on it, and at the same time be a supplicant. I think as the
system evolved it became less open. You know, a lot of insider stuff
was always going on where people who were on these panels would
have their own publications come up for discussion, or ones that they'd
been associated with. Yeah, I think I can attest, having handled hundreds of thousands of dollars—I never counted how much it came to
altogether—of public money, that on the whole it has certainly not gone
to the neediest, nor has it gone to the most deserving, but it's gone to
the people who are the best at the game and who are doing something that
is very comprehensible and eminently respectable and where there is
some immediate recognition of the names of the people they're publishing and the right connections and so on.

I was once asked if I would serve on a literary panel for the New
York State Council on the Arts. I rather foolishly announced that it would
be one of my objectives to eliminate the conflict-of-interest situations on
the panels, and then I was disinvited. I never did get on the panel. I
probably should have just said all the right things, gotten on a panel,
and then raised hell. Artists and writers in general are worse than other
people, less sensitive, about the conflict of interest stuff, because the
attitude is "anything we do is okay because we're artists". Among the
minority publishers there's a tendency to say, "Okay, here's a system
to be used. We're finally in a position to use it and we're going to use
it to the maximum and that's the way it should be." So I think there's a
lack of openness. There's a lot of insiders' advantage.

On the other hand there are some things that just have to be
funded. You know, if you start something new and it's in the right

174

minority area—now, my wife applied for a grant for a company called the Irish Bronx Theater Company, where she became the artistic director more or less by default, and knew that if they just filled out the forms right, NYSCA [New York State council on the Arts] would have to give them some kind of minimum support, which is what happened. But on the other hand, if you have something literary, and it's general and it's not minority, you'd have a tough time getting funded, even with a track record.

I think nowadays, if you have a niche, whether it's ethnic minority or whatever, you have a market.

Yeah, that's true. I suppose you could consider the grants organizations giving public monies as just a peculiar kind of market. And of course a lot of the small publishers now are getting good at really reaching certain segments of the market in sales. I'm fairly good at helping other publishers in various ways—finding distribution and that sort of thing. I'm just so disorganized, unpredictable, frequently unscheduled in what I do, it's harder to help myself.

I was looking through your catalogue. You have a lot of wholesalers listed here.

Yeah, that's who I have—just wholesalers. I don't have any true distributors.

Have you ever had any?

I haven't. I had one opportunity, with Atrium, a few years ago. And I suppose there would have been other opportunities, but the way they do things doesn't particularly make sense to me. I have one book which got into the chains and was selling very well at that time and went into an immediate second printing. It's called *The Cleveland Indian*, by Luke Salisbury. It got great reviews everywhere from *USA Today* and *Baseball Weekly* to *New York Review of Books*. It made the top-headlined essay that week, by Stephen Jay Gould, who was also a baseball fan. Well, great if somebody like Atrium would take that on, but the same year I published *Matriarch*, a book of poetry by Glenna Luschei, and a bunch of things I didn't think really belonged in most stores or needed to be in Atrium's warehouse. So they wouldn't have wanted to handle everything, but what would have made the most sense is just to handle some titles. I have another recent book which has gotten good reviews, John Bennett's novel, *Bodo*. It's being translated into Czech. I'm very hopeful that there will be a German edition soon. Now I've not had any distribution for that.

I was publishing so many funky little things—in most cases, books of poetry—many years ago, it just didn't seem to make sense. I once had a salesman, a salesman for Grove Press—a guy named Len Schmuckler—and he was great. He placed great quantities of all my books in a lot of stores. But most of them came back. So having learned that lesson—I actually had my own salesman, a very capable guy who traveled all over the country—he went all over the place: he was in the East, he was in the Midwest, he was in Portland, he made several sales trips a year. Len was great at getting the things in there, but I discovered that most of the things I publish can't sell in a typical bookstore. A few of them can. The essays by James T. Farrell, Farrell's novels, something like that. But some poetry just belongs in special places.

So when you do a book, you're pretty much at the mercy of the reviews.

Yeah, that's right. Reviews call it to the attention of the librarians who may want to order it. When the authors make appearances, sometimes the books sell well. One recent book that's excellent and made a little money is called *A Sense of Direction*, a book of poetry by Karen Swenson. She probably gave about thirty-five readings within a year after the book was published. It got very few reviews. It was selected for the National Poetry Series. So it didn't get reviews, but because of the appearances it made money. It still sells. In the same period I published a book called *Working Firewood for the Night* by Lloyd Van Brunt, and it got great reviews everywhere. Well, not everywhere, but in literary reviews. It got a terrific review in PW [*Publishers Weekly*] "Forecasts," it had glowing blurbs from Norman Mailer and poets like David Ignatow and Gerald Stern. It scarcely sold at all.

I've always found it hard to predict. Sometimes things that go unnoticed at the beginning become noticed later. Back in the middle '70s I published something which is a satire on the poetry establishment of the time. It's called *A Modern Dunciad*, by Richard Nason. It was actually done in rhymed couplets. And it satirizes people like John Ashbery. It was greeted with total silence by the New York literary establishment. Reviews started to appear though in places like San Francisco and Los Angeles and Denver. Then finally one showed up in a Metropolitan area newspaper, *Newsday*. It never did get any attention in the *New York Times*, but about a year, year and a half after the book was published there was a two-page article in the *Village Voice*— pictures, all of that—about how this book had become an underground classic and a small press bestseller. And since then there has been a continuing demand for it over the years.

I was very ambitious at the time. I think I printed something like four thousand copies. I still have them. Most of my press runs these days are about a thousand to fifteen hundred copies, depending on what it is. A book of poetry might be eight hundred copies.

I do have lists. I have my own list of buyers, people who have followed the press over the years. Of course, many people on the lists who are just interested in, say, John Bennett, there's not necessarily going to be a crossover, but I use those lists too. When I market my new books [a collection of Menke Katz's works], I'll show them at the Association of Jewish Libraries and stuff like that. We'll advertise them in the Yiddish-language papers. And then I'll do a somewhat large edition of the English translations. I hope that that will be done this year. It could be successful.

I'm doing fewer books, but I need to slow down now with publishing. I'm involved with other things, among them projects with Arts End Press. My friend Marshall Brooks who worked at The Smith right after high school, started his own press some years later. We'll be doing some things together. I expect that probably next year we'll have the first joint imprint.

I've had some cooperative projects with Birch Brook Press. Tom Tolnay. We've collaborated on two anthologies edited by Peter Bjarkman, on baseball. I've been going at the rate of four or five books a year recently. It might be just a couple with somebody else two years from now.

I wanted to free more time for my own writing, and then I got involved in all this stuff with Loris Essary and International Titles and doing things with and for other publishers.

177

I was going to ask you about your involvement with International Titles.

Well, it came about because of COSMEP which, of course, is now defunct, or merged with PMA, Publishers Marketing Association. I was one of the founders of COSMEP along with Len Fulton and Richard Morris back in 1968 in Berkeley. Of course there were others involved in the very beginning, like Jerry Burns—Goliards Press. He's dead now. He lived in the state of Washington, in Bellingham.

People got together as a kind of gathering of the tribe and formed a trade organization—COSMEP. Later it had the subtitle of International Association of Independent Publishers. I started to work with Loris on these exhibits [i.e., the American Booksellers Association trade show, the American Library Association conference, various book fairs], and of course we spent time together there, and I was promoting my own books, and so on. I was just a member among members of the board; I had nothing unusual to do with the running of the organization. One exception was when I helped them out when they met in New York City at NYU in the early days, when they still had their big conferences in the universities. Then they went to a more businesslike format of having conferences in big hotels and that sort of thing.

I made arrangements for Loris to extend the exhibit services to the Frankfurt Book Fair. Then I got to like working with him and when COSMEP folded, to my considerable surprise— When I left in the beginning of 1994 a seventy-thousand-dollar surplus was being predicted for that year. We had a lot of successful new programs, cooperative advertising in *Publishers Weekly*. All kinds of good things were going on. A large surplus was predicted. Then a year later, after a lot of inner conflict, I hear they're more than eighty thousand in debt. They merged with the PMA and fired the executive director, Richard Morris, at the worst possible time, just a couple of weeks before their annual conference.

Anyhow, when COSMEP died, people had already registered for the ABA and the ALA, and Loris was in terrible trouble as a result of all of this, so I decided to step in and make it a business relationship with Loris, to do the big trade shows in the U.S., to pick up COSMEP's obligations, if you will. People paid money to COSMEP to register. I actually saw very little of that money. Despite the fact that it was a total financial disaster, it wasn't all that bad. Overseas publishers—we had a lot of Italian art books at the ABA. Scholarly books from different publishers. Some of them we were representing in other ways, in other venues. I just got word from Loris today that a Singapore publisher for whom we exhibited in London last year wants to be with us in the U.S. show this year. He's an English-language publisher, quite a few titles. So that's working out reasonably well and we've done a lot of good for some of the publishers.

For your own press, are subsidiary rights sales or leases very important?

Well, it's starting to be. Like John Bennett's book, *Bodo*—it's not a lot of money; the advance is fifteen hundred dollars. I split that with the author. We're both awfully glad to get that, with royalties to come. I recently got paid for the forthcoming Czech edition—the money just showed up in The Generalist bank account one day. They never sent me back the signed contract; I hadn't heard about it for eight months. So this activity has certainly helped my press, and it helps other people too.

Small presses generally are now in a position not only to have access to various marketplaces in the U.S., but in the international marketplace. A lot of business that we're doing is with countries that used to be behind the iron curtain. All these recently created private companies in Russia and Poland and Czechoslovakia and other countries—all the major publishers didn't want to touch them with a ten-foot pole in the beginning. We were very quick to make deals with them, and it's working out very well.

I don't have any more questions. Is there anything else you want to go into?

No.

Juris Jurjevics
Soho Press

Daniel Simon
Four Walls Eight Windows; Seven Stories Press

"In any industry uniformity of product is a big goal. You can have it in six colors, but it needs to be the same thing. And business is very uncomfortable when the product is not that, when it's very individualistic... A lot of the people from the business side...didn't really get a full grasp of it, and their idea of uniformity obviously doesn't work. Really, the way they talk, you'd think they were sending out to a delicatessen for 'six more of those.' And it doesn't quite work that way. You aren't offered the menu, whether you like it or not."

"I think there's always been this...dynamic tension between the values of authors-are-important/editors-are-important and authors-aren't-really-important/editors-aren't-really-important—what's important is the marketing and distribution, packaging. There's always been that tension."

Juris Jurjevics was born in 1943 in Tukums, Latvia, west of Riga. Following the end of World War II, and after half a decade in a displaced-persons camp in Germany, he went with his parents to the United States, to New York, where he spent the remainder of his childhood in the Bronx.

Dan Simon was born in 1957 (Jurjevics: "'Fifty-seven?'" Simon: "Yeah." Jurjevics: "I'm leaving.") in Bromley, England, outside of London. He came to the United States with his family as an infant. His father is a research scientist at Harvard Medical School, his mother an educator and arts administrator; for a time she ran Goddard College's graduate program. In college—Columbia—Simon began as a music performance major, then switched to English literature, taking a B.A. and then an M.A.

Jurjevics did not go to college; he laughs when I ask if he did.

180

"What did you do instead?" "I bummed through some colleges" for a couple of years, he says.

Both Soho and Seven Stories are general trade publishers, publishing fiction and nonfiction. Jurjevics: "We [at Soho] don't do practical books; we don't know how to. We don't do any of the reasonable kind of things you would do [as] a small press. There is some immunity if you do reference books. The reference book is self-sustaining if it's about something practical, like building a house or planting a tree." Each press puts out around twenty-five titles a year. At the time of this interview, Seven Stories was most successful at publishing hardcover fiction, "which is interesting," Simon says, "because it's the hardest area to publish." Simon attributed Seven Stories' success in fiction to publishing well-known authors.

Subsidiary rights sales—primarily paperback reprint rights—are important to both presses, Soho especially, whose rights sales account for fifteen to twenty percent of its yearly gross income. Seven Stories is not as successful in this area. "We're not as smart as Soho. Historically, we haven't been as smart as Juris."

I interviewed the two publishers together on Wednesday, March 26, 1997, an overcast morning. We met at a small bakery in Manhattan—the Jon Vie—on 6th Avenue between 12th and 13th Streets. It had rained earlier, the rain coming in behind a blasting wind. Now both wind and rain were gone and the air was warming after several days of freezing and near-freezing temperatures. In arranging for the interview, I had not been aware that the two were friends. The interplay between them, much of it silent, taking the form of facial expression or head twist, was a pleasure to watch.

Let's back up. You went from college to...what?

Dan Simon: One of my advisors was Ann Douglas at Columbia, and her editor was Alice Quinn. And when I was sort of shuffling my feet about whether or not to continue in academia, she put me together with Alice and Alice got me thinking about publishing as a possible career.

Juris Jurjevics: Our Alice?

DS: Yeah.

JJ: Good.

What does "our Alice" mean?

JJ: If it's the same one.

DS: She has a Juris connection.

JJ: I never knew that. Oh, this is going to get too crazy, transcribing this.

This is neat. I did this once before. One of the most fun interviews I've had. Um, so you went into publishing from graduate school?

DS: Right. So I went from, um...right. I finished the MA and then I looked into publishing as an alternative to continuing with a Ph.D. I went to Harper in '82, and began there. And then to Norton in '83. And then I went from Norton to Sheep Meadow Press—it's a poetry press—which I ran for Stanley Moss, who's the owner. Then to Matthew Bender, which is a legal publisher. I did a number of books. I sort of bummed around at a pretty stiff pace for about three or four years.

You started at Harper in editorial?

DS: In permissions. Worked for Linda Rogers. Permissions was a great first job because you read everything in their library. Book publishers call you up and they say, "We want to reprint these five pages. Is that okay?" You end up reading kind of a medley of some of the best things that they have published, and they're a very illustrious house that has a fantastic backlist. So that was great.

And then went to Norton in editorial, and spent about a year and a half there. That was by far the hardest I've worked in publishing. I was an editorial assistant originally, for two editors. Both of them were good, high-powered editors. Mary Cunnane and Linda Healy. And I was the only person at Norton at the time that read French language manuscripts. So these French language manuscripts would come in and I'd read them all, like a true sort of, you know, innocent. You know, I read all of these damn things. Nobody else who was there was that interested in them. "Oh, give it to Dan," you know. I read French comfortably but slowly.

What years are these?

DS: 'Eighty-two, '83. So I was reading, you know, a six-hundred-page biography of Marx that they would never in a million years publish. They should have said to me, "Don't read them, just glance at them and reject them." Instead, I sat and read the book. So that was a very hard-working year and a half. And then I left and went to Sheep Meadow Press which I managed for Stanley Moss. And that was wonderful. We published Stanley Kunitz and David Ignatow and Ed Sanders and Alberto Rios and.... It was a very distinguished list—all poetry—that Stanley had put together. Stanley himself was a fine poet, better than you would expect from a publisher. His poetry has been published by Harcourt, among others. He was a Yale Younger Poet in 1949. So that was great.

And then for a couple of years did medical books for Matthew Bender. And I did eight-million-dollars-a-year medical-book publishing for them, and started a medical journal. And...I don't know, I would get into these situations where, if you're in a corporate structure, you have to know how to give a lot, but also how to stop it. And—

Stop what?

DS: Well, I don't think corporate structures are designed for people to give totally of themselves. The people who survive best in corporate structures modulate their contribution and do a fair amount of withholding. That's healthy. That's how you should do it. I never understood that. So, again at Matthew Bender, I proposed this medical journal and they gave it the green light and I brought in medical people and put together a cutting-edge medical journal, which wasn't what that environment was set up for. What that environment was set up for, if people were to ask you—you collect a paycheck. So both at Norton and at Matthew Bender I kind of burned out. I got physically sick. At Norton I went into analysis. [Laughs.] I was just not controlling my contributions.

And, after a couple of years at Matthew Bender, I landed doing work for Glenn Thompson [at Writers and Readers] who I felt was a really brilliant publisher. He's brilliant as a publisher, which is an unusual thing. You know, there're a lot of smart people, good writers, et cetera, but somebody whose brilliance is actually expressed in publishing is rare, and I felt Glenn had that.

I began editing his beginners' books. And because there wasn't always money to pay his editors, at one point he offered me an imprint as a way to sort of keep it interesting to me. And I had been wanting to publish Nelson Algren and so that became possible. And Glenn made it possible for me to start this imprint and begin publishing Algren. That was in '85. Algren was completely out of print at that point, entirely out of print.

What was your imprint?
DS: On the book it was printed "Dan Simon/Four Walls Eight Windows Book". The first Four Walls Eight Windows book was Nelson Algren's short stories, *The Neon Wilderness*, which I still have in print. It's great.

That's the prose poem he did?
DS: That's *Chicago: City on the Make*.

Oh, that's right.
DS: *The Neon Wilderness* is stories that he wrote, including his earlier stories from the '30s, and then his war stories from the '40s. It was the book between *Never Come Morning* and *The Man with the Golden Arm*.

So the first book was this Nelson Algren short stories, and I had gotten enthused about Nelson Algren, and then as I was researching him I found out that all these books are out of print. So that was great. There was a crusade waiting to happen there. I mean he's one of America's most important writers and has a real following and his books are out of print. There are two prizes in his name, both of which are active, but his own work was not available.

So Glenn supported me on that and began publishing the books. And then it was the reverse of the corporate situation, where if you're in an entrepreneurial situation you have to give totally, you have to basically give of yourself in a nonwithholding way. And it's appropriate. You don't feel like you're being foolish as you do when you're that way in a corporate structure.

So, beginning as an editor at Writers and Readers, I began Four Walls Eight Windows, and then a year later—'84, '85, that winter—I took on a partner and we developed it for the next ten years and built it up to where it was a kind of annually break-even company that was able

184

to fulfill some kind of regular commitment to a certain group of authors.

Your partner was John Oakes?
DS: Yeah.

For those years that you were just breaking even, were you subsidizing the press yourselves?
DS: Initially we were subsidizing it ourselves. We kept our regular jobs and we were putting the money into it from that. Then we did a business plan and we raised, really, a pretty small amount of money. A little over a hundred thousand dollars, from a combination of people in the industry, people we knew, people we didn't know, a couple of organizations. And then, in the latter years, our distributor was able to float us a kind of unofficial credit line.

Who is your distributor?
DS: Publishers Group West. In effect, they were investors. They were our bank eventually.

Do they distribute for you now?
DS: They do, yeah. And then.... So then we had a divorce in '95.

You and Oakes, you mean.
DS: Yeah. In '95. And then I was willing to continue on my own, and the question was whether the authors, key authors in the house that I had been working with over the previous ten years, felt enough loyalty to me personally to leave an existing entity, and the implied stability of that, to go with me for an uncertain future. And that was a tough year, not knowing if that would happen.

And then—I was leaning a lot on this guy [indicating Jurjevics]— and then, one after another, they came with me. Annie Ernaux, Octavia Butler, Gary Null, Project Censored which does the annual censored book, and the estate of Nelson Algren—those were the key. Up until that point, my involvement over the previous decade in publishing was about my relationships with those people and their work. I had a sort of live-in relationship with those authors, even though some of them were dead. Even in the case of Nelson Algren, that was a very passionate relationship for me, an ongoing relationship. So if there was going to be continuity there, then nothing else mattered that much. And it looked like there was. So those people's backlist, their future publishing programs, were going to stay with me. So then it was fine, and whatever kind of static there was between me and my former partner was in some kind of perspective.

And so we came to an agreement, not easily and not amicably. We came to an agreement where these authors, me, and my backlist would reinvent ourselves, and in exchange I would leave behind my half-interest in the company, I would give up my rights to the name of the company, et cetera. So what ended up happening was painful but organic. It was a long process. And the company [i.e., Seven Stories] has basically stayed on track. We've added some new names. Charley Rosen is this basketball novelist. We've had a lot of success with him. Paul Krassner. Next fall we publish the Nobel Prize winner, Aung San Suu Kyi. She's the head of the democracy movement in Burma. And some other very exciting new authors. And we continue to publish the authors that we have this ongoing commitment to. We haven't lost any. So what makes it exciting for me is the relationships, including collegial relationships and relationships with the writers, and those are constantly changing and surprising.

I also am kind of interested in this business of what a publisher is, which I think is not an easy question. And I think there are these people—Juris and I have spoken about this before—people like Barney Rosset or George Braziller, who I think is one of the great publishers and is underappreciated, and these people, they're almost like another species, like bison or something, that we and society are in danger of losing. And I really don't think we can exist without them, because they do something that's not generally appreciated, but they have a certain way of being in the world that's unlike [the way of] any other human beings. It's unlike the way of writers, unlike the way of readers. It's a different kind of existence, and it's very, very valuable. They're mediators, obviously, but I don't know how it can happen without those kinds of people. There's all the difference in the world between a Barney Rosset or a George Braziller and Alberto Vitale or a...who's the head at Disney?

JJ: There are strong editorial people in the corporate—

DS: —remaining, right—

JJ: Oh, absolutely. There just used to be more at a higher level. Now there's one Nan Talese. At one time there were at least half a dozen editors who were at that level, who could almost, you felt, command the front page of the *Times*.

DS: Right. Nan Talese. There are some. What's-her-name at Putnam—Faith Sale.

JJ: Yeah. She was really junior to that era, but there are really strong pockets. Riverhead, which is within Putnam, which is now within Penguin, which is within Pearson, which is about to be within something else. [Riverhead] is very strong and they've got three terrific editors. I think they're all in their mid-thirties, late thirties. And they're buying at a very expensive, very high level, and they're really, really wonderful editors. They're giving out numbers on first novels that are just incredible, and backing them with some success. So there's a corporation betting on editorial sensibilities.

DS: That's good. It's good to see that.

JJ: The marketing machine is serving those writers very well.

DS: It's like a snake shedding its skin: It's healthier than it seems.

JJ: I think it is healthy. It's always fluid. [Publishing] is always very volatile. Just as I'm mostly worried about the distribution, at the same time the distribution has also injured mass paperback. They've lost—they estimate eleven percent of their revenues. It looks more like twenty to twenty-five percent to me. As a result, there's more emphasis on trade paperbacks, and so there are unprecedented sales figures now in trade paperback. Unimaginable, unheard of before. The industry needs to supply that format, but that means that the content level has to be higher. So there's a tremendous growth in that one area, in trade paperback.

How do you distribute?

JJ: I went and pleaded with Farrar Straus Giroux. I harassed them so much that young Roger Straus agreed to have Soho, give its imprimatur and shop it. So we have the protection of Farrar for collection, for our titles and for distribution.

They act as an independent distributor would act for you? For a percentage?

JJ: Yeah. But it gave us some cachet.

Did you like them especially, say, rather than Norton? Harper used to do it. I don't know if they still do.
JJ: Harper was one of the first we checked, actually.

Norton takes on smaller—
JJ: Yeah. I thought of Norton. The process seemed to work, like production and design. But Norton, frankly, hadn't been that strong in fiction. They're much better known for nonfiction. They have their fiction list, but they've been unpredictable, where with Farrar Straus, it's really the house karma. And I thought that would be ours as well. And it's certainly proven out.

Where did we leave off with you? School. What did you do after you'd bummed through college?
JJ: I came back east and went to work. Working for a book company. A bookstore. Barnes and Noble. Early '60s.
DS: Was it called Barnes and Noble?
JJ: Yeah. Sure. They were really college oriented more than anything. The college campus stores, some of them, they'd go around and visit—really, how it all got started was the book exchange for students. It was very cash-rich twice a year.
DS: Was it on Eighteenth Street then?
JJ: Yeah. Eighteenth Street.

How long did you stay with them?
JJ: Um. A bunch of years. Until I got drafted.

Huh. So you were in the military then.
JJ: Yeah.

[To Simon:] Were you?
JJ: Dan was in the Peace Corps, I was in the War Corps.

What?
JJ: Dan was in the Peace Corps, I was in the War Corps.

188

The War Corps. Okay. So you got drafted by the army?
JJ: Yeah.

What year was that?
JJ: 'Sixty-six. Went over in '67.

To Viet Nam?
JJ: Yeah.

I was there '65 and 'six. Where were you? What unit were you with?
JJ: Two Corps. A signal company. I was attached to...you went too?

I was in Two Corps. I was in Special Forces.
JJ: How about that. I was in Phu Bai. I knew a lot of Special Forces.

I was in—well, my C team was at Pleiku. I worked on an operational detachment at Plei Me. We got hit, late '65. They broke up the team, put a new team in.
JJ: Right.
DS: When you say you got hit, that means wiped out?

Not wiped out, but we were hit so—we took so many casualties, among the Americans—I mean the Montagnards took worse casualties. We started with four hundred of them and still had almost three hundred left when it was over. But we started with nine Americans and there were only three of us when it was over.
DS: You called it the mountains or the—?

Montagnards?
JJ: Montagnards.

They were indigenous—
DS: Right. In northern Laos.

189

Well, they were all throughout what used to be Indochina. They're actually part of a very...a periodic migration from China south. It's still going on.

JJ: Which of you is going to publish Gerald Hickey's volume on Montagnards. It's out of print now at Yale. You know Gerald Hickey?

Yeah. Which volume are you talking about? The big—?
JJ: Yeah. There're two volumes.

I have Ethnic Groups of Mainland Southeast Asia. *I'm not going to publish it. I don't do books like that. I'd like to put it out, I just don't do books like that.*
JJ: Yeah.

[To Jurjevics:] You were there in '67?
JJ: 'Sixty-seven and '68, yeah.

And you were with a signal company?
JJ: Right. Attached to MACV.

So you were in Pleiku.
JJ: East of Pleiku. We were the only Americans in the whole province other than a couple of Special Forces encampments. When you were there, who were your best pals?

Excuse me?
JJ: Who were your best pals in Special Forces? Who do you remember? You were a lieutenant, or a captain?

No, I was there as a sergeant.
JJ: Me, too. Hmm.

My best friend survived, actually. His name is Roy Hubbard. We were at Pleiku and then he went to Dak Pek, up on the Laotian border. We corresponded for a while, and then—I don't really correspond with anybody. But, actually, most of the people I knew were killed. I worked a couple of operations with Project Delta. The first Project Delta. The one commanded by Charlie Beckwith. They got wiped out a month after I left. Delta was later reconstituted. So I knew Beckwith, and I knew a lot of the people who were with him, but they were all killed. Most of them.

JJ: A story still to be told is Rheault's. He's up in Maine, I think. With Outward Bound. Colonel Rheault. He was head of the Special Forces—

He was after my time, yeah. We had a Colonel McKean. I wrote a novel about this. If I can remember, I'll send you a copy. Colonel McKean was.... Well, when my camp got hit, Beckwith came in to take command. We had a captain, Beckwith was a major. When Delta came in, he took command. And they had such a stranglehold on us that—this was the first time North Vietnamese fought in their own units, as opposed to being integrated into VC units. We were fighting two regiments. Together they were almost division strength. This was the battle that led to the Ia Drang. It was just a few weeks before the Ia Drang where they sucked the 1st Cav—

DS: Where they—?

What?
DS: Where they what?

They sucked the 1st Cavalry, the 1st Airmobile—
JJ: It only took how many, twenty years, to write that book [*We Were Soldiers Once...and Young* by Lt. Gen. Harold G. Moore and Joseph L. Galloway]?

Yeah. So. So when did you get out? 'Sixty-eight?
JJ: 'Sixty-eight, yeah. April '68.

So you were in for two years. And you were sane afterward?
JJ: I was sane afterwards. Well, in a manner of speaking, yeah. I went to work at Harper and Row on May 21st, 1968.

Just as soon as you got out?
JJ: Yeah.

How did...? All right, here you are: You had not graduated from college, you were a soldier, a proletarian—
JJ: Mm hm.

You weren't an officer. And that makes a difference—
JJ: Right.

How did you get a job at Harper and Row?
JJ: In the contracts and copyrights department. In the dungeons. I cranked out copyright and contract registrations. I'd run all over the publishing company getting signatures and whatever. You'd see the whole operation.

DS: Right. You know, we both had our first jobs at Harper. I worked in the permissions department. That was my first job. It was so hard to get work in publishing at that point that even though I had—I had connections with Ted Solataroff who was helping me, and I had a graduate degree, and still I had to get a permissions job. And I remember my salary was ten, four.

JJ: It was very blue-blood. Very exclusive. Wonderful setting, though.

DS: Yeah.

How did you survive on ten thousand a year, living here?
DS: Did a lot of free-lance writing. I did a lot of medical articles. It was crazy.

You must not have made very much either.
JJ: Oh, man, it was pitiful. I went to a lot of book openings. Crashed a lot of cocktail parties. [Laughs.] Whenever I could get into them. It was fairly honorable then. Yeah, it was crazy. It was minimal. Eventually made it into editorial.

DS: How did you make the transition from—it's a big jump from contracts to editorial?

JJ: You want to turn it off?

If you want me to, I will.
JJ: Yeah.

192

[The recorder is turned off, then, after several minutes, back on.]

JJ: You want this on the record? [Laughs.]

Well, I'd like as much on the record as you're willing to give, but if you don't want to do it, we just won't do it.

JJ: Well, as I said, I got involved in labor organizing. Harper and Row had a house union left over from the '40s, and a couple of us sort of tried to make it serious. They were very heady days. They had teach-ins at Harper—

Teach-ins at Harper?

JJ: Yes. The whole company stopped at one point and.... Panthers came and talked, Robin Morgan talked, Margaret Mead came and talked. This was the wild, heady '60s.

Why at Harper?

JJ: It was going on everywhere, in all the companies. There was quite a radical element at Random House—

DS: And Harper must have been—I mean Harper was the publisher of Martin Luther King. It was the publisher of Howard Zinn. It was the publisher of...of...so it must have had some really opinionated editors.

JJ: Yeah. More at Random House, but there were a few at Harper's. Certainly the list was much more liberal then.

What year was this now?

JJ: 'Sixty-eight, '69. And, as I said, this eventually led to some problems for me, and I wound up at Avon. Dennis Dalrymple found me a job, and Dennis was a Yippie. In fact—it comes back to me—when Dennis set up the job he had to excuse himself that summer, because he was going to Chicago, and he was busted in Chicago for running pigs dressed as sailors. So the FBI came to visit us, and were doing double takes between Dennis and me. So they thought they had my number. But he was a terrific guy, and worked at Warner Books forever. He knew I was in trouble at Harper so he got me a job at Avon with Peter Mayer. So I worked there for a while. In those days [Mayer] was in his thirties, and it was a very hot house. It just had tremendous luck. Even when they made

193

a mistake, it turned out golden. They had wonderful editors. And Peter was in his glory. I think the first paperback reviewed on the front cover of the *New York Times* was [Henry] Roth. *Call It Sleep.* To get the front cover of TBR [*The New York Times Book Review*] was a big, big deal.

DS: You mean this time around, or—?

JJ: This time around. The Avon edition.

DS: Yeah.

When was that? I thought it just came out.

JJ: I'm talking about in the '60s. The '60s publication.

I thought it went from the '30s to the '80s.

JJ: No. It went '30s to '60s, and that's one of the cornerstones of Peter's reputation, is that. And he was the golden young guy of paperback in its time. Paperback just kept growing in power. The money concentrated. With very small staffs. They worked six, seven days a week. And you bought for ever larger amounts of money. I think Peter was the first person to pay a million bucks for paperback rights.

DS: At Avon?

JJ: Yeah.

DS: Which was at that time part of, as it is now, Hearst?

JJ: Right. Anyhow, I did some editorial there. A couple originals, some reprints. Small stuff. Started editing. Published a young publicist who worked on the set of *Love Story* and started an editing job at Popular Library, which was then owned by CBS, or had just been bought. And they were empty, had no inventory at all, so in the short time I was there I bought several hundred books. We would buy them by the barrel.

DS: Who was the young publicist from the set of *Love Story* that you liked?

JJ: Nicholas Meyer. Who came up in my next publishing phase. I was hired to do hardcover editorial by E.P. Dutton. And Nick Meyer showed up. His mother actually showed up for the novel he was having trouble getting through. Harcourt Brace had a lien on it, interestingly. But they wouldn't take it because of copyright complications. I thought it was going to be a great hit and so I signed it up for Dutton. It was *The Seven Percent Solution.*

DS: That was the Sherlock Holmes continuation.

194

JJ: Yeah.

DS: It was good. I saw the movie.

JJ: Yeah. He did another one. He did two of those. Sherlock Holmes. It was a lot of fun. Then it was, what? 'Seventy-seven, I think. At this point I went to Dial Press.

DS: You could do whatever you wanted at this point, because you were golden.

JJ: No. It was a real battle I went through. About a year after I got there the publisher left to start up his own company and took some people and took a lot of books with him. So they were planning on getting somebody experienced, solid, and aged in there. But Mrs. Meyer said it's Juris. I had just blown up a Xerox machine, and I thought I was being called on the carpet for running a manuscript through it. You weren't supposed to copy manuscripts. I'd burned out a lot of these machines, so they knew where to look.

DS: Then you [became] the head of Dial?

JJ: Yes, editor-in-chief of Dial. And I did that until '82. It had some successes. It published James Baldwin. He was a house author. Then wound up in '82, '83— Basically what happened was, Dial was owned partially by Dell, then wholly by Dell, then Dell was bought by Doubleday which then was attempting to strip itself down, and everything that it owned, for—we didn't realize—for eventual sale to Bertelsmann. They went from—Dell alone, without Doubleday, was about six hundred employees. It went down to—I'm making a number up—it went down to, what? Twenty? Just like that.

That's Dell?

JJ: Actually, yeah, that was Dell. Doubleday Bantam Dell, et cetera. They basically kept the editorial components—this was under Bertelsmann—and collapsed the rest.

DS: And they closed Dial.

JJ: What it amounted to was I didn't think it was viable after that. They stripped us down in '83. Tried to move us over to Doubleday. I didn't think it was going to work, so I bailed out. Anyway, by then I sort of saw the publishing scene as getting larger and larger. It was just sort of...corporatization. Corporatization was just a tremendous, tremendous push at that moment. If you look at the March 17th [1997] issue of

The Nation, you'll see what it eventually was all about. Give you an idea: I think—I think—when it started at Random House, they might have been at forty million annual gross, and I think they were over four hundred million when all this conglomeratization was going on. They were buying companies. Today it's one point something billion. They're pushing toward two. There was tremendous accelerated growth. During the same period Harper, I remember, bought Lippincott, bought Basic—the whole idea was simply, obviously, instead of fighting for market share, you buy it. It worked very well, up to a point. But it was not a lot of fun to be in that melee.

That's an expression that a lot of people have used.
JJ: Which?

That it's no longer fun. What does that mean?
JJ: Well, it was incredibly exciting. The editorial departments had—at Harper and Row, you had just fabulous editors discovering new writers, and it was very, very exciting. And all the excitement was sort of shared and passed through the house.

That's when it is fun.
JJ: Yeah.

But when it isn't fun?
JJ: Oh, instead of editorial decisions, they're basically run from the marketing side.
DS: Yeah, I agree. I think that what it means—it's an interesting question, because I also have met a lot of people who left publishing who say that it isn't fun anymore. And I think that that's it. I think that it's at least partly code for "We weren't appreciated anymore." And, you know, if you're there doing a fantastic job, staying up till two in the morning and weekends, fine-editing a manuscript and putting it through its paces and making something that editorially is good, and nobody in-house has the time to read it and they ignore you, what you did, and they don't value what you did, it's not fun. If you're not getting positive feedback, if you're not getting a sense that what you do is important, you've got to do something about it.

196

JJ: In any industry uniformity of product is a big goal. You can have it in six colors, but it needs to be the same thing. And business is very uncomfortable when the product is not that, when it's very individualistic. And so there's a real drive to get into the genres that are obviously lucrative, and they stay there until they develop the authors in those genres. And the genres that weren't so lucrative, they want to stay away from. A lot of the people from the business side—there was a big MBA push in the business schools—

This is the '80s you're talking about now?

JJ: Yeah. And because of the mergers, too, they needed to speak to people who spoke that language. I know quite a few. They didn't really get a full grasp of it, and their idea of that uniformity obviously doesn't work. Really, the way they talk, you'd think they were sending out to a delicatessen for "six more of those." And it doesn't quite work that way. You aren't offered the menu, whether you like it or not. And the business side wasn't that comfortable with it. They like it downmarket and controllable.

DS: I just want to say I'm so glad that you said that. I think there's always been this extreme dynamic tension between the values of authors-are-important/editors-are-important and authors-aren't-really-important/editors-aren't-really-important—what's important is the marketing and distribution, packaging. There's always been that tension.

Always, do you think?

DS: Yeah. So the kind of publishing side/editing side was never all that much fun. Even when Juris said it was, it was still borderline. But there was a dynamic tension, and you did sometimes get the rewards. You got to do the work, which itself is meaningful. But now it's gotten much worse. You get people who really ought to be in the back room, you know, like Alberto Vitale, who are basically determining company policy and who have basically no appreciation of what writers do or why authors are important or why he can't do his job without them. And those people are in charge now. So there's a terrible kind of... I mean, who reads in publishing now? Exceptions—there are people who read something sometime. But do editors, as a rule, read? Do salespeople, as a rule, read?

You mean on their own. Are they readers on their own? Is that what you mean?

DS: And even what they're selling. Do they have time to—is there a place for reading? Because if the whole thing takes— It used to be that editors read and the salespeople kind of didn't, but somebody in the room had read the book.

Is that at the point of acquisition, or—?

DS: Well, at some time. Either then or at the sales presentation or the—because now you get this whole kind of...you sometimes have the experience of thinking everything is coasting along with the book, and then nobody.... I think it's okay if you have a room with ten people who are working on publishing a book and only two of them have read it. I think that's all right, because those two will say key things and the other people will have, in a sense, vicariously experienced the book. But if you have a room with ten people who are publishing a book and none of them have read it, then that's a drastically different situation that doesn't bode well for writers and editors and readers.

How did the book get there? The acquisitions editor must have read it.

DS: Not necessarily. I don't...I mean I can't...I can't really give meaningful testimony on the...I don't know of a situation...I'm just repeating rumors, really. [To Jurjevics:] Do you know of a situation where nobody in the room has read the book?

JJ: Well, if you're in a fairly large publishing situation, the meeting's being chaired by somebody. Now it's mostly being chaired by the marketing person or the publisher. If it's the publisher, the odds are it's a former marketing person, not a former editorial person. Most of the publishers are now coming out of marketing.

DS: It's a big change.

JJ: Yeah. And one or two editors in the room will probably have read it. And their supporting documentation will be in a pile in front of the chairman's seat. And on top of that will be sales/marketing estimates, and on top of that will be a profit-and-loss statement. Then there will be some kind of synopses and other supporting material. It's like being the president of the United States. As the pile of paper grows larger, the paragraphs grow shorter, and it's only condensed on top. And the sales department says "We project we can sell so many of this. And this is what you're going to make, or lose." If it's in the red [makes a clicking sound with his tongue], out it goes. So the crucial impetus from the sales/marketing side is that magic number. And then from there on it's really ongoing relationships, what the particular editor's track record is. They'll often defy the paperwork if the editor is a known commercial gambler; and they might gamble on the gut instinct of that editor.

If it's a small, beautifully done novel, and they're projecting a four-thousand-copy sell—I worked with a fellow who, on several occasions, fortified himself with a couple martinis at lunch and went into this pub and instead of asking for the four thousand dollars to publish the book, he hit them up for forty thousand, on the theory, of course, that the higher the numbers, the more likely they'll be impressed. So he made a couple of agents and authors extremely happy.

But the small book is not of interest to the large operation. The accounting is screwing them up; it's hard to allocate the overall costs. If you segregate each title that's absolutely doable, and it hits short of the annual overhead—obviously the volume of poetry or a first novel can't sustain that kind of pressure. So unless the publisher overrides it as a favor to whoever, it's not going to happen. Which is, I think, where the small presses come in. Because a large operation's break-even is nine or twelve thousand copies, and most books sell far below that number. And I think the small presses have a chance—until now, this latest development, which is the stricture at the point of distribution. That's becoming a problem.

What do you mean?

JJ: I don't know if small presses can compete with the large companies for shelf space. I think it's analogous to saying if John Sayles finishes his movie, he can't find a screen—

DS: There was something that happened where it kind of opened up ten or fifteen years ago, and it was possible for companies like ours to actually get books out there on an almost even playing field. And something in the last few years has happened where the large presses have kind of done a little bit of an end run, and they're monopolizing shelf space again.

Do you think the large presses are taking you into account when they do this? They're just competing against themselves, aren't they?

JJ: Yeah. Absolutely.

DS: Yeah, but nonetheless, it seems—I don't know, but it seems like maybe— The marketplace, it seems to me, was not fully controlled, it was a little bit of a jungle, which was good. And now, even though in lots of ways it's better—if you have a book that's working, you can get it distributed better, faster, than ever before, even as a small press—it still feels like it's being controlled. Again.

Is this showing on your sales statements?

JJ: I don't know, it's hard to say. But the simple thing of— Twenty-nine years ago, when I started, you could get a reprint in a week. No problem. Now it's up to three, four, five, six weeks, depending on what time in this particular season you're going to press again. So your worst-case scenario, it takes you six weeks to produce the book in the fall, and another six weeks to get it processed into the system, which it often does—you're talking about three months out of stock. It's too perishable a commodity to take that. So you're gambling tremendously when you're first printing. And the situation is very volatile. Added to that, the chains and everyone else have reduced the amount of time in which they order stock. So the window is much smaller, and, they don't realize it and they probably wouldn't care, but they're actually forcing a shake-out.

Who is? Who's forcing a shake-out?

JJ: The whole system, basically. The wholesalers, the chains. So the time in which you can make the book is much narrower. The amount of stock they take from you for that initial testing is much smaller. So now you're guessing even more on your first printing. The risk increases exponentially.

Those are all my questions. We can talk freely now.

JJ: So when did you get out, and how many years were you in?

John Oakes
Four Walls Eight Windows

"The lesson to me...was that if you sell your press to an outside entity, you'd better be prepared to either be kicked out or else to work on the other people's terms. This may seem self-evident, but I think when you're running a business for decades...you start to identify yourself with the company and you think, well, Four Walls Eight Windows is...me. And once you have shareholders who own more of it than you do, it's not."

I interviewed John Oakes at midmorning in a small partitioned cubicle in a corner of the offices of Four Walls Eight Windows on West 14th Street in Manhattan on Thursday, March 27, 1997—a sunny day with many people wearing light jackets or heavy overshirts in lieu of winter coats. The weatherman had promised this morning that the temperature would reach sixty degrees. Indeed, the bitter wind of the previous day had been replaced by a breeze that was balmy by comparison. Before I began taping we exchanged catalogues and talked a little about James Sallis' work. I had published some of Sallis' more experimental writing and, as it happens, Oakes is a fan of Sallis.

When I telephoned Oakes to request this interview, he suggested that I also interview Barney Rosset, saying that Rosset was responsible for his, Oakes', going into publishing. In fact, I interviewed Rosset two days later.

Born to a father who was a New York Times *editorial page editor and a mother who was a book reviewer and teacher, Oakes was raised in Manhattan. He graduated from Princeton, then went to Paris to the Ecole de Sciences Politiques for graduate work. ("I did some work that was ostensibly study. I mean I basically had a good time—I studied politics in Paris.") Returning to the United States, he got a job with the Associated Press in New Orleans. But then Barney Rosset called, and...actually, Oakes' career in publishing had begun before this phone call, but he wasn't aware of it then.*

I did a thesis on Samuel Beckett, which is actually how I got into publishing. Should I expound?

Sure.

I actually chose Beckett because I'd heard so much about him, and I knew nothing about him. And I thought he was one of these guys, you know, I'm never going to read on my own. At the time he seemed like sort of a daunting edifice, a literary edifice. And I thought the one way to get to know him was to do a study on him. So I did. And in the course of writing this thing, I got in touch with Barney Rosset who was then publisher of Grove Press, Beckett's American publisher. I had a list of questions which Rosset was good enough to take to Beckett. And so Beckett answered these questions, and then I wrote the thesis and Barney gave it to Beckett, and Beckett read at least some of it and commented on it to Barney, and Barney got back to me. And that's how—anyway, the thesis was a great success. Barney and I stayed in touch, and then later I did an interview with him—which was, actually, originally for the *Paris Review*, [and] which Plimpton told me how much he loved, and never published it. And then I got sick of waiting and finally gave it to the *Review of Contemporary Fiction*. And they published it in their Grove Press issue, which was actually a wonderful issue, aside from my interview with Barney Rosset.

Anyway, I did that interview with Barney and then after that he and I went our ways and I went to Paris and studied and wrote, you know, did freelance writing and worked for the Associated Press in New Orleans. And then in New Orleans I got a call from Barney Rosset. And he said, "How would you like to come up to New York and be an editor?" [Laughing.] And I thought, Oh, God, you know, what a terrible thing, because I was just getting started in my life as a cub reporter. But how could anyone in his right mind, or her right mind, turn down an offer like that? So I chucked everything, came up to New York, and....

It wasn't easy at the beginning, because the people at Grove didn't know who the hell I was. Barney was the only one there who knew me. They just knew that all of a sudden this new guy showed up. So at the beginning they weren't too receptive to my presence. But Barney told me he saw me as a—at that time he had just sold Grove

Press to the Gettys, to Ann Getty. And I think he saw me as a counter-weight to Ann Getty's son, Peter Getty, who was, I think, younger than I was. At the time he was like twenty-two or something and I was like twenty-five or twenty-six. And I was sort of Barney's boy, and Peter Getty was sort of the other young punk there, was Ann's delicate—

Was Barney out now?
No, at that time he was still running things.

But he didn't own it anymore.
Right. He was an employee. And that arrangement, as you probably know, very quickly collapsed. Because Barney is a quintessential independent. And the Gettys...you know, the Gettys weren't used to this sort of thing. They were used to, you know, owning Texaco or...I don't know what the hell they own, but, you know, stocks and bonds, and they weren't used to.... Ann Getty wanted to have some sort of cultural connection, you know, thought it would be fun. And it is fun. And to my mind and, I think, anyone else's, much more interesting than Texaco or whatever. But it also has its financial irregularities. I mean it's not.... As you know, if you're publishing books to make a lot of money, either you're doing computer books or reference books, or else you're just stupid. Or ignorant, maybe that's a nicer thing to—

Anyway. So that collapsed. The Getty-Rosset connection collapsed in a huge fire storm and explosion and nuclear warfare and horrible stuff, and people—it was really a terrible thing. And Barney half quit, half was thrown out. I tried to organize a little petition, you know, getting writers to switch— Actually, the *Times* did a little story about it—not about me, but we wrote up this petition and got all these writers to sign it—

Grove Press writers?
Yeah. Well, all sorts of writers. Beckett. All sorts of people signed it. I think Burroughs. All sorts of big cheeses, as many as I could think of. To make sure the Gettys kept Barney. But it was no use. But at least it was embarrassing to them. So Barney was out, I was still in, and then they brought in...it changed. It was interesting to see how it changed. It just got worse and worse, and they moved the Grove Press

offices, and then I quit. But before I did, they had moved Grove into these very elaborate offices for a time there on 53rd Street, and then they were linked up with Weidenfeld and Nicholson, which was actually—Weidenfeld was the architect of this thing—but I'm talking more about Grove than Four Walls. But anyway, it was interesting.

The lesson to me, which was, I think, a good one, was that if you sell your press to an outside entity, you'd better be prepared to either be kicked out or else to work on the other people's terms. This may seem self-evident, but I think when you're running a business for decades—I mean, Barney had been running Grove for thirty years—you start to identify yourself with the company and you think, well, Four Walls Eight Windows is...me. And once you have shareholders who own more of it than you do, it's not. I think that corporate mentality is very difficult sometimes.

Do you think it's because he was the founder of Grove—I guess I could ask him—do you think it's because he was the founder of Grove that he identified so strongly, or because he was there for so long?

Well, I think it was a combination, and then also his personality, which is very...independent, as they say. I think also it doesn't matter so much if you're the founder or not, but if you're—you know, technically, he bought Grove Press from people in 1953. But they had done like three books. I think if you're at some place long enough, you make it your own. Who cares, you know? Who cares about Mr. Simon and Mr. Schuster? Maybe they had very noble intentions. Now it's just a subsidiary of Viacom or Disney or whatever the hell it is.

Yeah, I don't know which one. It doesn't matter.
I think it's Viacom.

Do you make your living from Four Walls Eight Windows?
Such as it is, yeah. Yeah, I do. My wife works here and I do, too, and, yeah, I get a modest salary.

Do you write, yourself?
I used to. And I still write nonfiction. But I used to write fiction, poetry. What I think killed it was reading people who I thought were...I

204

personally believe that everyone—everyone, without exception—has something to say, and has a...a.... I'm very curious about everyone's background, and how they came to be where they are. And I think that applies to myself, too. It's interesting, what psychological molecules make you the person you are. But I don't think that necessarily translates into a skill at written communication. I used to—in fact, I wrote a novel, but I guess....

When I was at Grove, I came across this writer whom I now publish. It was actually sent to me by Louis Menand, who is now a big-cheese New York intellectual type. Used to be a cultural editor at *The New Yorker*, and now he's a sort of certified New York big cheese. You still see his articles all over the place. And, actually, he was a professor of mine at Princeton—sorry to back into this—whom I got a good relationship with, and stayed in touch with, and then I was an editor at Grove, under Barney, and then Menand sent me this book by this guy called Michael Brodsky. And I read it. It was published by a press that's now out of commission, that's been out of commission for a couple of decades, with the unfortunate name of Uranus Press, or something like that. Spelled like the planet. One of the worst names for a press I can come up with.

But I read this guy, Brodsky, whom I'd never heard of, and I thought, Jesus, you know, this is...there's no point to my writing fiction, because this man is so far ahead—it was like seeing a living master. You know, it's different if you read Shakespeare or even Beckett or something, you feel they're in the past, they're in a museum, they're not living, working, breathing masters. But, to me, reading this guy, Michael Brodsky, was a sort of revelation, and I thought, Gee, if I can, I want to publish him. And when Four Walls had its first list, which was in the fall of 1987, one of the books on it, I'm pleased to say, was Michael Brodsky's. It's a novel called *X Man*. No hyphen, just X M-a-n.

And since then we've published a number of his books. He has a small but devoted readership and gets some very good reviews, and plenty of reviewers who are wondering what the hell he's doing [laughs] and make fun of him and say this is just pretension. But I always remember—my background in Beckett is helpful, I think, in this instance, because—I don't have a good memory for quotes, but I do happen to remember what John Updike wrote about Samuel Beckett. He wrote a review in *The New Yorker*—this must have been the 1960s, or '50s, even—he wrote a review of a book of Beckett's called *What Where*, and in it he said that this was "a plastic job for the intellectual fruit bowl." Which is a very nice phrase, but I think we would all agree that Beckett is one of the great thinkers of...of...period. You know? One of the great innovators and somebody who, if you're reading it and you don't understand it, it may be that you don't have enough depth to—but I think he's established through his body of work that he is a—I mean he's a literary Picasso.

And for me, Michael Brodsky is on that level. It's been a tough, sometimes very lonely road for him, and, I guess, somewhat also for his early publisher. But you pick up one of his books, there are plenty of great quotes from people who say, you know.... I doubt he'll be picked up by the Oprah Book Club.

Did you send it to her?
No.

When you do one of his books, how many do you print? Do you do his in hardback or paper?
I do Brodsky both, simultaneous. Try and get the library market and get a broader readership. We try now never to publish less than four thousand copies. So it might be three thousand paper and one thousand cloth.

Have you always been with PGW [i.e., Publishers Group West]?
No. We started out with Consortium, which was then a very different organization from what it is now. From what I gather, they're much perkier than they were when we started out with them in 1987. I wanted to move from Consortium, because I did not want to be typed. And I still hate it, being typed as one of those "cute little small presses." I admire the people who do this sort of work, but, to me, small presses are associated with marbled pages and hand-set lettering and—

Fine printing.
Fine printing. And I admire that. I even own a number of books like this. But I'm not interested in doing it myself. I'm interested in

doing books that I enjoy and that are strong works and that, hopefully, reach a broad audience. I get frustrated when we sell, you know, a small amount. I want to reach a wide audience. And I work—we all work hard—toward that end. I mean, we do have a very commercial side—or more commercial side—and it's people like the woman you see out there, JillEllyn Riley, who will keep me honest. She pulls me back to a moral imperative. She has been with Four Walls now about three years. She has been a very good and helpful influence. And I started out with a partner.

Actually, I interviewed him yesterday.
Oh, you did?

Yeah. Dan Simon?
Yeah.

Yeah. He didn't talk much about—he just said he had a partner, and you got divorced, and then—
Yes. Yeah. I actually initiated that divorce in 1995. I think when we started out, it was a very good connection, and we were very helpful to each other. But I think as time went by, [it became apparent that] we had very different ways of working, and different philosophies about publishing, and just how to deal with people. And it got to be very difficult. And it got worse and worse. And I think we both were miserable. And then we had the split-up, which was very difficult. Jesus Christ! But it's certainly for the best. My God, it's been a very good thing.

You know, you both seem very nice and very earnest and very dedicated. It must just have been a difference in taste, I suppose.
It was more than that.

We don't have to go into it if you don't want to.
I don't mind. Let me just say that I feel it was more than a difference in taste. It was a difference in working styles, in our connections with people. And, yeah, I wish him the best. But we have no communication, no contact. And I think that's best that way. It was

tough. But, yeah, at the beginning I think there was some sort of a good symbiosis. But, for whatever reason, we grew apart and...yeah.

When did Four Walls Eight Windows get started then? He had started it, and you came in a year later? I think that's what he said.
Well, he had published one book with Writers and Readers. A Nelson Algren book. Actually, this one: *Neon Wilderness*. It was a Four Walls Eight Windows/Writers and Readers book. He had done this one book. And that was it. And I met him at a party. And we got talking, and I felt we shared political viewpoints and some appreciation for the arts, and I think we did, at that point. And I said to him, "Well, why not start a full-fledged publishing house? You know, why not get the whole thing going?" He was a little, you know, gingerly.... He said, "Well, gee, you know...." I guess I pulled us both over this precipice. [Both of us laugh.] And then, to Dan's credit, he went right in there and he brought in some very good books, you know, great stuff. So, to say he had started it is true in a sense. He had one book out. And that had been, I think, two years before. But then we started a real publishing company. And...yeah. I think I learned from that experience, that association with him, that if you go into a partnership you ought to have a contract with the other partner, no matter how friendly you are, for both your sakes, you know? So that if, for whatever reason, you want to go your own way, there's a clear understanding of how you disengage.

Getting back to Michael Brodsky, or literary writers—
Yeah.

If you can sell three or four thousand copies of a literary book, you're doing a lot better than almost anybody I've talked with.
I didn't say I could sell them. I'm saying we print—it depends on the book. We have done very well with some. I mean, I'd say overall we've done pretty well with Brodsky's books. I'd say the better-selling Brodskys may sell up to three. But that's a struggle.

How many titles do you do a year?
Sixteen. Sixteen, eighteen, something like that.

Do you do poetry?

Well, not if I can help it. We have done a couple of poetry anthologies. And then we did one book which—there was sort of a funny experience at the sales conference, because I was talking about the book and I was avoiding the use of the word "poetry" because I knew if they heard the word "poetry" they'd say, "Oh, we're going to advance twenty-three copies." Then all of a sudden, somebody said, "But wait a second, John. This is poetry." And I said, "Well, sorta." Everyone laughed.

This is this book that just came out that I should mention. I'm trying to tie it into reading groups. It's called *Simple Annals*. And it's quite an important book. It's by a guy who, until he was thirty-one, he'd never been to school. Ever. He'd never been inside a movie theater, never ridden a bicycle, never gone out on a date. He was born in 1949 in very rural western Tennessee and brought up by elderly relatives who taught him to read from the bible and comic books. And this book is about his family. Two hundred years of his family in Tennessee.

This is poetry?
Yeah, there's some poetry—

I read poetry. You don't have to be defensive with me.
I know, but it's a mixture. It's sort of prose poems and poetry and, you know, some folk tales and stuff. I think it's just great. It reminded me of *Spoon River Anthology* by Edgar Lee Masters. I don't know if you read that, but at one point, around the 1920s, it was a very important book. This is, to me, in a very attractive American tradition of populism. You know, the tradition that comes from Woody Guthrie and—it goes back to Steinbeck and sort of this simple—not simple in the sense of being stupid, but, you know, people who don't have a lot of material resources, but have a—

It's really a simple environment. It isn't that the people are simple.
Yeah.

I was trained as an anthropologist, and this became a big issue with me. When we talked about the evolution of simple to complex,

graduate students would confuse that with being—
Smart or stupid.

Not so much that as that people who live simply think simply.
Yeah.

And as we grow into an urban environment, we think more complexly. Actually, the inverse is true.
Sure. Because in a complex environment everything is done for you. You step in a cab and it takes you where you want to go; you don't have to hitch up the horse and direct it. Right. I agree with that absolutely, yeah. So that's a book I'm very pleased about. And who knows? I've always said about that book that it may be a sleeper and will sell.

What's his name?
His name is Robert Allen. You'll hear about him. Great book. Lovely book.

Getting back to Barney Rosset—why'd you do it? Why'd you change from journalism to publishing?
Well, Barney as a person was very attractive to me. As you'll see, he has a tremendous amount of energy and there's a real electricity around him. I think that sometimes can get in the way of running a business operation, or even a cultural organization, because you have to sometimes subsume yourself, right? In the interests of the company. Of the publishing company. And I think Barney has always—to his credit, in a way—has always had a tough time doing that. His mark is very much on that company, on what he does, on what he's associated with. And that can be difficult. But that's also what attracted me to him. I really liked the fact that he was somebody who did what he wanted to do. And I thought that was a very attractive way of working. And also it came at a nice time. Because at the Associated Press, as you may know, as a wire reporter you write sometimes two or three stories a day, extremely superficial, very fast, and it's a very hectic atmosphere. While publishing certainly can be hectic, at least you're working on books that take a little more time to produce. Personally, I feel there's much more

210

satisfaction in that. Even if your name isn't on the cover, if you've edited a book that is worthwhile, I think that's better than churning out...more satisfying to me, anyway. So that's why I got associated with Barney.

Also, I grew up—I was born in '61, but I grew up— My older sisters had been involved in student movements and stuff, and even as a little kid—I was just thinking this morning how I volunteered for the McGovern campaign, of all things. And I grew up—in '72, I guess it was, yeah, I was passing out leaflets—and I was thinking, I think I always sort of regretted having missed, having been too young to really fully participate in that era. And Barney, to me, represented—you know, he was at the heart of much of the cultural activity in the '60s, with *Evergreen Review* and stuff, and I found that very sympathetic.

This same issue came up with Dan, actually. I'll tell you what I said to him. I've met a number of people in the past ten years, say, who are in their twenties and thirties now, who seem to be intensely inter-ested in the era, not having been part of it. It was a terrible time. It was just horrible.

Yeah.

But I guess that isn't what's carried through.

We-e-l-l, don't put me in the category of people who see it as sort of a paradise or an Eden. I remember riots, and I was very frightened. The police were very threatening. There was a lot of chaos. Everyone was very worried about Viet Nam or being blown up by atomic bombs. That's not so much what I'm talking—I mean I'm not so interested in Woodstock and stuff like that, but I think there was a collective sense that it was much more acceptable to be pushing for change. I think now a lot of that stuff has been co-opted, for example, by this terrible president we have, you know, who I think has done—to be "perfectly clear," to borrow the words of another president, I think Clinton's a great flag bearer for the right wing, and he's not what he pretends to be, which is a liberal, and I think he's done a terrible disservice to the country.

I think he's betrayed a lot of people.

I think he had opportunities to do things that were wanted and needed. Four Walls, by the way—I think politics is a very important part of what we do. I think that it literally infuses everything we do, from a book like *Bike Cult* which is a nonfiction, one-volume encyclopedia about bicycles versus the car culture, to—JillEllyn did a book called *Dead Meat*, about the meat-eating culture.

Kind of muckraking?
The book or the publishing company?

You said Four Walls takes politics very seriously.
Yeah.

Do you mean in the sense of muckraking?
It could be, yeah.

Not in the sense of yellow journalism, but exposing—
Yeah, I'd say that I'm interested in that, though I'm not a big fan of conspiracy theories and stuff like that.

Is this a 501 (c) (3)?
No. No.

Do you have any feelings about—?
Well, we thought—years ago I flirted with doing nonprofit. In fact, I even registered a name. Then at one point I thought I'd have a subsidiary of Four Walls, like Moyer Bell has a subsidiary nonprofit called Asphodel Press. And I thought at one point we'd do that, and for all I know our name is still registered. New York Books was my nonprofit entity. But it never took off, because the paperwork for maintaining a nonprofit is tremendous, and then you also have to go on your knees, or your belly, or wherever else, to foundations or the government, getting money, and I'd much rather do my business books, or whatever other books, to try and pull in the cash. Although, God knows, it's difficult. But that's just— I have nothing against nonprofit organizations. I just don't have the patience to fill out, you know, to apply to foundations and crap like that.

212

I didn't know you do business books also. So you do fiction, a little poetry that you don't want to talk about as poetry [Oakes laughs], and your nonfiction is...?

Well, we do biographies. We did a biography of Thomas Paine. I'm trying to edge us more into science books. We did a book, sort of a brief history of mathematics. We have a book about the universe coming out this fall. And this spring we did a book about Boeing versus Airbus. And before that we did a book about Lloyds, the insurance company of London. And we have another one in the works that I can't mention. We had a book about the IRS, which counts as a business book. We have a book about the nature of infinity coming out in the spring that should be fun. We have a book about the cult movements at the end of the millenium coming out; that should be a good one. And I hope to be doing something about the Mormon church, the history of the Mormon church and some of its darker sides—you know, very involved in politics, very instrumental in the Reagan administration also. So we have eclectic interests.

What percentage of your gross income comes from the sale or lease of subsidiary rights?

It just took a huge jump with the publication of *Fermat's Last Theorem*, which is this book on mathematics. It has sold literally everywhere from Finland to Japan. We've probably sold a hundred and fifty thousand dollars worth of subsidiary rights, of which half goes to the author. Also we sold paperback on that to Dell. So if that trend keeps up, I'd say...fifteen percent. I don't know. Yeah, maybe that's right. Maybe ten percent. Ten, fifteen percent.

Do you see Four Walls as.... Can you define a mission or purpose?

Yeah. I know it's there; it's hard to define it. [Laughs.] Our mission is: to put out books that are well edited; that look sharp; to use an obscene word, that are in a good "package," the content of which is first-rate in whatever field it is. Also, it's to do innovative publishing. Also, I think the progressive outlook is part of what we do, and informs everything we do. I mean, I just could not take on a book by—if Jesse Helms offered me his, for no advance, offered me...I know for a fact I couldn't do it. That's an easy example, but I think it's very much a driving concern. That said, there are books we take on that hopefully provide fuel for other books. [Shouting through the partition that separates his cubicle from the rest of the office:] JillEllyn, can you define our mission?

JillEllyn Riley [calling back:]: You're doing fine!
John Oakes: What?
JR: You're doing okay!
JO: You shouldn't listen to me when I talk.
JR: I'm not listening.

You probably get thousands of submissions a year.
My guess is about three thousand.

I get about fifteen hundred. My experience is that many of them, I would say more than half, are at least competently written.
Yes! I'm glad to hear you say that! Because I've often seen in print, and I've heard fancy editors and publishers say, "Oh, there's nothing out there," or "Most of the stuff that comes in is trash." I would say that—I would modify that to say most of what gets sent to us is totally inappropriate.

That's right. I would say the same thing.
Yeah. But I'd say a fraction of three thousand is still a hell of a lot of manuscripts. A fraction is interesting. And of that, a smaller fraction would be appropriate for us. And of that fraction, a tiny fraction I might jump on. But the fact of the matter is I don't have time to even open the mail, the submissions. We have interns, and we tell them what to look for. But just physically, you don't have time to do that. And people don't understand that. They think you ought to be reading—they're shocked when I tell them that. If I open an unsolicited submission, I'm going to read the cover letter and maybe the first couple paragraphs. And I'll get a sense of whether it interests me or not. And it's true, we have turned down stuff that in another incarnation—or if we were another, bigger publisher, I would take on.

214

That's it. Anything else you want to talk about?

No, not really. Just that we're trying to be innovative as far as distribution goes. We're now being distributed in Africa. We've always been distributed in Australia, in England. I'm very eager to pursue that sort of thing—you know, alternative methods of selling. I guess that's it.

Alexander Taylor and Judith Doyle

Fiona McCrae

Judith Roche

Charlie Winton

Marianne Nora and Lane Stiles

Harry Smith

John Oakes

Clockwise from top:
Barney Rosset, Allan Kornblum,
Peter Rosset

Top: Eric Kampmann
Bottom: Jim Bodeen

Clockwise from top: Daniel
Simon, Emilie Buchwald,
Pearl Kilbride

Vito Perillo

Top: Bob Harrison
Bottom: Dee and Chuck Robinson

Barney Rosset
Grove Press; Blue Moon Books; Foxrock, Inc.

> "I always thought of myself as an amoeba that spreads where, you know, it meets less resistance, and goes into that corner. But an amoeba with a certain amount of intelligence."

Barney Rosset is a legend in the publishing world for a number of reasons: he was the driving force behind the move to change the censorship laws in the United States; he was Samuel Beckett's American publisher; and he built a tiny literary press—Grove Press—into one of the most prestigious publishing houses in North America and then had it taken away from him. Some of the most significant of the books he has elected to publish are those which have advanced the causes he considers important. He is known to other publishers as one who has continuously reinvented himself. A number of younger publishers idolize him, though they may also point at a seeming penchant for self-destruction in Rosset's personality. Still, he is one of a handful of twentieth-century American publishers who is considered "great" and perhaps the only one regarded as heroic.

I interviewed him on Saturday, March 29, 1997 in the living room of his Greenwich Village apartment. As one would anticipate, the walls were lined with bookcases densely stocked with books he had published, as well as others. At a glance, the latter appeared to be mostly nonfiction, mostly books of political interest written for the educated, nonacademic reader.

He spoke slowly and thoughtfully, and while there were many pauses as he looked for the best way to express what he had in mind, there were no wasted words. It seemed to be important to him to be accurate as far as who said what and what it meant was concerned. Specific dates seemed to have less value to him. He laughed often throughout the interview, usually with irony, sometimes ruefully. It was my good fortune to interview him during the period when he was working on the first chapters of his autobiography: he had been reviewing his life, and much that had occurred more than half a century earlier was clearly on

216

his mind. At the time of the interview he was the publisher of Blue Moon Books and of the Foxrock imprint.

I began by asking when and where he was born (May 28, 1922; Chicago) and if he had gone to college.

I went to a few of them. I went to Swarthmore one year. And then—that was 1940, '41—I went to the University of Chicago for one quarter, which was very lucky, it turned out later. And I went to UCLA for one semester. Then I joined the army for almost five years. And then I got out, I went back to the University of Chicago where they had to let me in—because I had been there—on the GI Bill. Although I had never passed a course, I never flunked one either. I never took an exam. So I stayed there long enough to get a two-year degree. By now it had taken me about twelve years. And then I came here to New York in 1947 or 'eight. And I actually got a BA at the New School. That overlapped Grove Press.

You started Grove Press while you were at the New School?
Yes. Well, no. Right after.

It must have been in your mind while you were at the New School. No?
No. No. It was not on my mind.

It was an impulse?
It was an impulse. Yes. It was. But going back over my life, you could see it was inevitable. From my background in Chicago, the school I went to. When I was in the eighth grade I had a newspaper called *Antieverything*. First we called it *The Sommunist* and then we changed the name to *Anti-everything*.

Who is "we"?
A classmate whose name is Haskell Wexler. He became a famous cinematographer. Actually, he made his own film—he had many, he won Oscars and so on—but he did one film called *Medium Cool* which takes place during the 1968 Chicago Convention. It's about the convention. It takes place in the middle of the convention.

I remember the title, but I don't think I saw it. Was it a documentary?

No. No, no. It's fiction. One of the interesting shots in that film is [where] the tanks are rumbling through Chicago and somebody says, "Haskell, Haskell. Those bullets are real." That was accidentally picked up from off-camera. It's true.

But it wasn't a documentary?

No way. It's about a young woman from the South who has a child, no husband. There's a TV news guy in Chicago who has an independent frame of mind, politically, and they somehow hook up together during the convention, and she loses her child in a riot at the convention. They actually put her—this actress—into the middle of the goddamn troops who were marching around and so on. And she's asking the National Guard, "Have you seen my daughter?" And the TV guy is doing TV work. He gets killed in an automobile crash. It gives you a very good idea of the convention, of what was going on. Haskell does John Sayles' films, most of them. He did that one alone, but he does most of Sayles' films and got Oscars for *Who's Afraid of Virginia Woolf?* and *In the Heat of the Night.*

But that's all to the side. When I was in the army, I ended up in China where I was in charge of a photographic team. And after the war I tried to make motion pictures. And I made a feature in 1948, '49. Only one. When I was finished with it I was finished with film-making. But later I did produce Sam Beckett's only motion picture, called *Film*, with Buster Keaton. Allen Schneider was the director.

Was your own motion picture distributed?
Yes.

What was the name of it?
The name of it was *Strange Victory*. It's a...I don't know what you would call it now. Fictional documentary. It's about racial problems in this country. When you see it today, it looks more immediate than it did when we made it. I've never seen any other film vaguely like it. Although I've seen a lot better ones.

218

Where were you in China? I studied under a man who was in China from 1944 to 1949. During the war he was with OSS [Office of Strategic Services] 202.

I was with OSS a lot. I was in—I just went back in November for the first time in fifty-one years. To the same place. Kunming. That was our starting place. From Kunming we fanned out through China. I was actually in Viet Nam. A little. And ended up, for a while, in Shanghai. I was there when the war ended. Accidentally. We went there to film the peace ceremony. It never took place—there. It was on a battleship, the Missouri.

They were anticipating it being in Shanghai though?

Yes. So I had the good fortune, really, to be there. Then when I left—I was sort of thrown out. Then I flew back to Kunming, and from Kunming to India. And, really, you could see the beginning of the publishing right there.

I read *Red Star Over China* when I was in the ninth grade, and also *Man's Fate*. Malraux. Two books that are extremely important to me. One of the earlier things I did at Grove was to republish *Red Star Over China*. *Man's Fate* was published by Vintage or somebody, so I did *Man's Hope*. It was nearly the same book, but anyway.... So all these books were key to me in China, and that's what got me thrown out of Shanghai. I kept telling my American superiors, colonels and generals, that they should spend their money and have a good time, because Mao was coming [laughs] and they were just crazy to be putting their money in the bank, which they were doing. Buying gold. Real estate. And I was doing quite the opposite. Finally at four o'clock one morning I was told, "You've got one hour to pack. You'll be downstairs. A jeep will be waiting. And you'll be put on a plane." And it happened. As for the beginning of publishing....

Somebody called me the other day—it was a very weird coincidence—and said, "Is this Rosset and Dunlap?" I was probably the one person in the world who would be ready for that question. I said, "No, it's not. There's a 'G' on it." And this person said, "Oh, there is?" And I said, "Yes, it's Grosset and Dunlap." Because when I was in the eighth grade, we had textbooks that were published by Grosset and Dunlap,

219

and I used to cross out the Gs in all of my textbooks. So you can see—that was the beginning.

It sounds, from the background you've talked about so far, like you could as well have become a journalist as a publisher.

I could have, but the filmmaking experience, which took me two years of concentrated work, and when it was all over I didn't really like the film—I needed more immediate gratification. [Both of us laugh.] Book publishing is immediate. I had just gotten divorced from a fellow Chicagoan, a great painter named Joan Mitchell. Joan became, I think, one of the most important women painters of this century. She's had— she had; she died—one-woman shows at the Museum of Modern Art in Paris, the Whitney here.... Recently the Museum of Modern Art took down the big Monet that they have in a separate room, and put a painting of hers up for three months.

Anyway, Joan and I grew up together and we should have left it that way, but we got married. In France, actually. Her mother was at one time the editor of *Poetry Magazine* in Chicago. A friend of hers and of mine—a young woman then; we'd been students at the Art Institute in Chicago—had a friend who had started a publishing company called Grove Press. Published three books. That was 1947, 'eight, 'nine. Two guys, and they published three reprints. Then they quit. And she came along one day and Joan said, "Maybe you'd be interested in this." I was at the New School, actually. And I said yes.

You and she were married at the time?

No. We were divorced. We got divorced, she moved a block away. Long before we got divorced she moved a block away. I kept saying, "Joan, come back." And she'd say, "Yes, I'll come back. Just wait." [Laughs.] So I waited a year and I said, "Come on. It's not right. [Laughs.] If you don't come back I'm going to get divorced." She said, "Oh, that's ridiculous, don't do that." So I did the ultimate bluff. I went to Chicago and called her. I said, "If you don't come back right away I'm getting divorced, like tomorrow." Chicago, even then, had this incredible law that you could get divorced immediately if you were a resident of the state for a year. I'd been there all that time, and there was no opposition, so...I did it. The judge who divorced us was the one who was the judge of the Chicago Seven trial years later.

Hoffman.

Julius Hoffman. A trial which I attended. So anyway, I took the three books, the poetry of Richard Crashaw [*The Verse in English of Richard Crashaw*], the religious mystic, and Melville's book, *The Confidence Man*, and *The Writings of Aphra Behn*—she was an early woman writer; she was a feminist of her day, actually, a playwright and so forth. Eighteenth century. So those were the first three books. And they were going to publish another book, *The Monk* by Matthew Lewis. This is a book that I really liked, and which they had set the type on, and then had stopped.

Who's "they"?

The two people who had started and then abandoned the thing. And I continued with it. Only I took a whole different attitude towards it. They were only interested in the historical background of the book. They even did an edition which gave all of the typos of the first original edition, as compared to the fifth, the sixth, the tenth. I was really interested in the book, and I got John Berryman, who was teaching at Princeton at that time, to do an introduction, along with the introduction by the academic maniac who was interested in all the misspellings and nothing else, and hated the book. And we kept that in print as long as I was at Grove, and it is still in print. I think *The Confidence Man* and *The Monk* are still in print. I don't know about the other two.

So, taking off from there, I took home the books that were left. One of these is the original [showing me a copy of *The Verse in English of Richard Crashaw*]. That's one they did [showing a copy of the first Grove Press edition]. And I found myself with three books in suitcases in the top of a brownstone on Ninth Street. I mean it just seemed like a natural thing to do. I always thought of myself as an amoeba that spread where, you know, it meets less resistance and goes into that corner. But an amoeba with a certain amount of intelligence.

So I found myself in book publishing and so, what do you do then? One of the first things I did was go to Columbia and take a course in publishing. There, the student sitting next to me was Donald Allen who became my first coeditor of *Evergreen Review*, which I started in

221

'57. He's now in San Francisco, or outside of it. The professors were marvelous. Each one was a leader in his area of publishing. Ian Ballantine was one, for example. The best man in advertising in book publishing in the country was another. So I learned a lot through these various people whom I got to be friends with.

And then I set out trying to sell the books. I'm sure my story and yours are not very different—all of the travail of selling and getting sales reps, et cetera, et cetera, et cetera. I think I've gone through every form of book distribution that exists at one time or another. I think I was innovative in that. For example, I had books distributed by Dell whereas other people were selling them books—paperback rights. I never did. I did them myself and had them distributed. And it was very important because one of the books that I published, for example, was *Transactional Analysis*. I think we did his [Eric Berne's] first book originally as a paperback. Did two or three thousand copies as a paperback and finally sold them. Then he sent me another book, *Games People Play*, and that sold even more slowly for a while. But then it began selling and selling and selling. So when it came time to do a paperback, I went to Dell and just had them do it for me, for Grove. I don't know what they sold, but certainly, it was over a million.

You had Dell manufacture the paperback for you?

I manufactured them. And they were very happy and I was. Some of the books I did they would never have published. Like *Last Exit to Brooklyn*. Dell distributed it. It was the first mass market paperback to sell for more than a dollar, and it worked. And they distributed the paperback edition of *The Autobiography of Malcolm X* for us, the same for *Lady Chatterly's Lover*, the same for *Tropic of Cancer*. We almost never sold the rights to anything.

Dell worked on commission?

Yes. And it was a good relationship. But I wouldn't really call that being a distributor, because they were taking one book at a time.

Oh. So what about your backlist?

We did it ourselves. At one point we had a good sales staff of our own. At other times we used commission sales reps. We had

222

Random House during one period, and they weren't good at selling our books. So then I made an arrangement with them whereby they did the billing and shipping and collecting. That was good. Because people paid them. [Both of us laugh.] They were cooperative. People thought that they had to pay us. Because if they didn't, they wouldn't get Random House books. It was not true, but people thought so. [We laugh again.] And that went on for like twelve years. It was still in effect when I left. But that wasn't distributing either, in the usual sense.

But you have had a distributor, you've—
I've gone through three in one year. It's a disaster. I was doing it myself until one year ago.

This is Blue Moon Books?
Mm hm. I was doing it until a year ago. Almost a year ago. Then I had Consortium. Who were very nice people. Who didn't have a clue how to sell my books. [Laughing.] Well, I'll take that back; they had more of a clue than the next one. It was Lyle Stuart who was doing his own books and took on mine. It was a totally disastrous error. And so now I'm alone again, without one.

So you're pretty much at the mercy of reviews then, to create a demand. No?
No. No. I'm trying to go to the wholesalers. Well, at Barnes and Noble—I got thrown out of Walden. They were our biggest customer, and because of our Reverend Wildman in Mississippi two years ago, they one day sent all the books back without telling me beforehand.

What's his organization? I don't remember.
Wildman? Oh, I don't know. Something probably about "decency." In Mississippi. He attacked the National Endowment and us. It's quite a compliment. And, I think, *Playboy.* Burger King also. Because they advertised on bad soap operas. He went to Kmart actually, and told Kmart that if they didn't get our books out of Walden, which Kmart owned, and probably still own a good part of, he would organize a boycott of Kmart. So the first thing Kmart did was tell Walden, "Get rid of the books," and Walden got rid of the books. And so did Barnes and

Noble, who were our second biggest customer. But they changed after about two years. They were very good about it, actually. They came to me, said they'd made a mistake. Took back the books.

That's interesting.
Anyway, that's the major buyer, which certainly wouldn't be my choice. But being the amoeba, I had to go where the books might go. It's not the right audience, but...that's what it is. No Walden. But Borders finally started buying some books. Barnes and Noble is buying less. Ingram comes and goes. Lyle Stuart denounced them a few months ago.

I remember that.
Publishers Weekly mentioned that Lyle Stuart said that he wouldn't sell them any more books, so Ingram said, "Okay, as you distribute Barney Rosset's Blue Moon Books, they're out too." [Laughs.] I wrote to Ingram and said, "Look, I'm a civilian casualty of your war. Please don't kill me too." They were actually friendly, but the damage was done.

Is Blue Moon a nonprofit press?
No. Never. Being innately capitalist somehow.

When did you start Blue Moon?
About '86.

How many titles have you been doing per year?
Well, that hasn't been the same each year. It reached a peak of probably about thirty or forty, and at the moment it's almost zero. It varies. Nothing goes smoothly.

Barbara Wilson—she was one of the founders of Seal Press—
Yes.

She said that she thinks that the reason people do this sort of thing—small, independent presses—is that they like risk. Some people are just drawn to risk.

That's right. I think that's the legitimate truth. [Both of us laugh.]

Do you sell subsidiary rights, or try to? Reprint rights or foreign rights?

I have. Inconsistently.

Can you estimate what proportion of the press' income that would account for? One of the things I'm trying to do with this book—in the West, in the Northwest, at least, very few people sell subsidiary rights. I would think, being here where the big houses are, it's probably easier to do. To find the connections. That's a hypothesis.

It's a hypothesis that I could not prove or disprove. Almost accidentally, I've sold—most of whatever I've gotten out of Blue Moon in subsidiary rights has come from Spain. I have no idea as to why. And some few things from England. But that hasn't been of particular value, because that's our major market—selling the books themselves [to the English market]. So I haven't pursued it much recently.

Looking at how you sold Grove Press books, and how you sell Blue Moon books, has the world changed so much that—I don't know, maybe you are doing really well with Blue Moon. Are you doing well with Blue Moon?

No.

Has bookselling changed so much? Or publishing changed so much? Or are you doing completely different books?

I think it's changed very little. I mean compared to other aspects of life. Books? The major innovation, I think, was paperbacks. Trade paperbacks. We started Evergreen Books. Doubleday started Anchor Books around the same time. Vintage and so forth and so on. I think that was a major, major shift. There already were pocket books coming out of the company with that name, from before World War II, I think, or during World War II. And that was a terribly important phenomenon. Not much has happened since that I know about.

People worry so much about the conglomerizing of publishers, which is maybe true, but much more so is the conglomerizing of book-stores. I'd say that's the major feature of the last generation, is the putting together of large book chains which, in a sense, dominate the selling of books. When I started, Brentano's was a major thing. But they were nothing compared to what goes on now. I don't know how you deal with that one. Our bookstores were people like City Lights and so on.

But, see, whatever I do always leads to trouble. When I published *Lady Chatterly's Lover, Tropic of Cancer*—I read *Tropic of Cancer* in 1940, long before I ever thought of book publishing. I was at Swarthmore. I read *Tropic of Cancer* because somebody told me to go to Gotham Book Mart in New York and buy this book, and I did, and I read it and I was just absolutely knocked out. So much so that I thought, "Who can stay at a place like Swarthmore after reading that book?" And I left. But when I ran out of money I had to come back. And I wrote my—the one year I was there, I wrote my English paper on *Tropic of Cancer* and another book of Miller's, *The Air-conditioned Nightmare*, which came in very handy at a big trial in Chicago twenty-some years later. So when I published those books, immediately I was denounced as being an obscene pig and so forth and so on, as if I had done them because of the erotic character. The odd think was I never felt that that book was very erotic. When I read *Tropic of Cancer*, to me it was a denunciation of the American way of life. I never even noticed the sex until many years later. [Laughs.] Almost the same with *Lady Chatterly's Lover*.

Lady Chatterly's Lover, to me, was a part of one of the few plans I ever made that actually sort of came out the way I intended. As soon as I got into publishing it became my objective to publish *Tropic of Cancer*. But how to go about it? I actually thought of a very good, sneaky plan which was to publish *Lady Chatterly's Lover* first, because D.H. Lawrence, after all, was a writer of some distinction and known to the world as a great writer, whereas Henry Miller was thought of as a pretty bad person, a reprobate and so on. And so if I could get *Lady Chatterly's Lover* okayed, then I would be a step closer on the road to *Tropic of Cancer*.

And we did exactly that. We planned our whole thing with *Lady Chatterly* so that the post office would arrest us. And they did. Fell right into our net. We had a wonderful trial in New York at the post office, which we lost but won on appeal. And, of course, the book was out of copyright, so everybody immediately started publishing it. Especially

Pocket Books. I refused to sell the rights to it. They offered me what was a pretty big hunk of money at that time and I said no. So they said okay, and they went and published it. [Laughs.] I think their edition was thirty-five cents; we had had a hard-cover for the huge amount of six dollars. So we immediately had to fight back, and Dell distributed our fifty-cent edition and we took out big ads in the papers saying that Pocket Books were pirates. It took a lot of guts on the part of my advertising guy whose biggest account was Simon and Schuster. That's who we were up against. But we did it.

They owned Pocket Books then, too?

Yes. In fact, the head of it, Leon Shimkin, was the head of both. And so they sued me. And they hired the man who ran for president—Dewey—to be their lawyer in Brooklyn. So we went to Brooklyn and hired the head of the Bar Association. And the judge threw us both out, which was exactly we wanted. And we outsold them, I don't know, two, three, four to one. I don't know what it was. We did everything we could to disgrace them. We put on our cover "The One And Only Grove Press Edition". It was actually a lot of fun. And even mildly profitable. And we didn't have any arrests. Then I did *Tropic of Cancer* and we were arrested all over the United States.

Because of local laws?

Local laws and so on. And we pledged to defend everybody. And we did. Wherever there was a lawsuit.

When you say you were arrested, you mean booksellers were arrested all over the United States?

I was personally arrested in Brooklyn. I was charged with conspiracy to have commissioned Henry Miller to write *Tropic of Cancer*. In Brooklyn. First of all, I'd never been to Brooklyn. Second, I would have been about fifteen years old if I had done it.

It was a grand jury thing first. And Henry wouldn't go to Brooklyn where he was born and raised. He was, sorry to say, afraid. So I went. I got arrested and fingerprinted and so forth and so on and went before the grand jury. And the district attorney, who was quite well known, said to the jurors, "This man has published a book which your children are reading, it's on sale at the book stand near the school, and he's going to corrupt them and destroy them," and so on. And I said to the grand jury that if their children had bought *Tropic of Cancer* and actually read it from beginning to end, they were to be congratulated as parents. And they liked that. So they refused to indict me.

So the district attorney gave out an information, which, if they can't get an indictment, they can still try to go ahead. And at that point the *Saturday Review*, which was a big magazine at that time, published a marvelous article absolutely devastating the district attorney in Brooklyn, and claimed that I had done this amazing good thing by Miller. So that was my arrest. In the rest of the country it was bookstores and distributors, and we fought for them. We finally won before the Supreme Court. Well, we won a unanimous decision of the Supreme Court of California early on. But I think the case that got to the Supreme Court of the United States was from Florida. And it was never heard before the Supreme Court. We won without their having to hear it. They refused to accept the government's case. They also refused on *Lady Chatterly*. We won. We won before the Supreme Court although there was no hearing.

Did Grove Press produce the film Tropic of Cancer?

No, but a friend from UCLA days, who was here two nights ago, made the film. Joseph Strick. Still a very dear friend of mine.

It was a fine film. I saw it.

He did *Ulysses* and *Tropic of Cancer*. *Ulysses*, I think, was his finest.

I saw Tropic of Cancer—

I was there, in Paris, with them and Henry when they were shooting it. Anyway, we did all of that and finally did win *Tropic of Cancer*. *Last Exit to Brooklyn, Naked Lunch*—we had the major case for the latter in Massachusetts where we strengthened the [existing] law by using it. We got into a political fight in Massachusetts without knowing it, between the Democrats and the Republicans. The Republicans were the good guys. They had a senator, Brooke, and...I think he was the lieutenant governor then, and the guy who became the attorney general under Nixon and quit—Richardson. Elliot Richardson. They were the two Republicans. And there we were, arrested—a bookstore owner was arrested—for *Naked Lunch*. The police took a typically sleazy bookstore for that time and thought they could terrorize the store. And we got them to use the law so that it was an attack on the book itself, the object, and, thereby, the publisher. And we defended it in Boston and we won. And that law helped.

Was the ACLU [American Civil Liberties Union] helping you with any of this?

No. Well, once in a while. I mean I talked to them, but I never was too closely associated with them. No, we did it mainly ourselves, with two or three attorneys. At one point I went to NYU law school. I thought, "I'm in court all the time, I might as well become a lawyer." Shows you how bad the aptitude test can be. I had to take the law school aptitude thing. I think I came within one percent of the top percentile, so they let me in. And I went to NYU for one semester and I took Contracts, a basic law course, and I noticed that the professor was calling on me too often, because there were about three hundred people in this damn course. And I finally realized what it was—he was using me as the example of how *not* [both of us laugh], how *not* to do this. I was getting a mirror image—I was getting things reversed. After the first semester— I worked very hard and I think I got a D or C—I quit.

Now at Blue Moon Books, which is really a continuation of Grove, I went through the same thing again. Not with lawsuits, but the contempt of certain people in the book business. The stores who bought *Last Exit to Brooklyn* and *Naked Lunch* and so forth wouldn't buy Blue Moon books. To them, there's a kind of eroticism involved which disturbs them. Sadly, City Lights is one.

They won't buy them?

No. No way. And City Lights had given me a party which spilled out into the street there, Columbus Avenue, when the Gettys bought Grove Press—it should have been a funeral party—and I have always remained personally friendly with Lawrence Ferlinghetti. We met, for example, in Nicaragua. He and I went to a book fair in Managua. I think we were the only American publishers there that year for the Sandinista event. My son Peter was there for ten years, so I went to

Nicaragua a number of times.

So it's the same battle again. But now we've lost a lot of the good stores, so we have to rely on the worst. [Laughs.] The old and the chains, in lieu of all the places we were in. It's disheartening.

That is really ironic. I don't think any independent publisher likes the idea of having to deal with the chains. But you have to deal with the chains. Eighty to ninety percent of the trade—my trade—is through the chains.
And you're not alone in that dilemma.

I know. So you need a dis— Well, there are more and more distributors. You have to be really careful nowadays. A few years ago, there was Inbook, there was Consortium—
They come from the West Coast. It's interesting. Publishers Group West and Consortium. And Subterranean—aren't they in Oregon? [The Subterranean Company went out of business in 2000.]

Yeah, but they're not really big. And they use the same, or some of the same, sales reps as Consortium.
Oh, yes, they all—PGW [Publishers Group West] has their own.

Yeah. And Inbook. They were really the three major distributors for radical or literary titles—PGW, Inbook, and Consortium.
Inbook?

They were part of Inland.
Oh, right. Which went out of business.

They went bankrupt, yeah. So Inbook doesn't ex— Well, Inbook was absorbed, or taken over, by Login.
I never even heard of them.

Login has three major divisions, and Inbook is one of them now.
Really? And I've never even heard of them.

You might—if you wanted—

No, I don't. No, I'm finished with distributors. [We both laugh.] No, no, no. No, I have one book. John Oakes of Four Walls Eight Windows and Dan Simon, who was with John at that time, and I formed a company which—I think I'll take credit for the name—it's Foxrock. That's where Samuel Beckett was born. It's a suburb of Dublin. Beckett was the author I most valued at Grove; I published him from 1953 until I left. And when I was thrown out of Grove by the Gettys, Beckett stood forth—as did John Oakes, then a Grove editor—stood up and said, "What can authors do for their publisher?" And one thing an author can do is give him a book.

And he wrote something. Well, first, he gave me a play. It's called *Eleuthéria*. He wrote it before *Waiting for Godot*. It's the only three-act, full-stage play he ever wrote. It hasn't been put on to this day. He wrote it in 1943 or thereabouts. Then he wrote *Waiting for Godot*, and he couldn't get it produced. He wanted either one to be put on the stage, and *Godot*, which had one set and three major characters, was a lot cheaper and easier for Paris, and they put that on. It's also better. And so *Eleuthéria* went into his suitcase. It was never done. It was written in French. So when I was thrown out at Grove, he brought that to me in Paris. He gave me the manuscript and then realized that it had to be translated. So he started to translate it.

Beckett himself did?

Yes. And he came back to me very shortly thereafter and said he couldn't do it. Little did I know he was going to be dead within about three years. And he said that it was too late, he was too tired, but that if I would forgive him, "if I would forgive my unforgivable Sam," he would write something new for me. And he did. He wrote a very short little book called *Stirrings Still*. And I published it. Marguerite Duras also gave me a short work which I published.

It's interesting that he had the energy to do something new, but not to translate.

Translation was a tremendous, tremendous job for him. When he translated, he transformed the work. It was a lot more than just translating. And then he said he didn't like the play anyway, he didn't want it published, which he had said to me about many of his books throughout his career. He had written books which were published in England before the war. And he took an aversion to English publishers and he wouldn't allow those books to be republished for years and years. And I fought with him, and argued and argued, and ultimately I got every one of them published.

You did his first novel, didn't you?

Yes, *Murphy* is a major novel. And a wonderful book of short stories called *More Pricks Than Kicks*. So I figured, well, someday he'll let me do *Eleuthéria*, but he double-crossed me: he died. [We both laugh.]

So six years went by, and Stan Gontarski—he's a professor at Florida State; he's been the head of the Beckett Society, amongst other things. He's an expert on Beckett, but in a less academic way than some others. And he came to me and he said, "Barney, you've forgotten you have that manuscript of *Eleuthéria*." And I said, "Oh, yeah, you're right." So I said, "I'll publish it." Well, the literary executor of the Beckett estate was Beckett's French publisher, Jerome Lindon of Minuit Editions, and he said, "You can't do it. I won't let you. Beckett said he didn't want it published; it cannot be published." So we proceeded to have one hell of a battle. And I pointed out that if the executor of Kafka, Max Brod, had done that, then we wouldn't have any of the major works of Kafka who said exactly the same thing, only much more strongly. He said, "Burn everything."

So I was threatened with lawsuits and so forth. Anyway, I went to John Oakes and Dan Simon and said, "Let's form a company together, and own it half and half." And PGW would be the distributor. So we did it. And the lawsuits were being threatened, and one day, almost simultaneously, Dan Simon and I each came [on] the same solution, which was that we would print the book and give it away. [Laughs.] And John said, "If that's what you two think, okay, I'll go along with it." So we announced that we were going to print the book and give it away. There'd be no damages then. So the *Village Voice* picked it up and ran a big article, with the headline saying "Free Beckett". And *Le Monde* in Paris picked it up and did a big article on...it's one of those funny words, it doesn't translate. Giving something away and being free are not the same word. And so *Le Monde* did a big thing on this funny idea of Beckett being both of two kinds of free—gratis and libre. The paper's headline was "Beckett libre (gratis)". And the French publisher panicked. And he said, "Okay, do it," and proceeded to publish it ahead of us [laughs] which I'd asked him to do in the beginning.

So then, when that happened—okay, fine, we did do a small edition as a giveaway—but then we also printed it to sell when Lindon caved in and published it himself. And it's still available. It's now in trade paperback. And Dan and John split in the meantime and I got John to agree to get out and now I have that shell of a company with one book. But, I don't know, maybe I'll be able to use it now to publish some more books.

People have an idea of me as a sort of pornographer, I guess, because of the last ten years of the Blue Moon books. Again, it was a catch-22. If I'd published these books—and many of them I think are very good contemporary novels—as hardcover books they would have sold maybe three hundred copies, four hundred. As Blue Moon books with the aura of eroticism around them, I could print ten thousand, fifteen thousand, and very easily distribute them. Which I did. But, of course, there were no reviews. So, unfortunately in one way, there are some very good books lurking under the Blue Moon imprint, and none of them got recognized.

Also, although I am certainly interested in publishing work that has an erotic quality, I've been even more interested, throughout my whole career, in political books. But these have been shut off from me. So I'm hoping, maybe through Foxrock now, to go back more like Curbstone Press and.... I mean last night, about four this morning actually, or five, I got very excited about the idea of doing—not that it's a great new idea, but it's something that particularly bothers me—is the role of illegal drugs in the world today. The political influence of drugs throughout the whole goddamn world. And, too, I feel very strongly that drugs should be legalized. To me it's Prohibition replayed. The same pattern of damage. I've had the feeling, for example, that if you took the power of oil—petroleum—and illegal drugs, and traced how they're being used today with each other and around each other—there's a lot of political information to be spread around. Not that it isn't done by many people, but it could be more. It particularly interests me. Interests *me*—I mean I feel chopped off, that I haven't been able to go forward. And *Evergreen Review* was a political magazine. We were bombed on Eleventh Street.

Oh, I'd forgotten that. When was that?

It was twenty-five years ago. It might be '70. By anti-Castro Cubans. That very month we had a marvelous portrait of Ché Guevara on the cover. Fred Jordan, of Grove, and I went to Bolivia, looking for Ché.

He was killed in '67.

We had gone there though, right after he was killed. We had gone and brought back parts of his diary. He was dead by the time we got there, but just. And I went to Cuba with Dick Seaver, the other important person at Grove. And you see how it carries on: my son Peter has been in Cuba a number of times in the last year. He somehow has gotten permission from the United States government to go. And to take people with him. He's very much involved in agriculture and the role of food in the world, vis-à-vis Food First Books of which he's the director. He's actually lectured in Cuba.

He spent ten years in Nicaragua where the American powers that be saw and put up with him, although he was teaching at the University of Nicaragua and running agricultural stations.

Well, when I got to Cuba, you couldn't go. I got in fantastic trouble when I came back—the stupid Cubans had stamped my passport. [Laughs.] But I did not like China this time. In fact, I got extraordinarily upset. I mean I literally had nightmares while I was there. I had to get out. I found the oppression was worse now than it was when I was there under Chiang Kai-shek.

I was very outspoken against him, and there I was, an officer in the American army. As I say, they finally got rid of me, even though the OSS had taken me in. I didn't know it for twenty-five years, at least. Maybe more. I found out that I had been a member of the OSS. That was a sort of typical madness. But the OSS were the only people who fought, including the whole Chinese army. The OSS guys, what they did—and I worked with them, moonlighting from the army—was go behind the Japanese lines and blow up everything. And if it hadn't been for the OSS the Japanese would have captured all of the materiel, et cetera, et cetera, that we had given to Chiang Kai-shek.

Well, the U.S. army issued an edict against me. I had an in-country pass, as a photographer. I could go anywhere I wanted on any plane, except to Yenan. That was Mao's headquarters. But my men could go. And I sent them. I have wonderful photographs of Mao and Chou En-lai, and Hurley, our wild Indian, reprobate ambassador who was sent to China to try to make peace between Mao and Chiang Kai-shek. And he damn near succeeded. I mean, Mao said fine. But not Chiang. He wasn't gonna share nothin'. Anyway, that was a major part of my life. In back of you, you can see photographs, some that I took in China.

But this time, it was such a terrible feeling—the oppression. The freedom to open your mouth is just gone. It was awful. I mean, to me. An unbelievable thing happened. We were in the street in Kunming—a pretty crowded street, a main boulevard—and a man carrying a child comes up to Astrid and me, a three- or four-year-old child, put the kid on the sidewalk, and in perfect English said to me, "Would you like to read something?" And I said yes and he handed me a hand-written document. A protest.

In English?

In English. Broken. Slightly scrambled English. About a ten-page thing, read like a short story—it was very simple—of what had happened to two people who were driving a truck and accidentally, I don't know, splashed water or something on a police truck, it turned out, and the police came after them and beat them up and killed one. And then the families of these two guys went to the police.

To tell the story from there, get Kafka. The more they tried to get some kind of justice, the worse it got. They never got anywhere. And the story breaks off and somebody is talking to one of the Tiananmen Square leaders, and that guy is saying, "The situation is hopeless, but we can't quit." Like Beckett's "I can't go on, I'll go on."

This is this trip to China?
Yeah, it was this last time there.

It's a wonderful line.
That's exactly how I felt, but I felt this time I can get the hell out

235

of this country before I go to jail. I'm sure in three or four more days there you would never have heard of me again. What struck me as being so horrible was the total cooperation of the United States with these people. I decided to call it Capcom. Capitalist communism. I mean, well, you ought to know—you're in Seattle. They had in *The Nation* recently that Boeing, unto itself, is the fiftieth largest economy in the world. Just Boeing. And China has got to be their number one or two customer. Well, start from there and go on to the oil companies, and so on. I mean it was so sweet to see our vice-president there the other day. So here I, who was a Communist—I was actually a member of the Communist Party at one point. After the war. And I quit in disgust! Not in the sense of ever denouncing it, but....

You quit when?
I quit when I went to Czechoslovakia. I went to Prague just as it became Communist, in 1948. I took my film there to show it to them. And I was so upset by Prague—I never was as upset again until I went to Kunming this time. This was a very similar feeling. In fact, in the nightmare I had in Kunming I was sort of back there. Prague and New York City suddenly had moved to Kunming. And there were riots in my dream.

You were in Kunming last year?
Yes. In November.

Only four months ago. So you really haven't had time to absorb it all yet.
Well, it really goaded me into trying to write an autobiography. And I wrote a chapter. And it starts off in Kunming. Because that really gave me a flood of feeling. Not particularly about China, but about...everything in general. And especially *Red Star Over China* and *Man's Fate*. They represented the two sides of me. *Red Star Over China* was the idealistic Communist and *Man's Fate* is the decadent side. The first time I read it, it was a revolutionary figure, but this time when I read the book it was the businessman that intrigued me the most, who is tricked by a girl—a young prostitute or a very fancy call girl who asked the Frenchman to bring a bird to her hotel in a cage, and at the hotel there's another guy with a bird.

236

When I was in Shanghai—it was absolutely unbelievable, but I stumbled on some of the eighteen thousand German Jews there. Stumbled on them. In a park. I didn't know they were there. In a park in Shanghai. They were living in a ghetto. They were ghettoized. They weren't put in prisons. During the war. The Japanese didn't know what to do, really, because the Germans told them, "We hate Jews, and you're our ally." So the Japanese sort of compromised. They put Americans and Dutch and British into really terrible prison conditions. But the Jews they put in a ghetto, and they could leave the ghetto every day.

They put buildings in the park—?

No, no! This was just a way of enjoying themselves. It was a party I came upon. They had a band and were dancing. And when they saw us it was like the sky had fallen, like the UFOs had landed. Myself and two of my photographers. And we're standing there and suddenly the music stops and the people start looking at us—the war was actually not formally over. And they ran over to us. Somebody ran home immediately and got me a Roliflex camera that he had kept in a box. And there were some very attractive young women. And I picked one, and suddenly they said, "Oh, my God, it's curfew." Like "Okay, it's nice to see you fellas, but it's curfew, we got to run home." And I said, "No, you don't. The war is over."

The war had ended then?

The fighting had ended but there was no formal peace yet. And the Japanese were traumatized. In Shanghai. They assisted us in keeping order. I got my hotel suite from a Japanese officer. He bowed to me and gave me his suite. So I took one of the girls, who was very beautiful, and said, "Come on. We're going to go and sit in the park on a bench past curfew." And the other two guys did the same thing. And along came a Sikh cop. The Sikhs were the police of Shanghai. The Japanese weren't very innovative. They took over the police force from the British and kept it. God knows, maybe they're still there. Anyway, a Sikh officer came up to me and I was shaking; he had a gun, I didn't. And he saluted, said, "Good evening, Sahib." And I turned around and I said to everybody, "See? The war is over. Come on back and dance." [Laughs.]

And I was given credit for liberating these people. I mean, it was fun. And that girl became my girlfriend. And she became like the girl in *Man's Fate*, to me. What the hell had she been doing all that time in Shanghai? A very beautiful...in this ghetto.... She didn't have to go back for curfew. [Laughs.] And she knew the French quarter of Shanghai, which was big. It was like a city. And the international settlement was a big city. Not what I had imagined. And I loved her very dearly, actually. And I was told, in the middle of the night, to get out of Shanghai. Given one hour to go. I woke her up and got her to go downstairs, very unwillingly. I had a riksha outside. I put her in it and I piled everything I owned, literally, on top of her, including sacks of money. And said good-bye. And never saw her again.

But a few years later she called me from San Francisco. She said she took all the money I gave her and got out, to San Francisco, where she was very happy. Wanted to call me and thank me again. [Laughs.] So, you know, it had a nice ending.

That's a sweet story, yeah.

It was all very important to me. The sexual, erotic side of *Man's Fate* was as powerful to me as anything else. It was even more than that. One of the major revolutionaries was killed because an old man wouldn't stop playing roulette, to warn him. To me, that also was very intrinsic. That scene.

He was sent to warn him, but he got distracted by gambling.

Gambling. I was reading it again. He had a fantasy of losing. He enjoyed losing.

You know, he reappears in Anti-Memoirs, *the same guy.*

Really? I didn't know that.

I can't remember his name.

Baron de Clappique.

Yeah. He's always saying "Not a word."

And then the other guy, the Russian agent who gives up his poison at the end—cyanide—that was the most heroic act I've ever read described. He gives up the cyanide to two comrades and then he's going

238

to be thrown into a boiler. So those scenes...and then Lincoln Steffens who was with John Reed in the Russian Revolution and afterwards, was back home saying how great the Soviet Union was, and so on—actually, he wasn't back home; he was on the Riviera. And he was questioned by reporters: "Well, Mr. Steffens, if you think it's so goddamn nice there, why aren't you there?" "Oh," he said, "I've seen the future and it works." And they said: "If you've seen the future and it works, why aren't you there?" And he said, "I'm too old." [Laughs.]

I never went to the Soviet Union. I must have had a feeling: "Don't go there. You're not going to like it. It's not the land of your dreams." So I never went there. But I sure as hell went to other places. You know, I gradually changed, but the total change was in Kunming this time. Sad. I end my first chapter with saying, "Some day in Paris I'm going to run into Chou En-Lai, that handsome, aristocratic Chinese, in a bookstore. And I'm going to say, 'Comrade, I've got some bad news for you.'"

Did you see this book? [Indicates a book on the coffee table in front of us.] One thing I did get in Kunming was *Lady Chatterly's Lover*, in Chinese.

It's in English. It's got a Chinese cover, but it's in English.

You're right. You're right. It was in a Chinese foreign book-store. I'll tell you why I said it's in Chinese. It's heavily annotated in Chinese. I don't know what they had to say about the book, unfortunately. [Flipping through the book:] Look, all the annotations are in Chinese. God knows what they've said about it.

[He hands over a book on the OSS in China.] It was a strange war. Anyway, the OSS—I thought they were wonderful. They threw me out. I found out when under the Freedom of Information Act I got thousands of pages of information about myself from the FBI. It started when I was twelve years old.

I sued them. I sued every head of the CIA from its inception through Colby. I sued them for money, but the real thing was information. And they each hired a law firm, a private law firm. The *New York Times* reported the GAO [General Accounting Office] complaining about the money being spent to fight my lawsuit. I mean one guy alone had spent eight hundred thousand dollars on a fancy law firm. But all I wanted was more information.

Finally we offered to set up an ombudsman. And we said if this person is acceptable to me and to them, then the CIA heads—former heads—if they tell him that they had nothing to do with me, we'll dismiss them from the suit. And if they say they do know something about me, they will give any information they have to this person who can then decide if it's secret. There was nothing I did that was secret. And my attorney picked as the ombudsman, to my utter amazement, the general counsel for the CIA. You'd think they would accept that person. I wasn't sure why I was doing it, but I took my attorney's word, Ed de Grazia, who had fought with me on *Tropic of Cancer*, et cetera, et cetera, et cetera. (He had a very big book recently—I mean by "big", thick—called *Girls Always Lean Back*. Random House. It's a story of censorship in this country. Semi-documentary.) And Colby wrote me a letter saying "I think this is a fantastic idea," et cetera, et cetera, et cetera, "but they'll never accept it." And he was right. He knew. Finally, the lawsuits dwindled to a stop; I ran out of money. I did get help from a very liberal institute in Washington because it was an enormous burden.

They started with me when I was twelve, in 1934. I was a delegate to the American Student Union convention at Vassar—as a college student, but I was really in the eighth grade. I was elected as a college delegate. Another eighth grader, Quentin Young, became the health commissioner of Chicago; he and I were the delegates to the American Student Union convention. It was an anti-war moment, and Joe Lasch, who was certainly not a Communist, was the head of the American Student Union. And Jimmy Wexler, who became the managing editor of the *New York Post*, was the secretary. And we, the delegation from Chicago, went through winter storms and blizzards in an old bus to Vassar.

It was also interesting because for that week they put up male and female students together—1934—and Manchuria had just been invaded. To me, the most exciting moment was when a bonfire was built outside in the snow and the girls took off their silk stockings and put them in the fire. [Laughs.] The *Times* had a photograph of this little episode. And, boy, I didn't even understand why, but in looking back, I thought it was very sexy, all those beautiful legs—these beautiful girls.

240

All of whom were much, much too old for me.

Sex and politics together.

Sex and politics together, right from the beginning. [Both of us laugh.] It's never changed. In the last few years, you would think it was the sex. If you read some of the Blue Moon books, you'd see—it's in there, the other side.

Do you want to talk at all about your leaving Grove Press?

Just a little bit. It remains a mystery to me. I knew George Weidenfeld. He's a lord. He was, I would not say a friend of mine, but I'd known him for a number of years, and actually had worked with him on something called the International Literary Prize, of which Grove was the American member. It was Gallimard from France and...anyway, it was all big, important publishing companies, except us. But we were chosen by the others to represent the United States. Our reputation was much bigger in Europe than here. Although they had chosen Kurt Wolff, or Pantheon, to be the company, Kurt Wolff said no, he was not American, it should be Grove Press. Which made me love him from then on. I'd never even met him. And Weidenfeld was representing England.

So, over a number of years, we got to know each other pretty well. And he came to me—this was years and years later, and I hadn't seen him in years—here in New York and said, "Barney, I've met a wonderful woman who will give me anything I want." George had had a series of incredibly rich marriages—Marx and Spencer, and then a Whitney, and an Astor on the side—and he said, "She's a wonderful woman and she'll give me anything I want. I'm finished with England anyway." And I said, "That's great, George. What do you want?" He said: "I want you. I want to buy Grove Press and you will be the head of it and run it. You could do anything you want, there'll be money." We were just drifting along, doing what we could do, and I fell for that. Grove Press was publicly held, and so I did know how to run a business.

When you had it alone, was it publicly held?

No, I took it public. I made it public. I was a shareholder, but not a majority one. So he gave me a low price. To be exact, it was two million dollars. I knew of other companies being sold for ten and twelve at that time who really did not compare, even commercially, to Grove. But there was a promise of enormous amounts of money to do good things. And I met with Ann Getty and I showed her our political books, and I showed her our sex books.

We had just done a book on the Caribbean, a whole series on the Caribbean, including two by my son on Nicaragua, and others. One was called *The Other Side of Paradise*, and it was the other side of the Bahamas and so on, the exploitation by American oil companies. So I gave that book to Ann Getty and she said, "Oh, don't worry about that." She and her husband had sold the goddamn Getty Oil Company to Texaco for, I don't know, a couple of billion dollars, two or three billion. They were supposed to be the richest people in the world. Close to it. She said, "So I don't care. You could say anything you want about the oil companies." And as for the sex books, I gave her one with a wild title—I think it was called *Lashed into Lust*. She laughed and she said, "Oh, don't worry, I read a lot of those books in college," and so forth.

Okay. So I did it. And I never got any money. I ran the company for a year just as if they weren't there. And then one day they held a meeting and I discovered I was no longer there.

"They," meaning George Weidenfeld and—

And Ann Getty and.... Ann Getty had a financial person who is the head of a company called Petroleum, Incorporated. To this day. In Washington. And who is a very, very close associate of the deputy director of the CIA. I'm just telling you facts.

They threw me out. And this guy told me that—I couldn't believe it when I felt it in the room. And I turned to this man who was sitting next to me, much closer than you are now, and I said, "I don't get it. Am I hearing straight? I'm no longer running Grove Press?" He said, "Oh, you knew that. You knew the day you signed that contract we were going to throw you out as soon as we could." He was the one who convinced me to do it, this particular character. So I...all I could think of...you know how something will flash into your head? All I could think of was the Chicago Black Sox scandal. There's the famous story of a young kid who goes out of the stands, goes up to Shoeless Joe Jackson—"Tell me it ain't so, Joe." As I'm looking at this guy, that's all I could think of. [Laughs.] "Tell me it ain't so." Well, he didn't. He

242

was as guilty, or more so, than Jackson. So I said, "I guess I'd better leave." I got up and I left.

I never got an explanation. And when I left they started pouring money into Grove. And lost, I was told, over fifteen million dollars. They tried to sell the company and, through John [Oakes], I got together a group of people who I thought were crazy. I got John and Dan and several other small companies as a nucleus, and then I got outside backers, to buy back Grove Press. They were auctioning it off. They would not sell to us. We offered a price. Think of this: I sold Grove for two million; it certainly was in no better shape when they wanted to auction it off—I think much worse. We offered eleven million. They turned it down. And ultimately they didn't get a bid at all. From anybody.

Why do you think they turned you down?

I think I was almost afraid they would accept. [Laughs.] We tried to get the head of PGW to join the group, and he wouldn't.

Charlie Winton?

Yeah. He wouldn't. I didn't even know him. But I did try. I called him. He said, "You've got to try it alone." So I don't really know. And it was a very traumatic thing.

I would imagine so. What year was that?

It was '86. It was only...that life only lasted about a year. John Oakes wrote about it in the *Review of Contemporary Fiction*. He tells the story about how insane it was, because Grove Press was in my house. It was just like this, except it had four floors, in a house I built on Houston Street. I was there for eighteen years. And John said you'd go in there and it was so confusing because the editorial part was on the top and my then wife was running that, and he said I'd be stretched out on the floor a floor below [laughs], unconscious. More or less. And that was how life went on for a brief time, after it was sold. Then I had to sell the house. And came here.

So—what now?

I've also been working with somebody who started a company called United Publishers Group. Gabriel Morgan and I formed a little imprint called Rosset-Morgan and we're giving this UPG three books. Three novels.

What do you mean, you're giving them three novels?
Well, I'm giving them—they're paying. I mean, I'm the editor. Sort of a cooperative thing. It's just right now beginning, but those three books are definite. Hopefully there'll be more, and maybe I'll be able to work Foxrock into this thing—I hope—and do something political. [Laughs again.]

I don't have any more questions. Do you have anything more you would like to talk about?
No.

Thanks. It was a great interview.

Late in 1997 Rosset filed for Chapter 11 bankruptcy for Blue Moon Books after Barricade Books, its distributor, filed. In 1998 Avalon Publishing Group acquired Blue Moon and a controlling interest in Foxrock, Inc., hiring Rosset as a salaried consultant for the former and as the director of Foxrock. Also in 1998 Neal Ortenberg of Thunder's Mouth Press and Dan Simon of Seven Stories Press announced their intention to copublish Rosset's autobiography, to be called The Subject is Left Handed *(see Reid 1998a and 1998b).*

244

Bruce McPherson
Treacle Press; Documentext; McPherson
& Company, Publishers

"[I]f there is one central attitude or approach that I take, it is that I'm interested in the intersection of the arts rather than the limitations of genre or the definitions of what constitutes a particular discipline... The books I do are in almost every case intended to try to push the definitions...."

I talked with Bruce McPherson on Sunday morning, the last day of August 1997, at Bruegger's Bagels on First and Mercer. He was in Seattle to participate in the small press book fair at Bumbershoot, the city's annual arts fair, at Seattle Center, three or four blocks up Mercer. "Bumbershoot" is an archaic word for umbrella; the fair, over Labor Day weekend, purports to coincide with the beginning of the Pacific Northwest's rainy season, and it often does. But today was sunny and promising, and both of us were looking forward to large crowds of book buyers.

McPherson was born in 1951 in Atlanta to a pediatrician father (who later quit his practice to go into pharmaceutical research) and a mother who had "various employments," including office manager for a law firm in Atlanta and running a girl scout council in Indiana. In 1960 the family moved to Evansville, Indiana, and in 1961 to San Mateo, California. A couple of years later they moved back to Indiana where he went to high school—"did time," as he says. He went from high school to Brown University, led a kind of peripatetic life for a while, then settled in Kingston, a town of about thirty-five thousand, in New York's Hudson River Valley.

He is married, has a small son, and runs McPherson and Company from his house—"Office in the attic, warehouse in the basement." The house is what he calls "Sears style. You know, catalogue houses. The builders in those days"—the '20s—"were doing an early kind of development. You could have your porch on the left side or on the right side. You'd get one bay and it could be on the first floor or it could be a projecting bay on the second floor. You go down the street and you often see houses which are remarkably similar, but they'll be asymmetrical, or have the same elements in different combinations. It's kind of an interesting approach."

Let's back up. You got your B.A. at Brown?
Yeah. English lit.

You said you were at the Annenberg School of Communications when we talked earlier [several days before, in setting up the interview].
After college I didn't have any particular direction. I wasn't thinking of publishing, although I'd been involved in a small press at Brown. It was called Hellcoal Press. It had been founded in, I think, '69 by two undergraduate students who sort of jettisoned the old-fashioned college literary magazine, using the money they had cajoled out of the student government. They were publishing pamphlets from visiting poets and writers. Their names were Steven Heller and Chris Coles, and so they wordsmithed their names together into a metaphor.

When you say you were involved with it, what does that mean?
Well, first I fell in with a group of writers—

Were you writing?
I was trying to. It interested me. But I sort of got swept up into the press, became—we sort of gave each other our own titles; I became managing editor and a poet named Jon Klimo was editor-in-chief. I think he was from New Jersey; I'm not sure. He's now on Long Island somewhere. And then after Klimo the press sort of fell into my hands for a year or two. There was a fairly large number of people involved originally, a dozen or more, though attrition was high. It was kind of amazing, the literary politics in this little town—I guess it's the normal aspirations of nineteen- and twenty-year-olds in academia that leads to their inability to hang together.

A couple guys spun off and did a magazine in conjunction with some people from RISD [Rhode Island School of Design] which is

246

adjacent to Brown, on College Hill. And a couple of other people got involved in different publishing activities. But actually, one of the models, both for all of the spin-offs and for Hellcoal Press itself, was the publishing operation of Keith and Rosemarie Waldrop—Burning Deck Press. It's a famous press. It's a little press. I mean, originally it did letterpress editions of a hundred and fifty to three hundred copies. But I don't think it's terribly well known that they're probably responsible for the language movement. The language poetry movement. They didn't name it but they were publishing almost all of those people in small editions when they were very young poets in the early '70s. Even the late '60s.

They have a very broad, ecumenical grasp of the international scene. They both translate. Rosemarie's German; she translates from German. Keith translates from French. Rosemarie does French as well—in fact, she's the translator of Edmund Jabes. Jabes is a French...I think he's Egyptian. An Egyptian-Jewish Frenchman. Jewish-Egyptian Frenchman. French-Egyptian Jew. I'm not sure exactly in what order—

Was he self-conflicted?
No, he's totally resolved. In fact, now he's dead.

That'll do it.
But he's the author of *The Book of Questions* and some other absolutely remarkable books that, I think, Wesleyan University Press publishes. Although the first of them was published in the early '70s by a small press in...Santa Barbara? David Meltzer's Tree Books. It's called *Elya*.

They [i.e., Burning Deck] also published people like Jackson Mac Low before he was quite the elder statesman of the movement, and various other figures. They have the most eclectic poetry list I think anybody has ever imagined. And what they have been teaching anyone willing to pay attention is that the true dimensions of poetry—or what people think of as the dimensions of poetry—are not to be found within the confines of academia. It's all a great continuum, finally, from the Modernist movement, with all kinds of interruptions—you know, Dada, Surrealism, Objectivism, Expressionism, and Duncan and Black Mountain, et cetera. All the really interesting poetries.

247

You were writing during this period?
Yeah, I was still trying to.

Poetry?
Poetry. Oh, I tried to.... I was a total failure, I think, as a fiction
writer.

Were you publishing poetry?
I published a few poems. Here and there. Before I learned better.
I'll tell you why I say that. It's because...I'd published four or five
books by other writers, and I was still trying to write as late as about '77
or '78. And I realized that I was competing with my authors. And I
thought, as a publisher and an editor, to be competing with my authors
was an extremely self-defeating mind set. I had to finally admit that I
was publishing people who were far better than I would ever be. And it
was a lot more important that I should become a good editor, a good
reader of other writers, than that I should be having feelings of competition toward the work that I was publishing.

That's interesting. You know I publish myself.
Some people can do it, some people can't.

*But I've wondered. The sense of competition is there, though I
don't think as strongly in me as apparently in you. But that may be why
I've gone more and more into surrealism, not in my own writing but in
other people's, whereas I remain a realist. So there won't be that competition. I haven't thought about that, and I'm not sure I'm right. But it
could be. I do find myself drawn more toward publishing writers who
deal in surrealism. But I don't write it.*
Well, good surrealism is not only hard to find but extremely
hard to do. The real stuff. I mean there's always the cheap variety of
pseudo-surrealism that crops up in every college literary magazine in one
way or another. But the stuff that sticks, the stuff that really matters....

*Surrealism or, in one form or another, magical realism, has crept
into mainstream writing. So you can write whatever you want and say it*

248

has surrealism or magical realism in it, and you may be right. But that's not really what I'm talking about.

Right. Well, enough about me.

So you went from Brown to Annenberg? Or was there a break in there?

I spent two years toiling in the admissions office of Brown University.

Did you find that interesting?

Well, being highly judgmental— There were eight or nine of us who got to deal with about ten thousand applications every year. Those were, I guess, my real salad days in terms of reading—speed reading. It was self-defense, you know.

Speed reading admissions applications?

Admissions applications. Otherwise you were just absolutely snowballed. That was a very interesting job. We worked eight hours a day and then took home fifty file folders a night for six months. It was brutal.

It was salary, or—?

It was salary. I knew that question was coming. And so, in a way, my publishing operation at Hellcoal initially was partly a defense against that. After I finished school I said, Well, that was that. I mean, at Hellcoal we did something like seventy pamphlets [and] all kinds of on-campus, off-campus publications: student anthologies, chapbooks by visiting writers, an annual anthology that was two or three hundred pages long—

Were you selling them or giving them away?

We did both. But one of the features of the *Hellcoal Annual* was that probably three-quarters of the work was from off campus, was from around the country. So we were really participating in the burgeoning small press movement. Klimo had tied it all in, because he had connections previously with a variety of...everyone from Richard Eberhardt to— Plus, we were drawing on the resources and contacts of on-campus writers, mostly poets, such as Edwin Honig and James Schevill, a very

249

important poet who had come to Brown in the early or mid-'60s from San Francisco where he had run the Poetry Center for a long time. So we really reached out. And we tried to get our publications distributed a little bit. Places like City Lights and Gotham Book Mart. Then we also let it be known that we were interested in receiving manuscripts, and we got lots—an unbelievable amount. We were publishing all kinds of people, and tapping into the scene.

In the '60s there was a huge ferment of literary activity. It was enthralling, exciting. It was coming out of the student movement, it was coming out of the anti-war—so it had a literary component, a political component, it was coming out of the free speech movement. It was the mimeograph revolution, which gradually went over to the offset revolution. And there was also a kind of response to or outgrowth from the underground newspaper phenomenon and the cooperative bookstore phenomenon, all kinds of alternative approaches to information—development, presentation, et cetera.

Why do you consider the mimeograph revolution a revolution? I've heard only one other person refer to it in that way, and when I mention it to other people, they don't regard it as a revolution. Offset, yeah, I think everybody agrees that the development of offset printing did produce a revolution.

Well, a lot from the small press movement was done on mimeograph.

You're not really talking about the technology.

No, I'm not really talking about the technology. I guess I'm talking about the first time people really started thinking about.... I'm not going to say "first". I don't like speaking in absolutes, but rather in continuums. There were literary magazines throughout the '50s and '60s that were independent of academia and that were operated by a variety of entrepreneurs, and collaborative ventures by poets and writers, et cetera. And they were usually tied up with letterpress printing. This is true of Creeley's magazine that was done in Majorca, and a lot of printing was done in Majorca or in England in those days because there was often cheap printing to be had, depending, I suppose, on currency fluctuations. And that was sort of the high end, even though it was

250

down-and-dirty printing. I mean we say "letterpress," but a lot of that stuff was dashed off, it was very conventional in appearance—it was not fine printing per se.

In those days, you know, most towns had letterpress printers who were a rough equivalent to today's copy shops. They were the stationery printers—they had linotype machines in their back rooms. It was simply the way one created typesetting. Use of the mimeograph machine for literary publications was, in a sense, a bit of an act of rebellion on the part of outsiders to the academic or the established magazine scene. And it was also so fast and so cheap, anybody could do it. And it was a kind of revolution because it became an acceptable format.

Probably one of the earliest and greatest expressions of it was Ed Sanders' *Fuck You: A Magazine of the Arts*, which was a journal in the early to mid-'60s. I think it remains one of the best. And poets also would self-publish. Important work, sometimes in very odd formats, in small editions.

When did you start McPherson and Company?

Well, first there was Treacle Press. It was conceived in '73 and the first book came out in the spring of '74. The first book I did was a novel by a woman named Jaimy Gordon. An extraordinary writer, in fact, one of the best of her generation. It was going to be a one-off press. You know: one book, one time, one edition.

I know how that works. What was the title of the book?

Shamp of the City Solo. I'd gotten to know Jaimy—in fact, she was instrumental in introducing me to Jon Klimo and getting me involved in Hellcoal Press. And the year I was the editor at Hellcoal, I insisted that she be the associate editor of the annual that we did. So we edited that together. She was an MFA student who, after getting her MFA, went into the doctoral—the DA [Doctor of Arts] program that Brown offered in those days. It was an extremely good writing program. I mean John Hawkes, R. V. Cassill, Schevill, Honig, Waldrop. Cassill was the guy who founded the Associated Writing Programs. And there were some extraordinary students, as well. John Keeble. He was in the MFA program at the same time. A very good writer.

So, let's see. I finished school, I got a job, I knew Jaimy—I'd been watching the gestation of a novel. Everyone was kind of astounded by her because she was far advanced over all but a few other writers, such as Keeble. I mean among the MFA people. They were just blown away. Where was this stuff coming from? She writes on three or four different levels. It's, I would say, a form of surrealism, getting back to where we were before. I've got two Gordon novels on my list now, and she's got another finished manuscript and a fourth that she's working on. She's won some prizes but hasn't had the success that she deserves. Maybe it's just a matter of waiting for the right book. I think she's going to be a case like Cormac McCarthy at some point—a writer who will have a lot of readers go back to her earlier work. His first novels, as I recall, sold two or three thousand copies when they first came out. You know, they dived below the event horizon soon after their first appearance, until *All the Pretty Horses*.

So, let's see. I had a job, so I had some cash. I had an apartment. I was still hanging around in Providence.

This is still when you were at the office of admissions?

Right. And Jaimy could not get her novel published. Bill Goyen had taken it on her behalf to some editors. An east Texas writer. His books have been brought back into print by Triquarterly Press. Anyway, Goyen had come to Brown and met Jaimy and read her stuff and said he couldn't believe it. He'd been an editor with some house in Manhattan. So he showed it around. Had no luck at all. So I told her, from my experience at Hellcoal Press, that we could publish the book. I would form a press, we'd do the book, get some reviews, and then we'd turn it over to a commercial house. Seemed like a perfectly good idea at the time. There is a flaw in there somewhere, but I'm still looking for it. [We both laugh.]

And it worked, of course.

Actually, it had an astounding success. *Succès d'estime*, you know, where we got reviewed in the small press journals. In many cases, people just could not believe that there was a small press that was publishing a novel, because there were not that many presses publishing novels at that time. It was early '74. There were a couple that were beginning to. Len Fulton brought out a novel about the same time, and Harry Smith—The Smith—I don't think he had a full-scale novel on his list, but certainly he'd published novellas. But still, it was quite rare. Most of the small press scene was short stories and poetry, mixed genre publications, small anthologies, poetry chapbooks—a zillion of those—and the feeling was that novels were the province of the commercial houses because they did require a fairly substantial outlay. But I thought we could sell enough copies. And we pretty much sold out the first thousand copies in a few months. We did a lot of direct mail promotions, using all of our lists and personalized letters, things like that. And we got some wonderful reviews, and we were off and running.

The first review we got, I think, was a *Library Journal* review. It hated the book. So I thought, Oh, God, we'll never get over this. But fortunately it wasn't fatal. It was damaging but it wasn't fatal. I'll still never forgive them for that. But it's good to know what you're up against. So much of our perception of writing is a misreading due to conventional expectations, where the whole purpose of this kind of writing is counter-conventional. It's to counter conventions of under-standing, of reading—

We do it because it's different and it intrigues us. But because it's different and intriguing, it upsets certain people. And then we get upset because they're upset and they have clout. But we have to expect that, because—

Oh, making people upset certainly should be considered an aspect of success.

An aspect of innovation or literary success, yeah. But it does keep sales down.

That's another bag.

I'm just saying how our own critique tends to be loopy. I know that my wanting to publish something almost guarantees that a lot people will not like it.

Well, don't you find it curious that in presidential campaigns the difference between a winner and a loser is a percentage point or two in popularity? If you do anything in this country, automatically half of the

253

people are against you. If you make a move, if you utter a sound, half of the response automatically is going to be disapproving. The other half might be approving. It comes with the territory. Universal approbation is a total myth. It's something not to be wished for at all. It's a kind of death.

You're right. But when I was first starting out fourteen years ago, I probably could have accepted that in the abstract, but it would have hurt. But, yeah, if I had a book on the best-seller list now, I would think, What have I done wrong?

If you had a book on the *New York Times* best-seller list, you'd probably be driven out of business.

That's true. I couldn't capitalize it.

You couldn't capitalize it. You'd have to put so many books out into the distribution stream to maintain the sales to stay on the best-seller list—it's put a lot of smaller publishing operations out of business.

I know. But I don't expect that to happen.

Let's hope we don't meet with great success. Jack Shoemaker told me once that when they set up North Point Press, they set it up so that they would be flexible enough to deal with a best-seller. They had three or four.

*They had Evan Connell's book [*Son of the Morning Star*].*

West with the Night [by Beryl Markham]. And a few others. But it was very careful advance planning. That operation was built to withstand it. And I think he said that at one point it almost didn't. It was almost too much for them. But, as you say, it's not likely to be a problem for either of us. Although you never can tell. In which case you may have to make alternative plans, like finding a publishing partner or selling the rights to somebody who can do it.

Okay, so you're still at the office of admissions. And you started the press for Jaimy Gordon's book. Did you do more than one printing?

Actually, at that point we just did one printing. We had a lot of fun, and I expected eventually to sell the rights. And I was thinking of

254

doing another project, because we did have so much fun. Clayton Eshleman sent me a manuscript. He's a poet we'd published in the *Hellcoal Annual*, and the editor of *Caterpillar* magazine. He was also a Black Sparrow poet. So, anyway, he sent me a suite of poems and told me to get in touch with a friend of his, an artist named Nora Jaffe in New York City. And I did and she produced a complementary suite of drawings for the book. So I published my second book, in an edition of five hundred copies or four hundred and fifty copies, something like that. Strange format. French-fold binding. A cover that wrapped. I had a nice success with that book, pretty much sold out quickly.

So then I did a third book which was a long poem by Keith Waldrop. My idea, actually. I should mention here that one of the things about *Shamp of the City Solo* was that we enlisted Jaimy's friends and family to help. Jaimy's former boyfriend, James Aitchison, a considerable artist, did a dozen drawings of which we incorporated eight or ten to illustrate *Shamp*. Aitchison's a very, very good painter. He has a local reputation, but he doesn't have the national reputation that he should have. And her brother Adam had a silk-screen operation, so he silk-screened the cover, four colors. At that time I was thinking that all the books I would do would be illustrated by various artists. Poets and novelists usually know visual artists at least as well as they know other writers, so I would ask my authors if they knew artists who could accomplish work to go with theirs. And in the case of Keith Waldrop's five-hundred-line *Poem from Memory*, he turned me on to a woman named Linda Lutes. She was an interesting artist, living somewhere outside of Manhattan in one of the boroughs. And she did a suite of thirty drawings that actually was almost like a flip book. And we put twenty lines on a page and she illustrated the poem and produced a silk screen cover—a marvelous cover—using a technique that's rarely used in silk screen but that was often used by printers at that time. That was called "split fountain," where you take the primary colors and put them in the ink tray for the press, in order, and you get a rainbow effect that would tend, over the course of a press run, to start merging [its colors]. The effects were somewhat unpredictable but very delicious. She did that with silk screen. Sunburst effect—it's just great. So that was that. Treacle Press was up and running. Three books, two of which were poetry. While I had success with the poetry books, my real interest was the fiction, so I moved on to it.

You moved on to McPherson and Company at this point?

No, I moved on to graduate school. The Annenberg School at the University of Pennsylvania. I spent a year there, and I was also still running the press. I was publishing something called the Treacle Story Series. Short stories in those days were hardly published at all by commercial houses, and longer short stories didn't often have a place in literary magazines, so my idea was to create fiction chapbooks—one or two stories by a single author, illustrated with original drawings, photographs, whatever—and to present them as an alternative approach to publishing short fiction.

Did you sell them primarily through your mailing lists?

Well, also bookstores. But, you know, we were dealing with a thousand copies or fewer. And I was distributing through Bookpeople. At that time Bookpeople was the main distributor for things.

So you did that while you were at Annenberg. Did you graduate from Annenberg?

No. I spent one year there and I left.

What did you want there? Why did you go?

Well, I was interested in expanding my understanding, or conception, of publishing, to include all forms of communication. I wanted to study it both in the theoretical sense and in terms of direct understanding of how things operate—what the systems are, socially and commercially.

I didn't know Annenberg had a publishing program.

Publishing, no. But I felt that I could extrapolate, perhaps wrongly. Although it didn't hurt me. But it didn't immediately help me.

They do mass media, don't they?

It was a lot of mass media. Of course, publishing is, at least potentially, a mass medium. I actually think that what we've been learning more and more lately is that broadcasting has given way to narrowcasting. When you have thirty channels on a cable, you're actually

256

witnessing not broadcasting, but narrowcasting. There's a lot of self-selecting of the audience.

Niche casting.
Yeah. Niche. Narrow, niche, however you want to describe it.

So you went from Annenberg to where?
Well, I stayed in Philadelphia for a year. I don't know how I lived that year, to tell you the truth. I did some publishing. I did a Philadelphia Book Fair. This was 1976, '77. Right after I left Annenberg I did the book fair and...what did I do for the next year? Spent a little bit of time in New York, spent some time in Philadelphia publishing the Treacle Story Series, and then wondering what I was going to do and where I was going to go next. I was involved a little bit with—there was a poetry project at the Philadelphia Y, and I came to know a lot of poets and people involved with that. Anyway, I made it through the winter somehow. I'd begun working on a project with a performance artist, Carolee Schneemann, and we fell in love and I moved to upstate New York outside of New Paltz with her. And then for the next year or so I did freelance graphic design and was the art director for a small arts-and-culture magazine in the county that was being run by a fellow named Michael Perkins. And we worked on this project to create a presentation—she was one of the original creators of happenings—

Carolee?
Yeah. So we worked on this book, building a book out of an archive. It was really an extraordinary experience. It took us two years to compile it and for her to write it, then another year to get it printed. It's called *More Than Meat Joy*. Meat Joy was a famous performance that she created in London in 1964. 'Seventy-nine is when [the book] came out. In '78 I did a couple more books of poetry, a translation of Novalis, a book of poetry by Robert Kelly, but I was moving away from doing any poetry altogether. It was still Treacle Press, but when I came to *More Than Meat Joy* I realized that I couldn't use Treacle Press for it; it just wouldn't work. It was an international art book. So I created a new imprint called Documentext.

I was changing my focus, getting very involved in the art world.

She was very well connected in New York, so we spent a lot of time in New York City, and I came to know a fairly large number of artists. It was a whole different scene from what I'd known. There were some other figures from the small press scene that I'd come to know in the early '70s, such as Dick Higgins—a very important publisher in the '60s, Something Else Press—who were part of the New York art scene of the '60s and '70s as well. So suddenly I was an art publisher on the one hand and a literary publisher on the other.

It went along like that for a couple of years, and it led me to broaden my horizons in a number of ways, both in terms of the contemporary art scene and in terms of the possibilities of publishing, because it sent me to Frankfurt [i.e., the Frankfurt Book Fair] to try to find an international partner. I never did succeed at that, for [*More Than Meat Joy*], but I came to know a large number of publishers and the literary scenes of Germany, France, England....

Do you go to Frankfurt every year now?

I went first in '78, looking for a publisher. Then I didn't go back again until '84. I went in '84 and I've been every year since.

Is it worth it? Is it profitable for you? You go there to sell subsidiary rights, right?

Yeah. I would say it's probably a wash. But I have had some marvelous successes. It may be a wash in terms of the actual costs. I look at it partly as a long-term development project. I've had fiction and nonfiction published in England, France, Germany, Italy, Austria, Poland—never Spain or The Netherlands, but eventually those will happen, too. It's an entirely different concept of what your purpose as a publisher is in relation to your authors. Where you might not succeed here, you might very well succeed in another country. It's entirely possible for an American author to be better received in translation for his innovative work. I've found that in a number of cases. Actually, I've made money. Not a lot, but I've made some money with those deals. It's a lot of fun, too.

That's what I hear.

It's overwhelming. It's totally daunting. There's nothing that prepares you for it. You can't begin to do what you want to do, because

258

it's just too enormous. But if you take a sane approach to it, you can accomplish a surprising amount of good things that will take you the rest of the year to actually carry out. And the contacts. And it evaporates a lot of the feeling of insularity that you might otherwise have.

Cathy Hillenbrand [publisher of Real Comet Press; see Gold 1996] told me that she liked going to Frankfurt because no matter how off the wall she got, she was bound to meet one or two other publishers who knew exactly what she was doing.

Not only who knew exactly what she was doing, but who were doing something even more off the wall. It's a great thing. I mean you go looking for more courage.

That's a good point. For me, there's always a tendency to slide back into what's safe—and boring. Consistently, at some point I'll read something, or somebody will say something, that will bring my courage back up.

I need a little bit more coffee. If we could break for five.

[We went through the coffee line. While waiting to pay, McPherson began talking about his personal view of publishing. This continued after we returned to the table.]

All right, we're back.

I thought I would say at this point that one of the reasons I'm going through this chronologically is that my conception of publishing was never one attitude or one idea but rather an evolving set of conditions that would be responsive to changing interests, and would be flexible enough to accommodate the various kinds of artists or writers that I want to publish. My idea of what a book would have to look like was never fixed in my mind. And an idea of what would constitute the appropriate expression of the press—that is, the genre—was never fixed in my mind either. In fact, thinking it over, my wanting to have artists contribute illustrations and be involved with the publications I was doing at the very beginning of Treacle Press was part of feeling that if there is one central attitude or approach that I take, it is that I'm interested in the intersection of the arts rather than the limitations of genre or the definitions of what constitutes a particular discipline. That's why I've always been involved, to a certain extent, with experimental forms. The books I do are in almost every case intended to try to push the definitions, for myself as well as for anyone else who cares to look.

In 1978 you went to Frankfurt for the first time—
And in order to pay for the book, because it was so expensive, I took a job in New York City. I was a production manager for a company called Publishing Center for Cultural Resources which provided publishing services to nonprofit organizations such as museums and historical societies. Unfortunately it's no longer in operation. It was a nonprofit set up by a fellow named M.J. Gladstone with the help of the New York State Council on the Arts. I think he had been a publishing consultant to them and he had this concept of raising the quality of nonprofit organizations' publishing. For a good ten-year period, he succeeded.

Anyway, it was a great training experience for me. I learned everything about book production and every other kind of production, too. Everything from napkins to coffee table books, magazines, brochures, flyers. It ran the gamut. Duotone. Four-color process. Everything.

Were you still writing yourself at this time?
No, by that time I had closeted my urges. Or cloistered my desire?

Is that how it feels? Does it still try to get out?
Oh, sure. Well, I mean I write copy. I write catalogues. I write letters. I write constantly, in a sense. And I assume the persona appropriate for the communication. I'm a publisher or an editor or whatever. And that's a bit of a stretch sometimes in that I don't think one should ever take oneself too seriously in this business. The moment you start to think of yourself as a publisher, the publisher—even though I have to assume that persona in order to make my way through the business day, that's not really the way I describe myself.

How do you describe yourself?
I think I'm acquiring my education in the public eye.

What are you being educated in?

Everything. Life and all of its vagaries. And all of its arts. I think it was my father who suggested to me that it's an extremely good idea to remain curious for all of your life. It's the only cure to boredom.

Do you have anybody working for you now, at McPherson and Company?

I wish. I have in the past had quasi-full-time assistants. I have an editor for my Italian projects, who's also the translator. His name is Henry Martin. In a sense he's not an employee but a partner for that part of the operation. He gets royalties as a translator and as the editor, and we find whatever money we can for him as a translator through special grants. But also, he's discovering—well, he brought a couple of fabulous Italian writers into English: Anna Maria Ortese and Giorgio Manganelli.

Okay, so where are we now? About 1980, I think.

I had a job in the city for a couple of years and more or less paid off the book. After a couple of years in Manhattan—Manhattan drove me crazy; the city's a hard place for a country boy like me. I mean I grew up in cities, but that's just too much steel and concrete. So I moved upstate and got a job managing a type shop with a cohort, another small publisher named George Quasha. He runs Station Hill Press. At that time he had put together an arts center which had various components: a printing plant, typesetting, a theater, a restaurant, various other activities. It was very dynamic. He was a real mastermind. He'd made it work utilizing CETA [Comprehensive Employment and Training Act] grants. It fell apart pretty naturally when the CETA program ended.

So I did that for a couple of years, and then in 1983 I was feeling frustrated. I had a number of good projects I wanted to do, but I was not getting the kind of critical review attention that I felt I ought to have been getting. So I decided that part of the problem was that I was seen as two entities—by the art world as Documentext, by the literary world as Treacle Press—and that I ought to find a way to have Treacle Press taken more seriously. And I finally decided that the best way to do that would be to name the whole operation for myself, to take both credit and blame and stand behind it. And McPherson and Company sounds, of course, like a much larger and older entity than it is. And it happened to work. By 1984 I was getting the kinds of attention I needed to get. I was getting reviewed in the *New York Times*. I'd never been able to break into the *Times* before. I was getting into *Publishers Weekly* consistently. I was getting into a lot of other papers. And I was switching over to some of the first distributors: I was one of the first presses in Consortium—I think it was in their second year—but only for a year.

Why did you—?

Well, they didn't know how to sell most of my stuff. These distributors employ commission sales reps and the commission sales reps, quite rightly, I suppose, want to be able to deal with conventional product, books that can be described in understandable terms where you don't have to reinvent the wheel. But a lot of the most interesting small press publishing has to do with reinventing the wheel every six months or so. So that's more or less my story with distributors.

And then, for quite a number of years, I put together my own groups of sales reps who pushed my stuff around the country and in and out of bookstores.

You contracted with commission sales reps?

Yes. And all this time I was doing book fairs in various cities and going to the ABA on occasion.

What was your experience like, having your own commission reps?

They were some wonderful people. The people who chose me, or who would allow me to wind up with them, were never terribly effective. Some of them were better than others, but, by and large, they were all pretty terrific people. I mean, they weren't taking on my books for the money. And it wasn't just for a little bit of prestige either. They genuinely enjoyed the stuff. Being able to communicate that to booksellers, though, is hard, especially when you've got a very long list, a big bag, and you—I guess the biggest problem that I have with the commission-sales-rep approach is that on occasion they'd be able to get me into the bookstores for a copy or two of each of my new list, but I was still being regarded by booksellers as an utterly marginal publishing operation, and it was really hell to pay to get them to reorder if they did sell out of the books.

There's a curious logic that keeps small presses down: If you succeed a little bit, well, fine, but go away; then if you're too weird, fine, we don't want you in the first place. It's really damned if you do, damned if you don't.

Yeah. It's perception. It isn't the book, it's the bookseller's perception of the book.
Yeah.

So you started McPherson and Company in—?
In '83 I named it. In '84 the first books came out.

How many books have you done? How many individual titles?
Sixty, maybe.

But it's not consistently four titles a year.
No. I've gone up to seven or eight some years, and one—last year, only one. This year, three, including one new edition. Next year, five.

Do you make a living at it?
Well, my accountant thinks so.

[Laughing:] You don't work at another job?
I don't right now. I've from time to time picked up a little freelance work here and there for a variety of things, but, basically, ten years ago I decided to just do this. And that's what I've done.

Do you have another source of income?
My wife has a part-time job. I don't have a whole lot of debt, and I'm reasonably successful in selling my books these days. I had a very big downturn about three years ago and was flooded with returns and saw my sales drop by half, and they kept going down even after that. At which point I also realized that not only was I no longer going to be able to get any grants from the National Endowment for the Arts— I did not rely on but I did enjoy over the years a number of grants from

the National Endowment for the Arts literature program, and much smaller grants from the New York State Council on the Arts. I still receive from time to time support from NYSCA but nothing from the NEA for several years, and I'm no longer even eligible to apply. I'm not interested in becoming a 501(c)(3) literary organization.

Why not?

Well, I don't believe in institutionalizing the—I don't think you can institutionalize the reasons for doing this kind of operation in the first place.

Ruth Gundle of Eighth Mountain is not a nonprofit but publishes poetry. She wants to own her own business. [See Gold 1996.] That's fairly common thinking among literary presses that don't go for grants, who don't incorporate 501(c)(3).

Which I didn't do. But I did get grants for quite some time. The NEA somehow got around the restrictions in order to be able to fund literary presses that didn't have 501(c)(3), because at the very beginning nobody had 501(c)(3). And they wanted to be able to fund literary presses so they kept that going until a substantial number of their constituency went 501(c)(3). And they were pushing 501(c)(3) as much as they possibly could.

Now my objection to 501(c)(3) is that it's very hard, if the NEA goes under, or if the literature program goes under, to turn a nonprofit into a for-profit without raising all kinds of red flags and having all kinds of legal problems. The other objection that I have with it is that it institutionalizes the organization, and I think that in many cases the literary vision in a literary publishing company comes from the founder, and I'm not sure that there's a *raison d'etre* beyond him or her. It's a very hard thing to share literary taste and vision. The failure of most collectives shows this. It seems to me also that it grows with the institutionalization of arts organizations, generally speaking.

What grows with that?

The drive to "institutionalize" literary presses—not merely as a convenience for grants organizations, but it follows the same trend in many other fields, art, music, et cetera. There are a lot of people who

264

run arts organizations who have no particular abilities in any of those particular arts. They have, basically, MBAs, quote unquote, in arts organization. It's a master's in arts administration, whatever that is exactly. But in any case, you go nonprofit, you have a board of directors, you spend a great deal of time simply raising money.

Have you thought about what will happen to your press after you kick the bucket?
Well, it's more likely that I'm going to have to deal with it before I kick the bucket. I think it will predecease me.

Oh, really?
Yeah. Probably. Well, I'm healthy [knocks on the table].

Well, if the press predeceases you, that means you give it up.
Yeah, sell it or...yeah.

You must have a strong identification with it. You've been doing this all your life. You're one of the few people I've interviewed who went right into it. There were some deviations, but you were going in this general direction all your life.
Pretty much. But the identification is...well, let me take as much credit as anyone wishes to give me, but.... What can I say? What do I really think? I'm interested in, as I said before, conducting my education in the public eye. And maybe at the public's expense. I'm interested in the concept of there being a literary contest, a perpetual contest between commercial forces and the real artistic impulses. And it seems to me that the function of a small literary press is to fuel that, and to make the discourse as dynamic as it possibly could be. Art is never finished. And it's not that the arts are progressing. I don't believe that at all. In fact, it's hard enough just to keep up with the past, never mind any advancement.

Of course, artists themselves are constantly returning to the past.
Art is a dialogue with the past. Art is attempting to locate the present with reference to the past, and by projecting something into the future. The present is only created by some sort of reference to the past,

by definition. It's hard to.... I mean I certainly want to continue, and I have to make a living somehow, so I'm not going to go off the deep end. But I never did. My notion of experimental work is not something that is experiment for experiment's sake. It's art wherever you find it. If somebody wants to describe work as experimental in pejorative terms, that's really more their business than mine. I think that the rules of all of the arts are there to be broken. That's one of the things that makes us interested in reading the work of new writers. There are certainly enough writers dead and gone to afford you a lifetime of reading pleasures. It's maybe wanting to tap into the Zeitgeist that drives you to discover what people's dialogue is at this moment. It's, you know, it's a guide to yourself, to your own thinking, to your own position in the moment.

In the interview I did with Barney Rosset, it was apparent—he may even have said this, but whether he did or not it was apparent to me that he regarded publishing as a form of self-expression. The books he selected to do and how he chose to do them were his way of expressing his interest in his own self.

Sure. I would agree. I mean I have to claim these children as my own, in a way, and try to make sense of my list for myself if for no one else. I don't think that publishers discover writers; I think that writers discover publishers. At least I prefer that formulation. Editors shouldn't take too much credit. Their batting average, if you look at the long term, is something on the order of well under .300. Maybe one out of eight or ten. Let's give the credit—I mean if they really knew what they were doing, you would think it would be a little higher, wouldn't you?

The idea of professionalism, or science, in publishing is just ludicrous.

That's for the public.

Lane Stiles and Marianne Nora
Mid-List Press

"One of the things I love about being in book publishing is all the things that come together. I like the physicality of books. I like the history of books. I like literature. I like designing. I like the visual aspects of it. I even like writing promotion and getting into marketing and those kinds of things."

"[E]verything that's learned in this society seems to be overheard in a conversation on the way to the bathroom."

I interviewed Lane Stiles and Marianne Nora at their home, which is also home to Mid-List Press, in south Minneapolis. Coming down the interstate that morning, I ran into a gloom so dense I had to turn on my headlights. It was not mist, nor rain, nor any kind of precipitation, but it was a day grayer than any I'd seen outside of Asia. The monsoons of tropical Asia come in on a dark sky, but this, whatever it would prove to be, sucked the color and light out of everything, substituting the gray of homespun. In the south, lightning flashed behind the clouds like an intermittent strobe. Yet there was no thunder. Two or three minutes before reaching the house, the sky crashed down in a roar of water. As I was gathering my things together after stopping the car, wondering how I was going to get the sixty feet or so to the house without getting myself and my pack soaked, Stiles came out with a large umbrella. He is a tall, slender, sandy-haired man who reminds you of the youthful Henry Fonda. He said that storms like this one were uncommon in September, but occurred regularly in July and August. That evening, a television weatherman said the storm was "phenomenal for this time of year."

We sat over coffee in the dining room. At the rear, where apparently there had been a porch or a mud room, there was now a workroom where Marianne Nora sat at a computer, and for the first part of the interview there was in the background the sounds of the telephone and the rhythmic humming grunt of the printer in operation. It was Tuesday,

267

September 16, 1997.

Stiles was born in 1952 in a little town in Missouri called Nevada. "Nevada is the same town John Huston was born in. I don't think anyone knows that. There's some kind of apocryphal story about his father being fire chief there, and the city burning down one night because he was drunk or something, and they left in the night. I don't think there's a bit of truth to it."

He grew up mainly in Joplin. His father is a retired insurance salesman, his mother a secretary. Both come from farming families. They are not readers, have no interest in literature. "I think about that often. Why did I come out this intellectual in this anti-intellectual climate, this person interested in books in an anti-book world down in the bible belt in rural southwest Missouri? I don't believe I was genetically programmed to do this. I can't tie it to any particular teacher. It seems like I've liked literature as long as I can remember, but it's a miracle to me. Now Marianne, it's easy to understand, because her father's very literary, very academic. Her mother is an actress, a former teacher, who's acted at the Guthrie—"

Nora, from the workroom: "I was supposed to be a doctor."

Stiles: "On Marianne's father's side, everybody's a doctor."

Stiles took a degree in English at Rice University but wanted to make films and enrolled in the University of Texas' MFA program in film-making. He decided he needed to go to Hollywood where he could work his way into movies by writing. During this period of decision making, he visited a friend in the Twin Cities and met Nora. They went to California together. "We actually got no closer to the movies than I am right now. But we started working in a bookstore there. Hollywood Book City on Hollywood Boulevard. It's right in the heart of Hollywood. We lived there about a year, decided we were too midwestern to take the culture and the weather, and moved back here to Minneapolis." He worked as a sales rep for The Bookmen, a book wholesaler and distributor, then as a bookseller. He returned to school, got a degree in elementary education and taught elementary school for five years. Then he went back to school—the University of Minnesota—for his doctorate in English.

Lane Stiles: I haven't finished my dissertation yet; I'm one of those. But during that time, the time when I went back to school, that was when Marianne and her father started up the press, in 1989, and I started helping with that. It was actually Marianne and her father who began the press. Her father lives in Washington, D.C. now. James Nora. He was a well-known cardiologist and geneticist who had written a novelization of his experiences with a heart transplant team in Houston—De Bakey and Cooley. They were the two notorious surgeons involved with the heart transplants in Houston. He tried to get it published for years and publishers all told him it was a mid-list novel and they weren't interested in mid-list novels. So he decided that what he would do was found a press that would publish mid-list books and he'd call it Mid-List. A kind of in-your-face to New York.

We've been told often that we should change our name. Marianne went to New York a few years ago to talk about paperback reprint rights with some presses. They all said, "The first thing you have to do is change your name."

You have to change your name before they'll consider sub rights?

LS: No, it's a piece of advice that they were happy to throw out. They liked our stuff. They just thought we should change our name. But I like the fact that it is somewhat prosaic.

Well, it's certainly making a statement. I didn't know much about your press except that it was a literary press. And I knew from the name of the press that it had something to do with the fact that so many mid-list writers were without homes now.

LS: Yeah. That became our mission then, to find other writers. And it primarily came down to first-time writers who are the mid-list writers who have the greatest difficulty getting published, as you know. So that was one reason why one of the first things we did was to start the First Series. The only conditions for submission were that you could never have published a novel or a book-length collection of poetry. We excluded chapbooks from that.

Now we have the First Series For The Novel, the First Series For Poetry, the First Series For Short Fiction, and the First Series For Creative Nonfiction. The latter two were added in the last few years— 1995 was our first year for Short Fiction, '96 for Creative Nonfiction.

Leslee Becker's *The Sincere Cafe* was our first Short Fiction winner. It's done really well. I don't know if you know Leslee or not. She's teaching at.... [calls to Nora in the workroom] What is the college that Leslee teaches at?

Marianne Nora: Fort Collins. Colorado State.

LS: Colorado State.

Is there a cash award associated with these prizes?

LS: We give a thousand-dollar advance and publication, and then a regular royalty deal. The poetry is a five-hundred dollar advance.

Are these all original paperbacks, or do you do hardback first?

LS: Most of our books are paperback. It's just been the last few years that there's been a shift to trade paper as a kind of literary form. People seem to prefer it. And the cost. And it doesn't seem to make that much difference to libraries anymore. In fact, there are some that even prefer the paperback since they're going to put on their own covers anyway. We brought Alfred Corn's first novel [*Part of His Story*] out this year in hardcover because we thought we had a good chance at subsidiary rights—paper reprint rights.

The first book in the series, *Same Bed, Different Dreams* by Hugh Gross, did come out in hardcover first. Simultaneous hardcover and paper.

What became of James Nora?

LS: He still provides guidance. He's still the publisher. When he was living in Denver, we split some of the functions of the press between Denver and here. What year was it that we moved everything here? We moved our entire operation—

MN: Nineteen ninety-three.

LS: 'Ninety-three. December '93 we moved our entire operation to Minnesota from Denver. Since it's moved here, Marianne and I have taken over everything.

One of the books that Marianne's father gave us to help us start the press was a medical and trade book that he'd written, called *The Whole Heart Book*. He'd gotten it back from Holt Rinehart, and he revised it and brought it out as *The New Whole Heart Book*, and that helped fund the press and get it off the ground. We were a for-profit press to begin with and we used projects like that to help us fund the literary aspects of it.

When he was running it, was he doing everything himself?
LS: Not everything. But it was primarily he and Marianne. He started out doing the typesetting and arranging for the fulfillment and production.

Was he accustomed to operating a business? Does he have his own practice?
LS: He wasn't really accustomed to doing business. That was one thing Marianne was good at and took over and has really improved immensely. Marianne has handled most of the accounting, and she standardized that and took care of it. He's still the publisher. Now he mainly provides editorial advice and support for us. He evaluates manuscripts and that sort of thing. Does some copy editing, other editorial kinds of functions. Marianne, as associate publisher and executive director, handles most of the day-to-day business—orders, accounting, shipping and fulfillment. I do all the design and typesetting, and then we both share editorial and marketing. My title is senior editor. [Both of us laugh.] You know, titles in small presses, you can hand them out. We sometimes hire freelance editors to help us out.

Are you working now outside the press?
LS: Yeah. A little over a year ago I took a job as senior editor with Fairview Press, which is a division of Fairview Health Services. And Fairview Health Services is a large complex of hospitals, clinics, health providers; it's now affiliated with the University of Minnesota hospital system. Essentially Fairview is a trade publisher within a large corporation. It's not really a publishing arm of the hospital. It's more just a trade publisher associated with the hospital, doing books that relate to health. [In 1998, Stiles was placed in charge of Fairview Press.]

What were you doing until then?
LS: I was teaching at the U. Teaching composition.

Did they give you a certain amount of time to finish your dissertation?

LS: I still have time to finish it. I've got about two years left, if I want to sit down and do it. I'm just so busy; I come home and work on this at night and weekends, and it's really hard to get around to it.

Yeah. I did one too, in another discipline. They gave me ten years to do it; I took eleven. [We laugh.]

LS: So did they approve it? Did you—?

Yeah.

LS: I should really do it. I mean I got this far. All I have to do is finish the dissertation. I actually had a book come out with U. Mass. Press. This is the paperback version of it. I was the coeditor on it. The article I wrote for that was going to be the basis of my dissertation. So I have the research done and I started writing it, but I— This is my scholarly interest: history of the book and studies in print culture. This book [Moylan and Stiles 1997] helped inaugurate U. Mass.'s new series in that. It's a really rapidly growing field, interdisciplinary.

I wasn't aware of it. But I'm not in academia anymore.

LS: The basic thesis of this book is that there's a very important interaction between material aspects of books and their textual aspects, or textual interpretation. And these are essays that historically tie together literature in America with aspects of material production and dissemination. Reading a book by its cover is a kind of cliché that's developed around that idea, but I don't think there are very many books quite like this. It's an approach, really, to interpretation, is what we wanted, because most of us were coming from English lit. Although there's an historian who wrote in this too.

One of the things I love about being in book publishing is all the things that come together. I like the physicality of books. I like the history of books. I like literature. I like designing. I like the visual aspects of it. Yeah, I like working with the graphic artist putting together the covers. I even like writing promotion and getting into marketing and those kinds of things.

That's the one thing I don't like. I do it, but I don't like it.

LS: It's frustrating, given what the market is right now. There are a lot of books being published in the English language. It's topped a hundred and sixty thousand a year. I don't know what it is in the United States, but it's—

Close to sixty thousand.
LS: Yeah.

Actually, England produces more books than we do.
LS: Yeah.

Smaller population. Presumably they print fewer copies per title. But they produce more titles.

LS: There's an enormous lot of books out there, and to get attention for the small number of books that we produce is getting more and more difficult. When we started in 1989 it looked like this infatuation with frontlist was about as bad as it could get, and it's just gotten worse and worse.

Now your series is called First Series. Do you do second books by the same authors?

LS: That's another thing that we've tried to grow into. We've started doing second books by authors. We're going to keep with them. There are a lot of first-book contests and first-book awards out there, fewer second books. And we feel like we're obligated to our writers to stick with them for more than one book. So last year we brought out *A Step in the Dark*, a second book by one of our First Series winners, Stephen Behrendt. He's at the University of Nebraska. A well-known scholar in British romanticism. This year, in another couple of weeks, this will be a second book [*Settling*] by a First poet that we published, Mary Logue. That's a galley for it there. Then next year we're hoping to do a second book by Neil Shepard who's the head of the *Green Mountains Review*. And we've done some second novels by people. The *Same Bed, Different Dreams* author, we did a second novel by him.

Does that revitalize the first book when you do a second by the

273

same author?

LS: You know, we're really not large enough to see that. And the time difference between when one comes out [and then the other], we haven't seen a huge effect yet in sales on the other books. Poetry, you're not going to see major sales anyway. I think maybe as we do start doing more second novels, even third novels, we may start seeing more things happen with the earlier books.

I do publish second and even third books by some authors. Fiction. And it does help sales on the first books. So maybe with the second book I can sell another hundred copies of the first book. Still, it's a hundred copies.

LS: Yeah. Yeah.

When you've printed only a thousand or fifteen hundred copies in the first place, that means something. But I find that cover art changes so much. If the book came out six or seven years ago and you still have that same edition in print, then store buyers are reluctant to take it because the artwork is dated.

LS: Yeah, we have been very careful in how we go to the trade. We try to stay out of the trade, actually, as much as we can. We're only doing paperbacks, and the returns—you can't handle the hurt books, you can't handle the shipping and so forth that some of the larger publishers can. We go to libraries. We do some direct mail.

How do you target libraries?

LS: Well, one thing that's always helped us is that we've gotten pretty good reviews for our books. And we find that a good *Kirkus* review will sell a thousand books without us even announcing it. We do some direct mail to libraries. That seems to produce sales. I think if you produce a quality product and just go through the review process, that's a long way toward selling it. And that's something we've been real fortunate in from the very first. The trade journals have been good to us and we've gotten major national reviews. Not always kind, but most of them have been. It's a real crapshoot with those journals, because they have two hundred and fifty words and two hundred and forty-nine are summary, and then it's, what is the one sound bite gonna be? And what kind of mood is the reviewer in? Are they gonna be serious about the book or are they showing off, or what? Sometimes it's tiresome how much showing off goes on, how shallow some of the reviews are.

Sometimes it's just funny. I just came out with a book. When Kirkus *reviewed it, they started off by comparing it to Ovid and Kafka. Actually, it didn't occur to me to compare it to either Ovid or Kafka, but it works, in a way. I mean I can see where the reviewer—he's having fun. But then the last line—you know how* Kirkus *is, they gotta zing you on the last line—I guess he couldn't figure out anything else to say because he liked the book, obviously, so he said, "But when you compare it to"—and he named some popular thriller—"But when you compare it to" this popular thriller, then it's "too literary by half." [Both of us laugh.] I just loved it.*

LS [still laughing]: How can you win when they say something like that? I mean, what can you do?

Well, of course, anybody in the trade who is used to reading those reviews knows what's going on.

LS: Yeah. If you compare it to Marvel Comics, there's not nearly enough pictures.

That's right. [We're still laughing.] Oh, let's see. Are you a 501(c)(3)?

LS: Mm hm.

When did you—?

LS: In December of '93 is when we decided to go—when we moved everything here we decided we were going to go nonprofit, and that's when we filed with the IRS. We were approved about a year later. We're different from a lot of the other small presses here in town in that we haven't done a lot of grant writing. We've really relied on book sales. We still maintain a kind of trade approach to what we do. For philosophical reasons, in that we have our mission and we want to do what we want to do and we don't want to create projects for grants. We also want to be able to build a plan, have steady growth, and if you're at the mercy of funders and you lose a major funder, suddenly your revenue picture changes drastically. But the main thing was that we didn't want our acquisitions to be driven by the needs of our funders rather than what we wanted to do.

Then why go nonprofit?

MN [from the workroom]: Well, there's different kinds of funders. You've just gotta have a combination—

LS: Yeah. We found out—like the state arts board, we get funded through the local arm of the state arts board, the Metropolitan Regional Arts Council. That's a process that we have gotten involved in. In fact, we're going to put a grant application in in a couple of days for that. And that's worked for us. It's open and the issues are clear. We don't really have to tailor what we're doing. What we're doing already fits what they want. We have gone out to some funders, but we don't let that drive what we do.

MN [coming into the dining room]: Actually the purpose of being a 501(c)(3), for a small press like Mid-List, is that most of the support would come from individuals, and that gives them a reason to support worthy causes. Another thing is that we put in for aesthetic awards, and usually they want 501(c)(3) status. But we're pretty choosy about it. I don't know if you saw the article in *Time Magazine* that was done on arts funding in the United States. It said that for corporations and foundations, funding for the arts has always been driven by public relations. A lot of foundations try to do public good works, and often that's at odds with aesthetics. I mean, you can see what's happened with the NEA. It's happening with foundations and with corporate funders. They'll decide one year that their whole focus is going to be children and families, and so a lot of arts organizations will try to cram their aesthetic to fit that. Which means that they acquire on that basis, they edit on that basis, they market on that basis, just so they can achieve their funding goals. That's just not very interesting to us.

LS: The only reason we're doing this is to do the books that we want to do, and if a funder will help us do the books we want to do, then that's great. They may not want to do the stuff we want to do, and that's fine, too.

MN: The problem is not just in literature, but it's in music, it's in theater. Basically, if you're a small press, foundations and corporate funders say you have a product to sell. So either do our product or do your own. Pay for it yourself.

LS: One thing that's easy to forget is that thinking of literary presses as nonprofit arts organizations is a fairly new idea. Scott Walker really started doing a lot of that with Graywolf [i.e., Graywolf Press], convincing funders that that was something they should fund. I think the IRS is still a little hesitant sometimes to grant nonprofit status if your mission is primarily literary as opposed to educational.

I think Curbstone—I don't know if they were the first, but they were one of the first—they got their nonprofit status in the '70s, and I think Scott Walker did in the early '80s.

LS: Yeah. That's when he came here [i.e., to the Twin Cities].

MN: Milkweed Editions was in the '80s and Coffee House—I think they started as educational before they switched over. [She returns to the workroom.]

LS: Did Curbstone find that funders were immediately interested in them? I was thinking that funders' being amenable to funding literary presses seems to be somewhat more recent. In fact, some still think of it as a different entity than an orchestra or a ballet company.

It took Curbstone years to get nonprofit status because there was so little precedent.

LS: Are you nonprofit?

No. For the reasons that you cited about doing what you want to do, I haven't gone that route.

LS: Yeah. We can have essentially the best of both worlds if we want. We can act like do-what-we-want-to-do, but we can solicit contributions from individuals who are sympathetic to what we do. If funders match with us, we'll go and talk to them; if they don't, we don't have to.

I do go for awards, but my own rule is that I have to sign the contract for the book before I go for it. Because otherwise I find myself slipping into that frame of mind—

LS: Yes.

—where you start looking for a book that will win the award.

LS: Yes. That's a kind of integrity that's easy to lose. There's a little slippery slope I've seen in the nonprofit world where people slide into that pretty easily. Because you're always on the edge anyway; it's just such a hard battle.

Yeah, that extra thousand or five thousand or seven thousand dollars, when you do get it, it's just amazing—I mean the feeling you get—and it isn't a matter of quality. At least I don't think that the quality of what wins that award is better than that of a number of other books that are, or could be, up for consideration. It's just having that relief from the financial pressure for a while.

LS: Yeah. Yeah, I know the feeling.

You know, I talked to Barney Rosset—I was telling you earlier before we started taping. When he sold Grove Press, he sold it for two million dollars, and he said that was actually about half of what his family had put into it over thirty-five years. It's interesting that a press that size—one of the largest presses in New York in the '60s—lost half the money they put into it.

LS: That doesn't seem to mean much anymore. You just look at HarperCollins cutting a hundred titles off their list. And the mergers. There are so many hyphenated names out there, I don't know who owns who anymore. I think two or three major media conglomerates own everything.

There are eight. Six are American and two are European, according to the article that appeared in The Nation *last spring [see Miller 1997].*

LS: It's very interesting sociologically to consider that at the same time that you have this mass consolidation of the larger publishers, and the media reduced down to just a few companies, you have, on the other hand, through the desktop-publishing revolution, a gigantic rise in small presses and alternative presses out in the hinterlands.

In the literature on underdeveloped nations, there is what they call a dual economy. There is that gross economy at the national and

278

international levels, and then there is the way that people deal below that. Often, in poorer countries, it's simply barter. In the United States I think what we're seeing is cottage industries starting up again. And small presses are part of that. It isn't only small presses. People sell tee-shirts, for example. They buy them, put a print on them, and sell them. The United States is generally regarded as a developed country, but perhaps in some ways, some segments of our economy have more in common with the secondary economies of underdeveloped countries than with the economies dominated by the megacorporations.

LS: I think, for a small press, an important issue is, how do you avoid marginalization? How do you make a difference with what you're doing, rather than just becoming part of this barter-trade segment down here? How do you get where the power is? And because there's a lot of politics and power involved in literary reputation, the institutionalization of these texts— I don't know whether you should be content to play in your little arena down here, or whether you should try to be devious and subversive and figure out ways that you can break into those—you know, get your books out there, play the big guys' game a little smarter than they do—kind of a guerrilla attack on the huge mass market out there.

Yeah, I used to call it guerrilla publishing. That's the same question I wrestle with all the time. Because you want to have an impact. Regardless of why you get started, if you stay with it, you're eventually going to want to have an impact. I suppose course adoptions is part of it, if you can do that. The frustration comes from knowing that we do better work than the bigger publishers, but we don't have the mechanism to get it to market like they can.

LS: There has to be some kind of turning point in this frontlist mania. Like the superstores—their niche came when the B. Daltons and Waldenbooks were stocking twenty-five copies of only a couple thousand titles, and they found out that if they had two copies of seventy thousand titles, then they'd sell more books. I think the big publishers are going to realize that there's a limit to how much money they can keep throwing into this frontlist market and get payoff. I think they know it now; they just can't get out of it. They're trapped in it.

MN [in the dining room again]: But the logic seems to be screwed up. Did you see this article in the *Fort Worth Star-Telegram* [Guinn 1997] on the fading midlist and HarperCollins? It was talking about how much money Ballantine lost on Johnnie Cochran's book. They paid him four point four million dollars—

LS: That was the advance.

MN: —and made like nothing. So they say that the only way to fix it is to get rid of midlist books. [All of us laugh.] It's fascinating.

Not the blockbuster, but the midlist books.

MN: Exactly.

LS: We've started a correspondence with a literary editor at Avon. They're going to start up the Bard line again, and make it a literary line.

Yeah, they called me too.

LS: He was talking about establishing a relationship with us, because he thinks a lot of the most interesting work is being done by small literary presses. I don't know if that's going to mean anything or lead to anything, but I think there will eventually develop an audience need for something that's different, a little better, and since small presses are getting the better work, they're going to start making deals with small presses. They'll use them the way literary agents moved in and did some of the work that manuscript readers and editors used to do at some of the houses. And the small presses will be developing the material which the larger presses can then use some of their mass-marketing skills with.

Well, one of the points that Eric Kampmann [see interview, this volume] made when I interviewed him was that larger publishers look at the small presses as farm teams.

LS: Yeah. That's a good metaphor.

But they're looking at the books we develop or the authors we develop as fitting into their market. I'm not talking about quality. Quality doesn't matter. We're talking about the market. In fact, when I see that a novel is published by Random House or Doubleday, I assume it isn't worth my reading. [Stiles and Nora laugh.] Occasionally I'll scan one in a bookstore to see whether I'm wrong: I'm never wrong.

LS: It may not matter if they have no sense of quality if they go ahead and distribute quality books. If they don't understand what the market mechanisms are, why people might be interested in quality, but they realize that they sell, maybe it doesn't matter.

But they would have to realize that they sell.
LS: Yes.

There's a mind-set against quality books—
LS: Yes.

—if the book is categorized as quality. I was recently talking with somebody who used to rep for me, and he said, "Well, of course, your books—there are only a few independent stores who will carry them." But actually I sell most of my books through Barnes and Noble, proving that my books can be sold in general trade stores. And he could not comprehend that. It was the way he thought about it.
LS: Yeah.

Somebody has to present the book to the store buyer, and it has to be packaged in a way that the buyer finds attractive. They don't read the books. They base their decision on how it looks.
LS: Right. There was an article about publishers essentially becoming book packagers for the chains. There was an example of a publisher running a cover by Barnes and Noble and letting Barnes and Noble decide what the cover of the book was going to be [Carvajal 1997]. The final cover didn't really reflect the contents or the quality of the book at all. There isn't always any connection between the inside and the cover. Marketing may not read the books.

Well, they won't. I shouldn't say they won't: it's not likely that they will. I discussed this issue with Juris Jurjevics [of Soho Press: see interview, this volume] who worked in corporate publishing for a long time. I had been told that in corporate publishing the editors and marketing people don't read the book, that they decide whether or not to publish a book without having read it. So I asked Juris if that was so. I was interviewing him and Dan Simon of Seven Stories. Simon said he had heard that, too. And Juris said, Well, it's possible that nobody will have read the book. Or maybe of the seven or nine or twelve people who are sitting at the conference table, one or two or them will have. But that's not the issue. What you're looking at is projected profit and loss. That's what it comes down to.

LS: Yeah.

What they do is, they categorize the book. They'll say, "This is personal essays," or creative nonfiction, however you want to term it, and they'll look at other creative nonfiction that they've published and they'll say, "We can expect to sell this many and we can anticipate that the production of the book and the overhead for the book will cost this much. Do we want to do this?"

MN: But wouldn't you think that, given that kind of scenario where they're trying to make as much money as they can with a book, that they would—they're not going to read it, and the marketing people aren't going to read it—don't you think that they would give the author more input into the process? Most authors get no input into the marketing plans for their books, or cover design, or any of that. So if they don't read it and they don't know what it's about, how in the world—I mean every book is written for a specific audience, and the author knows that. So you get all these mismatches—I read someplace that out of a hundred books sold in the United States, only ten of those are actually read.

Really?

MN: Yeah.

I didn't know that.

MN: They don't bother to read them. I mean, you get it for a gift and someone said it was good, and, you know—everything that's learned in this society seems to be overheard in a conversation on the way to the bathroom. Nothing is firsthand anymore. So people buy books and then they don't read them. We know ours are read. I mean that's for sure, because we do hand-selling here. You've gotta want our books to find them. [Stiles and I laugh.]

Well, I don't know why....I think the question you asked me was,

282

Why don't they let the author know why his book was rejected instead of letting him feel that there is something lacking in the quality. I think it's a matter of their intentionally allowing the author to believe in an illusion. Allowing the public to believe in an illusion. Because they do promote themselves as doing quality work, as doing good work. Those of us who know better don't talk about it very much. It really isn't in our interest to talk about it publicly.

MN: Well, we just got a whole bunch of stuff from Avon. And I'll tell you, that stuff is good. There is good work that's being done by the big publishers.

Yeah, there is good work. But it's as though the good ones are hiding out in these little crannies.

MN: Well, I think it is frustrating to have a literary book pulled into a marketing venue, and people discussing things that they haven't read. The last time I was in New York I went to see some of the big publishers, and because I have an imprint called Mid-List they were kind of like, "Eewww. Oh, that makes us feel so bad." But every one of them said, "You do the kind of book we would like to do." And I'm like, "Well, why can't you do it?"

The impression I get from editors who have seen my stuff at the BEA—they would react in that same way—the sense I got from them is that they're ashamed.

MN: Yeah, they are. And I'm surprised by that. I suppose it is this bottom-line mentality. I used to work in the brokerage business, so I'm rather familiar with the bottom-line mentality. But it seems strange that they're always wrong. I mean, if profitability is what they're really looking for, then they should produce books that people want to read. If I was head of Simon and Schuster and someone came to me and told me, "Well, people buy these books and then they return them"—because everything's a big lending library out there—"and they don't like the books, and they think they could do better writing their own books," I'd say, "Well, we'd better change our aesthetic then." It's not the marketing that's the problem, it's the aesthetic. And then people will buy them, and they will share them, and books will do what books have always done, which is being passed from one person to another.

283

LS: There are still audiences out there. In the frontlist world, if that audience does not exceed fifty thousand, they're not interested. So a reading group of fifty thousand—which to me is huge—that's not sufficient to sustain a book anymore. That's why the midlist books are not being published.

MN: Well, what is sustaining books?

LS: Mass media. Marketing campaigns.

MN: It's nothing but marketing if the books aren't actually being sold. Because they're all being returned; eighty percent of them come flying back in your face—so they're not being sold. They're being marketed for sub rights only, and a lot of small presses are starting to do that too.

Some small presses are taking on books from even smaller presses and doing them as paperbacks. I believe [a certain press] does that. They only do about twenty-five titles a year, but they're really good at subsidiary rights sales.

MN: Well, Permanent Press. You read the "My Say" [Shepard 1995] from the head of Permanent Press. He has the same kind of concept, although he is for-profit. He looked at places like Graywolf and Coffee House and Milkweed, and he was so envious of these huge grants they get, NEA and Lila Wallace and all this stuff, and he just decided it's not worth it. Stay small, get the work out there, sell the subsidiary rights, the foreign rights, and you'll be fine. The big publishers are just trying to sell movie rights. It's all movies. There's this huge industry that's so hungry. Every one of our books—I'm sure they call you, too—rrrring! There they are again, send them a—

Every time the reviews come out.

MN: They get all sweaty, you know. You think something's going to happen.

LS: I love those people who call up and say, "Are the rights available?" And then, "Goodbye." That's a nice job if you can get it.

MN: But it's a very hungry market. With all the new cable stations popping up everywhere, people are trying to turn everything into a visual art. Because of that, that's where the money is. And the big publishers, they don't have a love of the book. It's either audio or it's going to go to movies.

The big publishers are owned by the movie companies.
LS: Yeah. Time Warner.
MN: So it's just feeding this—

It's a closed loop now.
MN: Yes, it is.

And there is a lot of frustration—at least I sense from the people I've talked with in that part of the industry that there is a lot of frustration on the part of some editors.
MN: Yeah. This is the cultural artifact that they love and that they're used to dealing with, and it's really pretty much being swept aside. Because the focus is on getting the two hundred and fifty thousand dollar advance from the studios. It's not the same sort of match that it used to be. It used to be, for an editor, he had this vision of somebody sitting there, reading it. It doesn't happen anymore.

Yet.... One of the authors whose novel I published also wrote a grammar. And he sent it to Random House and they kept it for a year and a half, sending it to one publisher after another within their group, because two editors liked it. Essentially they acted as agent for it within their own group, but they still could not get anyone to take it. Their publishers felt that they would not sell enough copies to justify publishing it. Actually, I can see where they would be suspicious of it, because it's very good writing. It's very fine writing. You've got a fine writer who is producing a grammar, and I could see where it would frighten Random House and Crown and whoever else. I could see them saying, "God, what a great idea. If only he wrote worse." [All three of us laugh.]
LS: Well, that's what we thought when we started the press. It is an opportunity. There should be really high quality books out there that we can publish, and it seems to me that there are. I think it's easy to forget that historically books and commerce have always existed tenuously together. We were just talking about marketing not matching up with what's inside. There's a nice essay on Melville, about how Harper marketed him as a travel writer, travel writing being a genre that

285

everyone could understand in the mid-nineteenth century. *Typee* and *Omoo*, even though they were a little idiosyncratic, fit into it in a way. When he started producing stuff like *Moby Dick* and some of his more eccentric work, they still marketed him as Melville, author of *Typee* and *Omoo*, and audiences didn't know how to read him. They still wanted to read him as a travel writer. Melville's relationship with his publishers was pretty terrible. But the up side of that story is in the 1920s, when American literature was institutionalized in the academy, Melville was one of the first saints of American literature; he was resurrected. So it tells us that the institutions that we can look to—like you were saying, course adoptions—ways that we can get our books to readers, get our books out there—

MN: Also, part of our mission is to work with other 501 (c)(3)s. And we do fundraisers for them where we use our books and our authors to bring people in, and to introduce our authors to different audiences than they're used to reading before. I think that's—you gotta get the hay down where the goats can get it.

LS: One thing we say a lot when we talk about what we do is that when we publish books, we want literally to publish them in the sense of making them public, because it doesn't do any good to kill a lot of trees and put out this artifact. You've got to have readers engage it. So that's one reason why having a trade look for our books, making them look professional, getting rid of the preconceptions people have about a small press look— We want to play the game smart. That's so we can get the book to readers, because a book doesn't mean anything unless it's read.

MN: All publish means is to make public. Got to get it out there.

LS: That's one reason why we feel good that it gets in so many libraries. We think it gets to more readers that way.

I read something by Gary Snyder recently where he said that he wished he would have gone out on the road and read publicly earlier in his life. He hadn't realized how important it is for a poet or an author to establish a following. I think that's so. Of course, you don't know what's going to happen after the death of the author. Still, I think that the best information is passed by word of mouth. Somebody sees you and tells somebody else about you. That's why I think course adoptions are impor-

286

tant—not that they always adopt the best books—

LS: No.

—but you've got one generation handing over to another.

LS: Yeah, you need some kind of literary institution, or what Richard Broadhead calls a "paraliterary institution," to take it up somehow. And that word of mouth is more powerful if certain kinds of people are talking about it. Certain networks.

Yeah. Agents of influence.

LS: There seems to be—I don't know if anyone has ever done a study of this—there's an issue of culture and book clerks and handselling and how do those.... Like, say, in Borders bookstores, a whole bunch of clerks will—there's a culture where somehow they communicate. I don't know how it is, but they'll take up a work that they think has some quality. What was that, *Snow Falling on Cedars*, wasn't that the name of it? I think that was like a Northwest Coast independent [bookstore] and then a Borders-handselling thing that caught on locally and then went national.

I don't know who the publisher was, but I think they bought into one of those Barnes and Noble promotion schemes. That's what I was told.

LS: It was?

MN: It was.

LS: So they bought into—okay. I thought there might be a kind of informal culture there.

How many books a year do you do now?

LS: We're doing at least five a year. That's set. We do the four in The First Series and then we do one second book, at least, of poetry. And then we see what we can do after that. It's a comfortable number of books; we can handle that.

I can see why you're not finishing your dissertation.

LS: Yeah. We get so many submissions. For The First Series, we get well over a thousand submissions. And we try to be very diligent about reading every manuscript. I think that's one thing—if writers knew that some real person actually reads the manuscript and treats it with some respect, they'd be a lot more inclined to come to a small press. It's a privilege that a lot of writers don't experience anymore.

My experience has been—and John Oakes [of Four Walls Eight Windows] said the same thing—that most of the manuscripts I get unsolicited, which is almost everything I get—
LS: Yeah.

—are pretty good. But they've come to the wrong place. Is that your experience?
LS: Yes. We try to set no preconditions on manuscripts. We want to be open to anything. But we have tendencies, and they're going to come out. Plus, we have guidelines for submission. You know, there are certain times of the year that we read poetry submissions; if you've not published before, we prefer you send the entire manuscript during this time, rather than querying. If people would write first for guidelines, it would save everybody a lot of trouble. And then read the publisher's works for appropriateness: Does your work fit into—? Our personal taste is that we shy away from stuff that seems overly experimental or academic, because we really do want books to reach their audiences. These audiences don't have to be huge. If a thousand people get some value out of it, that's a big enough audience for us. But if it's fifteen academics, I'm less interested in that, whatever tour de force it is. That's just our taste. There are plenty of small presses out there that devour experimental work. Readers need to educate themselves about that.

How big a print run do you do of, say, a novel?
LS: A novel? We've done as low as a thousand, as high as twenty-five hundred.
MN: Three thousand. We did three thousand.
LS: We did three...? Oh yeah, we did three because that's gone back to print. This one here, we haven't even begun to market this one like we could. *The Latest Epistle of Jim* [by Roy Shepard] got a starred review in *Kirkus*, a starred review in *Booklist*, and really nice reviews in *Publishers Weekly* and *Library Journal*, and that just took off with the

288

libraries. And we did three one-thousand-run printings. It's a very nice little novel about a Midwestern minister who's in a middle-age crisis about his career. It's a very nice little book. I think we could take it to religious bookstores and it would do real well. I think there's a lot of potential left in it.

[Looking at a copy of the book:] This is a book, had it been offered to me, I would have taken seriously just from the way he constructs his sentences.

MN: He's a poet. Because of the First Series Award, a lot of people come to us who have published poetry before but have never published a novel, or have never done creative nonfiction. Most of them have done something else. Usually they come from poetry or, if they're novelists, then they're doing their first book of poetry with us. I think what's good about the book is that it really strikes a chord in terms of what's going on with religion and the search for spirituality. David Hare's new play at the Guthrie is about that. There seems to be a lot of interest in what's happened to our institutions, the institutions that our parents built. They're pretty much crumbling.

We feel that they are. They may not be, but we feel that they are. I think it depends on what we regard as an institution and how we look at it. I think the idea of a dual economy that I was talking about earlier is a profitable way of looking at it.

MN: I think we find ourselves, especially because of television and the tabloid press, fearing that we live in a broken world. So there's this major urge to find our spiritual center, to create instead of destroy. Yet churches are closing, universities keep raising tuition, which makes it more and more difficult for people who are not extremely wealthy to become educated—

For certain, the world is changing very fast, and in ways few of us like. At least the country is. The boundaries between socioeconomic classes are becoming so much more rigid. Nevertheless, all the people who may have been middle class in our parents' era, or even in our era, and whose grandchildren or children will not be—those children or grandchildren are still going to be there, they are still going to be living people who are going to do something with their lives.

MN: Well, I sure hope so. I mean, I come from a generation that says he who dies with the most toys wins. And they're not building the institutions of faith and learning and art and culture.

But your father started this press. It's on a much smaller scale than what we would like to see, and many of these presses die within the first couple of years. Nevertheless, some persevere. You've been going since 1989, right? That's eight years. I've been publishing for fourteen years. It's a matter of accepting the losses, and going ahead. You have your own way of dealing with it financially, but I'll bet you're underwriting a lot of it yourselves.

MN: We don't take salaries. So that helps. [She and Stiles laugh.] And we survive on the sales of books. When everything breaks down to money and how to get money and how to get even more money than you had before, you lose your sense of what a mid-list book is. I guess I want to leave you with that. Because a lot of people get rejected from large trade houses and even from literary houses that say, "This is a mid-list book." Now what the publisher is saying is, "I'm not going to make any money with this." What the author needs to know is that mid-list is an aesthetic term.

LS: It's a trade term, but it means it's well written.

MN: Faulkner was a mid-list author. Hemingway was a mid-list author. Let's face it, this is where new and emerging writers were nurtured by their publishers. And there used to be a great deal of pride in that. I think if every one of the major publishers went back to that sort of publishing, they would see their book sales increase instead of fall. You can't go any place in this country where you don't trip over bookstores. We went into a fabric store, picking up something for a book Lane was doing, and they had a huge table in the middle of the store, with the polyesters and the tattered lace—books, seventy percent off. These were novels. Stop at any grocery store now, they'll have a big bin of discounted books by the front door.

What it says also, I think, is that people will buy books if the price is right. But because there are so many middlemen between the publisher and the public the price is driven up to where most people

290

can't afford them.

MN: Sure. But I think we're just drowning in books, because most publishers overprint. And they're left with them in warehouses. I mean, sometimes I have nightmares about this—I get all sweaty, ugh. I mean, there're just all these books and we're drowning in them.

LS: I was just thinking that the practical aspects of what we were talking about, of who is going to be reading these books—are you going to be talking to Emilie Buchwald [of Milkweed Editions]? I know she's very conscious of the fact that we create what can possibly become rarified artifacts unless there is a literary culture that continues to sustain it. It has to be more that just a small press publishing boom. It has to be something that sustains readership too. That's why she started those adolescent books of hers. They're a little higher quality fiction than they get in some of the baby-sitter, book-club stuff. We need to think about those institutions too. How do we continue to develop readers out there?

I think it definitely is linked to quality of education. The quality of public school education in the United States. I'm a counselor in a prison for adolescents. And sometimes I'll read to some of them. I'll pick books that I like and that I think they might like. And they know the difference between something of quality and something not. They know. They have not been educated that way, but they know. They know because they feel something.

MN: Right.

LS: It is a matter, then, of getting it out to them.

Yeah, but that's the question we go back to: how to do it on a scale large enough to have an impact. Regardless of how we get the books out there, we don't seem to be able to get beyond a certain threshhold.

LS: That's the next thing we have to start doing. We just jumped on the web this week.

MN: I've gotten four calls in the last couple days from Amazon [i.e., Amazon.com] because they're hot-linked to us. And I think that's a great way to sell books.

LS: There are some issues. We were talking about—we're doing an event at Barnes and Noble and we're hot-linked to Amazon.com.

291

What's our relationship to the independents? I was real cautious when I was putting our site up. Am I gonna hot-link us? How am I gonna do that, you know, because I thought.... I just see the internet as a wave of the future. And I think we gotta get the books out there any way we can. And I think we'll do what we need to do without capitulating ethically.

Allan Kornblum
Toothpaste Press; Coffee House Press

"I'm a child of the Left... [M]y parents moved when I was a year old. They integrated the building they were living in. When they moved out they transferred their lease to a black couple. It was an all-white building. I heard Martin Luther King's 'I Have a Dream' speech. My father took me to it when I was fourteen. To have a book I've published listed as an ideal teaching tool in a magazine called *Teaching Tolerance*—that made me feel real good."

Allan Kornblum and I sat in a small conference room in the midst of the Coffee House Press offices in Minneapolis, surrounded by the comings and goings of staff. He warned me that it got stuffy in this room, but that if we opened the doors, the noise would interfere with the interview. It did not get so stuffy that we had to open the doors, though it was only a couple of hours after the terrific rainstorm I drove through in order to talk with Lane Stiles and Marianne Nora [see their interview, this volume]. Now, in the afternoon, it was still humid, even if the sky was clear and the sun was out.

I told Kornblum that we had met once before, when he was at Elliott Bay Book Company in Seattle to talk about book printing and its history. He calculated that it must have been in 1993, but he didn't remember me. At the time of this interview, he had been married for twenty-five years and had two children. The older was about to begin her first year of college; the younger was in grade school.

Kornblum was born in mid-February 1949 to a mother who was a teacher and a father who was a social worker.

I lived in New York City from birth till about the age of one. My parents then moved to New Jersey, then to Everett, Massachusetts, then Chelsea, Massachusetts, and I went to junior high school and high school in Wilmington, Delaware. I went to NYU in the fall of 1967 as a voice-education major, envisioning myself in the future as a high school choir director. And I dropped out in March of 1968 as part of that whole generation of people who turned on, tuned in, and dropped out, feeling that college was somehow, at least at that moment, irrelevant to my life. I moved to Boston in the fall of 1968 and then back to New York in the fall of 1969. So I lived for one year in New York as a young adult, then a year in Boston, then another year in New York before moving to Iowa in 1970. And I arrived on July third, and as I got off the bus from New York I picked up a paper and saw the account of the bombing in Madison. And there were pictures of the four young men who were wanted, and one of them was the brother of a girl I had a crush on in high school. David Fine. I don't know if David ever turned himself in or got caught, or what. I think he may be the one who never did get...uncovered. Wherever poor David is, I wish him well. In any event, I stayed in Iowa from July of 1970 to August of '85. Which is when we moved here.

Were you in Iowa City?

I lived in Iowa City from July of 1970 till August of '72. So that's about two years in Iowa City.

You were in the creative writing program at the University of Iowa?

Yes and no. Formally, the creative writing program is a graduate program. The way they structure that, or did at that time, was to have four fiction writers and four poets on staff each year. And then each of those had a graduate assistant. If you were an undergraduate and wished to participate in the creative writing program, each semester, prior to the semester, you would send in a sample of your work. The best students studied with one of the four poets or fiction writers who were guests of the workshop for that year. The remaining students would study with a graduate assistant. During my period there, whenever I submitted work I was accepted by whoever was the teacher, who was, you know, one of the real poets. So I studied with Don Justice and Jack Marshall and Anselm Hollo while I was there.

I'd say Anselm and Jack might share a sensibility, although they're a little different. They're about as different from Don Justice as one could imagine. But I was really impressed by Don Justice's ability to work with students whose work was drastically different from his own. I recall students at times asking me to explain the strategy of my poems, and I really did not have the critical vocabulary to articulate what I was all about. And although my work was just absolutely on another planet from Don's, Don completely understood what I was doing and was able to explain it to the rest of the class. I was so impressed, and rather flattered, and I still hold him in very high regard. He's a great poet, I suppose; his work doesn't speak to me. But I have the highest regard for his integrity as a person and as a teacher.

Anselm originally is from Finland, and spent about eight years in England as a news broadcaster for the BBC. This was in the late '50s, early '60s that he worked as a broadcaster, and fell in with a lot of poets in that area. He also spent some time studying in Germany, and then he began corresponding with poets in the United States, and Paul Blackburn brought him to SUNY at Buffalo, I believe in '68. And Anselm has been in this country ever since, sort of vaguely associated with the New York school of poets and with Black Mountain.

Did you get a degree from Iowa?

No, I dropped out in '72. In 1970, when I moved to the University of Iowa—well, let me back up. When I dropped out in '68, I started reading a lot more, and when I was working at a book distribution warehouse in Boston I came upon an anthology edited by Paul Carroll, called *The New American Poets*. And I noted that, of the poets I admired in the anthology, the ones I liked the most, about half of them were associated with the St. Mark's Church Poetry Project, and quite a few of the others were teaching at the University of Iowa. So I began a plan. I thought, Okay, let's move back to New York, spend a year studying at St. Mark's, and then apply to the University of Iowa and start college there. And that's exactly what I did.

During that year in New York, during which I did the midnight to eight-thirty shift at the post office in Grand Central Station and attended classes at St. Mark's Church Poetry Project and at the New School, I came to get this feeling that one of the coming-of-age rituals for a young poet on the make was to edit a little magazine for a year or two. When I was accepted at the University of Iowa I had just made a group of friends in New York, I had high hopes of meeting a new group of interesting friends at Iowa, and I thought that mix would form the basis of an interesting magazine. And I announced to the friends I had made in New York that I had been accepted at Iowa and would be moving there in the summer, and that I was going to start a magazine and that, as soon as I got there, they should send me work. And as soon as I got to Iowa I started making the rounds of people who seemed to be interesting, asking them for work. And by August I had produced the first issue of my mimeographed magazine, *Toothpaste*.

That September, while looking at the catalogue of courses offered by the University of Iowa, I noted that a course titled "Intro. to Typography" was offered. In my mind I envisioned Harper and Row, which was what they were called at the time, someday publishing my book of poetry, and I thought that if I took this class I would know how they were doing it. I was certainly unaware that I was about to take a class in letterpress printing and that Harper and Row's books hadn't seen metal type in many a year. Nor did I realize that there was a whole universe, a whole little world of fine-press printing. And I certainly did not know that the professor with whom I was about to study was internationally regarded as one of the great living fine-press printers in the world—Harry Duncan. I, with the arrogance of youth, assumed that the classroom lectures were not going to be of great interest to me, since what I wanted to learn was how they actually printed books. So, to my shame, I admit that I skipped at least half of Harry's lectures. I produced a letterpress pamphlet of six of my poems that showed absolutely no sign of either talent or taste. It is a graphic mishmash of minor disastrous proportions.

Did you feel that way at the time?

Well...yes and no. I knew immediately, once it was done, that it just hadn't jelled. What then happened was another student in the class approached me and indicated that he was something of a minor collector, and that his idea of a collection was to get projects that were done by students of a typography laboratory in Iowa City, and in some instances to continue to collect work by students of Harry Duncan. And would I trade my project for his?

I was more than happy to do so and I gave him my little pamphlet and he gave me this stunning little thing. I doubt that it was much larger than three by four and a half inches. It was a collection of very, very short poems by an excellent poet. It was printed on Wookey Hole Mill paper, which was a hand mill from England, long since folded. It was what's called a cold press paper, which means that— A hot press paper is smooth. A cold press paper is much bumpier, has much more "tooth." And on this somewhat toothy paper, he had printed these poems in ten-point Bembo. Ten-point Palatino looks pretty large; ten-point Bembo is real tiny type, with very delicate serifs. Even at that point in my life, when I had no real knowledge of what was hard and what was easy, it was quite clear that he pulled off something in this little book that was stunning. I couldn't seriously believe we'd taken the same class. I later found out he had been a hobby printer for years before he took the class. So what was for me an introduction to printing was for him a kind of brush-up and an opportunity to pick up some fine points from the master. So we had started at very different points. But, in any event, I was just flabbergasted at the beauty of this lovely little pamphlet of poems by a guy I later became friends with, Dave Morice.

And I asked Professor Duncan if I could do another project, even though the class was over. I said, "You know, I think I muffed it. If you could pick a typeface that probably none of your students in the next semester are going to use, could I come in off hours and just try another project?" And he looked at the project I had done, and he looked at me, and he rolled his eyes a little and shrugged, and said, "Yeah, all right."

Rushing in like a fool, where angels and certainly more experienced printers would fear to tread, I received some poems in the mail from another friend of mine who I've kept in touch with over the years—Rochelle Ratner. They were ten or twelve poems about the Zodiac, or constellations—they weren't the exact Zodiac signs. And I had this wonderful idea of printing white ink on dark blue paper. That's exceedingly difficult to do, even for an experienced printer. But I went ahead. I bought some Strathmore text.

Then I heard that dampening paper can make it more receptive to the ink. And I clearly remember walking into the typography lab with this stack of paper, prepared to dampen it, and suddenly realizing I hadn't a clue about how one went about dampening paper for letterpress printing. And I began practically drenching both sides of every sheet.

297

About ten minutes into this process Harry Duncan walked in, took a look at me, stared for a minute, and then walked into his office. Ten minutes later he came out; I was still dampening both sides of every sheet, practically drenching it with a sponge. He looked at me, he fidgeted for a minute of two, he opened a window, and went back to his office. Five minutes later he came out—there I was, still drenching both sides of every sheet—and he said, "You *can* do it that way."

And I said, "How do you do it, Professor Duncan?"

He said, "Well, I put down two dry sheets. And then I quickly whisk three of them through a tub of water and put them down. And then I put down two dry sheets, and whisk three through the tub of water. Then I put them in a plastic garbage bag, seal it, put a board over it, then a weight on the board, and let it sit overnight."

I said, "That sounds a lot faster than sponging both sides of each sheet."

He said, "I think you will find it so." [Laughs.] He gave me a little time to do it wrong before he came in and told me how to do it. And actually it came out relatively credible-looking.

Did you go back and do it as he recommended?

Well, I did the rest of them that way. The sheets that I had drenched scarcely printed at all. You can get paper too damp for letterpress printing. That's another story for intaglio, but for letterpress printing it should be barely damp. The test that Harry later told me was if you put the sheet to your cheek it should feel cool.

That's very subtle.

Yes. Yes. If it feels cool to your cheek, you've probably got it just right. But if it feels damp, it's probably too wet. A nice sensual image. So, anyway, that project looked better. Then my wife, although we weren't married yet, decided to take the class. She had benefited from watching the first two projects I had done.

Harry, at the time, had a live-in apprentice. Actually, he wasn't living in Harry's house; he was living next door. He was the son of somebody from Mexico who was very wealthy. This family had enough money to allow this kid to spend a year renting a house next door to Harry Duncan and working for Harry for free. But the kid wanted to go home for Christmas, and that's when Harry had time off to print. So Harry asked if I'd like to volunteer, along with the guy who had actually given me that luxurious little pamphlet, Al Buck. And Al and I wound up hitchhiking each day ten miles east to West French, Iowa where we worked on a book for Harry. And I really fell in love with letterpress printing, watching Harry work, and got a sense of what it was all about.

Harry was an extraordinary person. He published first editions of Wallace Stevens, William Carlos Williams, Robert Penn Warren; he'd done Robert Lowell's first book. He was something of a living legend. And although I came of age in the '60s era, I very rarely, even at the time, and still very rarely, use the term "aura." But Harry had an aura. The spirit of craftsmanship seemed to hover about his shoulders. And it seemed reasonable that such a person would have a letterpress shop in his home.

That was around December '71 through January '72. Around February or March I bumped into this guy who had taken the same class. I hadn't gotten to know him very well, but he asked me if I wanted to see his letterpress print shop. I said, "You mean you've got your own shop?"

He said, "Yeah, yeah. It's in the basement of my frat house."

I said, "You've got a print shop in the basement of your frat house?"

He said, "Yeah, yeah. It's all my own stuff." So I went to look at it. And whereas Harry, as I said, seemed so extraordinary that it seemed entirely conceivable that he would have a print shop, this other guy was just a decent enough, ordinary joe, living in a frat house. And he had a print shop. And I thought, Oh, if this guy could have one, maybe I could, too. So I asked him how he got all that stuff. And he said, "You know, it's mysterious. I just told one or two people that I was looking for a press and within two weeks somebody I didn't know walked up to me and said, 'Hey, I hear you're looking for a press. There's one for sale along with a whole bunch of other equipment.' So I bought it." So I looked at him and I said, "All right. Tell you what. I'm looking for a press. Send out the word." Damned if two weeks later somebody I'd never met before didn't walk up to me and say, "I hear you're looking for a press. They tried to auction one off at a community auction hall that has auctions every week, and no one bought it. So it's for sale for thirty-five bucks to anybody who'll plunk down the money and haul it off." And that's how I got my first press.

I think we bought it around late March or April and we moved it into Anselm Hollo's garage, and then we got kicked out of our house by Urban Renewal. At that time in Iowa City, Urban Renewal was offering this deal that, even if you were renting, if you wanted to buy a house they'd give you two thousand dollars plus half the difference of a down payment. Well, Harry Duncan had just got a job to teach at the University of Nebraska at Omaha and was moving. So my wife and I looked at each other and we said, "Let's buy Harry's house." Because we knew he had strengthened the floor of a room in order to be able to hold the presses. And that's what we did. We bought Harry Duncan's house. He had been printing there for about twelve years, and we put in another thirteen, printing. So for twenty-five years, that house was a print shop. And we got married in August and moved in in August and set up the Toothpaste Press.

Does Toothpaste Press exist now?

No. The Toothpaste Press was almost exclusively poetry. Of the seventy-odd books and pamphlets that we printed between 1973 when we really got going and 1984 when we closed out the imprint, I'd say fewer than half a dozen were prose. The remaining books were all poetry. And they were all letterpress. They were all either hand-set or cast in monotype, with the monotype shipped to us, printed at our house. The books were hand-folded. All the pamphlets were hand-sewn. The books with spines were Smythe-sewn and then the covers were glued on.

So it was a fine-printing operation.

It was a fine-printing operation. However, rather than using handmade paper, or even mold-made paper, on the whole the books were printed on the better grades of American machine-made papers. Mostly Strathmore and Curtis. We were attempting to compete in price with those books that were being produced with IBM Selectrics and then sent off to Ann Arbor to be turned into perfect-bound books. So we were putting in tons and tons of labor and fine materials and then trying to be competitively priced with much more cheaply produced objects. As a result, we really never got out of the hole financially. But at the same time I did learn the craft of book design and I learned the craft of

300

letterpress printing and then, as the years progressed, I learned more and more about the book business itself.

Many of the fine presses in this country are run by people who were introduced to letterpress printing in an art department. They were studio artists or somehow associated with studio art. So for them—their friends were selling paintings for three hundred—to sell books for three hundred was not a stretch. I was a young poet whose friends were doing mimeo magazines or cheaply produced offset books. Our inspiration was not Grabhorne but Auerhahn. The Grabhorne Press was the sort of fine press that did three-hundred, five-hundred, thousand-dollar books. Auerhahn was a press run from about '58 to '63. And during that period they did first editions of books by Philip Whalen, Jack Spicer, William Burroughs—they were part of the San Francisco Renaissance. They were doing, as I was attempting to do, letterpress books on a slightly higher-grade, American, machine-made paper rather than handmade papers from Europe. And they were trying to price them so that they could sell to the literary community. They were running a fine press and at the same time trying to make it a press that was part of the literary community and that responded to the needs of literature, not fine art. So that was my inspiration.

And by the end of the '70s and early '80s I began to realize that letterpress simply was no longer a medium that could serve literature the way I felt I wanted to serve it as a publisher. Also we had started having children, and living on three thousand a year plus my wife's salary as a health administrator was starting to wear.

So you personally didn't have another job. This was it.

That was it, yeah. She was working full time as a health administrator, I was working full time as a letterpress printer and publisher. About all I ever took out of the press was about three thou a year. We put the rest of the money back into the press, buying more type, buying more equipment.

How were you distributing the books and chapbooks that you were printing?

Well, we did flyers, we attended book fairs and started to build a mailing list which eventually was entered in the computer and is in our computers to this day. Some of those names were added in the early '70s, over twenty years ago.

I remember attending the second New York Small Press Bookfair, which was my first. And the first two days I had this idea that selling poetry was something somewhat dignified, and I didn't want to be too forward about it. And so I sort of sat there politely with my hands folded, trying not to aggressively catch anybody's eye. The first day, despite the fact that there were probably five to ten thousand people walking past my table, I think we sold about twenty dollars worth of books. The second day we hadn't sold a thing until we were packing up, and then somebody walked by and said, "I'll take two of everything." And I almost tried to talk her out of it, I was so flabbergasted and foolish. The third day I decided to take a different tack and started standing and shouting, "Step right up! Come see the most beautiful books at the Small Press Bookfair! We've come all the way from Iowa to show you these beautiful books! Don't be another blasé New Yorker! Come right up and take a look!" Well, we took in about two or three hundred dollars. And that was the last time I acted like a funeral director at a book fair.

And I began to realize that sales could be a fulfilling part of the publishing process, and, in fact, began to realize that it was the completion of the publishing process. And that anyone who thought that their job was done when the book was printed didn't really understand what publishing was all about. David Godine calls the attitude that the book is done when the book comes back from the printer "privashing," not publishing. To publish is to make public. And I was one of the early small presses that grew out of the antiestablishment world of the late '60s and early '70s to buy into the idea that it wasn't selling out to try to sell a book.

Around that time I became acquainted with and then became close friends with a guy named Jim Sitter who started his career, as did many people, working at the Hungry Mind Bookstore in St. Paul, and then worked for a guy who had just moved to town with a small press distribution service, David Wilk, whose distributorship at the time was called Truck. In 1978, I believe, David got hired to be the literature program director of the National Endowment for the Arts. And it's my understanding that Jim bought Truck Distribution Service for one dollar

302

with the additional agreement that he'd buy one of David's cars for about fifteen hundred.

At that time, there were about a half dozen small press distribution services in the country. Small Press Distribution; the New York Small Press Association was one, Truck was another; there were a few more. Each of them was receiving about thirty-five thousand dollars a year in support from NEA. Most of them were grossing about twenty thousand in sales and they had to find volunteer labor to get the other half of their one-to-one match, you know, to say they got in-kind services in order to match their thirty-five-thousand-dollar grant. When Jim Sitter took over Truck Distribution, which he then renamed Bookslinger, he brought a new level of organization, of energy, of entrepreneurship to small press distribution than had existed before, at least among small press distributors that were focusing exclusively on literature. That excludes Bookpeople, which was not exclusively literary and really was making it as a business. These others—they were pretty laid back. I don't mean to cast aspersions on anyone; there weren't any good models.

Jim Sitter initiated a new model. Jim started making sales trips. He'd pick a part of the country each year. He'd fly there, rent a car, and put together a string of appointments. All the way up the West Coast one year, and all the way up the East Coast one year, and just get in his own car and drive all over the Midwest one year, and meet booksellers, and really make sales calls. Within a year or two, whereas everybody else was taking their thirty-five thousand and leveraging it to gross about twenty, he was grossing a hundred to a hundred and twenty. And he recognized in me someone who was willing to meet him halfway and work with him. And we kind of inspired each other. He inspired me to work more closely with bookstores, I inspired him to take what was working as a model and build on it even further. We both worked our asses off, and we each knew that the other was working hard. He'd call me at ten o'clock at night on Sunday and he'd say, "Where are you?" and I'd say, "I'm in my press room, printing." And he'd say, "I'm over at Bookslinger, working. Let's talk."

Then in 1980 I attended my first ABA. I walked in with a carton of these lovely little letterpress books and pamphlets on my shoulder, and I took about ten or fifteen steps into the building and a woman wearing only a slip walked up to me and handed me a brochure for a thirty-five-dollar book called *The History of the Negligee.* I took another half-dozen steps and another woman wearing a New York Ranger hockey outfit approached me and handed me a brochure for her book about her attempt to become the first female pro hockey player. I took another ten steps and there was a guy with a drugged baby tiger on a leash who handed me a brochure for a book on animal training. And I said to myself, "What the hell have I gotten myself into?" But as absurd as all of this circus-like atmosphere seemed, I also was attracted to the real business of selling books, and I began to feel that I wanted to try my hand at going beyond editions of three hundred to five hundred copies. I wanted to get my foot in the door to real trade publishing.

And that led to our decision to close out the Toothpaste Press as an imprint and reorganize as Coffee House Press, a literary publisher of trade books with a nonprofit status that would enable us to solicit the funds needed to run a publishing operation the way I wanted to see it run. In '84 my wife and I put our house up for sale, drove up to the Twin Cities, and incorporated the press here. Then we drove back and waited for a year, trying to sell the house.

How did the decision to relocate here come about?

Well, I considered that Bookslinger was located here. I had started attending book fairs here and became attracted to the Hungry Mind Bookstore, to the many exciting writers who were in town. I was attracted by the fact that The Loft was part of this community. And, with all due respect to the state of Iowa, its motto at the time was "A Place to Grow," and, if you're in the arts, you kind of reach your limits of growth there after a while. And I did feel that if I was going to grow as a literary publisher I had to be in a more urban environment. And this place seemed like the right step.

I may be remembering incorrectly but I seem to recall that when Scott Walker [founder and former publisher of Graywolf Press] moved from Washington state to St. Paul, he said that he had been offered twenty-five thousand a year by...somebody...for five years, guaranteed, to do what he wanted to do anyway, and that was why he made the move. That doesn't sound familiar to you?

If Scott said it, it's probably true—

304

I'm not asking you to verify—

—but no one gave me a similar offer. It would have been nice, but no, no one made that offer to me. We were aware that there was a different funding environment in Minnesota than existed in Iowa, but, actually, in our first few years I was more concerned with learning where the grocery store was and getting the press a little better established so that when I approached people for funds I could point to an ongoing program. We moved here in '85 and I believe it was really not until '87 that we started to approach the funding community and began getting the funds that we had been hoping for.

Why did you decide to go nonprofit?

Well, you know, the deal is that publishing is a capital-intensive occupation. There are three ways of going about publishing. One is to be independently wealthy. Unfortunately, that was not an option open to me. Option two is to seek investors—who will then want their money back. And publishing literature isn't something that you can guarantee will be a profitable enterprise. The third is to go nonprofit and solicit donated funds with the argument that what you're doing is a genuine contribution to culture. And donors don't ask for their money back. So that's the route we took. It would have been nice if my father had been in the steel business, as James Laughlin's had been, which enabled him to found New Directions. But that wasn't the case.

Distribution. You're distributed now by Consortium, right?
Mm hm.

Consortium didn't exist in '85, did they?
Actually, they had just begun. I believe we signed on with them in '86.

And you have an exclusive arrangement with them?
That is correct.

How does that work for you?
Well, in order to have a successful relationship with a distributor,

305

both sides have to have an understanding about what each side is responsible for. It's Consortium's responsibility to get our books into the stores. It's our responsibility to get them to walk out of the store in a buyer's hands. Consortium does an excellent job of getting our books into the stores. They do an excellent job of packing, of shipping, of invoicing, of collecting, and their reps are excellent. Many sales reps in the book business don't actually read books.

I know.

The reps at Consortium are real readers. It's a great group. Sometimes our books sell real well. Sometimes they do modestly well. Sometimes they're a disappointment. But I can't ever blame Consortium if a book didn't sell well. I have to look at myself for having picked it. I have to look at the cover and wonder if it was the right cover. I have to look at the times and wonder if, gee, maybe the book would have done better five years ago or two years from now. But it's not Consortium's job to make sure the customers buy the book. It's Consortium's job to make certain that our books are professionally presented to the book trade. To booksellers. From that point on, it's up to us. They do a good job, and we continue to try to grow in our responsibilities and adapt to a very rapidly changing marketplace.

Do you try to sell subsidiary rights?

Yes. In fact, we have just received a grant from the Cowles Media Foundation on behalf of the five nonprofit Minnesota literary presses—Coffee House, Graywolf, Milkweed, New Rivers, and Holy Cow!—to jointly hire a subsidiary rights director who will, on a full-time basis, be responsible for selling foreign rights, film rights, paperback rights, book club rights, et cetera. I believe last year we grossed about seventy-three thousand in subsidiary rights sales.

About what proportion would that be of your gross income for the year?

Of our gross earned income, or our total income? In other words, we took in about two hundred and thirty thousand in book sales, another seventy thousand in subsidiary rights sales, and maybe another three hundred thousand in donated income.

That's a pretty high proportion for subsidiary rights.
We had a fair amount of growth in the last year.

Whatever happened to your own poetry? Do you still write poetry?
Very, very rarely. I decided I was a better editor and publisher than a poet.

Do you miss it? I guess it didn't become part of your life's routine, or maybe it did. It just got away from you?
It just got away from me. The press took all my time. You know, you look back and you think, Well, you miss some things, but what are you missing? Are you missing writing poetry? Are you missing publishing little pamphlets? Are you missing your youth? It's always hard to tell what it is you're missing. I'd say I'm writing about a poem a year. Maybe two. If something strikes. I remember reading one after I'd written it, and thinking, If this came in the mail, I would say, "Nice guy. I share his values. Not up to the level of competition."

I don't have any more questions. Is there anything else you would like to say?
Well, I'd like to say that there are a number of satisfactions in running the kind of press that we have now. In some instances, we've made careers. It's always hard to tell when somebody's jiving me, but I've accepted manuscripts from people who've said, "You're the twentieth publisher who's seen this and if you had rejected it, it was going to go into the bottom drawer of the desk, never to be seen again." Some of those books have gone on to win a number of awards and become their authors' launching pad. That was a story we were told by Karen Yamashita, that she had sent it all over and we were that book's last chance. And the book won two awards and we sold about seven thousand copies. It's still selling. It's become the subject of papers delivered at MLA [Modern Language Association]. *Through the Arc of the Rain Forest.*
I called an author one time to tell her that we'd accepted her book, and she was out. So I left a message on the answering machine. It

turned out she was out for dinner, celebrating her fiftieth birthday. This was her first book. She had starting writing in her early forties. And she was so thrilled she popped the tape out of the answering machine—to keep the tape forever. I think at the time our advances for a novel were fifteen hundred dollars. They're up to about three now for novels. And she won the Barnes and Noble Discover Award. She got five thou for that. Then we sold paperback rights for twenty-five thou and then her agent was able to sell her next book for a hundred and twenty-five thou. We changed her life. We changed her life by publishing her book.

We've had one book listed as an "ideal teaching tool" in a magazine called *Teaching Tolerance*. I'm a child of the Left. I mentioned that I was born in New York and my parents moved when I was a year old. They integrated the building they were living in. When they moved out they transferred their lease to a black couple. It was an all-white building. I heard Martin Luther King's "I Have a Dream" speech. My father took me to it when I was fourteen. To have a book I've published listed as an ideal teaching tool in a magazine called *Teaching Tolerance*—that made me feel real good.

It's a small scale compared to the movies with audiences of hundreds and hundreds of thousands of people. Or millions. But I still believe in the power of the printed word and I believe that the people who do read our books are the kinds of people who can influence the course of the future for the better. That's one of the things that keeps me going.

Do you think that any good book will find its publisher?

Not necessarily. I think that there are people who are easily crushed. There are people who are juggernauts, who will roll over any obstacle. But there are quiet, sensitive people who can give up if they don't receive encouragement at the right moment in their lives. And one never will know what great things they might have been capable of doing had they received that encouragement at that key moment. Would Jack Kerouac have become the alcoholic that he became if *On the Road* had been published within a year or so of its being written rather than ten years later, and then receiving that snotty little note that this wasn't writing, it was typing? He might have still become an alcoholic; he might not have. He might not have drunk himself to death. I don't know. But I do believe that it is entirely possible to lose the work of a gifted writer if that person does not receive encouragement at a key moment in life.

My reason for asking—I agree with you—but my reason for asking is that I've found that it's difficult for somebody who feels he has a mission in publishing to turn something down. And one of the ways by which we rationalize it is by saying somebody else will pick it up. We all have limits on how many titles we can publish per year.

Mm hm.

And here comes one more and you know you just can't do it. At least that's my experience. As much as I like it, I know I can't commit myself.

I would say that if I receive something that is just clearly screaming at me to be published I'll take it even if we're full and just put it on the list for later. What we sometimes wind up sending back are those interesting books that are intriguing, are intellectually interesting—they may not be the most vital book, but they deserve to be published, they're interesting books. They're the ones that sometimes we very regretfully send back. But if I'm really, truly passionate about something, we take it. We take it. Particularly in prose. There is poetry we sent back that I dearly wished we had room for, but I don't think I've ever sent a novel back that I just absolutely had to publish. I've sent novels back that I had a lot of second thoughts about; part of me wanted to do it and part of me wasn't certain. Or it was an interesting book, well written, and yet there was something that didn't quite get me all the way, and so it was a book on the bubble. Those books should be published by somebody else who does feel passionate about them.

What we do get sometimes—what you want in a literary press—is a book with a prose style that just knocks your socks off but also has something to say. What you wind up getting are books with something to say by writers who don't have a compelling prose style, or writers with a compelling prose style who don't have anything to say. It is rare that you get a writer who has both and can really entertain the reader and can tie the thing up. Man, it's hard to write a novel all the way through to the end and tie the damn thing up. I have read some books that started out well and then just sort of dribbled off. The author lost the timeline. All of a sudden you don't know what day it is, what month it is, what's going on in the main characters' lives, and it just fizzles. But, as I said, I don't think I've ever sent a novel back that I felt passionate about. We don't get that many novels that I like that well.

Thank you very much.
My pleasure.

Emilie Buchwald
Milkweed Editions

"I'm an enthusiast for good writing. I think most of us who are literary publishers swoon over outstanding writing. It gives a visceral response when you read something really wonderful."

Before beginning the interview, we talked about the possibility of forming an association of independent literary presses, of both the for-profit and nonprofit varieties. I had recently written an article in the guise of a letter to the editor of Poets & Writers, *suggesting this (Gold 1997). In the same issue in which the letter appeared, the formation of the Literary Publishers Alliance—an association of nine nonprofit publishers—was announced. Nothing has come of my idea and, as far as I know, nothing of consequence has resulted from the Literary Publishers Alliance.*

We met late in the afternoon on Wednesday, September 17, 1997 in Milkweed's offices in Minneapolis, not far from those of Coffee House Press and New Rivers Press. It was a warm, clear day in which small, white clouds hung on a pale sky. It was a great day after the monsoonlike rain of the day before. Buchwald blamed me for bringing bad weather from the Pacific Northwest and insisted on taking credit for today's clemency.

She was born in Vienna on September 6, 1935, though she believes she's not really a Virgo. "It's a mistake. I'm not mathematical, neat, or precise. I'm more simpatico than analytical. It's an error." She came with her parents to the United States in 1939. Family members who remained in Europe perished in the Holocaust.

Until she married, she lived in Queens, then afterward in Manhattan where her husband was in medical school. She had matriculated at Barnard; now she got her M.A., in English, at Columbia. When she and her husband moved to Minneapolis for his residency, she entered the University of Minnesota's graduate school and took a Ph.D., again in English.

At the time of the interview, she and her husband had been

311

married for forty-three years. They have four grown daughters and several grandchildren. An observation on having children: "The people who grew up when I was growing up never thought about not doing what was considered sort of the routine: getting married, finishing whatever course you set out on, having children. The option of even thinking about having children is, I think, something quite new. Just this last generation has really thought about whether they would be better off not having children, for all sorts of reasons, from purely selfish and hedonistic to thinking about not bringing more children into the world. The fact that it's a serious option now has made a big difference. Two of our children are not married."

How does it feel, being a grandparent? I'm old enough to be a grandfather, but I'm not. Did you suddenly feel older with your first grandchild?

No, because it didn't happen for a long time, not until seven years ago. I thought it was way past time. I was certainly ready. And they were ready; that was the important thing.

Do you have a teaching position?

I don't. When I left academia I decided that I didn't want to do that. I decided I'd had enough of secondary sources and footnotes and the infighting that goes with academia, and although I've always been involved and interested in books and writing, that I would not do it in that way, I would not continue my interest in that way.

Sounds like me. I got my doctorate in anthropology, but by the time I was ready to finish my dissertation I knew I didn't want to stay in academia.

Right. It can be just a dreadful place.

It's very narrow. I went into anthropology because I thought it would open the world to me.

I was going to say—anthropology, yeah. Sounds great.

It was, at one time. I mean some of the people I studied under

312

obviously had a great time. But it's become so institutionalized that—
Yep. Exactly.

You graduated, you got your doctorate, so how did you get into publishing?
Well, when I was living in New York, in the summers, I worked at various magazines, from *TV Guide* to *Madamoiselle*. They had this college board thing, and I was a fiction editor one summer for them. It's like an internship. It's a nice opportunity. I've also edited a journal of obstetrics and gynecology—it's called the *Sloan Journal of Obstetrics*. I've done a lot of medical editing and proofing. And I was also writing. I had my first short story published when I was in college, and it made it into the O. Henry Awards. So I published fiction and poetry when I was still in college. And I continued to do freelance editing while I was doing the other things I was doing.

Here in Minnesota I edited the Poetry Society of America's centenary issue on Wallace Stevens, and then after I left the university I taught at The Loft, which is our writing center. I taught writing poetry. I taught writing for children through the university's continuing education for women. I wrote a couple of novels for children during that time that Harcourt Brace published. I think that writing for children is a wonderful art and—we'll get into it, but Milkweed began publishing fiction for middle graders in 1993, and I'm very, very interested in doing more of that.

My friends who are in commercial houses have told me that around 1993 they slowed down [in] publishing middle-grade fiction because they were doing series books, picture books, and they were making a lot more money. And I thought that's a very good reason for a nonprofit literary press to publish fiction for eight- to twelve- or thirteen-year-olds, so we began to do that. I love children's literature, so that's a great interest of mine. To make a long story short, I've always been an editor or a writer, teacher, involved with books in one way or another.

Do you continue to write?
I haven't written anything for...I think at least four years, because, well, you know, publishing takes you over. It just swallows you up.

313

That's why I chose to remain small—so I could continue to write.

Good for you. Good for you, that you can do it. But right now, it's just impossible. I feel people do what they want to do. If I really wanted to write, I'd find a way to write, so I must not...want to at this point? need to at this point?

If you don't feel the need—I wouldn't do it if I didn't feel the need.

Yeah. I think the energy is being spent vicariously in editing other people's work, which I like. I like to edit. I'm an enthusiast for good writing. I think most of us who are literary publishers swoon over outstanding writing. It gives a visceral response when you read something really wonderful.

I just received a wonderful manuscript. It happens occasionally, once or twice a year. You get one that stands up and shouts.

I know.

My response to it amazes me. I don't know why it is, but it's there.

I think that's what it takes. Because you have to do a lot of unpleasant or difficult things in order to sustain the pleasure that you get from finding the good ones.

So when did Milkweed start?

Well, I was on the board of The Loft in the late '70s, and I met a visual artist and designer named Randy Scholes. And we talked about the fact that there was no journal that brought together the verbal and the visual, poetry and visual arts, that literary journals treated art as an add-on or a decoratif, and that it would be great fun to have the synergy of those two art forms together. We talked about it for awhile, and then we decided that because we were ignorant, we would try to do it. [Laughs.] That is definitely the reason. In 1979 we incorporated as Milkweed Chronicle. We are the second oldest Minnesota nonprofit organization. *The Great River Review* is the oldest. They still exist. In November of '79 we came into existence officially, and in February of 1980 the first issue of *Milkweed Chronicle* came out. We were funded by grants. We were told by the funder of the first issue that there had to be a second issue. That was the proviso with which we got the grant. And so we went on in a very hand-to-mouth kind of way for those first few years.

Who was your funder?
The Jerome Foundation.

I keep hearing of them.
They're wonderful. Wonderful people. And we were interested in collaboration. So the first Milkweed book grew out of...well, a friend of mine and I had been collecting poems about the visual arts and we decided that this anthology would be better served in a book format than in the journal format. So in 1984 we published that. It was called *The Poet Dreaming in the Artist's House*. It's still in print. It was distributed in bookstores and we were thrilled by that. A few bookstores anyway.

Nationally?
Yeah. And it got good reviews, and was named by *Bloomsbury* [*Review*] as one of the best small press books of 1984. It was a nice beginning. The next couple of books were collaborations that we asked for through the journal. We asked writers and artists to collaborate, and we published the next two as collaborations. And then we published a collection of short fiction by Carol Bly called *Backbone* that got a major *New York Times* review. And suddenly we were book publishers. Up until that time we considered it really an extension of the journal. At the end of 1985 our board said that we should, over the next year or so, make a decision about whether we were going to continue the journal or continue books, because we were obviously going to kill ourselves in the effort to do both. We agreed that we would phase out the journal over the course of a year or two. We gave all our subscribers credit in books for any unused part of their subscription. Actually, we gave them a fifty-percent additional credit. We just decided that the books were getting out much further, that we were doing much better for the authors we were publishing, as well as for Milkweed.

In 1987 we found ourselves in the Advancement Program—the NEA Advancement Program—which was very helpful, also extremely time-consuming. They told us when we went in that we would probably lose staff members. Not that there were so many of us then; I think there were five. And I think at the end of that time, all but Randy and I were gone and we had to sort of start again. Because it took so much time and energy just to go through this process. As you know, these are all major burn-out things. When you spend a lot of time in meetings and you can't do what you're supposed to be doing to run the press, it's very frustrating. But it helped. Organizationally, it helped. We were stronger by 1989.

We've had distribution from 1986 on. First we were with Consortium, until 1992, and since then we've been with Publishers Group West. One of the reasons we changed distributors was that we wanted to publish children's books, and at that time Consortium did not call on children's book buyers; they didn't have a children's book catalogue. And they weren't, we felt, helping us to break out in sales. So we decided to look for other distribution. Which helped us.

I know Seal Press made the switch too. It must have been around the same time.

Yep. We did. We switched in the same year.

They really broke out.

We doubled our sales. That change made us very eager to plan certain things. For instance, we planned to do our first issue-oriented nonfiction title. We planned to do a fiction title that we thought had a chance of really selling well, and PGW helped us with that campaign. We planned—this was in '93—to start publishing children's fiction. So those were very busy years.

What does PGW do differently?

I think that it's not so much what they do differently—especially now, because Consortium is a strong and very well managed distributor. What was different for us was at PGW we were not one of a group of literary presses. Because when Consortium took all the books to the stores, they would decide, well, we have maybe ten poetry titles; let's skip these. Or if what we had for fiction wasn't their favorite, they might skip presenting that. We felt we were in too similar a group of publishers. And with PGW, at that time, we were one of only a few literary

316

publishers, so we stood out and that made it easier for reps to sell us. Their interest was a big help.

And then I felt they got into more stores. As I told you, they saw children's book buyers. And I felt that working with management and with the sales reps, at that point in time—I don't know what it is now—was more analytical than it had been with Consortium. I suspect that's probably not true anymore, because I hear that they do a very good job and that the reps do a good job.

So—what's Milkweed's mission?
Milkweed's mission is to have a humane impact on society through literature. It's just a small mission. We aren't taking on much.

Why the emphasis on children? Is it your personal interest, or—?
Well, our publishing falls into adult fiction, children's fiction, poetry and poetry anthologies, and we're now going to focus on nonfiction in Literature and the Natural World.

Our nonfiction has really been all over the place because I've looked for the best writing on subjects that I care about, and published it. It's been in education, in women's issues, in writing, in ethics. And we've decided that it no longer is possible for a press to publish, in miniature, all subjects. At least so it appears to us at this point in time. As we tried to decide where we wanted to focus, we looked at what we've been publishing and we saw we'd published books about the natural world. That's a real interest. That's going to be the future of our nonfiction program.

You're very open about what you choose to publish being an extension of your own interests.
Absolutely.

Are you the one who makes the decision?
Yes.

[Laughing:] You remind me of Barney Rosset. Even when he had three hundred employees, he would see everything first. [Buchwald laughs.] He would go in in the morning and he would be the first one to

317

look at manuscripts.
I understand that.

How many employees do you have?
There are nine full-time and several freelance people.

Is Randy Scholes still—?
Randy burned out one time too many in 1993. He decided that he was no longer doing his own art work, he was spending all of his time designing book covers and books, and that he did not want to do that any longer. And so, in a mutually amicable way, he retired from the press. We still commission him to do book covers and art for us, 'cause he's great!

How many titles do you do a year? In all three divisions.
Thirteen to fifteen. We're looking at seventeen next year, but it depends on what happens in terms of funding. As you well know, publishing is a capital-intensive business and [capital] limits you enormously in what you can do.

Do you sell subsidiary rights? Oh, you did. From Montana 1948 *you made a bundle.*
We did. And we continue to do pretty well with subsidiary rights.

Was that your first sale of subsidiary rights?
I think we had sold one or two small things, but that was certainly the first major rights sale that we made. And it translated wonderfully because we sold foreign rights to ten countries, in addition to paperback and audio. We optioned film rights. Everything that could happen happened for that book, and for Larry Watson [i.e., the author]. But, as I told you, that was our plan when we went to PGW: to provide them with a book that, together, we could think about how to break out. And we did. That was not an accident. It was the right book at the right time.

How did you know that?
It felt right. [Laughs.] That's about as scientific and analytical as I get to be. We thought about it. It's a well-written book. A literary western, if you will. Relatively easy read. What we found when we had

people reading the manuscript was how many different kinds of people it appealed to. There's sort of a universality about that book that is not true for most of what we publish. So it seemed to us that that was the right book to make this effort with. And when one of the major houses was bidding on it, they said, "You know, everyone from the janitor to the president has liked this book." You can't say that about most books.

Since then, as I said, rights have become a more important part of the business for us. We count on making those foreign rights sales and some of the other subsidiary rights sales. We hope to do more of that in the future.

Did you have agents for foreign rights before that book?
No.

Do you go through Writer's House?
No, we worked with a New York rights person, Linda Michaels, for a couple of years, and now—perhaps Allan [Kornblum] told you—five Minnesota presses have gotten a grant to hire somebody to do rights sales for us. We're going to see how that works. We're keeping our fingers crossed.

There was—I guess it could be called an exposé—in the New York Times *about how Barnes and Noble sells various things for promotion.*
Mm hm.

Actually, I got caught up in that recently. Essentially you buy a review that's published in-house. You know, those little pamphlets that they distribute in their stores for genre books?
Yeah.

Was Montana 1948 *involved in any of that?*
I can't remember if it was a "Discover Great New Writers" title or not. We found that the program was not always a good thing, because if there were returns they were major. That's not something that we have continued to be involved in.

Where does Milkweed go from here?

Well, as I told you, we're going to continue to publish adult fiction; fiction for eight- to thirteen-year-olds; we'll continue to do poetry anthologies; for individual poetry, we've just joined the National Poetry Series. We'll see how that works for us. Five publishers agree that they will each take a book that comes out of a national competition in the next year. It's Norton, Penguin, University of Illinois, Sun and Moon, and Milkweed. And then we're going to have a concentration, a focus, on The World As Home: Literature and the Natural World, and we hope to expand our nonfiction. I won't even say I hope to; I plan to expand the nonfiction.

Do you have a formula for how many titles from each emphasis or discipline—?

Yeah. I would say we'll want to do four fiction titles for adults, four for children, two of poetry, and the rest will be nonfiction. And there will also be, opportunistically, books for writers, but only very good ones.

What happens with Milkweed when you leave?

We're already planning that. We have a wonderful executive director and he is now running the business of our business. When I transition out of this, we'll hire another acquisitions editor with certain kinds of skills, contacts, background. Probably for a year or two I will acquire in one or more of the genres, and we will have freelance people acquiring and substantive editing as well.

But, really, we are a mission-driven press. It's pretty clear from the books that we've done, the kind of books that we're going to do in the future. Of course, with the taste of a new editor, that will change too. But I think the mission is big enough and interesting enough so that there's a lot of opportunity for the person who comes in.

You have nine employees. After the transition is complete, will your permanent staff be fewer?

Probably not. I mean, it depends on the industry so much, what you can do in terms of staff. I think we're at the point now where there are probably more of us than there would be if we were not doing as much with each of the books as we do. I mean there's a lot of attention that's paid to production values and...I just think we're at max for staff right now. If we go in any direction it would be to get smaller and to do more on a contract basis. It really depends on what happens over the next three to five years.

Do you pay health benefits?
Yes.

Do you have a retirement program?
We have no retirement program. We would like to have one. People can participate in a voluntary program whereby part of their salary goes into a program that's run through an insurance company. We aren't able to provide retirement benefits, but we do pay for health care.

That seems to be a critical factor as a, probably any kind of company, but certainly as a publishing company grows.
Right.

I talked with Barbara Wilson [see Gold 1996] and—
I've never met Barbara.

She mostly writes now. She's not—
Is Faith [Conlon] involved with Seal Press still?

Faith is the one now.
Okay. She's the one I know. Faith is great.

When they made the transition to...to being an organization, to getting larger, they left off doing fiction, except for some mysteries. The choice was, would the organization serve itself, would it be able to maintain itself and grow, or would they continue to be literary? And they opted to grow and do other things.
Right.

Those things are worthwhile; I'm not putting them down at all.
Yeah! Oh, no! No!

But that was a choice they had to make. They knew there was more money in other things.

Yeah. It's absolutely true. Fiction is wonderfully soul-satisfying, but it's very difficult in terms of backlist. A few of our fiction titles have backlisted well, but for the most part it's very hard to continue to sell. And that has a great deal to do with American reading habits. I should clarify what I mean. I mean that because the book industry, and bookselling itself, is so frontlist-driven, that readers, too, are thinking about what's new, what's the new book that I can get, rather than what are some wonderful books that have come out over the last five or ten years that I haven't gotten to. We're programmed to think that way.

I agree with you. Interestingly, all the writers I know don't pay any attention to frontlist. Most of those I know don't read modern American writing.

They're busy trying to catch up with all the good writing of the past and thinking about what they're [i.e., writers of the past] doing. That's true.

I have one writer who still prefers late nineteenth century, early twentieth century to anything else.

Well, I understand that. I love late nineteenth-century fiction.

I don't have any more questions. Is there anything else you would like to talk about?

I think that the only thing that probably everybody should be thinking about and speaking to is: How can you change the distribution system? How can you reach readers in a less indirect manner? How can we keep the middlepersons in our business from taking the money that should go to authors and to publishing companies that are trying to sustain themselves? Right now there is no good answer to that. It's such a burning issue that I don't understand why there aren't better efforts being made. They would have to be made by someone, or a group of entrepreneurial people, who can help us figure out what to do. We will try direct marketing on the net. If a consumer can push a button on his or her television set and order a book, it might happen. So that's a possibility.

That would change everything. I just feel that the way we are distributing now is incredibly wasteful. Sinfully so. The only people making money are the truckers taking books back and forth from one distribution center to another. The uselessness of printing too many books and having to either shred them or destroy them in some other manner—I mean it's absurd. So, to me, that's the burning issue that needs to be addressed. That's all. That's all I wanted to say.

Another aspect of having the distribution system that we have now, having so many middlepeople involved, is that it's driven the price of books up.

That's right! I'm glad you said that. If the price of books could go down, people would say, "Wow! I can get the new 'X,' or I can read what's supposed to be a pretty good new fiction title, and it won't cost me more than going to a movie." So that is an absolutely essential part of the equation. I'm glad you mentioned it. We're pricing ourselves out of the market.

I mean, people count on remainders. I count on remainders. I can't afford twenty- or thirty-dollar books.

I know. I was going to say, I wait till things go into paperback or I go to a second-hand bookstore. And that tells you a lot. The system that we have now is great for browsing, but not for buying.

Good point. Yeah. Okay. Thank you.
My pleasure.

C.W. Truesdale
New Rivers Press

"[T]he thought naturally pops into my head: How do I want best to be remembered, as the New Rivers Press publisher or as a writer? There's no question in my mind that I would rather be remembered as a writer."

I talked with Bill Truesdale at New Rivers Press in Minneapolis' warehouse district on the afternoon of September 18, 1997. I had talked with Randall Beek that morning and into the early afternoon [see interview, this volume] and the sky then had been a powdery blue behind towers of white cumulus. But through the day it had grown cottony, and by four o'clock, when I arrived at the press, the low cloud cover was a plate of polished steel. By evening, as I drove back to my motel, the radio was carrying a tornado warning.

Truesdale was born in St. Louis where his father was a physics teacher at Principia, a Christian Science high school. "I was raised in Christian Science. Mary Baker Eddy is now one of my 'wicked witches.'" He has lived all over the United States, partly because his father was a Christian Science War Minister during the Second World War. He went to high school in Rantoul, Illinois, where the navigators school at Chanute Field was. Then he moved to Alexandria, Louisiana, near Camp Claiborne, and then to Fayetteville, North Carolina when his father was assigned to Fort Bragg. Following the end of the war, he returned to Principia to continue high school, then graduated in Richmond, Virginia. He returned to Principia for college, but in his junior year left to marry the woman who would become his first wife. "I followed my wife-to-be out to California where she was a student at Stanford. We lived in California for a while, and then we got married in Seattle because the tuition was a lot cheaper up there. We moved up there in March 1950. We lived there for about four years. She finished up there, and I finished my undergraduate work and went right into graduate school" to study comparative and English literature. He got his doctorate in 1956. By then he had already taught for a year at the University of New Mexico. After receiving his Ph.D., he taught for six years at Virginia Military Institute. "It was just a horrible experience. It was basically a madhouse. I just hated that place. But I got into farming and foxhunting and stuff like that." In 1962 he got a job at Macalester College in St. Paul. Five years later he moved to Nyack, in New York's Hudson River Valley, then a year later to Manhattan where he remained for nine years before returning to Minnesota.

Throughout the first part of the interview, while amiable, Truesdale seemed reluctant. His responses to my questions were often laconic, and he did not volunteer anything. Only when we began to talk about marketing and his experience in trying to sell his books did his speech become animated so that I did not have to ask questions as much as guide the drift of the conversation. Several weeks after we talked, he wrote me that he was not satisfied by what he had said in the interview, and enclosed several chapters of his unfinished memoir of his life in publishing. With his permission, I have taken excerpts from these and incorporated them as notes. I believe they add flesh in some places where only a skeleton came through during the interview.

You started the press in '67?

'Sixty-eight. February '68. I started it in Nyack. I was living in Nyack at the time.[1]

Were you teaching there?

No. I'd quit teaching. I basically was writing. I didn't start teaching again until... I started part-time teaching at The New School and then later at Cooper Union.

Why did you start the press?

Basically because I had trouble publishing my first book of poetry. Once that was published in Mexico by El Corno Emplumado, I got into it.

From having worked with another press, you—?

Well, I got to know Meg Randall, who was the publisher of El Corno Emplumado, very well. She doesn't live in Mexico any more, but

325

she and her husband, Sergei Mondragón, lived in Mexico City. I got to know them pretty well. They did my first book.[2]

The purpose of your press then was...?
I published only poetry then. I publish a lot of different things now. Particularly since I moved to Minnesota, I've branched out quite a bit. In my writing—the press has always followed my own writing. When I first moved back here in '78 I started writing short stories. So when I started doing the Minnesota Voices project in 1981 I did both poetry and fiction.

Don't you give a prize?
The Minnesota Voices project.

That's for both poetry and fiction?
Yeah. There are about six books a year in that series.

How many books a year do you do now?
Oh, eight or ten. Sometimes eleven.

How many people do you have working here?
There are three of us.

That's quite a bit for just three people, isn't it?
Yeah! Yeah, it's gotten very complicated. We're very dependent on fund-raising, and stuff like that.

Are you a nonprofit? Five-oh-one-cee-three?
Yes. In fact, we were one of the first small presses granted that status.

When was that?
In '81. There were some magazines that had it before us, but not small presses.

I think Curbstone got 501 (c) (3) status in the late '70s.
Oh, really?

326

They don't know if they were the first. They think they may be, because they had a very difficult time getting it, and they—

Yeah, we had a hell of a time getting it. Yeah, we got turned down by the IRS.

Yeah, so were they.

'Cause I didn't understand their special terminology. When I finally did, I got legal representation and we worked on through it. Got accepted, but it was a hell of a job. Now everybody has it.

When you first started out with the press, you couldn't have been making any money off it. It must have been costing you—

That's true. I still don't make a lot of money on it. Our earned income level is, you know, we make a lot more than we used to, but our expenses are a lot more, too. And we could not function without grant support.

There were thirteen years, though, before you had grant support, right?

No. We got NEA support very early and—

This was before you were nonprofit?

Yeah. We had some kind of umbrella organization. I've forgotten which one we used. And we got money from the New York State Council on the Arts. It was really difficult to get private foundation support in New York state at that time, so we virtually had just public support. But it changed quite a bit when we moved to Minnesota. There's a lot of foundation support here.

When you say "public support," do you mean sales?

No. I mean grants.

Public institutions.

Yeah. Unearned income. Because we did a lot of first books. And we still do a lot of first books. We did nothing but poetry at first. It was really hard to generate much interest in it. In my personal opinion,

327

poetry is a marvelous art in this country, but it's very, very hard to market it. For a long time I was lucky to sell three hundred copies of a book. And of course the prices were ridiculously low at that time. I mean we were selling chapbooks for fifty cents.

When was this now?
In the late '60s, early '70s. Now it costs me a great deal more to have a book typeset than it used to cost for printing.

When did you get national distribution?
SPD [Small Press Distribution] in California was our first one.

Well, they're not really a distributor though. Do they have sales reps?
I don't think they have sales reps. When I knew them—I don't know what they have now; they're still in business—they used to be called Serendipity Distribution.

Oh, really? I didn't know that. I'd heard of Serendipity, but I didn't know they had evolved into SPD.
Yeah. Because there was a Serendipity Book Shop and the owner of that bookstore was one of the founders of the distribution company, it was called Serendipity, which, when he went off on his own, became SPD. They started distributing us in the early '70s.

Did you also have Bookpeople?
No. I know who they are. When I visited them in California, they were mostly into New Age stuff.

Yeah. They're almost exclusively New Age now.
I'm fairly traditional in taste, judgment, and so forth.

One of the conclusions I came to in doing my first book [Gold 1996] was that the smaller, independent publishers today are really kind of a throwback to when publishing was a cottage industry. We're the ones who are the traditionalists. Random House and Simon and Schuster, they're the ones that, for better or worse, are going off into space.

Oh, yeah. I agree. You know, it's thought that New Rivers, in that respect, because of my background, is an academic press. I didn't study creative writing in college at all. I had one course of it when I was in grad school. I didn't like it very much. I had a very traditional background in literature. I still think about poets I studied. My favorite contemporary poets still are William Butler Yeats and T.S. Eliot.

Did you have a national distributor with sales reps before Consortium?

Talman was our distributor before.

When did you go to Talman?
I think we went with them in 1987.

And you were with them till...when?
We left them in '95.

Were they a big help to you?
Initially they were, yeah. Then, I don't know, sales fell way off, and stuff like that. Consortium is local and they seem to be doing much better, although our returns are just a terrible situation, thanks to Barnes and Noble. Basically, it's Barnes and Noble who's ruining the book business. The problem with Barnes and Noble is that they've opened so many new stores. When they open a new store they order a lot of books to make a big impression on people. And then they return them. So the return rates through Consortium have just been astronomical, and it's really cut back on our earned income a lot. Hopefully, that situation will change, but I don't know.

What is your return rate?
It varies. You'll have to talk to our marketing person about that. But I know it's been as high as fifty percent, which is really high.

Yeah. I've had the same situation. It has been that high. Mostly it's around thirty-eight percent for me, which is still very high.
Yeah, it's still high. Ideally, it should be somewhere around twenty-one, twenty-two percent, something like that.

Well, before I had distribution, when I just dealing with whole-salers, it was down around fifteen...less than twenty percent. Of course, I wasn't selling as many books, either. If you could change distribution in any way—I mean everybody complains about distribution—if you could change distribution in any way, how would you have it different?

I'm basically very practical. I'd like to sell more books. Reach a wider audience. But those are pipe dreams. We do our best. We market. I published one short novel by Patricia Barone called *The Wind*. The heroine is a physical therapist by profession, but a painter by design. The physical therapist is a protagonist, as is her chief patient, a Jungian therapist. So we had a literary market, a physical therapy market, and a Jungian market for that book.

How did you reach all those markets?

Well, we tried. I'm not sure we did it successfully. But we used a representative from each field on the back of the book.

Have you tried getting into course adoptions?

As much as possible. It's really hard. Especially—I mean, we've done a lot of translations. But it's been very hard to break into that area. A lot of English professors, the people who would naturally adopt our books, are very loathe to adopt them.

Why?

I don't know. They're just very traditional. We've tried quite a bit to reach into that market; we've had some success.

How did you try?

Well, we've gone to the MLA conventions. Sent out flyers. Especially to creative writing people. We've been to the AWP a couple of times, three or four times maybe.

Was that effective, going there? I'm thinking about going this year. I never have.

It's really hard to measure. In terms of overall sales, I don't think so. In terms of manuscript submissions, yeah. Same with MLA.

Because a lot of professors write books. And they have a hard time getting presses to publish them, so they go to small presses when they hear about publishers in their area. I'm being a little bit cynical when I say that.

We've published some books that really should be adopted. I did a book about ten, twelve years ago called *Poems from Italy* [edited by Dana Gioia and William Jay Smith] which is a really comprehensive anthology of poetry from Saint. Francis of Assisi up to the present time. And it's got a whole world of translators, from Geoffrey Chaucer to Seamus Heaney. And it's a totally bilingual book; it's the only bilingual book we've ever done, with English and Italian on facing pages. It's been adopted, but not by nearly enough schools. But when I go to book fairs or anything like that, that's always a popular book. People love it. People who don't know Italian can read the Italian because the translations are on the facing pages. We've published a lot of books that really would be very good in courses.

Have you tried book clubs? Have you had anything—?

Mainly small ones, like the Norwegian Book Club. We had a Norwegian-American anthology called *There Lies a Fair Land*. It was a local book club.

Does your press have a mission? What do want for it?

Basically I want very good writing. When we do an anthology, for instance, the quality of submission is paramount. Much more so than, say, the theme. We've done a lot of ethnic anthologies but, again, the primary requirement is that it be very good writing. Our editors know that. A lot of presses don't do that. Some of [other presses' anthologies] have pretty good writing, but a lot of it is very polemical. And, frankly, I'm not interested in polemics. I don't have a central and political agenda. Personally, I'm probably left of center, but New Rivers is not an ideological press.

Most of the writers that I published during the Viet Nam era were very much opposed to the Viet Nam war. The writing I got during that period was just awful, most of it. It was very polemical type stuff. And, actually, I wasn't interested. The best poem I ever saw about the Viet Nam war was written six years before our active involvement in it.

331

It was by my friend Jim Wright. It was called "Autumn Comes to Martin's Ferry, Ohio". It's a generational poem. It's about fathers who insist that their sons play football. It was so much like what was going on in the Viet Nam era. "Autumn Comes to Martin's Ferry, Ohio". It's a beautiful poem.[3] Robert Bly put that in his anthology, *A Poetry Reading Against the Vietnam War*.

So nowadays you publish poetry, you publish fiction—
Yeah, and a lot of anthologies. Sometimes we publish a nonfiction book—creative nonfiction, memoirs, stuff like that. But definitely with a literary cast. We don't publish criticism, although I've read a good deal of that.

Where do you publish your own writing?
Literary magazines like *North Dakota Quarterly*, places like that. I write mostly prose now. In fact, I got obsessed with writing about dreams in the early '80s. I have a three-hundred-page manuscript about dreams that's never been published. I revised it three or four years ago, but it was basically written about 1982, '83. A lot of that was published separately in little magazines. And I've written a lot of short stories and I've written a lot of essays. I had two essays on Wanda Gág, who's a Minnesota writer and artist.

What do you suppose got you interested in literature? I mean you came from a family whose reading, I suppose, is not the kind of reading you do.
I like reading though. Though I was still a Christian Scientist when I was growing up, my two favorite authors when I was a late teenager were Saint Exupery—*Wind, Sand, and Stars*—and, of all people, Ayn Rand—*The Fountainhead*. For a while I was determined to be an architect, because of that book. Now, God, I'm embarrassed to say it. But I got interested in writing when I was in college. I started reading a lot then. I was really a late bloomer. I started writing poetry seriously almost as therapy to get out of a really bad situation, a scandalous situation.

Abusive?

No. It was never—they weren't abusive.

I have a full-time job; I mean I don't make anything off publishing. I'm a counselor at a prison for juveniles.
You probably know of a lot more abusive situations than—

Yeah. That's why I immediately—
I don't think my father was ever physically abusive. He was certainly psychologically abusive. I had four brothers and sisters; all hated my father. Loved my mother.

You mentioned Wanda Gág.
Yeah. She's probably better known as an artist and illustrator. She wrote a book called *Millions of Cats*. It's seen like sixty-three editions. She died in...I think in the late '40s or '50s.

She wrote the book or illustrated it?
She did both. But she wrote a journal called *Growing Pains* which was published originally by Coward McCann. A friend of mine was a composer and did a song cycle based on that book, and that's how I got interested. So I read *Growing Pains* and just loved the book, and wrote a long essay on that, which has not been published.

I've talked to a number of publishers who were writers but who haven't written, creatively at least, in several years.
That's not true of me.

Does publishing interfere with your writing?
It can. Sometimes it does. Quite a few years ago I came to what turned out to be a really important decision for me. Because I'm getting older—I'm sixty-eight now—the thought naturally pops into my head: How do I want best to be remembered, as the New Rivers Press publisher or as a writer? There's no question in my mind that I would rather be remembered as a writer. And I see publishing as an extension of that, rather than vice versa.[4] I know that's not true of a lot of small press people. And I know a lot of—like Allan Kornblum [publisher of Coffee House Press] doesn't write at all any more, as far as I know.

He says he does about two poems a year.

Yes. And Emilie Buchwald [publisher of Milkweed Editions] used to write a lot of poetry and a lot of prose, but I don't think she writes much now.

She says it's been about four years since she's written. Bruce McPherson—I don't know if you know McPherson and Company—

I know of him. I know very little about his press. I used to see him at New York book fairs often.

He doesn't write any more. Sam Hamill—

He writes a lot.

But he also regards his editing as informing his writing, and vice versa [see Gold 1996: 401-427].

Yeah. I see a strong relationship between editing and teaching. Grading papers is, I think, a lot like editing a manuscript. And since I started off teaching rather than publishing, it's sort of a natural extension of that.

When you say you regard publishing as an extension of writing, do you mean the editing aspect of publishing, or do you mean all of publishing?

The whole thing. I mainly do editing now because I have a marketing person and a production manager, but I used to do everything. Absolutely everything.

When did you bring on other people?

'Eighty-seven. Thereabouts. Before that I was doing my own paste-ups, stuff like that.

So you got 501(c)(3) status when it was just you?

Yeah. I had a board. [Laughs.] That was important. You can't do it without a board. They had a restriction: you couldn't publish yourself. I don't know if that's still true or not. It certainly was then. Oh, I've done a little bit, but not very much. I just do translations, and

334

occasionally a piece of writing in an anthology or something. But basically I don't do my own books.

I asked Sandy Taylor—he felt he didn't want to publish his own stuff; he didn't think it was appropriate. On the one hand, he says there's a dwindling market for quality, imaginative writing. On the other hand, he says that any good manuscript will find its publisher.

I don't think that's right. I think there are a lot of good manuscripts that have never found their publishers.

I agree. I've seen some of them that I'm sure will never be published.

Yeah. There's a lot of good stuff. One of our roles as a publisher is bringing out first books, giving people a chance. We're doing as well as we can, by marketing. I have real strong objections to the NEA suspending support to small press publishers in favor of giving grants to writers. As a writer, I can say that. Publishing is really important. It's important to me that what I write gets out there.

I don't have any other questions.

It's been fun talking to you. I enjoyed it a lot.

Good. Thank you.

Notes

1. "New Rivers Press: The New York Years," (manuscript): "When I began New Rivers Press in February 1968, the United States had been directly involved in the Vietnam War for nearly four years. Though there were disturbing signs of its demise, the Counter-Culture, which centered in California, had been flourishing for perhaps more than that amount of time. In New York, its most visible appearance was in the St. Marks Place and Tompkins Square area on the Lower East Side but its influence spread throughout the city and was more visible and messier than any other revolutionary movement in this country had ever been. The temptation to be new and different was almost irresistable, as was the energy abroad in the city and almost all over this country, fueled by the hatred of our involvement in Vietnam and the desire to build a brand new culture. It was a heady and youthful time in America. And a time as experimental and chaotic

as that which characterized the early days of this country prior to the American Civil War, almost exactly one hundred years earlier.

"I vividly remember going down to the East Village several times in 1968 and 1969 to see for myself what it was all about and to hawk the early New Rivers Press books. Walking across Cooper Square towards St. Marks Place, I was set upon by dozens of young panhandlers, mostly young women dressed in longish baggy dresses, hustling me for money. I walked down St. Marks Place crowded with young drifters, past head shops and the blaring new music emanating from The Electric Circus and other hip establishments towards Tompkins Square where the Peace Eye Bookstore was located....

"To those of us like myself who had been born too late to be directly involved in World War II and too early by fifteen or twenty years to be in danger of going to Vietnam, it was a time immensely attractive and frightening at once. I was too old and had too great a sense of history not to be worried about the future and where all this new energy was going to lead, but young enough to be swayed by it too, to be caught up in its novelty and the hope (forlorn, I feared) that some bright new future would actually come about. In other words, though I was much attracted to this new spirit, I was too compromised by my past and too old to be a good revolutionary.

"Literature, along with the new music and experimentation in drugs, was at the forefront of these new times. Prior to 1960, for instance, literature was dominated by the then powerful Eastern Literary Establishment centered in New York City. This meant that a new writer, often a poet, would follow a more or less fixed path toward recognition and the accumulation of awards. He or she (much more often a 'he' rather than a 'she') would submit his or her work to three or four of the best-known literary magazines like *The New Yorker*, *Atlantic Monthly*, *Quarterly Review of Literature*, *Hudson Review*, *Partisan Review*, *Harper's*, *The Kenyon Review*, and perhaps *The Southern Review*.... (When I first started sending poems out, for instance, I automatically sent them twenty or thirty times to *The New Yorker* or *Atlantic Monthly*. None of my work was ever published in either magazine but that didn't keep me from dreaming of that kind of glory.)

"Beginning as early as 1960, this preeminent position of the Eastern Literary Establishment began to be challenged by an explosion of new literary magazines that began to appear all over the country, most often in California. By 1968, literally thousands of these new magazines—often little more than shabby and poorly designed mimeographed rags—had come on the scene. Small presses, of which there were perhaps only two or three before 1960,...now numbered in the hundreds. A few of these existed to publish the work of their editors but many grew into real distinction, like George Hitchcock's Kayak Press...in California, Sumac Press in Michigan,...Teo Savory's Unicorn Press

336

and The Jargon Society in North Carolina, and many others, most of which are now defunct. The quality of poetry published in...them varied greatly, but most of it was characterized by a rebellion against the Eastern Literary Establishment and celebrated a very different style of life and work. The poetry was much more open in form, wilder in subject matter, youthful, energetic, and tied to readings and other forms of public performance. Almost all of it was anti-Vietnam War and anti-Establishment....

"It was in this climate that I started New Rivers Press."

2. *Ibid.* "In 1966, I...spent some six months in Mexico on an unpaid leave of absence from my position at Macalester College in St. Paul, a position which for me had grown almost unbearably ugly and academically political—so much so that I was seriously considering leaving teaching altogether....

"In Mexico, I was befriended by Meg Randall and Sergio Mondragón who ran a literary magazine called *El Corno Emplumado* and also published a great many books under the same imprint. *El Corno* was widely known all over Latin America and was very left-radical and political in orientation, much more so than I was at the time. They were also very much in step with the revolutionary fervor of the Counter-Culture. For some reason, they decided to publish my first book there in the spring of 1966. *In the Country of a Deer's Eye* was certainly less political than most of the books they published.

"I was much intrigued by El Corno Emplumado Press—its relative success (that first book of mine, for instance, was out of print before it was even published!), its economics (a dependence on government and private funding), and the cross-cultural, international flavor of the literary work they published. In the back of my mind, I began to dwell on the idea of starting such a press when I got back to America in the summer of 1966.

"I did little about this, however, until I had left teaching a year later and moved to New York where I hoped (vainly, as it turned out) to be accepted by the Establishment crowd on the strength of my poetry and the reception it had received in Mexico.

"My family and I lived in Nyack, New York...from August 1967 until June 1968. It was in Nyack that I started New Rivers Press—really by accident. I did not much like Nyack. I could only write for three or four hours a day, and not having a teaching position any longer, I had a lot of time on my hands. My late ex-brother-in-law Bill Chafee and his wife Connie, who lived down near Bellevue Hospital in New York City, had bought a small farm in the hilly country around Southfield, Massachusetts. In a shed in back of this house, there was an old Chandler & Price letterpress which had been used by the previous owners to print captions on the silkscreen Christmas cards they produced. Bill told me that since I had always talked about starting a small press, here was my chance. He gave me that printing press, and I started printing books there in February 1968 even though I knew nothing whatever about letterpress or any other kind of printing and was not the least bit interested in hand-setting type. In fact, I lugged heavy boxes of lead linotype I had had set by a printer in West Nyack up to Southfield in the trunk of my car.

"One of the very first books I printed up there was Meg Randall's *So Many Rooms Has a House but One Roof*, a small chapbook of poems she had written celebrating her visit to Castro's Cuba in 1967. Meg also let me have her *El Corno Emplumado* mailing list, which became the nucleus of the New Rivers list.

"In all, I printed three books in Southfield, including Meg's and Al Greenberg's *The Metaphysical Giraffe*, before switching in 1969 to the much cheaper, more efficient, faster, and less time-consuming offset printing method which we still use."

3. *Ibid.* "Although I was strongly opposed to the American involvement in Vietnam and almost all of the writers I published were also strongly opposed to it as well, I had to acknowledge early on that most of the anti-war poetry I had read (a lot of which was submitted to New Rivers) was pretty awful. Much of it was strident and neither well-informed nor imaginative. I knew very well that neither in America nor in any other English-speaking country were there many really first-rate political poems, maybe only as few as a handful—like Sir Thomas Wyatt's "They flee from me that sometime did me seek," one or two or Shakespeare's plays, Andrew Marvell's "Horatian Ode," and in our own day Yeats's "Easter 1916" and James Wright's "Autumn Comes to Martins Ferry, Ohio." Why this was true of American and British poetry (and there are great differences between the culture and literary expression in those countries as well) and not of Latin American writing or that coming out of Africa (particularly South Africa), Eastern Europe and the then Soviet Union is no great mystery to me. While the American and Soviet empires had much in common, for instance, the writers in each of those areas were exposed to very different kinds of authority. The monolithic governments of the then Soviet Union and the Eastern European countries controlled by it were the major focus of the writers' attention. The immense popularity of Soviet poets like Yevtushenko and Vosnishenski, especially in their early, post-Stalin work, spoke, perhaps indirectly, to the thousands of voiceless and disaffected masses. No such mass appeal existed in America even during the Vietnam War, though that war and the hatred of the young toward the established government and President Lyndon Johnson almost, for a time, overcame the traditional hostility or indifference of the mass of American people toward poetry. America, after all, had a long history of freedom of speech, despite what many of us felt was the effort

338

to undermine that tradition during the Johnson and Nixon regimes. Though many American poets envied what they saw happening in Russia and the immense popularity of Soviet poets like Yevtushenko in our own country, their poetry at its best was rooted in private, subjective experience and tended to be much more personal than what was coming out of Russia where the cult of the individual simply did not exist....

"So I tended to read what political, anti-war poetry came my way in the late sixties with considerable irony and even distaste... What did affect me in those early days was the youthful, energetic, sometimes outrageous poetry that expressed the values of the Counter-Culture which I sometimes published if I thought it was good enough.

"The truth of the matter was that I really adored good poetry and knew that it was not usually the product of a particular school or movement. This was a very old-fashioned view of things in 1968 and I suppose it still is. For this reason New Rivers has always been and continues to be a very eclectic small press. As a publisher I have never been affected by nor have I looked for anything that is fashionable or trendy even when I have been told that such and such a writer will earn us lots of money and/or notoriety. I look with considerable irony at anything which proclaims itself to be "avant garde" or Black Mountain or New York School or L.A.N.G.U.A.G.E. or concrete or mythopoetic or formalist poetry or post-modernist or what have you, though I have often found among such schools individual poems and writers I really like...."

4. *Ibid.* "Writing has always come first for me. Publishing I saw as an extension of that, even though, at times, it has come to dominate my everyday life and has often been more than stressful. I can even say that I function much better as a publisher when I am deeply engaged in writing.

"When I started New Rivers I had no compelling literary axe to grind nor any clear sense of what I wanted to accomplish beyond publishing the best work that came my way. What was most important to me as a poet was that I say what I had to say as richly and originally as it was within my power and imagination to accomplish regardless of whether or not it was fashionable...or would lead me to some kind of enduring recognition (not that I was ever indifferent to such recognition and even fame). What was really important to me in publishing and became more so as I got into it was that those whose work I brought out did not necessarily have the same ideas or vision as I did but that they had...voices unlike the voices of any other poets, including myself."

Pearl Kilbride
Hungry Mind Press (Ruminator Books)

"[S]upposedly a manuscript was killed because the chains said, 'Oh, we can't take it.' I think that when you get that much influence, it is a huge—there are people who, if a book doesn't go in the chains, they're not going to publish it because they can't get the numbers. And that is very scary. Then you're entering very scary territory, and that's part of the reason we exist. If you allow that much power to [accrue to] a single source that ends up dictating what people publish, then what does that say for freedom of information/flow of ideas?"

Pearl Kilbride, publisher of Hungry Mind Press, was born and raised in Williston, North Dakota. "There was a small library, and that was about it. No bookstores. There was a bookmobile from a neighboring town that would come around, so once a month you could check out books from the bookmobile. Service Drug was where you would go to buy books. The drug store. Going to college was the eye opener for me." She graduated from the University of Oregon with a bachelor's degree in international relations. "I actually started off in cultural anthropology. The more I got into kinship groups and that sort of thing, the more I got interested in how people will group together on different issues, which eventually led me to the whole act-locally-think-globally thing." In her mid-thirties when I interviewed her, she appeared even younger; indeed, she has the enthusiasm of someone in her twenties. She has been married to David Unowsky, owner of Hungry Mind Bookstore in St. Paul, Minnesota since 1991. She and Unowsky live in St. Paul, within walking distance of the store.

I interviewed her on the morning of September 19, 1997, a Friday. We talked in the kitchen in the rear of the bookstore after exchanging catalogues, she giving me Hungry Mind Press' most recent, I giving her Black Heron's, my own press'.

(Note: At the beginning of 2000, Hungry Mind Press' name was changed to Ruminator Books. Hungry Mind Bookstore also took on the name Ruminator Books.)

This neighborhood, actually, reminds me of the area around the University of Montana in Missoula. Just the way it's configured.

It's a great neighborhood. It has a real home-town feel. Coming from rural North Dakota, this is like the perfect way to be in a larger city. You know, you walk up and down the streets and you always see people you know. I love that.

It's safe? Do you walk at night?
Yeah. I mean you have to be smart, but...yeah.

I live in Seattle, and there're drugs everywhere. Even in my neighborhood there's the occasional shooting.
Oh, no. That's too bad. Minneapolis has had some problems—well, we've had some problems, too, in St. Paul. It's sad once that happens; it's hard to get rid of.

Yeah. It's the only kind of crime that keeps increasing. The national crime rate is dropping; violent youth crime keeps rising.
Right. Well, I think there's a direct link between Reagan economics and the kids that are coming up now. I think you have to look at the picture in an historical context.

Yeah. The press isn't how I make my living. I make my living as a counselor in a prison for juveniles.
Really!

Yeah.
Interesting.

I do look at it in an historical context. On the other hand, I deal with them as individuals. I'm one of the trainers for new employees coming in. I tell them that, one, they need to develop a capacity for heartbreak, and, two, they need to find a level of paranoia that they're comfortable with, and stay there. [Laughs.]
Absolutely! I think that's very interesting. My niece came to live with us when she was fifteen. She was a troubled kid. We spent a

341

lot of time working with her. I mean, she's great. She's absolutely wonderful. But a lot of the friends that she found here were homeless kids. They were homeless for a variety of reasons. And it was truly amazing—these kids had so much potential; they were so needy and yet so distrustful of adults. You know, when some of the kids would come in we'd give them a big hug. And it was like, their whole face was like—

That sounds like the kids I deal with, except the ones I deal with, of course, have been convicted of felonies.
Right.

So. How did you wind up here in St. Paul?
Well, I was in Oregon, and I'd lived in New York for a short period, and when I graduated I was trying to figure out where I wanted to go. I didn't want to move back to the East Coast, I didn't want to live in a real small town again, and the Twin Cities was the most logical place. It wasn't a huge city, but it had some of the attractions of a large city, and it wasn't a really small town, but it had the feel of it.

Did you know somebody here?
Not really. My mother had some cousins who lived here, so I stayed with them when I first moved here. Actually, they were living right across from a crack house, and when I first moved in I was a little bit naïve. [Laughs.] I learned quickly a little bit of what was going on in the city. This was in Minneapolis. I lived there for about two years and then I moved to St. Paul. And this definitely became home.

What were you doing in New York?
I was working as a nanny. Coming from a small town, it was the easiest way to go to a large city. I don't think I would have done it any other way. At that time. Now it's a lot different, but being a scared kid.... Even getting into a taxi was frightening, 'cause you're always told, "Don't get into a car with a strange man." Well, that's what taxis are. It was terribly intimidating for me. So it was a big experience, a really good experience. It opened my eyes to a lot of things. Coming from a place where you know absolutely everybody and you've known them all your life and you know their whole family history, then you come into

a place where—the apartment building that we lived in had more people in it than my entire home town.

So you came to the Twin Cities.

Came to the Twin Cities. I worked for the [Nuclear] Freeze Campaign for a while. When I first moved to the St. Paul area—I think it was '86. The summer of '86—I had three part-time jobs. I had one day off a month. I was working at a restaurant, at a small bookstore called Learn Me, which is a children's specialty bookstore, and then here at Hungry Mind. And I did that for a few months, till I totally burned out. Then I went full time at Hungry Mind. And I've been here ever since.

You're the publisher of Hungry Mind Press, right?

Right. But there are other partners. Our first book was in the fall of '95. In part, when Andre Schiffrin left Pantheon, this was the impetus for us. And, working at the bookstore, we saw a lot of things becoming more and more commercial. The conglomeration of the large publishers meant that a lot of books were going out of print much faster. Mid-list authors were falling out of what could have been good career paths. We thought there was a need for those authors to have a home. And we also have a lot of people from Hungry Mind who, you know, they see the publishing world [as being in New York], and so they go to New York. You lose a lot of people going to New York, finding jobs in publishing. It was like, why can't we have a publishing house here? There's some good people here. And that was the impetus for it.

We had Page Cowles, who's one of our partners, and Margaret Wuertle, Gail See, who is a long-time book person—she's been the president of the ABA; she's been in the book business for a long time. And then David Unowsky and myself. That's how we started, and that was the perfect way to start. We started meeting in restaurants [laughs]— very low overhead—and we did that for a short period of time. Then in March of this year I became publisher and began to work full time at the press because we needed somebody full time. And we have a staff of two people, Dallas Crow and Nicole Baxter. He's the sales manager, she's publishing assistant. Both are great people.

The press started in '95, you say?

That was our first list. We do four books a season, eight a year. Because we were in a transition, with me taking over and the partners taking lesser roles, we ended up with just two this season, but we're back to four again. And, hopefully, that'll go up again. That's the goal.

Is it profitable?

It will be. [Laughs.]

How do you know?

'Cause I think that we are publishing books that have a life. We can do things where you don't have to have twenty-five thousand copies. We started off doing reprints. That was part of the program.

I read Reconciliation Road.

Oh, good. Yeah. So we do some reprints. That gives us a base, a backlist. We haven't been around for very long, and two of our books have already won awards. *Sleeping with the Mayor*, which is a book that was just released—there's going to be a review in the *New York Times* on the twenty-eighth, a San Diego paper is picking it up, we have him [John Jiler, the author] on NPR [National Public Radio], so things are happening.

You do all nonfiction?

We started off doing all nonfiction. For us that was a way to start, a way to get into the publishing business. We are looking at doing fiction now. Our base will still be nonfiction, but we'll do select literary fiction. We'll still do some reprints, but more and more we're moving towards originals. *Sleeping with the Mayor* is an original. It's about the encampment of homeless people, called Kochville, outside City Hall. It was when Ed Koch was mayor.

You're with Consortium?

Mm hm. Right. They're a national distribution company. They do a great job for us. When I was in New York, everywhere we went *Sleeping with the Mayor* was out there, in quantity. It was wonderful. They're a good company for us. They're nice people too.

Yeah. Randall [i.e., Randall Beek, CEO of Consortium] is very committed.

Well, he's been in the business a long time, he's seen the ups and downs, he knows how the business goes. I think that helps, to have that kind of history, where he can say, "Well, this is the way the industry was, this is where it's moving."

Lawrence Ferlinghetti, in an interview I read somewhere, talked about the relationship between City Lights Books and City Lights bookstore, and he said he was glad to have both, because during hard years for the bookstore he could use the press' funds to shore it up, and vice versa. Do you—?

We are separate. I mean, it's important for us to be near the bookstore. Part of the reason we started is the connection with the bookstore. You see things on a different level. You see what's out there. You can spot trends, you see what's selling, what's not. So I think it's an integral part of the press to be associated with the bookstore. But financially we're separate. It's a separate organization, [though] I am involved in both, and Dallas used to work at the bookstore.

Do you think you'll be able to sustain eight books a year?

Mm hm. We would like to grow eventually. We'll see how soon we're able to do that, but I would like to see it grow to at least fifteen. Fifteen to twenty books a year would be great.

You're not nonprofit, are you?

That is correct.

Why not?

Part of it, I think, is that we're used to running our own business. And when you have funders, you have various things you have to do, things you have to get approved. We wanted to be able to be decisive. This is how we run the bookstore.

I think there's definitely a need for nonprofits. There's a huge need for nonprofits. I think the role of nonprofits is to publish things that are a bit more daring, publish things that are not—maybe an author who isn't quite ripe yet—to give him exposure, to give him feedback. I think that the rules are slightly different for not-for-profit and for-profit. Depending on what your mission is, I think that the goals are slightly different.

One of the arguments against, not public funding, but against the individual press accepting certain monies, is that there is a tendency to publish what you think will get you money instead of what you want to publish.

Right. Right.

I think that's true. I think that's happened here in the Twin Cities. Not that they're choosing to publish bad material, but they were publishing other things until the NEA restricted its funding.

But, then, where is the difference? If the funding falls off and you have to find sources elsewhere, then your goal changes to having to be profitable to be able to fund your books, and so you go into a more commercial area. For us, we have to have a certain amount of commercially viable work in order to support other works we completely believe in and maybe isn't as—

This is how the independent publishers in New York look at it, none of whom are nonprofit. None that I interviewed, anyway. They have a commercial aspect to the press, and those books allow them to publish other works that they think are important. Even the commercial books—they're books on which they expect to make money, but they still regard them as important. As opposed to, say, a nonprofit press which publishes, or tries to publish, only work that it regards as important to literature or to literary history. That makes the nonprofit more dependent on their funding sources, because they're not devoting a part of their production to commercial work. I'm not saying it's better or worse, I'm just saying if Four Walls Eight Windows—they have a more commercial aspect and they have a literary aspect—is successful with its commercial work, then they can publish other, more daring, things. And they do.

That's true. Absolutely. You're right.

I asked John Oakes [publisher of Four Walls Eight Windows] why he wasn't nonprofit. He said he just could not bring himself to do the paperwork.

Yeah. [Both laugh.] Absolutely. It's true, it's true. I mean it does add a different element to it. Part of the press is like we've always been—on our own. It's what we're comfortable with.

Have you given the press a time limit to show that it's commercially viable?

I think it's like anything where you have certain goals—you see if you can meet them, and you watch your progress. You see how far you can go with what you have, and build on it. There's not a specific time limit, but there certainly are goals that we have to meet, or want to meet.

What happens if you don't meet those goals?

Then we sit down and reevaluate and say, "Well, why is it that we didn't meet the goals? What changes do we need to make to meet the next set of goals?" It's like running the business here. Every day you open the door—who's going to come in? You have this history, so you know what to expect. But you constantly have to look at your business and decide how to make changes in order to position yourself the best way possible. Same thing with the press. You constantly have to be looking at where you're at, where you fit in, are you getting the attention and support that you need. You're constantly trying to guess what the trends are, what's going to happen. In the bookstore we can sort of see trends. We have an idea as to what customers are buying, what direction they're going. The questions we get from customers as to what it is they're looking for—that helps us to predict a trend. And we try to move in that direction.

Have you been pretty accurate, using this store to predict a trend nationally?

I think so. For instance, Chet Raymo—we've done two of his reprints, *The Soul of the Night* and *Honey From Stone*. He is a scientist but he also grew up religious, and so his books talk about how you reconcile those two things. And I think that is very timely. I think a lot

347

of people are thinking in those terms, what their spiritual and religious life is and how they reconcile it with science. And part of that comes from what we see selling on our shelves.

Would you publish a book that you really didn't care about? Not one you dislike, but one where you just didn't care about what the author was saying.

Yes. If we thought that it was valuable. Sure. Just because I may not personally like a particular subject—for instance, I'm not much of a horse-race fan, but we're going to be publishing *Laughing in the Hills* by Bill Barich, which is—it's a great book, but it's not one that I normally would have picked up. But other people absolutely love the book.

So somebody else selected that book?

Actually, the marketing manager really likes Bill Barich's work. I mean it's something that we all have to believe in, but it doesn't have to rest on my personal taste. It's definitely not my personal taste that's going to dictate to the press. I don't think that's right.

Do you all vote? Do you have a meeting—?

We have an editorial meeting where we discuss the merits of the work.

So everybody's read the work before you sit down?

At least two people usually have read the work.

How many people are at the meeting?

Usually between three and five. It's usually Dallas, myself, David, and then Tom Bielenberg from the store sits on our editorial. That way we get different interests and input. Tom is like a partner in the store. He's been here for twenty years. He is the buyer. He knows the books inside out.

If you go from reprinting work to doing original work, will that be a shift in direction?

No. On our first list we had an original work. We have the

reprints; we just want to start developing more original work as well. Instead of one out of four books being an original, we'd like to make it at least fifty-fifty.

Do you try to sell subsidiary rights?

Yes. We do our own subsidiary rights, but we also have an agent in New York to sell foreign rights.

Have you sold anything abroad?

Not yet, no. Not abroad. We've sold rights, like *Crossing the Moon*, which is an original hardcover for us. Penguin has picked up the paperback rights. It's in their new catalogue; we just saw it yesterday, actually. So we have that sort of thing. But that stuff we do ourselves.

[Looking through the Hungry Mind catalogue:] What's "Hungry Mind Find"?

That's our reprint series. We get booksellers across the country to make recommendations to us as to what they think are good books that have gone out of print and that they would like to see back in print. 'Cause booksellers, within their region, know what's going on. They know what books have gone out of print that they think shouldn't have, or that they think have a steady, consistent life. And that's what we're looking at.

Linny Stovall of Blue Heron Press told me that she had read or heard—I don't know where her information came from—but she said that some of the big corporate houses are now running manuscripts by Barnes and Noble to see whether they think—you heard that too?

Mm hm. There was an article in the *New York Times* about that. I think that it's important for publishers to run things by a variety of booksellers. My problem is—supposedly a manuscript was killed because the chains said, "Oh, we can't take it." I think that when you get that much influence, it is a huge—there are people who, if a book doesn't go in the chains, they're not going to publish it because they can't get the numbers. And that is very scary. Then you're entering very scary territory, and that's part of the reason we exist. If you allow that much power to [accrue to] a single source that ends up dictating what

349

people publish, then what does that say for freedom of information/flow of ideas? We're treading on very dangerous ground, and I think people are starting to realize that. But I'm surprised it took this long for people to start understanding it.

Oh, I think certain people have known it. But how do you deal with it?
Well, there's a lot of short-term thinking—

Well, this has long-term consequences though. I had a book refused by Barnes and Noble. First there was one reason, then there was another; there was always a reason. It made me very suspicious; there was always one particular person doing the refusing. My sales rep wouldn't tell me her name—the name of the person refusing. I was very suspicious that that happened. Even though the book was reviewed—it got a great review in Kirkus, *got a fair review in* Library Journal. *But it was reviewed in those places and was reviewed in other places afterward. They still wouldn't buy it. Even though the author was doing readings—she's from Manhattan and she was doing readings between Boston and Manhattan. Finally, they bought, I think, a hundred copies, but they didn't want to. On the other hand, they bought more than I wanted to sell of another book.*
Mm hm. But then you watch for returns.

That's right.
I think it's very scary when—again, this article in the *New York Times* where one of the Riggio brothers was quoted to the effect that after three or four weeks, if a hardcover book is on the shelf and it's not moving, they want to go back to the publisher and say, Okay, I'm not going to pay you. You need to discount this even further and so you're going to have to give us a discount on it because it's not moving.
Well, in our business, you know that a book, in order to make it—especially if you're going to nurture an author—you have to have it on the shelf for a significant time. And that time period between when it's on the shelf and when it disappears, even for independents, has gotten smaller and smaller because of economics. Whereas before you could have a book on your shelf for six months and help build an

audience for it. And then you make a real book out of it. And that's the danger: You have this small amount of time to make it happen.

It's across the board now though. Well, Elliott Bay [i.e., Elliott Bay Book Company in Seattle] is good to me. There's no question about it; they really bend over backwards. But by and large the independents that I deal with mostly are imitating the chains. They're frightened, so they're trying to do what they think works, and they think that the chains are working. I don't know that that's true.

They're losing money. They're losing their shirts. And I think you're right. The ones who do try to imitate, they can't compete on that level. You have to separate yourself out. You can't compete. You can't do what they do. You have to be different. But you're right. I don't know that everybody gets that. The ones who do are making headway. But it's a scary industry that way and we've seen just way too many things shake out.

I'm going to publish something next year; I don't expect to sell five hundred copies but I think it's an important piece of work and it will attract some attention from some people. But it's not going to sell a lot. Now Barnes and Noble may take a few hundred copies, but they're not going to sell them. And so they'll come flooding back. On the other hand, the author will do readings at Elliott Bay and Village Books, the independents, and...[laughs] we still won't sell many copies. I know that that type of work is going to upset people, so they won't buy it. Nevertheless, some people will look at it seriously. That makes it worth doing.

Absolutely. Absolutely. That's part of the beauty of publishing, when you have a work like that that you absolutely believe in. Unfortunately, I think there're not that many people like you out there.

Well, I'm doing things that are unreasonable. It's not reasonable to expect somebody to—

But a few of the good ones do. Like the 'zines. A lot of those 'zines aren't making money. But they're doing it because they love what they're doing. I am so excited about what's going to happen in the next few years from that group of people. By that time a lot of stuff is

351

going to shift. We're in a transitional period right now. But things are going to shift, and that group of people are going to be coming up and they're going to be producing strong work, and I think that is the most exciting thing.

The thing that bothers me about 'zine culture is the same thing that bothers me about anarchism: There's a right wing and a left wing, and the right wing really offends me. Now they distribute their stuff by handing it out on the street. That kind of distribution, on a small scale, works well.

Oh, yeah.

Some of it is homophobic. Some of it is neo-Nazi. It has to be watched out for.

Right. Yeah. I agree. But I do think that there are 'zines on the other side. In the balance, you let people pick and choose. It's a discussion of ideas. Even something that's neo-Nazi, you get it in your hands and you say, "Ugh. This is total trash. It's awful." People talk about it. And that's the whole point of a lot of what we do—to discuss and open things up. When things just happen in the closet, I don't know.... But if you can get outraged, if you can be impassioned, even if it's in a negative way, then it's important. I'd love to see more people impassioned or outraged over a 'zine.

Let me ask you, from the point of view of the store, what are some of the problems you have working with publishers?

Um. That is a loaded question. It brings up a variety of things. For the most part, this is a great business, and publishers are into it because they love books. That's why it's one of the most rewarding businesses I can think of to be in. I think that unfair credit, where more credit is given to chains [than to independent bookstores], where they have longer terms of payment, puts a heavy burden on a lot of independents. If they get an extra thirty days to pay, it makes a big difference. And people have done that. That's a big problem. The same with co-op dollars [i.e., advertising expenses shared by the bookstore, or chain, and the publisher]. The frustration comes more with the unfairness, and not having a level playing field. Not all publishers do that, obviously, but the ones who do—it's problematic.

On simple levels, I would say there are publishers who are very, very good about shipping, getting things to us on time, sending an order out the same day we request it, giving us feedback right away on whether or not it's in stock—you know, those kinds of service things, for the most part, are good. But there are a few publishers who drive you up the wall because they don't tell you that something is out of stock. They don't communicate very well. But it's great to have reps come around. Most of the reps are very responsive. We complain to them on a particular issue, some of them will go to the wall for you. Others don't. It depends. You can't characterize the industry as a whole, really.

Fiona McCrae
Graywolf Press

"What we're doing is almost by definition difficult."

Fiona McCrae was born in Nairobi in 1958 and moved to England with her parents two years later. She was raised in Harpenden, twenty-five miles north of London. She attended state school until she was sixteen, then went to public school in Dorset for her last two years. She took her undergraduate degree in English at Bristol University.

She became publisher of Graywolf Press in 1994, after Scott Walker, its founder and first publisher, left by what was called "a mutual decision" between his board of directors and himself. Apparently the responsibility for a record deficit was laid at his feet, and he was ousted. For a while, following Walker's departure, some doubted that the press would survive. Walker had been highly regarded by funders, as well as reviewers and other nonprofit publishers (see Covert 1994). Because of the financial crunch, half of Graywolf's staff had been laid off. This was the situation McCrae stepped into when she was hired seven months after Walker left. We talked on a sunny Friday in mid-September in her office in St. Paul, Minnesota.

I had this idea that I was going to be a teacher. When I was in high school, I thought maybe I would be a French teacher. Then I tried not to want to be a teacher. But by the time I'd finished I decided that that really was the most attractive thing.

Why did you try not to want to be a teacher?
Well, to look at it, it didn't seem very adventurous. And then I think a lot of people go into it because they can't think of anything else to do. But I really wanted to do it. Up until then, the only jobs that I'd done were cleaning jobs, in a hotel and hospitals and that kind of thing. Though I had this idea that to go into teaching and to go to school, university, would be very narrow, and that I needed to get a taste of the

working world. So that I could go back and tell my students about it. And in those days people couldn't type, as a rule. We did all our papers in university by hand. So I decided to learn to type and then get a job in an office. I had the kind of naïve idea that a year or so in an office would tell me how the world worked.

When I discussed being a teacher with my mother, she said to me, "Are there any other things that you're interested in?" I remember mentioning publishing, but it seemed I couldn't get in. It seemed like a closed thing, from my perspective. So I didn't really think hard about publishing. I went off and did this typing-skills thing. Before I had done that, I thought, Well, all I need to do is learn how to type and then I'll get a marvelous job. When you read the small print in the ad, it has to do with speeds and everything; a lot of jobs needed high typing speeds, and I had. But I was still in Bristol; I had stayed on in Bristol to do that. And by then I felt a strong pull to be in London which, you know, I'd grown up near. I hadn't loved it when I was a teenager or anything; I hadn't been drawn to it. But suddenly I wanted it as the only place to be.

So I went to a couple of [employment] agencies and the woman that was sitting next to the woman I was dealing with at one of these places said, "I've got a job in publishing if that's what you're interested in," because she'd heard me say another job sounded interesting. So I ended up having three interviews for publishing jobs. And in one they said to me, "You won't want this job. It's sitting in a basement, telexing orders to Hong Kong." And I failed the typing test; I think I spelled "liaison" wrong. So I learned how to spell that. I forgot the second "i".

But then I got an interview with the design department of a then academic press, a medium-size textbook publisher called Cassell. Cassell, Limited. It was a very junior position. It was secretary in the design department. So I got on quite well with the art director, and got hired. It was very junior, basic work, but I did enjoy it and sort of bought into the company. I got on well with my boss so it was a very nice working atmosphere. I ended up working there only eight months. When I think back to that eight-month period, it was the only time in my life when I felt that my job was finished at five o'clock. I really enjoyed that after all those years of studying and having things hanging over you, so I really took advantage of being in London and made sure I got to the Tate Gallery and all that, although the salary was very low at that point.

It was 1982 and the salary was four thousand five hundred a year. Which would be the equivalent probably of six or eight thousand dollars here in terms of what it bought you—not necessarily doing exchange rates, but in terms of what you could buy for that at that time. It was incredibly low. But at that point I wasn't thinking of this necessarily as a long-term career. I had a place at the teacher training college. But then, after several months, I was so enjoying the publishing that I thought I would postpone the teaching for a year, so I put it off one more year.

Then Cassell got taken over by CBS, the American company. And all of us were summoned, and we were told that nothing would change until they had a closer look at the company. And I thought to myself, Well, that "until" is interesting. And the upshot was that they closed the design department. They made both my boss and the next person I was responsible to redundant, and I was to be moved to the production department, which was going to take over design. But I didn't want to go. And there was someone else who had come after me who was going to be made redundant in the production department, so there was a time when we thought we might swap—I would get the redundancy money and she would get to stay in the production department, but she ended up leaving also and I didn't get redundancy money.

Then I heard about this vacancy at Faber and Faber. This was an editorial department, which sounded more appropriate really to my long-term goals. And I interviewed over at Faber and Faber, and I interviewed also for a job with an advertising agency. And that night when I came home I thought, Oh, maybe advertising will be quite fun. But then over the weekend it struck me that this job at Faber and Faber sounded like where I'd been heading all my life. It seemed to make complete sense. And over the weekend everywhere I went I would see an interesting book and I'd pick it up and it was a Faber book. You know, a book on Stravinsky. And I was going past a second-hand store and I picked up a book and it was Faber.

But I had been told that the position was maybe too junior for me. So then I was worried that I'd given the impression when I went to interview that it was too junior a position for me. I think that that's a problem sometimes for people trying to get in, to convince the people

356

who are hiring that they're not going to be bored, that they really understand that there's junior-level work involved and that they're prepared to do it.

So I called back and she said, "Oh no, you're one of three." And then another week went by and they offered me the job. To begin with, it was working for three editors. And from the first day, more or less, I felt as if I was in heaven. When I was at university I'd stage-managed *Rosencrantz and Guildenstern* by Tom Stoppard, and one of the editors I was working for was the drama editor, and he said, "Come and take a letter to Tom Stoppard." I just felt so excited, even though I was only typing the letter, I wasn't writing the letter myself. I would have paid for being in that position, and here I was, being paid for being there. I wanted to put a little note at the bottom: "P.S. Dear Tom, this was typed by me."

So I didn't really have problems with being junior. I had been told by many people, "Don't think a degree in English literature is going to get you anywhere." So I didn't have this idea that I was particularly qualified, and saw this as a training apprenticeship. And I let the teaching go altogether. I felt that by a mixture of luck and circumstance I'd found a really nice place to be. But you know, I've always had that sort of parallel life that I may have been living. Sort of, you know, plagued by inner-city kids who couldn't read or, you know.... I would in some ways have been given a harder road—the teaching—than what I was doing, and not so fun, necessarily.

Later on I did some teaching and it was quite fun. You go completely away from where you thought you were going but you end up turning around anyway. Like if you go east long enough, you end up coming west. But there are the same qualities in publishing and teaching—I see it as a continuity. We're just doing something either earlier in the process or later, whichever way you look at it. Which is to do with promoting the work, and sometimes the relationship can be a teacher's dreams. We're producing books that the students then read. When I was at university we didn't really study much contemporary literature and that bothered me at the time. So it was fun to be part of contemporary literature-making.

One of the editors was the drama editor. It was a very good drama list. Tom Stoppard and Beckett and everything. One of the other men I worked for, Charles Monteith, died a couple of years ago. He was quite well known in publishing. This might be incorrect, but he was the next big editor after—he overlapped with T.S. Eliot. He took on William Golding for Faber and Faber, and Seamus Heaney. I think he died before Seamus won his Nobel Prize. But he brought five or six Nobel Prize winners to Faber and Faber. Czeslaw Milosz and Seamus and Derek Walcott and William Golding and one other who I forget. But he was sort of semi-retired by that point, so it wasn't like a full-time job, working for him.

After a few months they confirmed that I was staying on and I said I could perhaps take on another editor. Then I worked for Craig Raine who was a poet and the poetry editor both. He was very casual. So that was very interesting, working for him, too. Then, after a year, I started to work exclusively for Robert McCrum who was the editorial director. At that point he was called the "young lion" of British publishing. He had come to Faber and Faber in his twenties. I think, when I was first at Faber, he was still under thirty. He galvanized the fiction list at Faber. They had Golding, then they sort of missed out on the next generation. He took on Milan Kundera and Peter Carey. There was a lovely time when Faber won the Booker Prize two years in a row. It was an exciting time to be at Faber because he was young and the managing director, Matthew Evans, was young and they connected with the junior staff. There was a lot of serious work going on, but there was a nice spirit in the company.

There was the year of working for Craig Raine and then working for Robert, and over the next seven years my job title would change from editorial secretary to editorial assistant to assistant editor to junior editor to senior editor. During that time my job evolved from being the assistant to Robert McCrum—and he had about sixty books a year under him, that he was responsible for. His job was so big, and as well as that, he worked himself. Some of that time he was writing the television series, *The English Language*, that Robert McNeil narrated. It was on your television and our television. There was a book on it, too. So Robert McCrum would say, "Well, I'm going to Australia for a month. You're in charge of the office." So there was plenty of room to grow. He would go away and I would be having first look at the manuscripts that were coming in, and it began to be the case that if I

358

found something that I liked, he trusted my judgment, because we'd had so much exchange on fiction manuscripts that I could take them on and, you know, project them. He'd say, "Well, you be the editor then." Then it gets to the point where you're suddenly being your own editor, where you need your own assistant and he needs another assistant. That's virtually how I did it.

I have the impression that that's probably a different career path from some of the people who are running independent presses. Their apprenticeship was doing letterpress, running their own small press, which I never did. I was never involved in the production side, making things. My apprenticeship was being stuck under earphones with Robert McCrum's voice going in my ears, doing a series of rejection letters or something like that. But it was a great place to learn, and eventually you started to go to editorial meetings. You would have the drama editor, the poetry editor, the fiction editor, the medical editor, the children's book editor all sitting around in a circle—

Were the marketing people there too?

No. Not at the editorial meeting. Editorial meetings were exclusively for editors, and discussing general ideas. And there was a respect: if the poetry editor wanted to take something on, nobody would say no. That was what he was paid for, to use his judgment. And no other editor would challenge him. Sometimes somebody might want to take on something, like Robert McCrum might want to take on something that was, you know, and the poetry editor would say, "Well, you put it on your list, not mine." That kind of thing would happen. But we discussed what anthologies we might take on, or what biographies, that kind of thing. There, for a while, Pete Townshend used to come to some of the editorial meetings, the singer from The Who, and that was entertaining.

Why would he come?

He got involved with the press, with Faber and Faber, and contributed some ideas and brought things to the press. They sort of used people as satellites, you know, who weren't necessarily full-time editors. There was a feeling that the best editors were not the editors who were at their desk all day long. So you had Craig Raine who came in part-time, who was out being the poet. He was out reviewing, he was out living in the world that he was publishing. Robert McCrum would go off to Australia for a month to do his language series. He'd come back having edited Peter Carey. They started to work with someone who was involved with film, a man called Walter Donohue, who apparently has recently been made the overall editorial director.

But there was a spirit in the meetings of great respect for the writers, and the sense that Faber should do this book, and that kind of thing. As I was leaving, in '91, the commercial side of things got more intense. So there was more pressure and they started to break down the editors' lists—which editor was producing the most.

Faber and Faber was independent? They weren't owned by a parent company?

No, they're still independent. So there was that kind of pressure which hadn't been that explicit before. And marketing became more professional. As well as the editorial meetings there was something called—I think it was called the book committee, or—anyway, there was a publishing meeting once a week also. They kept changing around who went, but they would have representatives from marketing, the managing director. And then the editors would come up to that meeting if they had a proposal, and they would present the book and would come away completely crushed because their idea wasn't accepted, or elated because everybody bought on to their proposal, which would have circulated in advance.

Who would chair those meetings?

The managing director. But Robert McCrum had a very big voice in those meetings as well, as the editor-in-chief or whatever.

My reason for asking is that I was told by Juris Jurjevics [see interview, this volume] who came out of Harper and Row and Avon and Dial and all that, that the person who chaired the meetings, although he might be the publisher, tended to come out of marketing rather than editorial.

No, I think that the marketing side got more aware and more professional, but Faber has remained editorially driven. I think that's one of its successes. They didn't say, "How can we make money? I know: We'll have a film list." But Alan Bennett, who is one of the playwrights they published, wrote a very funny, very clever screenplay called *A Private Function*, and Faber saw it as their duty, in a way, to publish the screenplay because this was part of their writer's output. So then they're thinking, Well, maybe that's not so attractive, just a screenplay. Let's have some commentary about it to make it more of a package. And that did well. And the film list was born. Now it's one of the best film lists around. That's my model—growing out from where you are, rather than inventing something and working backwards.

That's my observation too, that that's how things happen that last: You make a small decision, and then you see possibilities.

Exactly. And also this idea of having different voices come in to the editorial department kind of plays into how I like to run Graywolf, not to be the exclusive editor, which I think is sometimes more the model of some of the small presses. Which is a fine model also, but I like the idea that you can bring in other people.

Can you give me an example of how you've done that here at Graywolf?

Well, we've worked with some outside editors as well as just me. And then there's another editor here, Anne Czarniecki.... I want to finish that line [of thought], so let's go back.

All right.

It got to the point where, because of the way I'd come up—I did a bit of fiction, a bit of nonfiction—and Faber was going more toward specializing—they had their fiction editors, their nonfiction editors, and there wasn't any more slack I could be given, or any more room— And then, at about that point, Faber decided to increase their investment and try and build up the American office of Faber and Faber. There was a...it wasn't a management buy-out, but the family reduced its holdings in the company to just over one-third, and Valerie Eliot, T.S. Eliot's widow, took a third and then staff and management had another third. And, in that arrangement, Faber, Inc. became a bigger player. Faber, Limited is London and Faber, Inc. is America. So, in a way, Faber, Inc. could be my bag. Instead of my being the fiction editor, I could go and be Faber, Inc.

I had visited that office once. It's just north of Boston. But I hadn't thought seriously about...there wasn't a precedent for one of the editors in London to go over there. But they asked me if I was interested to do it. And as the question was being formulated, I knew I would have to say yes, because of the opportunity to see another country and get to know American publishing, and an opportunity to just spread my wings, really.

I think, you know, other people sort of move around faster. I was eight years at Faber, going up the pole. Other editors my age have jumped faster sometimes. And sometimes it's hard, when you've come up from the inside, to be seen as a senior—people saw you at the Fax machine and sending telexes, and in a way I so enjoyed being there [at Faber], I didn't really want to leave. But this seemed a nice way, still being part of Faber. So I went to Faber, Inc. There was another editor there called Betsy Uhrig and we worked together on the editorial side. That gave me a taste for working in a smaller office and being outside the mainstream, and also being more senior. I was there for three and a half years.

You were the director of Faber, Inc.?

No, there was somebody else who was running it, but there wasn't a senior editor to answer to. Betsy and I were on the same level, editorially. I became art director after a year or so, but I was not the director of Faber, Inc. The lists were already established, and we were just building and perhaps taking the lists in some new directions. It was fun, working the ground in Boston to find who the writers were. There is a very rich community that way, and people were very generous to me. I went to a lot of the readings; there didn't seem to be any editors around from any of the other houses, so I felt like—

You mean like readings at bookstores and universities?

Yes. There was *Agni Magazine* out of Boston University. I ended up publishing the editor of that magazine, and he and I had some combined events at Boston University. Then there was *Ploughshares Magazine* out at Emerson College. That was when, in fact, I did some teaching. I taught a publishing course at Emerson College for a few semesters, so there was that nice feeling of coming full circle. I know it wasn't teaching high school children, but it was a lot of fun. I used to do that one evening a week. I've always done talks, you know, gone out and been on panels and things. I've always enjoyed that side of it, having that sympathy for people who want to be published or who want to work in publishing, who've got that sense of being outside, which I had so strongly, and just to kind of fill them in and—those things were not done when I was a student. We didn't have that.

The Graywolf job seemed to be a very natural next step after Faber, Inc., because it seemed to me a combination of Faber, Limited and Faber, Inc. in many ways. I started at Graywolf in the fall of 1994. October '94. Scott Walker, who had founded Graywolf back in 1974, had left that March. It was a big transition time for the press. They'd gone through a period of retrenchment just before I got here and a lot of people were so ardent about the press, for good reason, that they didn't know how that transition would go with a new person. But I think it was just one of those wonderful things, being such a good match. It wasn't about me coming in and changing Graywolf or doing a completely different set of books. I thought that I could come in and build on what he had done before, knowing that I was not the founder myself and had not been a founder. I'd always feel grateful for what he had built up and I could just continue. So, in some ways, it was a win-win situation.

I think there are new things, as there would have been new things if Scott had stayed. I'm sure there are certain books that I've taken on that maybe he wouldn't have liked—it's not exactly the same list that it would have been, had he stayed. But there's not a rift. You can't detect in the catalogue necessarily that there's been a complete change. Since I got here we've taken on new books by Eamon Grennan and Martha Bergland and Josip Novakovich, all authors that Scott took on and who I responded to as well. So I didn't put a stop to all previous Graywolf authors. One example of what I'm doing is the Graywolf Forum. It comes from the fact that there was something called the Graywolf Annual which Scott used to edit. It was very successful; it continues to be. There was one on multicultural literacy which he had done.

With Rick Simonson.

Yeah. So everybody wants to know what's going to happen to the Graywolf Annual. I wanted to do something similar but make it different. Plus anthologies are harder to sell these days. They don't get reviewed very much because they're previously published materials. This plays into what I was saying earlier about involving other editors. Which, you know, it wasn't as if they had never done this before. So I thought, Well, we'll have a new series. We went back and forth about changing the name, decided we would change the name. I wouldn't edit it but we'd give it to an outside editor, and the editor would change every time. So even if the editors had their own set of writers, it would never be the same set, because the next person would be coming along and the new editor would commission new material. Instead of going through books that have already been published and taking extracts, the guest editor is completely free to write to ex number of writers and invite them to contribute other pieces. Sven Birkerts, who I worked with at Faber and Faber, was our first editor. The book was *Tolstoy's Dictaphone*. Gerald Early is going to do the next one, on sport. It's in production now.

I think of myself as working in relation to this idea of building on Graywolf's past, not trying to change things. Why would you be, when so much of it is so good? We just had a very good success with Jane Kenyon's book, *Otherwise*. I set that in motion, that we would do that book, but it was based on a previous success with Graywolf and it contained many of the works from books that Graywolf had already published. That did very well last year, and it's doing well in paperback.

I also work with a man called Fred Marchant on the poetry list. He's a poet in Boston. He does some of the editing, taking it to the next level. And then we have the novelist, Debra Stark. She's sort of a consultant for us on our Rediscovery list. There's too much coming in for just one or two people alone to be reading or working on. An interesting poetry manuscript comes in: if I was going to do it, it would mean taking the next two days off work to really get into it. Some of that detail work you can farm out. I could do some of that sometimes, but if I was doing it all the time—

When you say "detail work," do you mean copy editing or proofreading?

More than that. I mean the editing approach from the line editor, the shaping editor, getting your eye as close to the writer's eye as possible. You can't do that twenty minutes before breakfast, or an hour.

You need to have the time to dwell inside the manuscript. That kind of work. Fred will have a poetry manuscript and will sort of see where it's trying to go, and then communicate with the poet. He's done that a couple of times. I've done that kind of work here with some of the fiction, and Anne's done it too with some of the books. I think Anne plays a larger editorial role here than some of the other—I mean everybody has their own way, but for the moment I'm directing fundraising as well as editorial. I find that an easy model to work with, and have Anne Czarniecki do a lot of the editorial work.

You didn't do fundraising at Faber.

No, that was new to me. I like it, in its way. Sometimes it feels a strain. The attraction of being nonprofit is, you know, here you are with a proposal [i.e., as at Faber] and you feel like you're having to plead with the marketing department. It can distort what you might start looking for; you want to preserve that purity. So you think, Well, if I had some subsidy, then I could preserve that purity. But then, coming over to nonprofit, you see that the temptations start sliding, not towards the marketing department, but towards the funder, which is trading one thing for another. So you have to stay on course.

And sometimes, the way publishing works, which is less measurable than some of the other arts institutions, it's difficult to communicate how you're contributing to the culture. Because we can't count the people who are coming into our place every day, and provide numbers. But because I'm not used to being funded at all, I'm still amazed that anybody gives us any money. Even a thousand-dollar check, I just think it's incredible, and a wonderful bonus for us. What it means is the press can be editorially driven. Of course we take notice of marketing needs. We try and be as professional as possible, and make every last penny as cleverly as we can, but all those decisions come after you've decided to commit editorially. Then you decide, is it better to do hardback or paperback? better to do it in March or September? That follows afterwards. We don't say, "Oh, no. Books on cyberspace are doing well. We'd better do that." If it doesn't make sense from what you're doing already, if it doesn't grow from the inside, then we don't do it.

There's a dilution in terms of my time, going off to do some fundraising, but there isn't a dilution in terms of having to be working on celebrity biographies or editorial content that you're not keen on. When I think back to Faber, Limited—I know that's not the only model, but it is a really fine publisher model—it has a nonprofit well within it. It becomes profit-making. You know, W.H. Auden, Philip Larkin. When they were first taken on at Faber and Faber they didn't make money, but they do now. That backlist of poetry is paying for a new list of new poets that Faber and Faber is committed to publishing. And they don't expect the new poets to make money. But without that extensive backlist, without something to help you, you cannot publish like that. It's not that we're any more moral or better publishers; the subsidy allows it. If we didn't have the subsidy, we couldn't do what we are doing, which is taking on work for the long haul, some of which perhaps never even breaks even. Perhaps what's happening with Jane Kenyon is a sign that Graywolf is benefitting from its years of publishing. Jane Kenyon didn't make money to begin with, but she has done now.

How many titles are you doing a year?

Sixteen. We're doing eight per catalogue. It seems that any less than eight books, you don't have an opportunity to get a profile. Any more than eight books, then you're starting to do two hardcover fictions, two unknown poets, and I think the reps and the bookstores give you a chance per season with one of those things. What we're doing is almost by definition difficult. So you can't load too many difficult books, I don't think, per catalogue. We like to mix it up: hardback, paperback; new writer, established writer; nonfiction, fiction; poetry. I can't put my five poets out all at the same time and then the next season do five hardcover novels. It's got to be a mix. Otherwise, you get the skip.

Get what?

The skip. You know, the book that doesn't get taken. Whereas if you'd spread it out more evenly, they would both get taken. When I was doing that publishing class I used to have people come in from the outside to give talks, and this agent came in—she'd made quite a bit of money with some shrewd moves—and she said, "Publishing really is just throwing it against the wall to see what sticks." [Laughs.] You know, it's a bit like placing bets, literary bets.

366

I have this thing: the list can consist of hares and tortoises. Maybe the frontlist, hardcover novel goes out the hardest, but it sure comes back the fastest, whereas a sort of innocuous paperback may sell consistently for five to ten years, but never in one month is it ever a significant seller.

Do you know what proportion of your earned income comes from subsidiary rights sales?

It's a small percentage. I think it's less than five percent currently. Yeah. That's the sort of area where you could have a windfall one season and be dry the next. But it's an area that we've put more emphasis on in the last three years. We have a rights rep. She's our sales director. So when she's in New York for a sales conference she'll take a couple days and go and visit paperback houses.

What about translation rights? Have you sold any of those?

Yeah. We have. We have a book called *Jack and Rochelle: A Holocaust Story*, which sold in Norway and Germany. We sold Chinese rights to something the other day. It's a steady trickle, I would say, more than an avalanche.

Actually, you've answered everything I wanted to ask.

Oh, good. I'm glad I told the truth, anyway. My story. There's a logic to it, don't you think?

SALES REPRESENTATIVE

Bob Harrison
Karel Dutton Group

"[T]he thing is, it's not like a big-score kind of sales thing where you go in and you make that big score and you're set up for six months and you go look for some place else to make that big score. Going in season after season after season—the biggest thing, the most valuable thing I have in my bag, you could say, is my credibility. And if I blow it one season, it takes a few seasons to get that back. Some buyers have really long memories."

I interviewed Bob Harrison in early October 1996. We met for coffee in the cafe at Elliott Bay Book Company in Seattle. It was late in the morning, and the day was gray and mild, oddly balmy, with a south wind threatening a storm.

I met Harrison for the first time two years earlier when I was presenting my new books—i.e., Black Heron Press' books—at a sales conference hosted by The Subterranean Company, my distributor then and one of Harrison's clients. He was quiet, though I saw a quickness in his eyes that I did not quite know what to make of. Having talked with him a number of times since, I have learned that he is indeed very quick with repartee, and enjoys verbal play. His humor is reminiscent of Woody Allen's in being both self-knowing and self-deprecating, but he seems also a little uncertain, perhaps about how it will be received.

He was born and reared in San Francisco, coming of age at a time in America (the first year of the draft lottery—his number was three hundred forty-six) when young men had hard choices to make, none of which provided for happiness or security. Some drifted, at least for a while. Harrison went to college "a few times," starting at the University of California at Santa Cruz ("I was working in a place as a receiving clerk—you know, just doing a job—and a guy offered me a job in the purchasing department. Scared the shit out of me. Two weeks later I gave my notice. I moved to Santa Cruz.") and finishing at San Francisco State, with a couple of junior colleges in between. "I finally decided I wanted to get a bachelor's degree to hang on the wall of the warehouse I worked in. So I went back to San Francisco State. I was about twenty-five." He had worked in a number of warehouses; now he began working part time in the campus bookstore as he completed his degree. Then he took his master's degree, working in the bookstore full time. Both degrees are in comparative literature. "For my sins," he says, laughing.

He is a commission publisher's rep now with Karel Dutton, representing Consortium, The Mountaineers, Globe Pequot Press, and a number of other publishers and distributors. "I have publishers that do pretty much every kind of book—children's books, cook books, art books, photography books; I'm trying to have a religious publisher. The idea in being a commission rep, in being an independent rep, is to have something in your bag for everybody, for every kind of store. Because then you can visit pretty much any store. There are five of us [at Karel Dutton] who have essentially the same bag. We have special strengths in two areas: in travel books and in literary titles through Consortium."

Harrison's father was a mechanical engineer, working for small companies for many years, but then "the final ten or twelve years of his career he worked for Bechtel. That's where he was able to build up a pension and get the big salary and all that. He finished up his career well." Harrison's mother was a librarian in a public library in the Bay area.

My mother was always reading. She read a lot. Her mother didn't read, but her father read a lot. My grandfather. It was great. I used to go over to their house and he'd be like—he'd be reading a mystery. Out of one eye he'd be watching a soap opera, be listening to the ball game, and maybe doing a crossword puzzle at the same time. The guy had this incredible divided focus. And my mother was always a reader. My dad didn't read much. He said he didn't read much because his finger would get tired. Maybe he had a little, like, dyslexia or something like that. He was a really smart guy. Had a great memory. He was really good at what he did. But he never read more than the newspapers.

Did you have any ambition to write?

Not really. No, there's too many people doing it. [Both of us laugh.] I think fifty thousand books a year is an awful lot.

More than that.

Yeah, whatever it is. I'm thinking of the fifty thousand I have to sell. Wait—strike that. [We laugh.]

Okay, we're into the career now. Oh, do you and your wife have kids? You gonna? Ever?

Mm mm. See, I wanted to jump straight to grandchildren. I wanted to have grandchildren. That always appealed to me. You get to play with them, but you don't have to take them home.

I used to know a woman who had never been married, and didn't want to be married. But she would have liked to have been divorced because everybody was getting divorced.

That's carrying fashion a bit far.

Did you read the book about George Scheer, Book Traveler? *Well, you know of George Scheer.*

Yeah. In fact, I used to see him at the ABA meetings all the time. But I never did read the book, no.

In the early '70s a New Yorker *reporter went with him on his travels in the Southeast. And one of the things the reporter found was that each book got only about twenty seconds when they were [Harrison starts to laugh]... Is that still true?*

Well...you know, it depends. It depends on the store. I mean, like, this store [Elliott Bay Book Company]—I give it as much time as they'll give me. I spend two full days, at least, here. I spend two full days at University Book Store. Some places, I go in for an hour, and I'm not presenting every book because not every book would be appropriate anyway. You know, little stores, especially stores— But yeah, I mean it's—I hate to think twenty seconds. There are some books that it only takes twenty seconds, really, to tell. Other books, you want to give them a little bit more time because it's harder to get the information across. I think twenty seconds is a little bit of an exaggeration.

The book rep, Scheer, spent a lot more time in the store than—
he might be in a store for several hours. But part of that time he's
helping at the cash register or he's helping to shelve books or he's
reshelving books or he's setting up a display. But when it actually comes
to selling a book, it's the covers and the catalogues. I assume that's the
same. It averaged, I believe the author said, about twenty seconds.[1]
Wow.

And, of course, that was just select books because, as you say,
not every book is appropriate for every store.
Yeah. Boy, I'm sure I spend more time than that per book. But
if you average out all the books that I have in a given season, you might
come to that. But that would include books that I'm not showing.
University Book Store, for example, was two and a half days this year.
And I don't have that many books. It's just, you know, it's a conscien-
tious buyer there and, you know—

You're talking about Mark Mouser?
Yes. Basically, I'll take as much time as the buyer will give me.
In most cases. You know, it varies. I mean it's hard to make any kind of
generalization about it. That's one of the things I like about the job: it's
hard to make any generalization about the sales presentation, sales call,
because it's different in every store. Different personalities of buyers,
different buying environments. I mean it could be sitting with somebody in a fairly—you know, a space like this, where we're not being
interrupted. Sometimes I'm sitting with somebody who will answer the
phone every five minutes. Sometimes I have to stand with somebody at
the register because they have to sell the books. Other times we go away
someplace to a coffee shop or something like that. That's really quality
time. You can get a lot more done in an hour when you're sitting at a
table like this than you can in an hour when somebody's answering the
phone or they're running the register. I never worry about that when
they're running the register though, because as long as they're running
the register and they're selling some books and making some money,
they can pay for the books that they buy. [Laughs.] I always think that's
a good sign.

374

But it varies. From store to store it's a completely different experience. You know, different buyers, different interests, different...different psychologies. Some buyers, you know, just approach things in a different way. You try to find out what works best with that person. It's an ongoing thing. It's not something that you walk in and you instantly scope out the right approach. Over the course of the seasons you develop a relationship with the buyer. You learn the kind of things that work with them, the kind of things they're not interested in, the kind of approaches that work with them, the kind of approaches that turn them off. It keeps it fresh. That and twice a year having a new crop of books.

How many books do you represent this season, for example?
Gosh. I don't know. A thousand. I don't know.

How many publishers do you represent?
Oh, fifteen publishers. But that includes, for example, Consortium [a distributor] which includes—

You regard Consortium as a publisher?
Yeah. I think of them as fifteen clients. I have fifteen clients. Of course, with Consortium, some of those [publishers distributed by Consortium] are one-title-a-season publishers and some of them have eight or nine or ten or twelve or fifteen. Theatre Communications Group, for example, they have probably twenty-five plays this season. Well, not everybody's gonna look at all those plays, so.... Yeah, if I were to count up all those publishers, I don't know what it would come to, but it's fifteen catalogues I'm dealing with.

One of the things about the end of the business I'm in—you know, I am kind of at the mercy, in a way—I don't want to put it that way, but I'm kind of at the mercy of the publishers. I sell the books they present me with, and with Consortium and Subterranean and another distributor that I represent, every season will be slightly—there will be a change. You know, that's the difference between being a commission rep and a house rep, is that as a house rep you know every season going in and out—you have the same backlist. You learn that backlist once and keep adding new titles to it every season. But a commission rep's bag

375

changes every time. Publishers come and go. That's also one of the things that keeps it fresh, keeps it interesting.

Have you ever been a house rep?
Mm hm.

Who was that for?
It was for Crown. Crown and Outlet. It was just before they were bought by Random House. Crown Publishers, which is now part of Random House, and Outlet, which was at the time the world's biggest remainder dealer and promotional book publisher. They had like forty percent of the market, or something like that. They're now known as Random House Value Publishing. Which is quite a mouthful.

Was Outlet with Crown before?
Yeah. Actually, Crown grew out of Outlet. Outlet started back in the '30s, or something like that, as a remainder dealer, strictly that. They would pick up the leavings from publishers and find outlets for them, find places to sell them. And they found that there were certain books that, gosh! you know, they'd get these remainders in and as soon as they'd sell them out they'd get more and they'd sell them out again—"We could just start reprinting these!" And out of that grew the publishing program, Crown. And Crown published like Jean Auel—*Clan of the Cave Bear*—and Judith Krantz and Martha Stewart and...you know. But also people like Douglas Adams. They had a fairly successful history. When they finally were absorbed into Random House they still maintained a separate imprint.

Anyway, I was a house rep for them. I started in the Bay area, and then they transferred me to Denver. Suddenly I was a very high-profile rep because I was the one selling Tattered Cover [one of the premier bookstores in the United States] and Gordon's [a book wholesaler, now out of business]. Everybody in the company was reading my activity reports. I would say, "This is happening at Tattered Cover." You know those old TV commercials that talk about some brokerage firm—I forgot who it was, Dean Witter or whatever—and everybody in the room suddenly is quiet. And it was sort of the way, like at a sales conference—"Well, at Tattered Cover..."—and everybody's [mimics people whispering].... It's similar to here, of course. When you're talking about Elliott Bay, everybody and his brother wants to know what's going on.

There's maybe half a dozen stores like this in the country.
Exactly. And I was fortunate to work closely with Tattered Cover when I was—it was only a year that I was in Denver. But then, you know, this opportunity came up. And I'd always wanted to move here. So, here I am.

Now you work for—
Yeah, the Karel Dutton Group.

They're headquartered in the Bay area?
Yeah. Howard Karel is in the Bay area and Dory Dutton is down in L.A.

Is she related to—?
Yeah. Dutton's Books down in L.A. Her brother, Doug, runs the big store.

Who's the one who does the L.A. Art Museum? It's a Dutton who does the L.A. Art Museum.
Well, she used to be there. Years ago. Dory Dutton.

I'll bet it's her. I interviewed a letterpress publisher, Malachi McCormick, from Stone Street Press on Staten Island, and she exhibited his books at the L.A. Art Museum. Wow. A small world.
Yeah, Dory was there until, I guess, eight, nine years ago. Something like that.

[Looking at my notes:] I'm getting scattered here.
That's part of my technique, you know. I get the buyer off guard and then I zero in.

Well, I kind of like talking like this, in loops. But there's a danger that I'll forget to ask something.

377

Good.

Enjoying this, are we? [Both of us laugh.]
Okay. Focused. On track.

Um. Got out of college. Went to work for—you had been working at San Francisco State.
Yeah. I started there doing textbook returns as a work-study student. And then I transferred over to general books. The manager saw me sweating one day and thought, "Oh, this guy works hard, gotta pay him for it." So anyway, I was working in general books, and gradually I was doing more and more things. I ended up doing some buying, I became assistant manager, and then the general books manager became the overall book department manager—he was doing textbooks—and I became general books manager. That was just after I finished my master's degree. In fact...I know the chronology's a little scattered.

Where did you go from there?
From there I took a job as the buyer for an ID [independent distributor] in the Bay area. Cal/West. They're not there anymore. They're in the Sacramento Valley now, I think. What IDs do, they're the ones who supply, well, magazines, of course, that's the main thing. And because their magazine customers want books, they also supply books. They're at Safeway and...you know. Like Adams News up here.

I was doing a lot of mass market books. Suddenly I went from buying for a college bookstore to buying Danielle Steele and Harlequin romances. And it was kind of fun. You know, it's like a new Danielle Steele would come out and I'd start with twenty-five thousand copies. 'Cause I knew that would cover us the first couple of weeks and then I could see what I needed to dump. That was kind of exhilarating.

Exhilarating, like—?
With those kinds of numbers, yeah, it was like—Woo-oo! It also was really amazing, because of the incredible waste in that business. You know, I'd see—they have these huge container loads of shredded magazines. You know, when they get the magazines back from the stores. They probably made more money selling shredded magazines as

pulp than they did on the book program. It was about a ten-million-dollar book program, something like that. I don't know how big it really was, but I mean it was amazing. Like I say, I was there for a year and the numbers really turned my head around.

I also bought trade books. You know, the big things were like Sunset Books and the kind of things you put in supermarkets. Or regional or local books. But also *New York Times* bestsellers, things like that. Anyway, from there I heard about the Crown job, so I went and interviewed for it and they gave me the job.

And then you went from Crown to Karel Dutton?
Mm hm. Yeah. I was with Crown for two years.

Do you prefer being an independent rep?
No contest.

Why? I was talking with the woman who reps for Cambridge University Press—I see her at the Pacific Northwest Booksellers Association trade show every year. She really likes working for them.
Well, you know, there are different kinds of companies. That would be a good company because it's not...it's not a seven-million-dollar division of a multi-billion-dollar international conglomerate. I mean all the big publishers now, these multinational corporations...I don't know, I think the large companies are not where I'd want to be working right now. I've never been a corporate kind of person anyway.

But the Cambridge job, that would be good, because you're working for people who are publishing books. They want to sell them, they want to make some money, they want to generate revenue, so they have a sales force and such, but their publishing decisions are not necessarily...let's say their publishing decisions are based on books that they feel should be in the marketplace.

What I like about being an independent rep is that I am independent. I have a lot of autonomy over my time. I decide where and when and how. Instead of having a sales manager who wants to track every minute of my day and is looking over everything I'm doing—instead, I look at the big picture and I get to do it that way. I'm my own sales manager. I've never worked really, really well under direction.

379

The first couple of times I saw you, you looked so reticent. But as I've gotten to know you a little, you look kind of devilish.

I'm always on my best behavior at sales conferences. [We laugh.] Well, you know, it's important. It's the only time—for a lot of these people, it might not even be twice a year, it might be only once a year that they actually make it to New York to the meetings. And, you know, I think I owe it to them to give them as much of my attention as I can and be, you know, sincere, and see what they have to say. After all, they're paying me. But once people get to know me, it's a little different.

Okay. So you rep the Northwest region.
Mm hm.

You don't go into British Columbia?

No. Most of my publishers don't have Canadian rights for their books. The same books might be published by somebody else in Canada. Or they hire a Canadian sales force. Most Canadian sales forces want the whole country. They certainly want B.C. I wouldn't mind having Vancouver and Victoria. They have some great bookstores there. They buy a lot of books, but...you know. I travel enough as it is. I do Washington, Oregon, Montana, Idaho and Alaska.

You work only on commission. You don't get any salary at all. [Harrison nods.] That must be kind of hard when you're first starting out, because there's no—you need to capitalize yourself.

Mm hm. Yeah. Yeah, 'cause all expenses come out of it. So basically I'm running a small business. But, once again, that's what I like about it.

Are the independent stores hurting as badly as they say?
Yeah. Yeah, they definitely are.

You don't want to say anything more about it?
Well, sure. I can say plenty.

Say plenty.

Well, naturally, that's the basis of my business, is independent bookstores. And other venues—there's Pacific Pipeline [now out of business; see the Vito Perillo interview, this volume] and large companies like REI. One looks to put books wherever they should be. It's kind of like—I always use the hardware store analogy. Twenty-five years ago, before Home Depot and before Eagle Hardware, whatever, you'd go to neighborhood hardware stores. Every neighborhood had a hardware store. And most of them are gone. You have to go to these big boxes. That's what they call 'em—big-box retailers. I mean it's happened in just about every other area of retailing, so now it's happening to books.

And it's distressing, because I see—certainly my customer base is declining. I can cite specific stores that have gone out of business directly because of a quote unquote superstore opening nearby. You know, it's business, it's retail, it's survival of the fittest out there. There's not much you can really complain about. I mean, you know, some people get morally outraged and such, but that's business. There are good points and bad points, I suppose. Good points being that in some of the communities where they're opening up some of these stores, they're opening the store with, what? a hundred thousand titles or seventy-five thousand titles, whatever they're doing, and certainly there are books there that have never been available. Whether they're ever going to sell them is another question.

So what I wonder about when I hear about a chain talking about opening up fifteen hundred superstores is, well, you've got to fill those stores, which means publishers have to print more books. And it seems to me that the space is perhaps outstripping the demand, and there could be a shake-out down the line. And it wouldn't just be my customers, and customers of my colleagues around the country, it could be our client-publishers as well, publishers both big and small. So it's a little disturbing. Here in the Pacific Northwest and on the West Coast in general, we've been relatively lucky. My colleagues in other parts of the country, the Northeast, say, Texas, for example, have lost many of their independent customers. Because that's where the chains really focused at first. They really targeted other parts of the country. Only recently have they looked at the Pacific Northwest much.

The good thing about that is that my customers have had time to watch what's been happening around the country and gird their loins, so to speak. So I don't know if I'll be hit as badly here as my colleagues around the country. Fortunately, I have some wonderful big stores, and wonderful smaller stores. They keep me very busy, and I'll see how things shake out.

You don't go to every store in the region, or do you?

Well, there are, what? four hundred and some odd members of the Pacific Northwest Booksellers Association. Impossible to visit all those. And a lot of them don't want to see reps anyway. They feel more comfortable ordering from catalogues, ordering from wholesalers. There's a certain scale of bookstore where you're probably better off ordering exclusively from a wholesaler because, except for those publishers who really kind of specialize, you can reach a higher discount level. Although that's changing. The discount structures are changing among publishers to make it more profitable for any size store to order from a publisher. What they call "flat discounts." Five books is forty-seven percent discount, period. I think Harper is doing that. Harper, I think, it's no minimum. One book or a thousand books, forty-seven percent. But there have been some positive moves in recent years toward making what they call a "level playing field."

Right.

So it's changing things a little bit. I would say I have probably a hundred accounts, active. You know, that I actively work with. It varies. Stores open up. In fact, after I leave today I'm going to go by—a brand new Judaica store is opening up in town—and pick up our opening orders. And it's like, hey, it's great. A new store opening up. So people are still doing it, people are still opening new stores. They get a dream, they get an ambition—I think the successful ones are some of the niche stores like this. There's not another store specializing in Judaica, that I know of, north of San Francisco. So we'll see how this one works out. But it's fun. You know, it's a new account.

Would you be in another line of business doing the same thing, selling something else, as an independent rep?

Well, it's different selling books than, say...I was just at the building supply store and the rep for the roofing material company was

382

there and he helped me choose the right adhesive. Okay, that's great. I'm glad he was there. I wouldn't want to sell roofing material. I wouldn't want to be selling shoes. I'm not really...I'm not in this because it's a sales job. I got into this because I was in books and sort of backed into it.

Most books are sold on a returnable basis. And so—it's funny, I see all these books, say, in the business section: *Closing the Sale* and, you know, *Going in for the Kill* and all this. It's not a big-score business at all. It's not go in and make that big sale of a hundred thousand radial tires, or whatever it is. Or get the account at the federal employees credit union for paper products, or something like that.

It's an ongoing thing. You go in and you try to place the right books in the right stores because if they don't sell they just come back, they don't do anybody any good. Of course, a certain level of returns is healthy, because you want to make sure you have things cycling through. I mean books deserve a chance. But it doesn't do anybody any good to go into a store that's not going to sell the book at all and sell them ten copies. It costs them money. It costs the publisher money, you know, handling the books when they come in as returns. The store has to ship it, handle it, ship it back; the publisher has to receive it, put it back on the shelf. The books may get a little messed up in the handling, they end up being remainders, they end up being hurts, whatever. So I try to, you know, keep that to a minimum. All my customers, I try to work with them that way. I sort of look at myself not so much as a salesman selling a product, but sort of like a temporary employee of the store—an inventory consultant. I go in there and say, "Here are the books from the publishers I represent. Certainly you're expert on these books. Let's work together and get the right mix."

I think that's the only way it works. Because the thing is, it's not like a big-score kind of sales thing where you go in and you make that big score and you're set up for six months and you go look for some place else to make that big score. Going in season after season after season—the biggest thing, the most valuable thing I have in my bag, you could say, is my credibility. And if I blow it one season, it takes a few seasons to get that back. Some buyers have really long memories. Others, thankfully, have very short—

But, you know, you can only pull the wool over people's eyes so many times. You know, it starts to itch and they don't want to see you anymore. And I heard plenty of stories—I was a buyer myself and I guess this is where it all comes from. Particularly when I was at Cal/West, I had reps coming in and they could make a lot of money off me in a hurry, because I was buying big numbers. And I hate that. I hated the way people looked—you could see that glint in their eye. And I never want a buyer to see that glint in my eye. It may be there [laughs], but I wouldn't want them to see it. Because, you know, it's an ongoing thing. It's a season by season by season thing. The best part about it is when, after a few seasons of going in, you can actually say to them, "Trust me on this one. I've got a good feeling on this one," and they say, "Well, okay." That's when I feel like I'm doing a real good job, when people are willing to take that kind of advice.

In general, what I try to do, concisely—this is where it gets down to the twenty-second business with the George Scheer book—I try, without wasting any time, to get across to them what the book is, what it's about, who the market for the book is, and why people who make up that market might buy that book in that store. So it covers the whole thing from editorial to marketing to publicity to sales, and trying to wrap that up in, maybe not twenty seconds, but maybe twenty-five.

You can't read every book that you represent.

It's impossible. There are some books that you don't have to read to know what they're about. Say, a travel book. Or a cook book. Or a nonfiction book in general. Creative nonfiction is different. I get reams and reams and reams of information from my publishers, and I can't say that I read everything I'm sent. But I try, at the very least, to handle each sheet of paper. I may read every word on that sheet, or at least look at it enough to make sure that I have what I need to sell that book. If it's a book that's very straightforward, very simple, it's not going to take me a lot of time to get that book down.

I'll often read at least segments, maybe the entire manuscript, of a new novel. Because you've got a first-time author, not too many people are going to want to take a chance. Every season or so, I'll find a couple books like that that I'll think are really good. I'll read them and I'll, you know, force them down people's throats. Try to make sure that people get them, because the books, I think, have a shot, both because they're really good and because I think, one way or another, word's going to get out about them. The best book in the world may have just been written and may be sitting on a shelf, but if people don't hear about it, it's not going to sell. So many elements go into that—cover design and publicity and all that. But I read a fair amount of material. It's all based on what do I think I need to have to sell it—to characterize the book properly.

Are literary fiction and poetry really as hard to sell as people say? [Harrison nods yes.] I remember at the last PNBA show my table was opposite Story Line's, and both of us noticed that the buyers, as they'd come through, they wouldn't look at us. They'd just keep walking, or they'd turn away.

Mm hm. I think a lot of buyers are...I don't want to say scared, but there is a tendency among buyers to shy away from small press fiction or poetry. The thought being, maybe rightly, that the literary fiction and poetry that's going to sell is the stuff coming out from the large publishers, people who have the publicity arms, the marketing departments that can spend the money, mount the big tours, things like that. There are exceptions.

Of course, in my bag I have quite a lot of small presses, literary fiction and poetry. And it's tough. You can't sell it everywhere. A lot of people, the only fiction they're going to carry is mass market and the trade fiction from the big houses. It's a challenge, and sometimes I feel a kind of a...well, it's a challenge. There may be a book that one of my publishers is doing that I know damn well that if one of the big guys were doing it, they'd go out with a fifty-thousand, hundred-thousand print, push the hell out of it. So I try to make up for that in my small way by at least giving the book a shot.

I read in Publishers Weekly *a year and a half, two years ago now where one of the editors at one of the major houses—and I don't remember who it was—was quoted as saying that ninety-four percent of literary fiction is no longer published in New York, and that by 2005 they expect none of it will be.*

Well, I don't know about the percentages, but I think there's definitely been a movement of quality writing—or a shift in the portion

385

of certain kinds of quality writing from New York publishers to the smaller presses, to the independent presses around the country, a lot of them nonprofit presses. And college presses as well: Yeah. That's a definite thing. I see that happening every season. I see my publishers picking up writers whose books used to be published by these other companies, and these other companies, in so many cases, are being run by accountants. I don't want to sound like Marlon Brando in *Apocalypse Now*, I don't want to call them grocery clerks, but there are bottom-line people looking at what's going to make money, and if a book is not going to make a certain amount of money.... It's a business decision. They have shareholders to answer to and that's.... That starts a whole 'nuther conversation on the issue of so-called shareholders' rights and things like that.

So it's a great opportunity for the publishers that I represent because they have access to better and better stuff. They have access to books and writers who would otherwise be left homeless by some of the New York publishers.

What I see happening, though, is that some of the small publishers are doing less poetry and fiction and doing more nonfiction.

Yeah. Well, that's what sells, certainly. It's a lot easier to sell even literary nonfiction than it is to sell fiction. Look at the best-seller lists. Nonfiction sells. That was your experience at the show. You have people walking by because they saw this is literary. This is fiction and poetry, whatever, they're walking by. It's the nonfiction—it's very easy to categorize, it goes here in the store, zap! You make a decision based on "Yeah, we sell books on military history pretty well, so here's a book on military history. I'll pick it up." Whereas "Well, I've got a novel here. Gee, I don't know. What's it about? Ah, I don't think so."

It's too hard to discriminate, because there are so many books published. It's a lot easier to categorize nonfiction. In fiction, how many categories do you have? You have mystery, historical, romance, whatever. Nonfiction has a zillion categories. So it's a lot easier to categorize it. I know I'm selling a lot more literary nonfiction than I used to. And it's great because it's easier to sell. And as a literary rep, it's nice to have books that are easy to sell for a change.

What do you personally like? What kind of books—?

I read fiction. I read a lot of novels. When I'm on the road I read more mysteries because it's easy to sort of block out the motel surroundings. When I'm living for extended periods in motel rooms, I find I need something that's a little bit more...more of a rush. When I get home I read more leisurely narratives. I might, like, when I'm on the road I'll read Lawrence Block. But I read a lot. I mean, that's my—

Do you think most sales reps do?

It varies. It kind of surprises me how many reps don't read much. I remember one time I was at a show and there was a guy had a book that I wanted to read. You know, he had a stack of them. "Um, would you like to trade for this? I'd like to read this. Is there something on my table you'd like?" "No, I don't read." It was a mass market rep and he had a dump, you know, he had like thirty-six of them, and he said, like, "Here, just take it. I don't need 'em. I'm just giving 'em out anyway." That's fine. He said, "I just don't read."

A "dump"?

A floor display. Thirty-six-copy floor display. We call them dumps. That's where the display ends up after the books are sold. George Scheer certainly was a reader, and a writer. I mean he was a historian. He was a Renaissance man, I guess. But I don't think he's at all typical of sales reps. I think publishers' reps tend to be pretty much like any other professional. Maybe more of them are readers because a lot of us came into it through bookstores. But by no means did all of us come into it through bookstores.

Years ago I had an agent, and one of the things—this was the first indication I had that agents don't necessarily read. And he's very successful. He's done pretty well by his clients, actually. I think he's a good agent. He's well connected. But in talking with him, my impression was that he had read certain things in college, whatever was required, and stopped after that.

Wow. I can't imagine going through a day without reading. I mean if I go to bed at night and I haven't read for an hour, I feel—it's like I didn't brush my teeth. It's like something I almost physically need to do. But that's just me. Maybe it's because I was a sickly child. I don't know.

Were you a sickly child?

Yeah. I had asthma. But, you know, I just—I love to read. And when people don't read, it just mystifies me. You know, it's easy to sit in front of the tube and watch TV. Certainly I watch some TV myself, but not all the time. It's funny. I think of an agent—I mean that really is a salesman. Because you're selling something, and selling it period. I would think that certain kinds of books—a literary agent, I'd think, would have to be a reader, but I guess maybe not. You just have to be able to characterize a type of writing and plug it into the right person, the right editor.

I was reading a few months ago—it just blew my mind—I thought, "Well, this is publishing in the '90s." I forget which company it was—it was one of the big New York, you know, corporate publishers, and somebody had just been named editor-in-chief or editorial vice-president or something, editorial director, whatever, and his claim to fame was...yeah, he was the editor who'd signed a bunch of TV star autobiographies, TV star memoirs and stuff like that. Of course, that stuff's going to shoot to the top of the best-seller lists. But on the basis of having signed all these books that made a lot of money for the company, he's made vice-president or whatever. Hey! he's got shrewd business instincts. Is he a literary man? Hell, no! If he were, he wouldn't have been given that promotion, would he?

So those of us—I'm fairly literary, I've read a lot and I continue to read. I'm not saying I'm Mr. Literature or anything like that, but those of us in the business who are literary, you know, we're not necessarily where the action is. Think of the big publishers that are left that have a literary person at the helm.

I don't think there are any.
Roger Straus.

Well, for however long he's there.

Yeah, he sold the company [i.e., Farrar Straus Giroux]. But he's still running it as long as he's there. Otherwise, hey! it's big business.

388

You're talking about some of the publishers now, what is it? Random House has over a billion dollars in sales a year now, or something like that. It's a big business. They don't want somebody literary, they need somebody with business instincts. Can't argue with that.

It's interesting. Friends of mine—I'm assuming these anecdotes represent something larger—they've stopped reading the New York Times Book Review *because it's tied in to the New York companies and, for the most part, it reviews only those books those companies produce.*

Well, it does seem that.... You know, there are things changing in this world. I don't particularly like the direction things are going. Hopefully, there are other, cyclical elements involved, but I don't know. It seems like nowadays there are so many demands on people's time. Even educated, reasonably affluent people who used to buy, say, two hundred dollars worth of hardback books a year are now buying half that many because they don't have time to read because they're on the Internet. They're working with their computer. There are demands on people's time now that didn't exist even two years ago.

Well, they work much longer hours. The corporations they work for demand so much more from people on salary.

And then the leisure time that is left—hey! you can get two hundred channels on your TV now. There's always something there that might be at least worth checking out. Even if there isn't anything on, it takes half an hour to find that out. And then, hey! something else might be starting, so you start the cycle again. I've done it myself. I do it myself. You get into that process. There are all these different processes that you get involved in. And we have so much less leisure time, time that you could spend reading a book.

Notes

1. See Bruce Bliven, Jr., *Book Traveler* (New York: Dodd, Mead, 1975), 46: "...Scheer was able to devote about ninety out of each hundred and eighty minutes to pure new-book selling— a little more than twenty-six seconds, on the average, for each of his two hundred and six new titles." The reference is to new titles as opposed to backlist titles. Others of those one hundred eighty minutes went to re-establishing relationships with stores' buyers through gossip, complaints about aspects of the industry, asking about each other's families, and so on. In addition, the buyer might also be the owner, the manager, or the cashier, and so periodically be distracted by the duties of those other roles.

WHOLESALER

Vito Perillo
Pacific Pipeline

"...I always enjoyed books, being around books. I think the people who worked at Pipeline liked being in the book business. You know, it's a worthwhile thing to be doing... It's always good to see a book sell, something that you like, and see other people like it and sell it. I think it's got to be a real thrill for the buyers to be able to pick a book in advance and take a position on it, on a roll of the dice, as it were. You know, see the stuff that you've read catch the hearts of other people."

Laconic at first, even abrupt, he didn't warm up until we started talking about Pacific Pipeline, building it up, hiring for it. Sometimes his choice of words seemed to imply a kind of flippancy about major cultural themes, as though he was embarrassed even to mention them. But perhaps he wasn't being flippant so much as ironic; it was clear that ideas of social responsibility, for example, are important to him, and it may be that he mourns the passing of their influence.

We met late in the morning on a bleak, chill weekday in early March 1997 at a bakery/cafe called Louisa's, in Seattle's Eastlake District. He looked very fit, very trim, neatly dressed in a blazer and slacks, hair freshly cut. He held himself erect, whether standing or sitting. His style, the way he presents himself, is a little more direct than that of most Seattleites and he is just a little more dapper than most men in Seattle, who wear the obligatory business suit as though acknowledging its obligatoriness, or else denims and, if not a flannel work shirt, a tee shirt or a work shirt of some other kind. I cannot imagine Vito Perillo in jeans and a flannel shirt.

Born and raised in Providence, Rhode Island, he went to Brown University, but also George Washington and the University of Maryland while he was in the army. After military service, he sold radio advertising on the East Coast, then came out to Seattle for a job as sales manager for a radio station. That was in 1971.

393

Did that for a year. Till about '72, '73. Just poked around, didn't do much of anything for about a year. I had a few projects going, waiting for something to happen on the radio side. A friend of mine in the U District [i.e., Seattle's University District] published a book on marijuana cultivation, *How to Grow Marijuana Indoors Under Lights.* Sun Magic was the publisher, the book publishing company. Anyway, he needed someone to help with marketing and sales and, you know, it was a heck of a lot easier selling books than it was selling advertising. I wouldn't say it was a runaway best-seller, but I'm sure we sold several hundred thousand copies over the years.

Not only in the Pacific Northwest though.

Oh, no. No, we had other distributors around the country. But there was no distributor in the Northwest who really wanted to take on the book. Raymar was here at the time. They were wholesalers head-quartered in Monrovia, California, with a branch in Bellevue. And the folks in Monrovia weren't interested in a counter-culture book. So there was no one to distribute it here.

Then, at the time I was taking this book around to the stores, I had another client who published a book on horse racing and handicap-ping and he said, "Hey, you go around to bookstores, you might as well take this one along." So I got in touch with the publisher and made an arrangement to carry his book in my satchel. But it seemed to me that it made a lot more sense to bill them together for the bookstores' conve-nience than to write up an invoice for this guy and an invoice for that guy. Now I didn't know what a sales rep was in those days. Didn't know that sales reps existed. But it was really the impetus for starting kind of an umbrella company, which I called Pacific Pipeline.

In both those transactions we used Bookpeople [a wholesaler; see the Randall Beek interview, this volume] as a model. We had a consignment contract: You give them [i.e., the wholesaler] the books and they sell the books and pay you the money. So I had that arrangement with these two publishers. And there was enough volume in those two books to move along and create some business. You go to the mailbox every day and you do a little mailing or promotional thing. You go out to the various bookstores, Waldenbooks, J.K. Gill, University Book Store.

What year was this?

This was '73, '74 when we started Pipeline. The marijuana book was published in the summer of '73 and I started Pipeline in August of '74.

Isn't there a wholesaler in Ballard [i.e., a Seattle neighborhood] now that carries similar titles? Homesteaders?

Homestead. Homestead Book Company. Yep, that's true. In fact, I had dinner with him last night.

Oh, really?

Yeah. We've known each other for twenty years.

Was he involved with you early on?

Oh, he had a...I believe he had a newsstand or a bookstore in Tacoma. It was called The American Dream. He was one of my customers. You know, we had a lot of head shops in those days, up and down the Av [i.e., University Way Northeast, in Seattle]. Any college town had smoke shops. That was the primary market. None of the local distributors would tackle that market. So Pipeline became sort of the de facto distributor to both sides of that market, to the trade book market as well as to the underground book market.

So it started off with you and a satchel and two books.

Those two books, and I had a book called *Cooking with Marijuana*. We had another book that we bought as a remainder. We were kind of counter-cultural in our approach for about eight years, I would say. Books on, oh, I don't know, things like wind-generated electricity and vegetarian cookery and organic gardening—those types of things that fit the model of the clientele we were serving. These books sold at Walden and they sold at J.K. Gill.

There was a good undercurrent of publishing going on in the Northwest. Pacific Search Press had a zucchini cookbook that we sold a lot of, and they had a couple of other cookbooks that went along with it. There was a company called The Writing Works. There were some small presses in Portland that we distributed. It was pretty much small-press, local distribution, that type of stuff. It kept us busy. We weren't making a lot of money; we were having a lot of fun. A couple, three hundred titles is all. And kind of growing. You know, just sort of take them as they come.

There must have been at least one quantum leap to go from you and maybe a couple of helpers to an organization.
I think that was the Mount St. Helens volcano in 1980.

Was that Madrona's book? [See the interview with Dan Levant of Madrona Publishers in Gold 1996.]
Madrona's book and the Graphic Arts book and the book from Beautiful America. Within six or eight weeks of the eruption, I think we had twenty-two books. The two biggest sellers were the Madrona book, *The Eruption of Mount St. Helens*, which was co-produced by the *Vancouver Columbian*, and we had another book—I'm not sure what the title was, but it was produced by a publisher in Portland, Beautiful America. They published paperback picture books, the kind of stuff you find at the airports. But, you know, they got currency in the book-stores as well.

Those were the two books that sold really well. I remember we were buying five thousand or ten thousand copies of those things at a time. Couldn't keep them in stock; they couldn't print them fast enough. The Madrona book went on to become number eight on the *New York Times* best-seller list. Of course, that gave them a lot of money. But also, on the distribution side, we made a ton of dough too. I think the first million-dollar month in the history of the company was that July. July of 1980. We just couldn't ship them fast enough. We used the profits and the momentum from that to pick up hardcover books from national trade publishers for the first time. That was the fall of 1980.

What was the advantage in dealing with hardcover books?
Oh, I think it's just a matter of market perception. You have to understand that about the same time Raymar—the distributor down in California—back in, I think, '77 or '78 got sold to Ingram. And there really wasn't much of a market here in the Northwest at the time. So in early 1980 Ingram left the Northwest. They closed the Raymar opera-

tion and consolidated everything into a big new warehouse down in California. About a month after they pulled up stakes, Mount St. Helens blew. We were the only ones that were doing anything in the area. So we started to take a look at distributing a broader assortment of books to the niche that Raymar slash Ingram had left behind. And the book-stores were very responsive.

About how many employees did you have then, in 1980?
Oh, I don't even remember. We might have had fifteen or twenty or thereabouts.

How many do you have now?
Well, we're in bankruptcy. But we had about a hundred and eighty. Of course, it would be more at Christmas time, into the two-hundred range. Not only Christmas, but after Christmas we had returns to do. And we always had marketing and promotion based on trade shows and what-have-you. But the normal staff was one-sixty-five to one-eighty, give or take. Mostly full-time. We had people who preferred to work part time, and that was fine. But what we really used were warehouse workers, pickers and packers, pretty much entry-level kind of things. You know, it's a rare instance where someone who's making five or six bucks an hour can afford to take just a part-time job. I mean, you've got your working mom who's got the kids in school and dad's got a full-time job, but we weren't really big at that. Whenever you want full-time committed employees, you give them good benefits, a good work environment, pleasant surroundings, a good, relaxed atmo-sphere, you know, "We're here to get the job done, but let's have fun while we're doing it." You build that kind of corporate culture. So we never really focused on getting part-time people into—you know, we wanted them to be part of the family.

In the fall when we had seasonal hirings, we'd hire people with the understanding that at the end of January they'd probably be out of a job, but at least they'd be full-time workers for three months. And usually you would have some kind of turnover, so the better ones that joined the staff in September, October would replace the people who would drop out after a year or two when they found other jobs or moved on or whatever.

I published my first book in 1984. Michael Brasky was the small press buyer then.

Right.

And I think Inland was just starting up around that time. Inland Book Company.

Yeah.

So Michael put me on to them for the East Coast.

Sure.

What kind of relationship do the regional wholesalers and distributors have with each other? I mean Michael gave me a list of regional wholesalers in other parts of the country—

Right.

—and he starred Inland. He thought that would be really good for me.

Sure. Yeah.

But somebody sent him the list. Or maybe he made it up, I don't know.

Yeah, we had—I won't say we had cooperative relationships, but we all cooperated with one another. I mean, "I've got my territory and you've got yours," and we referred people back and forth. It's not a secret. All you have to do is call one or two of the bigger bookstores in whatever region you're trying to penetrate and ask them who they get their books from. And they'll say, "Well, we get this kind of book from Inland and we get this kind of book from Koen or this kind of book from Bookmen." There are half a dozen or so smaller distributors. We never pretended to be a national distributor, and never required any kind of exclusive distribution agreement. I don't want to have that kind of responsibility to the publishers.

If you had this relationship with a local publisher, say, and if that publisher was just starting out, and he or she didn't have the experience to know how to get distribution in other parts of the country, did you then have a buying-selling relationship with Inland or Bookmen or whomever for that publisher's books?

No. Up to the publishers to set up their own relationships. We'd point you in the right direction and it would be up to you to do what you want to do.

Have you considered Pipeline to be a distributor or a wholesaler or a combination of the two, or— I know you have some sales reps, or you had some sales reps.

We do, yeah. It's always been a little different. You're a trade wholesaler in that you sell books to the trade bookstores. So we have the books that are in demand, the latest best-sellers or the new crop of paperbacks or the best-selling cookbook or whatever's on Oprah, that type of thing. You're a demand jobber essentially. The orders come in and you fill them. The trick on the wholesale side is to have a sharp crew of buyers to stay ahead of the curve. Anticipate demand. Have an instinct for what's going on.

The smaller presses are a separate challenge in that nobody is going to know about these books unless the publisher does publicity. So we became kind of a de facto publicity arm for these publishers, with our weekly newsletter and the sales reps. I mean that was our excuse to go into the stores and do stock checks. In the early days that's what we did. Went to the J.K. Gill stores. Went to the Walden stores. Whipped out a catalogue, checked their stock, put together a suggested order. That's how we did business. It's real costly to put the reps in the field. And it becomes more costly every year. You know, gas goes up, wages go up, the price of the car goes up.

They weren't commission reps?

They were just regular full-time sales reps. They weren't commission. They weren't on bonuses and all. We just gave them a thousand a month and a car, or whatever the going rate was in those days, and they went out and visited bookstores. But we had some pretty darn good reps. They'd go down to Portland and out to Spokane and up to B.C. We didn't really do much in California or Montana, although they'd go out there occasionally. We'd see the bookstores at the various trade shows.

We were really kind of marketing for the publishers. Some books sold real well and pretty much paid the bills for the publishers that didn't sell real well. It all came out in the wash, really. It seemed like we were doing okay. We didn't really have any kind of fine-tuned financial analysis that said, "This publisher's costing you X; this publisher's costing you Y; this publisher ought to be charged more." Or, "There were more returns on this book than there were sales, so therefore you're just spinning your wheels."

We had probably twelve or thirteen hundred small-press consignment publishers and they all get a monthly sales report, you have to cut them a check, and you have to order the books. It's just a lot of basic stuff you've got to do to get those books to market. And you're responsible for them once they get to market. Nobody's going to track down some small publisher in Bothell or Tukwila, so we'd get returns from bookstores all over the country. That's a bit of an exaggeration. We'd sell books to—in recent years we'd sell books to the Barnes and Noble and the Walden stores. Local publishers might be putting out things that had more general appeal, so you'd be selling books throughout the Midwest, into California, out to the East. If they sell—hey, that's great, we all make money. If they don't sell you just get them back, and now you're handling the book a second and a third time, and there's no revenue there.

In fact, you're losing revenue because the sale was cancelled, but you've paid for the pick-and-pack, you've paid for the box that the books went out in, and now you've got to have somebody unpick and unpack, then recycle that box, and then find a way to get that book back on the shelf or, if that became too tedious, we'd just put it back in a box and send it back to the publisher for credit. And then you've got to arm wrestle the publisher because, hey, the books aren't in good condition. So you've got to develop an understanding with the publisher that our job is to get the books to market; your job is to make sure that they sell because if they don't sell, the secondary job that we have to do is sweep up the mess, but ultimately you're responsible for the mess. That's the way the game is played.

To get books to the Midwest, did you have accounts in the Midwest, or did you sell them through—?

400

Barnes and Noble, Walden.

You would be the vendor of record for some—
Correct. We had vendor relations with Walden and B. Dalton going back twenty years.

Were the local Waldens and B. Daltons able to buy locally?
Yes.

Can they now? I don't think they can.
I'm not sure what they can do now. I think they've got sort of limited flexibility. But in the '80s we would go into a store, do a stock check, and write the order. And take it back and fill it and bill the home office, and sooner or later we'd get paid. So that wasn't a problem. We had a real good relationship with the individual store managers. They knew that if it didn't sell this month, we were going to be back in four to six weeks and we'd pull the returns, we'd sell the new books and keep track of the stuff we were selling. We always had good sales reps in the field, taking care of their customers, making sure they had stuff that was selling. If we were running short on something they'd call the customers and let them know we were running out of this hot seller, let them know what was coming.

The store managers tend to be—when you get to that level where they've got a chain, you know, like J.K. Gill or Walden or Dalton, it's pretty stable. You get to have a personal relationship with them. They may have you manage their regional sections, or take your advice on locally published books.

How many sales reps did you have at Pipeline's peak?
At the peak? Probably six. We had national reps taking care of Barnes and Noble and Borders. We had a computer rep who was taking care of the computer sections of the stores. We had a couple of small press reps. Sales manager. I was—not that I was much of a rep any more, but I'd go out and visit the stores as well. I'd keep in touch with the top twenty or the top forty accounts on the phone. As far as field sales reps, probably three or four in-house reps. But I always had telemarketers.

How did you come by your organizational ability? I mean, you built up from a single person to a multimillion-dollar company. Aside from the money involved, you had to organize to handle it. You just grew with it, or you—?

That's pretty much it, yeah. You hire good people and you stay out of their way, really. I think you set up an environment that breeds success. I don't know how you do it. I just... It's sort of an instinct, I guess. However, you've got to trust people. I had an interesting—this goes back to Sun Magic Publishing. The guy who was the publisher, the store owner—the guy that produced the book actually wrote the book, Steve Murphy, also known as Murphy Stevens—he was a pretty laissez faire manager. He ran his plant store in a pretty easygoing way. And the book got published, a marijuana cultivation book, and he got into it for a couple of months, but the busy season at the plant store started. Christmas was coming or whatever, and he pretty much turned over the keys to the publishing company to me. Whatever I wanted to do was fine with him. I went to the mailbox, I got the money, I deposited it, I kept the books. He had no idea what I was doing or why I was doing it. We just had this trusting relationship, and he trusted me not to play any dirty tricks.

That's how he ran his business with the employees he hired. You get to know them and you have a level of trust and.... Steve was always one to—you know, if it's snowing, "Let's close the store and go sledding." If the sun is shining, "Let's take off early and go to the beach." If it's raining, "We've got to stay here and do some work." And when we did work, you might put in twelve, fourteen hours to get something done, but when it was time to play, hey! But the work always got done; the atmosphere was always fun; it was always fun to be around in that kind of environment.

Anyway, that was in the back of my mind when I hired my first sales rep, a guy named Sherwood Hayden. Sherwood was an interesting guy. In fact, I sort of knew him in my former career. His background was radio advertising, as well. He was general manager of a station down in Eugene, Oregon. He moved up to Seattle as the sales manager at KING-FM, the classical music station. I don't know how I actually met the guy, but it turned out he wasn't going anywhere in his radio career at KING. I guess the rule at the time was that you had to be a graduate of an ivy league school to get anywhere in their organization. Sherwood was a good salesman, but I think he was looking for an excuse to get out. And I had this kind of counter-culture project and he was affiliated with a counter-culture radio station. So I said, "I don't have much money here, but we could have a lot of fun. Why don't you come and be the sales manager?" I had, you know, a few publishers that wanted to get distributed.

So Sherwood came on board and, by gosh, he was setting the town on fire. You know, the guy was everywhere at once, selling books, packing books, delivering books, just going crazy. And I didn't know the guy all that well, but it seemed like his heart was in the right place, and he was doing a darn good job. But, you know, he was the guy that all of a sudden has all your client contacts and—that was a hurdle I had to get over, that I was letting go of control. But I thought about that, and I thought, Well, you know, this is exactly what Murphy did with me, and I didn't burn him; I'm just going to roll with it. The guy seems energetic, has a good spirit. I recalled that when I was working for people, I just tried to do a good job. I mean that's what you get paid for. It's not the money as much as the satisfaction of getting the job done. So I didn't bother the guy, just let him do what he wanted to do. I guess that was the first hurdle. But once you get past that and you realize here's a real energetic, driven guy, you're not afraid of hiring other people who are competent in certain areas and just sort of staying out of their way. I was hiring them to do the job and treating them well, paying them well, creating a "corporate culture" I guess is the term they use, but providing the atmosphere to encourage them to succeed. And that's what we did. I always tried to hire people smarter than I was, and then let them do their job.

You know, when you're a small company it's pretty clear what needs to be done. You hire somebody to do sales and that's what they do. If they're not doing it, you can tell. But hopefully you've made the right hiring decision and this person is out there running around, making calls on bookstores and bringing back orders. On the accounting side, you get the bills paid and you get some kind of accounting system set up and the checkbook balances and then that job is done.

It's not like in a larger company where things get a lot more complex. It's not real simple or straightforward. There are longer-range plans, there are projects of a longer-term nature that have to be managed. There's an ongoing issue of resources. You don't just hire someone and turn him loose; you have to hire someone who's able to put together a team to get a project done. You've got to worry about the postage bill, you've got to worry about the printer, if he's going to deliver on time, the mailing lists have to be merged, you've got more titles to keep track of, more reports, more checks—

More of everything involves a different structure altogether, I would assume.

Well, sure. I mean you become more bureaucratic. You set a tone... How do you say this? You set a good example. I mean I'm letting you do your job, and hopefully you'll learn from that and let the people under you do their jobs. Make the right hiring decisions, don't stand in their way, don't take credit for the work they do, praise them and build a team. I'm not sure we ever got to that point. We just kind of evolved and we had a certain amount of luck. Some people we hired didn't turn out well and had to be fired.

That's the other key. If it's not happening you've got to cut your losses. I had—maybe I still have, I don't know—I had the reputation for being pretty brutal when it came to letting people go. I never thought I was. There were no surprises when I fired anybody. They knew they were going to get fired; they knew they weren't doing the right job; they knew that they deserved to get fired. "Deserved" is the wrong word, but they knew they weren't living up to my expectations. Then they were cut. But when it came it was never a surprise.

Did you find the Peter principle at work sometimes? You know, somebody rises to his level of incompetence.

Yeah. That does happen. And that causes difficulties. You know, someone rises to the level of accounting superviser, and the next step is to be a controller/financial planner. Well, you want to give this person the opportunity to do that, but they don't have the capability or the instinct or the background. The training or education. And as much as you want to give that person a chance to move up a notch, they're just not there.

The sales thing as well. We had some real good sales people over the years who got to a senior sales position, loved being out in the field—this happened in a couple of cases. But the next step after that was sales management. Out of the field, taking care of the top accounts, not going and doing stock checks, but managing the sales force. You talk to them, you put together a game plan, you try to articulate what their new responsibilities are, you get what you think is buy-in on it, and then they're back to their old job, heading out to the east side to stock-check at a lot of mom-and-pop bookstores. You know, "That's not your job any more."

Then what you've got to do is you've got to go outside the company and try to find a senior-level person to come in. "Well, why didn't I get the chance at that job?" "Well, you had the chance. You didn't make the most of the chance. You're a lot more comfortable doing what you're doing." And that always causes some bruised feelings. In some cases you can do that. Some people are very comfortable doing what they're doing and don't want the additional responsibility. And other people are upset because they weren't given the chance when, in fact, the opportunity has always been there. Once or twice I got the story that "I've got the responsibility but I don't have the authority to do anything." I never understood what they meant by that.

We had a situation in the buying department where we wanted to create more of a.... Well, we talked about Inbook and Inland and how they had a distribution mechanism. Basically, they had an organizational structure to take care of the marketing needs of all these small press clients. Publishers Group West is the same. Atrium is the same. National Book Network is the same.[1] You've got models out there to look at. And there's certainly a need to do that. And there's an understanding that our big concern is that something has to be done. And then you can't get that person to do anything. In this case, the vice president of merchandising understood that that's what I wanted to get done, but even then wasn't able to organize or orchestrate development within his own division. It does happen. The Peter principle does happen.

In fact, I thought I was going to get Peter-principled out myself. At the time the company got to sales of twenty-five, thirty-five million, I started looking for higher-level executives to come in and help manage the company. It turned out I would have been better served by continuing to manage it myself. But you have to wonder as the company grows, at what point are you over your head?

Don't you think that a lot depends on what you want as an individual?
Yeah, that's true.

What I'm thinking of is that some small presses—I interviewed Barbara Wilson of Seal Press for the first book I did [Gold 1996] and Seal had a sudden increase in income and therefore an opportunity to grow. But once they grew and put on permanent employees, they had to start taking care of their employees.
Yep.

And then they grew in a direction that—they had to put out books that were profitable—
Sure.

—in order to pay their employees.
Right.

But that isn't how they started. They started with literary books.
Sure.

I took a lesson from that. I wanted to continue doing literary books, so I decided not to grow.
Right.

It's what I wanted.
Sure.

One distributor—I've forgotten which one now—said that a small publisher needs a hundred thousand dollars to get started. I could see how he was thinking. He was thinking in terms of staffing first, and then acquiring the books.
Getting the product line ramped up. Sure.

Everybody I know who's lasted—of course, most don't—but ev-erybody I know who has lasted started with the idea for a book or a book itself, and then grew with it.

Right.

As you said about Pipeline.

Well, with Sun Magic, they had that marijuana one, but there were a number of others that started with one book. Madrona's a good example of that, too. They had some good local books, they got a big profit on that book about the volcano, and then started to grow beyond that. But he [i.e., Dan Levant] was almost forced to publish books to maintain them. You've got a staff that's capable of producing twelve or fifteen books a year and you're wasting your resources unless you produce twelve books a year. But if those books don't sell, then you've got a problem.

I did interview Dan Levant for the first book. He said that when you were first getting started you had your books in your basement. Is that true or was he exaggerating?

That's true. Oh yeah. It was a pretty low-rent operation. I was managing an apartment building on Capitol Hill, and there was a furnace room, a basement room, that was used for storage. And I cleaned it up and organized the storage and got it off in a corner. I strung a phone line through a crack in the floor and I had the phone downstairs. And I had a little packing table and a couple pallets of books, a little alley with a side door. I could load up my car for the trips.

Do you miss those days?

Well, those were fun days. You're not sure what you're doing but you're paying the bills, and who cares? So, yeah, those were good days. Do I miss them? I think I'm a lot smarter, a lot wiser now than I was then. A lot more carefree then. Although I can't say I'm loaded down with worries or concerns or anything. I do pretty well. Mentally, I'm fine.

Pipeline had problems a couple of years ago with the new computer software, is that what it was?

Yeah.

You never got past the problem, or you ran into new problems?
Oh, well, that was kind of the start of a lot of problems. The company had grown dramatically. Our sales at the high point were fifty million dollars. We were basically selling a million dollars worth of books a week. The organization was a thriving organization. But we were pretty much at the limits of our capacity as far as the computer system was concerned. And there was a demand to expand the business. I had an executive board of really talented people who wanted to see the company be more dominant, whatever. You could hire just drones to take care of the day-to-day stuff, but if I wanted to keep the spirit there, keep the excitement alive, you want that kind of people. It's fun to work with those kinds of people. But at the same time they're looking forward to, you know, growth and excitement themselves.

So we were looking for ways to expand. The market was changing. There were smaller distributors in other regions that weren't doing what we were doing. There was an opportunity to perhaps acquire one or more of those other distributors, or open up branches of our own operation. But in order to do all this stuff, we needed a bigger and better computer system. So a decision was made to migrate to new hardware, new software, a whole new state-of-the-art package.

The folks who were managing that project didn't know what they were doing. It basically melted down. We never did get completely converted. We couldn't keep track of our inventory. We couldn't bill the customers correctly. We couldn't ship books properly. Or pick the orders. The orders were picked to pack, but the orders were fragmented, they were going every which way. There was not a heck of a lot of integrity in the ongoing transactions with the customers. Customers were being very, very supportive, for the most part. But in lots of cases with large customers—I mean, in order to reconcile their accounts to active conversion it took them hundreds of man-hours to comb through the records, trying to match up statements with packing slips, but without the real invoices. It caused a lot of customer dissatisfaction. Inventory started to decay. We just didn't have the inventory records to buy books. Those were the biggest problems for us. Customer confidence eroded, as did sales. And in order to repair this thing, we had to

408

pour a lot more money in it than we anticipated. It was going to be a million-dollar project; it ended up costing us probably two million dollars—and the company.

So we're in bankruptcy now. We're sorting it out. The staff is down to less than thirty people. Sales and buying is no longer—it's pretty much down to the accounting group, putting together all the accounting records for the bankruptcy. Some warehouse staffers taking care of the last of the inventory—actually, waiting for a decision from the bankruptcy court to dispose of the inventory. It's all returnable but it can't be returned because of legal issues about preference to certain publishers. You got consigned publishers, you got trade publishers. You got secured creditors, like the bank. Those are the things we're sorting out.

You said that the market had changed recently. How did you mean?

Well, on the publishers' side you got a lot of consolidation at the top. Among the top five or ten publishers. That's still going on. On the retail side you've got the expansion of the superstores, which are destination stores. I guess, in some sense, they're creating new visibility for books, but at the same time they're detracting from the independent bookstores that have served the marketplace for a long time. A lot of them serve the marketplace real well, a lot of them haven't served it so well. I mean, you've got small-time operators out there. "Small time." That's a cliché, but people running those stores—some of them are better at running a bookstore than others, some of them are more successful than others. Some are going to go out of business anyway. They might have gone out of business two years from now, but they're going out of business now, instead. Some people want to be in the book business because they like books, but, you know, you shouldn't be in the supermarket business just because you like to eat, and you shouldn't be in the funeral home business because you like dead people. So there's always that kind of a shake-out. The market is changing. Bookstores, even the well-run bookstores, are not seeing any increases. Their sales are flat. They're having to look at their margins, look at their costs, scrutinize things like they haven't been used to.

I'm noticing that the independent stores that, say, five or six years ago, used to buy five or ten copies of a book, maybe more, now are buying one or two.

Well, that's part of the equation that the wholesalers have been propounding for a number of years. I mean, if you've got a wholesaler that can get you books tomorrow, you don't need five copies. You can do with two or three copies and as you sell one, you replenish them. As long as the wholesaler's got a broad enough inventory, you can always get them. You get a couple, three boxes worth of books every day, every other day, to replenish what you've sold and you can shrink your inventory. Or, better yet, you can take the same inventory dollars [and] instead of having five copies on hand, you have one or two copies, and instead of offering ten thousand titles, you can offer twenty thousand titles. The same dollar-investment inventory. But a lot of people don't look at the inventory in terms of dollars; they see books. But if you're going to say, "That's an asset and I'm going to manage that asset," how do you manage it? Well, you've got turnover. Every time you do a transaction you're making a profit. Increase your transactions. And the wholesaler is key to that equation: stock availability on an overnight basis. These are the things that a bookstore is doing, or catching on to.

Financial management, although they probably wouldn't say it's financial—just being careful about how you invest your dollars. They're being forced to change. Computers are having an effect on the retail side—on bookstores. There are various computerized systems out there that are helping bookstore owners do a better job managing their assets, managing their inventory.[2]

Clearly, the competition is Barnes and Noble. I can tell you a story that was related by a bookseller. It happened at a bookstore on Mercer Island. I don't know if you know him—Roger Page of Island Books.

I don't know him but I know the store.

Well, Island is a very good store. He always used to refer customers, when he didn't have the book. Of course, he could special order the book for you, the customer, or perhaps you could check at University Book Store, or the customer would say, "Well, let me check University Book Store first." That was the way it was for a long time. If Roger didn't have the book, University Book Store, or the customer would suggest.... It was almost overnight that the change happened. The customer came in, Roger didn't have the book. After a discussion about it, the customer said, "Let me check Barnes and Noble first." It was no longer University Book Store, it was B and N. It was a pretty telling statement. Roger's a pretty savvy bookseller, and he picked up on that immediately.

The chains are out there and their focus is no longer on the mall stores. Walden and B. Dalton are being phased out. Not entirely; obviously they're going to do what they can with what remains. But I know, in the case of Waldenbooks, for the longest time—this was in the '80s— two of the top five stores in the Walden chain were here in Seattle. Southcenter was neck and neck, sharing the number one spot, with their big store in Tyson's Corner, Virginia. And I think the number four or number five store was in Northgate Mall. A tremendous book presence. B. Dalton—one of their top stores in the country was in Washington Square in Portland.

But the malls are fading in terms of books. You know, you've got to take into account, too, that Target is selling books now, and not just paperbacks that you find in the Safeways and the Albertsons— they're selling trade books in book departments. You go to Costco— they're probably carrying three hundred book titles, but it's all the best-sellers. So the independent bookstores are not only competing with the—the best-seller business is gone, even for the chain bookstores. So they've got to find a way to make it with other product.

Besides books, you mean?

Well, yes, besides books, but also with a broader assortment of books. You only have, what? twenty or thirty books on the best-seller list; Costco can sell all of those. But what else is there?

The impression I get from listening to you is that throughout Pipeline's career, it was the activity that you were drawn to, not so much the books. Do you agree, or not?

No, I always enjoyed books, being around books. I think the people who worked at Pipeline liked being in the book business. You know, it's a worthwhile thing to be doing. It's clean and environmentally friendly, all those positive things. A friend of mine, one of the book reps, was taking another job in—going back east somewhere. There was a going-away party for him, and we went out after the party. And he said, "That was the most interesting party I've ever been to. Everybody had something interesting to say." Everybody had read something, or seen a movie, or commented about this or that; he was just amazed. I think if you run with that— I mean, at bookstores, people are articulate, they're well-read, they're interesting folks. This is a book milieu.

In terms of sales—I mean Boeing makes more in a year, selling jets, than the entire book-publishing industry does in selling books, and we're talking about textbooks and trade books and scholarly monographs, what all, spread across twenty-five thousand different companies—small presses, big presses, what have you. It's fragmented, but it's got that...I don't know, not intellectual culture as much as...the idea of social responsibility about it, you know, freedom of the press and all that kind of stuff. It's got a lot of positive things. So I enjoy being in that milieu...and the excitement of building a team and doing something worthwhile. It's always good to see a book sell, something that you like, and see other people like it and sell it. I think it's got to be a real thrill for the buyers to be able to pick a book in advance and take a position on it, on a roll of the dice, as it were. You know, see the stuff that you've read catch the hearts of other people. Other books, you think, God, what a piece of trash, and it goes on to sell a million copies—you just shake your head and wonder. But, yeah, there's a charge out of it.

I like the excitement of the management of it all. I don't know that I could be as excited about distributing, you know, auto parts. Maybe I could get excited about the wine business or the olive oil business or something, but...

What do you see for yourself now? What are you going to do next?

Well, I've got a couple, three months worth of wrapping up this bankruptcy deal. Then I'm not sure. I'm taking some personal time off, just sort of kick back. I've had a couple of inquiries about what I'm going to do. It'll probably be book related, because that's the only thing I know. I think there's a definite need, at a minimum, for a small press clearing house. A lot of small presses are going to need representation or distribution or some *thing*. Other distributors have wondered what I could do on a consulting basis. I've got some calls I haven't made, people who have expressed interest in me. One or two mail order things that I might get involved in, maybe book related, or closely allied. Frankly, I'm not too worried about it.

But you want to stay in the world of books somehow.
Oh, I think so. I think so, yeah.

Elizabeth Wales [a literary agent] says nobody ever leaves, once they get in.
Well, she's probably right. We'll see what happens. I've got twenty years' experience in the book business. If I can help people avoid making the mistakes that I made, that should be worth something.

Perillo left. I stayed back to make some notes. A woman sitting at a neighboring table asked if that was Vito Perillo I had been talking with. I replied that he was. She said that Pipeline still had her books. She had published one book and it had won an award, but almost all copies of it were in Pipeline's warehouse and she could not get them into the stores. She was angry. Bankruptcy Court would be meeting tomorrow on Pipeline's case; she intended to be there.

In July 1997, Perillo became president of Koen Pacific Book Distributors, one of two wholesalers that moved into the Seattle area to occupy the vacuum left by Pacific Pipeline's demise.

Notes

1. Publishers Group West, Atrium, Inbook, and National Book Network are or were book distributors. Inbook had already filed for bankruptcy at the time of this interview; Atrium has since gone out of business.

2. Perillo is describing "just-in-time" or what Randall Beek calls "almost-in-time" ordering (see his interview, this volume). This idea assumes that publishers will keep a book in stock that is slow to sell, and that bookstores will reorder when they run out. But at the end of the year publishers are taxed on their unsold

inventory, so are reluctant to keep a slow-selling book on hand. And, except for fast-selling books, bookstore buyers tend not to reorder after they've sold their original order of one or two. With a book culture oriented toward frontlist (the most recently published books), books published a year ago, or even four or five months ago, are usually not reordered, having been replaced in the bookstore buyers' awareness by newer books. Sales reps, especially commission reps, are at pains just to present each season's list to the buyers; they rarely have time to reacquaint them with backlist titles. All of this contributes to the sameness of titles available in bookstores.

DISTRIBUTORS

Randall Beek
Bookpeople; Consortium Book Sales & Distribution

"...I never thought about going into the book business. I didn't grow up saying, 'Gee, I'll be a bookseller.' But I loved to read. And then I loved the people who are in this business. And I love the passion. You know, all of this stuff about what's going on with the industry these days, you forget somehow that these are people who had a personal vision and were publishing books and believed in it, put their money into it, and were producing a myriad of ideas, from literature to how to fix your Volkswagen to occult sciences, to all of this stuff—"

Randall Beek, President and CEO of Consortium Book Sales & Distribution, is an affable, stocky man in his mid-forties. He conveys presence. When he talks to you, his eyes are on yours. I did not find him intimidating—I think he would be appalled if anyone did—but he was very focused, very much with me. He required little prompting: Give him a subject close to his heart and he runs with it. His style of discourse is linear and exploratory. He carries his topic to its end, examining each of its facets along the way. At first I thought he was, on occasion, distracting himself, or that he had a looping style of conversing, as I do, where he would go from one subject to another, then return to the first. But neither was true. Rather, he was exploring, sometimes almost as if he were talking to himself instead of to me. We began talking in his office in St. Paul, Minnesota shortly after ten a.m. on Thursday, September 18, 1997 and continued until almost noon, then went for lunch together and talked some more.

Beek was born in Washington, D.C. and grew up in Potomac, outside of Washington. His first love was music. In high school he composed and played guitar, trumpet, cello, and piano. He was accepted by the Berkeley School of Music in Boston, but turned it down. Still, music is "one of the things I can't live without. I still play guitar. I have something like three thousand CDs, mainly jazz. There's a very strong music-book connection for me."

His mother worked at Brentano's. Dropping out of high school his senior year, he went to work there too. Then he worked at a Waldenbooks in a strip mall in Rockville. Then he went to Greece with the woman he was in love with. When they came back in 1972 he returned to Brentano's, running the store on P Street in Washington for a while. Then he became assistant manager of a store on Embassy Row.

(Note: After I transcribed the tape of the interview, I sent a copy to Beek. He proofed it and added some historical context, integrating it into the text of the transcript. Though Beek is clear about when he was present at an occasion, and what he witnessed personally, the reader should be aware that some of the following was not part of the interview itself, but was added afterward.)

My former high school history teacher was my boss. That store really catered to the people in the embassies. People like Art Buchwald used to come in, and all the embassy people. Sheiks would send their Mercedes and their Rolls to pick up books—a very carriage-trade store. And then I started to work for RPM Distribution in Rockville.

It was run by David Marcuse. He had run something called the Community Bookstore, which was in Washington. Then he started RPM. I started working there in about '73. I think they started maybe in '71, '72. David now is part owner of a bookstore called Chuck and Dave's, in Tacoma Park, Maryland. Another guy who used to work for RPM and at Brentano's with me, Charles Dukes, is the other owner. David also had a store on Connecticut Avenue that went out of business recently. He came out of a more political arena—for instance, the Community Bookstore—and then he started RPM. He had a small warehouse in Rockville. One of the original small press buyers was Janie Tannenbaum who ran the New York Small Press Book Fair for years, worked at the Gotham Book Mart, spent some time working for Marsilio Publishers, who we distribute, and now, I think, she's working for New Press.

One of the things that put RPM out of business probably was the fact that they had a number of bookstores. They had a bookstore in Alexandria, Virginia, one in Lenox, and they opened up one in downtown Washington. You don't want to be a wholesaler and have your own bookstores. It created a number of problems, plus David had no money to do all of this stuff. He basically modeled the company on

418

Bookpeople which started in '68. He bought a lot of books—he probably bought a hundred thousand dollars worth of books from Bookpeople. That's how I got to know them. I used to go out on buying trips and hang out with the guys at Bookpeople.

RPM handled small press and also trade. So they did Random House and Simon and Schuster and Ballantine, and that was a lot of the money-making we had with independent publishers, and I ran that. I started out working in the warehouse. I used to unload the trucks. We had no forklift; I used to unload the trucks by hand. I remember getting something like twenty thousand copies of *The Joy of Sex* in one day. I had to touch every single carton; it was unbelievable. It was a small place. We ended up moving twice when I was there. We kept moving to bigger buildings. We did a small press catalogue. We had a lot of the publishers that are still around, like Capra and...all of these folks.

We started to go into exclusive distribution, and we distributed a book called *Roger Dean's Views*. It was a psychodelic art book and it sold about a hundred thousand copies. And then I signed a contract with these guys to do a book on the solar home. I think we sold about a hundred and fifty thousand copies of that and went out of business shortly thereafter. We were basically competing with Bookpeople, though in some ways they were more exclusive. Bookpeople at that point had about thirty or forty publishers you could only get through them—including John Muir Publications, Four Seasons/Grey Fox and Wingbow Press, which is their publishing company—so we did a lot of business with them. RPM went out of business in 1977. June first, 1977.

I remember going out to the San Francisco ABA and walking around and telling everybody we're going out of business. RPM was not my company, but even then I had personal relationships with people. I wasn't going to have them just call up and have no answer, so I went out there and I spent a couple of days and stayed with the guy who did the solar home book and—you know, we ended up owing him hundreds of thousands of dollars—and talking to people. It was a disaster.

I mean when RPM went out of business I was twenty-three years old. It was a very interesting experience for me because it was a small company and I got to do a lot of different things, from working on the receiving dock to buying the books, putting together the catalogue to going out on buying trips. We did all of the original small press book fairs in New York. One was in conjunction with the ALA [American Library Association], I think. There was one down in Battery Park. There was one under Lincoln Center one year. We went to the Boston Small Press Book Fair. We went out to San Francisco to the International Book Fair.

I attended my first ABA. It must have been in Washington, D.C., in 1974 maybe? It used to always be in the Shoreham Hotel in Washington. That year the air conditioning broke, if I'm not mistaken, and people were just sweltering with the humidity in that June weather in Washington. It was a nightmare. That was my first ABA experience. You know, it was tiny. It was in the basement of the Shoreham Hotel. It couldn't have been more than twenty-five thousand square feet, or something like that.

So in '77 RPM went out of business and I took a couple of months off. I met some people at Bookpeople when I went out for the ABA. I said I'd be interested in working—I always wanted to live out in California. I liked the Bookpeople organization. So they called one day—I think I'd been up all night, and somebody called me in the morning and said, "Well, we have a job for you." It was a job in the warehouse, seven hundred dollars a month or some ridiculous amount. Maybe six hundred dollars a month. And they said, "Well, can you come out?" And I said, "Sure." I think I started October first of 1977. I went out with my girl friend and she ended up working there too, actually doing computer work for the company. So for a couple of months I worked in the warehouse, packing books, pulling books....

Bookpeople is a totally employee-owned corporation. Anybody who works there owns a piece of the business, and the way it works is that after six months you became a shareholder or you didn't. You put in five hundred dollars and you got stock which you had to sell back to the company when you left. It didn't appreciate, so I got five hundred dollars back in 1992 when I left. We got dividends and various things over the years, but basically it was very egalitarian and totally employee-owned. You vote for the board of directors. Everybody had an equal vote. The board of directors, at that time, hired and fired the general manager.

So I packed books there for a couple months. At that point, Terry Nemeth was running the small press department and also publishing Bookpeople's imprint, Wingbow Press. They'd been publishing books for a while. They did a book on how to grow marijuana indoors under lights. They also published Ed Dorn, Diane di Prima. They did a book about the San Francisco Bay Area poetry scene. They did a book called *Bargain Hunting in the Bay Area* which sold ultimately several hundred thousand copies. So Terry was running that and also the small press department. And his girlfriend at the time, Aili Taback, was, I think, also there. Really, when I started going out with people at Bookpeople, it was Terry Nemeth and a guy named Bob Delapp who were the small press buyers. And there was a guy named Rich Rieheld who was the general manager of the company at the time, who now works for some computer company.

Bookpeople was founded by Don Gerard with his wife Eugenia and his good friend Don Burns. They originally worked for LS Distributors and decided to start their own company in the East Bay with initial funding by an outside investor named Toby. After Rich Reiheld was brought in to run Bookpeople, the Dons—Gerard and Burns—started Bookworks. Bookworks was to be the creative arm of Bookpeople. It planned to develop and publish books, act as author management. There was a plan to represent Dr. Hippocrates [*Berkeley Barb* hip health columnist], to expand his column nationwide. They were to provide Bookpeople with new national distribution properties (sign contracts, produce Bookpeople's national catalogue, act as liaison between publisher and Bookpeople.) They received five percent of the fifty-five percent discount that Bookpeople received to provide those services. Bookworks was also additionally funded by Toby.

Before Bookworks, Don Burns was a close friend of Stephen Gaskin and convinced him to produce *Monday Night Class* as a self-publisher. It was from that experience that it was decided that Bookworks could successfully develop their own books. Their first title was *Grow Your Own*, by Jeanne Darlington, who also had a local organic gardening column, I think in the *Barb*.

[Even though] *Whole Earth Catalog* continued to grow in sales, Bookpeople was increasingly losing money. Books came in at fifty percent after Bookworks' five percent commission and went out at forty percent—a rather slim margin for an exclusive distributor. When Terry started in February of 1970, they had three hundred accounts; by the

421

time the last *Whole Earth Catalog* came along there were over two thousand. Collections were a nightmare. The only way they could stay in business was by continued growth. At this time, Stewart Brand—the one so committed to West Coast values and anti-Eastern establishment principles—enlisted Don Burns to agent *Whole Earth Catalog* to New York publishers. Actually it was more of a distribution deal, but with a high advance. *Whole Earth Catalog* had total control and handled all of the production. Originally they had an oral agreement with Hal Scharlatt of Dutton, but reneged on that deal when Random House came in with more money.

Once it became apparent that there were to be no more *Whole Earth Catalogs* from Bookpeople, they knew that without a radical restructuring we were going to be history. During this same period of time they were having problems with Whole Earth about actual delivery counts. When new *Catalogs* came in, they were delivered on a flatbed truck in unsealed boxes. The printer packed anywhere between thirty-one and thirty-five copies per carton; Whole Earth wanted payment for a full thirty-five per box. With no more *Whole Earth* to sell, payments got behind to Stewart. Bookpeople owed them something like a hundred and ten thousand dollars at that point. Stewart threated to send Bookpeople into receivership if we didn't pay. After a lot of negotiations, they agreed to pay thirty thousand dollars right away and the balance over four to six months. It was the day after receiving that check that Stewart held the last Whole Earth party and proceeded to hand the same thirty thousand in cash to the audience.

Shortly thereafter, it became clear that Bookpeople was going down the tubes if employees did not take over the company. Gerard was still getting his share of the pie, they were distributing Bookworks books at the same five percent deal, and at the same time he was acting as agent to sell the best properties. There was a strike. They took all the account records, notified all the truckers who were friends not to deliver, and locked the door. That night a meeting in Terry's living room on Grove Street formed a negotiating committee—Terry, Karl Mills, Miriam Foley, and Bob Chieger. Initially Gerard was trying to stonewall them. But it became clear that he couldn't run it anymore on his own. Also, by selling it, he could get something out of it. Toby, the financial angel, would have lost all his original investment if they didn't sell. Toby was really the key; without him continuing the dialogue it probably wouldn't have worked out. Bookpeople eventually got bought for thirty thousand dollars in cash, with more to be paid out of receivables over the year. I mean these were guys who were gone by the time I got there. In '71 when the employees bought it, the guys who were running Bookpeople were taking money out of it.

But, you know, I was packing books for about six months and then they offered me the job. I thought I was actually going to be the buyer for both the trade and the small press books, but it ended up I was just the buyer for the small press stuff. I came there, I think there were about thirty people, we did about three million dollars in sales. We did the dishes every thirty days, 'cause that's how it was. We had somebody come in and cook and you got to clean up after. It was a wild place. I mean there were a lot of people dope-smoking and stuff like that. It was pretty hippy. At that point Bookpeople was on Seventh Street, which I think was the second location. They had a smaller place before I got there, on 9th and Ashby.

I basically took over from Terry; he moved into just publishing the books and I went into running the small press department. I used a lot of the things that I learned at RPM. I developed a structure where we took books at either fifty-two or fifty-five percent. At fifty-five you got a special mention in the catalogue, graphic and descriptive copy. And I boosted the number of publishers. I think they had like a couple hundred, and we had like three or four hundred in a couple of years. In 1983, I remember, we had about five hundred and fifty publishers.

I just came in on the tail end when they had a national catalogue that they produced, and those were all people who were exclusively available only from Bookpeople. The big ones at the time were the *Whole Earth Catalog*, which was a big book, and then *Trout Fishing in America* by Don Allen at Four Seasons. He was publishing Richard Brautigan. The *How to Keep Your Volkswagen Alive* from John Muir Publications—John Muir over in Santa Fe. John Muir is dead now. He died of a brain tumor. He used to come to Bookpeople with a parrot on his shoulder. He published a book called *People's Guide to Mexico*. They're still going. A several-million-dollar company now. I think they're distributed through Norton. I think it was the Atlanta ABA in 1982 when they were pulling out of Bookpeople and starting to do it on their own.

But we had a whole slug of publishers which were ours exclusively. Really, there wasn't any competition for distribution at that point. In some ways Bookpeople, I feel, is kind of the start of the modern small press movement and distribution. Because there were a lot of literary books also coming up, but there was all of this back-to-the-land movement, and owner-built home books. This guy, Vic Marks, did a book, *Cloudburst*; it was, you know, funky. It had a taped binding. It's now Hartley and Marks Publishing up in Canada. There were dome books, and fixing-your-sandals, and all of that stuff. It really came out of the culture of the time. It was the hippy movement. Things like the *Whole Earth Catalog*—there weren't books in that format. You know, it was a huge book. I don't remember what the size was, fifteen by—it was huge. And then things like *Handmade Houses* from Scrimshaw Press, which was about all these funky houses that people were building in northern California—a full-color book. I think we sold—we sold tons of that. Ten Speed Press was coming up with *What Color Is Your Parachute?* The San Francisco Institute of Automotive Technology. We carried books by Gotham Book Mart. They actually published for a while. Gotham Book Mart did a book of photographs of the Beat Generation. We had Godine. We had Jargon Society. Capra. Black Sparrow. Frontier Press.

When I walked into the RPM warehouse—you know, I'd [been working] at Brentano's—I'd never seen any of these books before. It was like walking into a candy store for me, because here were incredible books—a book on the occult, books from Four Seasons/Grey Fox, books by Colin Wilson—it just was amazing. At that point we all called them small presses; people like to be called independent presses now. "Small press" was the current word for what was going on.

You know, really, I saw Bookpeople grow. When I got there, we were thirty people, we were at three million. By the time I left, we were a hundred people, we were at twenty-two million in sales. We were greatly affected by the New Age explosion that happened. There was Shirley Maclaine's book and books like *Ramtha* which were coming out of the Pacific Northwest—these were books on channeling and crystals, but we made a fortune on that stuff. They really provided us with some healthy bonuses and we moved from Seventh Street—

thirteen thousand square feet with an auxilliary warehouse—we just moved down the block and expanded.

This was in Berkeley—2940 Seventh Street. Right now there's a Whole Earth...it's like a...they sell...goods. They took over our old building. I was in every single office in the building on Seventh Street. Then we moved into another place, and built a kitchen and hired a full-time cook. The buildings were starting to get larger, but I can't remember what the sales were. Then our final move was to Oakland. This was after the San Francisco earthquake, whenever that was. Nineteen eighty-eight? Well, whenever that was, we were still in Berkeley. We had a lot of damage. It was kind of amazing; a lot of the stuff just fell off the shelves. So after that we moved to Oakland. We had eighty thousand square feet. So that was the final move. I never want to move another warehouse in my entire life. I'm sick of it. But I think they've now got several thousand publishers. This is their current catalogue. It's huge. This is on their twenty-fifth anniversary in 1996. It's probably fifty thousand titles.

They date their origins from 1971 when they took over the company?

Yeah. Yeah. I was there for the twenty-year anniversary, threw a big party in the warehouse. A lot of the old people came by. It was interesting. The old people were a bunch of hippies. They really believed in what they were doing. People like Terry Nemeth and Bob Delapp—I mean it was the art of the book. Terry had Mudra Press. They did a Robert Bly book. They did a Basho book. They did beautiful, hand-sewn books. They did some trade books too. I mean they were really thoughtful book people. I think over the years a lot of things happened at Bookpeople so that the people were less involved in the books and more involved in the political nature of the collective. I don't consider Bookpeople a real literary distributor, although they carry a lot of that. But really, they do a lot of their work in the New Age market.

I think they do less and less literary stuff.

I think they do. They just can't sell it. But you have to give them credit. This is a company that's been around as an employee-owned company since 1971. They've never not paid anybody, they've always paid their bills on time through thick and thin, and they provide a real service for people. I think they act honestly with those people. People will disagree about that; people always think the distributors or wholesalers take too much to do their work. But I think they're a real cornerstone in this whole thing. They and RPM were the first real small press wholesalers/distributors in the country. PGW came along after that.

When you say that Bookpeople had an exclusive arrangement with some publishers, do you mean contractually exclusive?

Contractually exclusive. They would sign contracts which I think lasted for two years and then were renewed every year. I believe at that point we were taking twenty-five percent of net. So all of those books flowed through us. But we had no sales representation whatsoever. It was all done through catalogues. We did really interesting catalogues, with dinosaurs on them. They were really cutting-edge in their graphic design. A guy named Michael Cronan was their designer. Now he runs a large agency in San Francisco—Levi-Strauss is one of his clients. I mean they spent a lot of money on the catalogues. They worked with a company that did microphotography for a while. People actually invested in this company. Bookpeople was really important; a lot of good people passed through there. And a lot of publishers. [Bookpeople] helped a lot of people to sell a lot of books. And they didn't always get the credit that they deserved.

Now they're an older company. You know, they're another wholesaler. A lot of things they have, Ingram also has. They don't have exclusives anymore. They now have a distribution company called Words which primarily is going to be doing metaphysical-type works, spiritual-type things. But they have a couple of gay publishers there. I think Spinsters Ink, which is a publisher up here in Duluth, just signed with them. Sheridan McCarthy who was my assistant at Bookpeople for years, and who originally was the credit manager, now runs Words for them. So they have a commission sales force. It was something I always wanted them to do; they never did it.

When I started out we still had a couple of exclusives. The first big book I worked on was a book called *Hygieia*. It was a woman's herbal. I remember what I did was, I put together a mock-up of this book with the cover and some of the interior pages. And I sent this out to various wholesalers, and we sold ten thousand copies of this book without any sales force. It was pretty damn amazing.

We were the exclusive distributor for Gay Sunshine Press. Winston Leyland published a magazine. They published, I think, one of the first gay sex guides, called *Men Loving Men*. He's still publishing those. We did a book called *The Beatles' England* from this press called Nine Ten Press. They were just Beatles fans. It was a full-color book, printed in Japan, and it was about all the places in the Beatles' songs, full-color pictures and stuff. We sold ten thousand copies. They're not in existence anymore. It was these two guys; they were Beatles fanatics. But we had a great time doing it. They put together a video—they were also video people, so we had this great video with a song, and we had a party at the ABA. We had North Point Press when they started. Robert Sheldon was working at Capra Press. He came up—

I didn't know he worked there.

Yeah. Robert was.... I think first he had a bookstore in Boulder that went out of business. He then worked for Noel Young at Capra, which is when I first met him. And then he came up to work for North Point—Jack Shoemaker, William Turnbull. Then I hired him at Bookpeople. Actually, Terry hired him at Bookpeople to do marketing and sales. After he left Bookpeople, he started his own marketing company.

My wife, Mary Bisbee, worked for him. He introduced me to my wife. They came into the bar when we were hanging out one day and we met there. She turned out to live two blocks from me in Haight-Ashbury in San Francisco and we got together and got married. She's a freelance book publicist. She actually works out of the house here in St. Paul. Before that she'd worked for W.H. Freeman, and then she worked for Bedford Arts, which was one of the book publishers that Consortium distributed. They did these beautiful accordion-fold books, books that would fold out, full-color art books. She worked for Heyday Books for a while—Malcolm Margolin who's a great publisher in the Bay Area, does books on Native Americans. A fascinating, wonderful guy.

I never met him, but Les Galloway, who founded Black Heron Press with me—
Yeah.

—knew him and recommended a number of his books to me.
Malcolm's fascinating. I think he's brilliant. Talking to him is like exercising your brain. He's one of my oldest, oldest, dearest friends. Books about Native Americans is pretty much what he's done, and very successfully. He did a book with the Northern California Independent Booksellers Association, a guide to all the independent bookstores in the Bay Area. So Mary worked there, and she ran the Cartoon Art Museum in San Francisco. She worked as a photo-archivist at the Oakland Museum. And then when we came here she started her own company. It's called Beeksbee Books. She's done work with Graywolf, she's done work with Copper Canyon, she does work with Theatre Communications Group, and she now does a lot of English publishers. She does Serpent's Tail and Gay Men's Press. She goes to Frankfurt, she's doing some agenting. So we're both in the biz. Kind of fun. But...where was I? Robert. Then he worked for Lonely Planet Publications. And he worked for Clark City Press, which was Russell Chatham's press in Montana. And—

I tried to interview Chatham for the first book [Gold 1996].
Yeah?

We talked on and off over the phone for several months. It wasn't clear to him, I don't think, what he was going to do.
I first met him, I had a friend who was running a gallery in San Francisco. She had a show of his paintings, right? Which were very expensive. And so all of the Montana guys came down. Like James Crumley was there, Jim Harrison was there, Jack Nicholson was at this party. We went out to dinner with Russell Chatham. He's a great lover of food; we ate and drank to excess.

When I was coming out here in '92, Mary and I drove across country and we stopped at Livingston and hung out with those guys for awhile. Russell Chatham had a studio there. He had a whole floor and his gallery there. And they did beautiful books but they paid way too much money for them, and they weren't paying attention to the production costs. That was the first publisher that went out of business on me at Consortium.

He told me that when he went into publishing he wanted to be a hands-on publisher. And he wound up with a staff of five, and the more people he hired, the farther away he got from it.
Yeah.

And he wanted to get back to doing publishing himself. That was our last conversation. And then...I guess he just decided to call it a day.
Yeah. He's a great guy. He's a fly fisherman. He's interesting.

Well, Montana.
Yeah, he does Montana kind of stuff. I had a great time with them. But they went out of business. That was a major hole for me at Consortium. In 1992, '93, they went out of business. I mean five hundred thousand dollars worth of net billing. It was kind of disappointing. [Laughs.]

So anyway, Robert was around for a while. I think he's a fascinating book guy. He was at WESTAF [Western States Arts Federation] for a while. Then he went down to Gannon in New Mexico, which was a wholesaler that went out of business right after he came. [He's had] bad luck.

He lives in Seattle now.
Yeah, he does. At the time I knew him he was married to a woman who at one point was married to a Maytag, of Maytag washer fame. She also had a press; I can't remember what this press was. But they were both down in Santa Barbara. I mean there was this whole fertile scene in Santa Barbara, with Noel Young.... Graham Macintosh was doing fine printing. John Martin was there from Black Sparrow. Woodbridge Press was down there. And Noel Young, of Capra, was publishing Raymond Carver, Henry Miller. John was doing his thing, you know. It was a real interesting little pocket. So that was...that was Robert. He's a fascinating guy.

As we've talked, it's become apparent to me that your experience at Bookpeople was perhaps the defining event of your life.

I watched this company grow. I mean, when I was there, one of the things we did was write an employee manual.

At Bookpeople.

Yeah. We got rid of the general manager after a while. Jeri Riddle. She quit and then what happened was the board of directors started running the company. There were five people on the board of directors that basically ran the company. For years I was chairman of the board. A guy named Gene Taback, who was the trade buyer, was the president. We actually switched off being president and chairman for a while there, kind of playing around with that stuff.

But we ran the whole company, so we were basically reviewing all of the department heads. We put in the kind of structure that they needed in order to have critical reviews and evaluations of people, and tighten up the whole business in general, to write an employee manual, to spell out the rules. Because what happens, once you start getting thirty, forty employees, you have people who will get disgruntled, start suing the company and all of this stuff, so you have to have policies in place. And I think it was really helpful for the development of Bookpeople to have these kinds of things.

So you came to Consortium in '92?
Yeah. I was fifteen years at Bookpeople.

Wasn't, or isn't, Consortium owned by Mercury House?
The way it worked is that in 1991 Bobbi Rixx, who owned the company, lost her line of credit. The company was not doing well at all, and they were looking at various ownership options, including maybe selling it to the publishers, and looking for other people to buy it. Stephen Williamson, who was a sales rep for us in New England, was acting president for a while. He would commute back and forth. And Bill Brinton—William M. Brinton—who owned Mercury House at the time, had already been through a bankruptcy with Eric Kampmann, and I think had fought Kampmann over the issue of consignment inventory belonging to publishers as opposed to being held. When RPM went out of

430

business, all inventory was seized, including consignment inventory, except what I was able to ship back, basically illegally. I shipped back books to Bookpeople, Black Sparrow—whatever we could do; we stayed up all night and packed books up and shipped them out. You're not supposed to do that because it's a preferential payment, right? So what did I know; I was twenty-three years old. So Bill had been through this bankruptcy and finally, they were just screwing around, he said, "Well, I'll buy it." So he put about five hundred and sixty thousand dollars into the company. Into Consortium.

Bill's a wealthy man. He's made some money as an antitrust lawyer, plus he's a staunch Democrat; he's put his money where his mouth is. I mean he sent computers to Czechoslovakia, he supports a lot of great causes, he's Bill Clinton's good friend—but he bought the company and hired a guy who was working for him then, Po Bronson. And Po came out to look at the company, and then George Gibson came in to act as the interim CEO.

They started advertising. I had kind of started talking to them at the New York ABA which was like a year before that, 1990 or something. I had been at Bookpeople for fifteen years and I loved it, but I was looking for a little bit of challenge. I liked Bookpeople best when it was growing. When we were building, it was exciting. After a while it's like an old scene. And I was back at a Lila Wallace/Reader's Digest panel where we selected publishers for funding. This was when I was still working at Bookpeople. And we gave out a bunch of money to people and we also chose the next round. This was for marketing grants.

It was interesting. I agreed to do this. And I didn't realize how much work it actually was. My wife was like, "Oh, you can just read the stuff on the plane before you get there." Well, they sent me—you know, it was thirty publishers. I mean there were their plans, there were...all of the stuff. It took me weeks to read through all of this crap and look at them and analyze them and write something up about their organizational abilities, and all of this stuff. So I went back to this meeting. And Jim Sitter was there. And I was kind of like, "Should I take this job?" And Sitter says, "Well, can you do it?" "I think so." "Well, maybe you should."

And we went out to dinner with a bunch of people, and I was talking about RPM and how I'd sent the books back and, you know, we were drinking some wine, and I came back to the hotel and I called a friend of mine, Howard Karel, who was a sales rep for Consortium, and I said, "Set up an interview." And I went over and interviewed with Bill and Po. I then had an interview with George at the ABA in Anaheim, which must have been '92, '91. It must have been '92 because I came here in September of '92.

They had, I don't know, sixty applicants, whatever it was. They had narrowed it down to two people: me and another guy who was, I think, a little bit more three-piece-suit than I was, but had qualifications. They flew him to St. Paul. They flew me and my wife to St. Paul. I met everybody on the staff and talked with them and, you know, debated whether I wanted to move. My wife was none too happy about moving from California to Minnesota. I kind of wondered, "What's this going to be like?" But I liked the people who worked here, I liked the organization. I saw a potential to actually have an impact on what was going on.

Don't you think that's probably the most important thing about work, who you're working with?
I think so. I mean I never thought about going into the book business. I didn't grow up saying, "Gee, I'll be a bookseller." But I loved to read. And then I loved the people who are in this business. And I love the passion. You know, all of this stuff about what's going on with the industry these days, you forget somehow that these are people who had a personal vision and were publishing books and believed in it, put their money into it, and were producing a myriad of ideas, from literature to how to fix your Volkswagen to occult sciences, to all of this stuff—

We were talking about the 'zine people [before taping began]— that's what I like about them.
Yeah. They've got some fresh energy.

Yeah. S.P. Miskowski—I don't know if you know her. She was the managing editor of The Stranger *in Seattle. They were pretty influential under her leadership. Then she left. Anyway, she and I have coffee sometimes—in Seattle you have coffee instead of wine—and we were*

432

saying that it's the 'zine people who are going to be next. They're the ones you have to keep an eye on. That's where the innovation will come from next, I think, and she thought so too.

I think so. I think that other people who are around will continue to be doing books, and will become a bit more sophisticated. But the 'zine people are going to bring in some new ideas. And they're also going to attract a younger audience. It's the poetry slam, it's the connection between rock 'n roll musicians and punk musicians and—there's a lot of energy and enthusiasm, and that's why we brought on these new people. Soft Skull Press, for example. I mean they're not a press that fits our profile really, because, you know, they're not—I think their sales are like five thousand bucks or something. But I think they have the potential. And it also fits well with Incommunicado and Juno. We have a philosophy about bringing publishers on, and they kind of fit into it.

We just got Exact Change, they came over from DAP [Distributor Arts Publications]. They're a publisher of surrealist fiction. They're out of Boston. I think Exact Change came out of the rock 'n roll movement. They had a band called Galaxy 500 which was big in the '70s. So they were musicians. I don't know how they got into surrealism, but they and another publisher that we have, Atlas Press, which comes out of London, both do important, neglected surrealist work. Exact Change did the autobiography of Mina Loy, Alfred Jarry books—they've done a whole list of things, very interesting things. Same thing with Atlas Press. They were rock 'n roll musicians, too. We do a separate catalogue called *The Culture of the Void*. It's really things like Serpent's Tail/High Risk, Juno Books, Incommunicado, Soft Skull, Hard Press in Massachusetts....

How many presses does Consortium have now?

There's over sixty. So this is stuff that sells if we cross-merchandise into Tower Books and Records. They sell a lot of these kinds of things. Bob Koen and others, including Consortium, sponsor the Firecracker Book Awards at the BEA now. They're the alternative book awards.

Juno used to be Re/Search and they had a very bad partnership that split. They were with Subco for years. They came here and then

433

they had a kind of partnership discrepancy, and so she started her own company and he started his, called V-Search. His name is V. Vale. He's got V-Search and she's got Juno Books, but they both can use the logo Re/Search. That is complicated. Their big seller is *Modern Primitives*, body piercing kind of stuff.

I've seen quite of bit of their stuff. My daughter is a big fan of theirs.

Yeah, they sell thirty thousand copies. There's a big market for those kinds of books. And again, you involve the next generation in some form of literature, whatever it may be.

Does Consortium have a mission? A mission statement?

No. [Pauses, then laughs.] We don't have one. Well, we have a philosophy. But I mean, basically, when I came to Consortium, there were seventeen publishers, we had a reputation for being pretty much literary. I don't believe that was really true, because there were other books we were distributing that were not literary books. But we were pigeon-holed into that category. I felt that that was just too narrow. Not that I don't love literature, but I thought, for the company to succeed, we needed to expand. So the first two publishers we brought on were Theatre Communications Group. It's run by Terry Nemeth who used to work with me at Bookpeople. I'm godfather to his child—I didn't sign this deal; I had George Gibson broker the deal with him. And Feminist Press was the second one.

The idea of Feminist Press, for me, was—we considered them our cornerstone women's publisher. So we were able then to add on other women's publishers, like Calyx, Eighth Mountain, Aunt Lute, Third Side, and we put together a whole separate women's catalogue so that we had a critical mass in that area and could market those books. And with Theatre Communications—they're the premier theater publisher in the country. They did the *Angels in America* plays, for Tony Kushner—won the Pulitzer Prize. Two three-hour plays. Fabulous plays. Sold hundreds of thousands of copies of these books.

So I really wanted to stretch the boundaries of the company. And I started looking at other people that would complement what we were doing in literature, but also bring us to other segments of the market. And now our largest publisher is Alyson Publications which is owned by *The Advocate* in L.A. Alyson is a specifically gay publisher. This is a publisher who may do as much as two million dollars worth of business this next year. I knew Sasha Alyson who was the original publisher in Boston from my work at Bookpeople. He was with Inbook at the time. Was not happy. We now do a gay and lesbian catalogue. So, again, with them anchored—Mercury House has gay literature. BOA has gay literature. Graywolf has gay literature. So you combine the literature of the gay and lesbian culture with Alyson, you have a critical mass—you can go to a lot more stores.

I also brought in a press called Applewood Books. This guy named Phil Zuckerman, who used to be a literary publisher in Boston, now does books on America's past. He does the original Nancy Drew books. He does the original Hardy Boys. He does books from Disney. He did a book on Superman. So I mean it's really a stretch—it's not literary. But he was with Globe Pequot Press and he was a friend of George Gibson's and we met and we liked each other and he came on.

We've really tried to expand those markets along with adding the finest literary presses. Right now one of our hottest new publishers is Gryphon House. They're publishers of early educational materials for children. And this is a guy—Larry Rood—who I grew up with in Maryland. Actually, David Marcuse, who owned RPM, used to live in his house. So we've known each other for years, and he was looking around, and we decided he would be a good publisher for us and we met. He's got his own business in Maryland, marketing to the educational market. He's got a warehouse—forty thousand square feet, a five-million-dollar business. We brought him in to expand his business in the trade. I think his business has quadrupled with us. So it's a half-a-million-dollar publisher with a six-percent-return rate because it is a very tightly focused niche market.

And we've recently added Building Blocks which does, again, early educational materials. So we now put out a separate children's book catalogue. We had people like Tilbury House, who is no longer with us, but they did a book called *Talking Walls*—a four-color children's book. It's interesting to sell children's books. You have to have galleys and F-and-G's ["folded and gathered" signatures] and all of that stuff to different markets.

435

I just landed a deal—starting in January we're going to distribute HarperCollins Australia. When HarperCollins disbanded HarperCollins "World" they left the UK, the Canadians and the Australians on their own. This woman, Denise Barnes, came from Australia, met with us—it looks like they're going to give us fifty books a season, a hundred books a year. Children's books, travel books, cookbooks. It's kind of odd, they're not really a traditional, small independent—they're an eighty-million-dollar company in Australia. But it will solidify our place in the children's book market. So, I mean, there's a strategy, like this cornerstone building on publishers and creating a critical mass.

The same thing happened when I brought on Sandy Taylor and Judy Doyle of Curbstone. Because they were so strong on Latin American studies, they also brought along Latin American Literary Review Press. And then we started looking at all of our other publishers. Well, we found we had about three hundred books that were appropriate for the Latin American studies market. So we started to put out a Latin American literature catalogue and we attend the Latin American Studies Association trade show with Curbstone. They know all of these academics, so not only are we selling those books to the trade, but we have a whole academic marketing program that we work with. We work with a college textbook marketing group that presents books to professors for potential course adoption. We go to Latin American Studies, we go to MLA, we go to College Art Association—about twelve percent of our business is in academic text adoptions. That's another area that we've expanded into. We've really tried to stretch the boundaries of the academic market with people like Juno and Incommunicado.

We did a book with WGBH in Boston, which is a public television station, an eight-part series on genetics and genetic engineering called *The Secret of Life*. That book was originally supposed to be published by Harper, but they cancelled the contract, so these people wanted to do it on their own. It sounded like a good idea to me, eight-part PBS—we sold twenty-eight thousand copies of this book in hardcover. It wasn't your typical PBS book, like the baseball book, the Civil War book, really highly illustrated. This is a serious book about genetics and it had some color inserts in it, but it was something I don't think Consortium would have typically done. And usually we don't do one-book publishers, but I thought it was an interesting idea.

436

I talked to the sales reps about this. They said, "Gee, you're literary. You're going outside of your realm." I said, "Well, I have a different vision. We can incorporate these books, and not dilute what we do with literature." Forty percent of our business is with literary, nonprofit publishers. That's three million and some dollars.

We work very closely with the nonprofits. The Mellon Group basically ran a seminar here. They flew in "the Mellon nine." Nine publishers. Five of those are Consortium publishers. They brought in Gigi Bradford from the NEA to talk. And they brought in Sheila Murphy. And they brought in Jim Sitter. So what we did was we sponsored a day-long seminar here with Gigi and Jim and Sheila, and I flew out the buyer for City Lights Books, Paul Yamazaki, who does a lot of work with Jim, Sheila, and Celia O'Donnell with CLMP [Council of Literary Magazines and Presses], and I brought in Julie Schaper, our sales and marketing director, and we sat down with them for a day and talked about the realities of publishing books for the literary nonprofit market.

We basically shared with them all the information about sales and return rates and trends and our theory about why things had gone to hell. Nineteen ninety-six was probably the worst year ever in the book industry, and part of it has to do with there being too many outlets for books, and there are not the appropriate number of readers. We used to have only one bookstore here; now we have twelve superstores in the Twin Cities. Somebody's gotta lose in that equation. The computerization of bookselling. Just-in-time ordering. So advance orders are being depressed because bookstore buyers say "Well, gee, I'll only take a couple. But I'll reorder them just-in-time," or, as I say, almost in time, from Ingram or whatever wholesaler they're dealing with. The shelf life of books is decreasing; they're sending books back faster than ever before. There probably are too many books published in this country. There's an article in *Time*—a hundred and sixty-five books a day are published. I think there's an information overload at some point which paralyzes people, really pushes returns rates up. Ours is now about twenty-eight percent, but we have publishers with thirty, forty and sixty percent returns. So there's a lot of competition, particularly in fiction.

Poetry had a real renaissance in the last couple years. It started out with National Poetry Month and Bill Moyers' special, which actually did, I think, a great deal to increase the American public's consciousness of poetry. And we were able to tie in with that. We've sold twenty-five thousand copies of Jane Kenyon's *Otherwise* in hardcover from Graywolf. And we've sold over ten thousand copies of Hayden Carruth's book, *Scrambled Eggs and Whiskey*. which won the National Book Award. And we've met with people like the Academy of American Poets in support of National Poetry Month. So there's a lot of stuff going on.

But it was fascinating to have all of those people from the nonprofit sector come in and talk with us. They really enjoyed it and we try to keep up that conversation. Whenever we have time, Jim Sitter, Paul Yamazaki and I try to get together and talk about what's going on, various trends. I'm going back in October for a Lila Wallace meeting that I think will include Ira Silverberg from Serpent's Tail, Jim Sitter and Celia O'Donnell, and I think Paul Yamazaki will be there and a woman named Connie Sayres who works at Marketing Partners—I don't know her very well. This is the second such meeting that we're having with these people.

So we try to do a lot of work with those people. It's important to meet with funders. Talk about what we can educate people to do. The realities of the funding base. Since forty percent of our business is literary nonprofits, it can make me nervous on certain days. Because NEA is basically not doing what they once were doing.

You know, I think one of the things that makes Consortium unique, and one of the reasons I really enjoy working here, is that whereas at Bookpeople we dealt with thousands of publishers, but I could only do a little for each of them, at Consortium we're actually involved a lot in the publishing process. We just completed what we call pre-sales and marketing sessions with the publishers. What they're doing is, they're sending us tip sheets, catalog copy, sample chapters from books, covers.... So we're talking about titles, subtitles, prices, formats—hardcover versus paperback—release dates. We're talking to them about marketing plans. And we read a lot. We read manuscripts. We like to read stuff before they talk to us about those books. Something that George Gibson started with the company, and it's a really good idea, to get together and talk with publishers and strategize.

I see part of our mission as being educational, part to develop new publishers. Although there's a certain pressure not to have five hundred and fifty publishers. But people like Soft Skull and other people that we've brought in where I think there's some potential—I think that's something we'll always be doing, not just going after the bigger publishers. Right now when people come to us, we say, "We're looking for people that are doing two hundred and fifty thousand in net sales and are publishing five to ten books a year and have a substantial marketing program" and on and on and on. But of course that's just a rule; we can't help everybody; we need to be selective.

You know, all of these are hand-picked people. I like all of these people. I like their publishing companies and I work very closely with them. At the end of the day they do what they want to do. But we like the idea that we have the ability to speak openly and honestly about these books. I think we make some very good suggestions because of our cumulative experience in sales and marketing in the book industry.

If you look at one of the major houses, let's say Random House as it was under Bennett Cerf and Donald Klopfer, and look at the different functions of production, marketing, promotion and sales, then what that one company did is what the modern independent press plus its distributor do now. What I'm saying is that what we call the publisher is really the publisher and the distributor together. I'm not suggesting anything be changed. I'm just trying to find a model to describe the way decisions get made.

Well, I think it's valuable, if you're publishing books, that you have a marketing program. It's more and more critical these days that you have a marketing plan, that you have an idea about why you're publishing this book, that you can articulate that idea to the sales reps and to us, so that when we go out the book has the best shot, because the time frame, the shelf life, has become so small that when the reviews hit for the books, you have to have all of these coordinated, and the better you do that, the more you talk about it, the better shot the book has of not having fifty percent returns. We are certainly not a publisher, and we certainly do not dictate to our publishers what they should and shouldn't publish. Basically, we're working as a consortium and as a partner.

Okay. But if you look at how decisions get made, say, within a New York firm, it's marketing driven—not market driven, but marketing driven. It's the marketing people who drive it.

Yes.

As opposed to, say, twenty or thirty years ago when it was editorial driven. That older relationship between marketing and editorial now applies to the relationship between the distributor and the independent publisher. It is a partnership.

I think so. I think we're very clear about that. That's one of the things that we do, we work very closely with our publishers in partnership. Our catalogue is based on publisher identity. It's laid out by publisher. Other catalogues are laid out by release dates, and the publishers are jumbled together. We have a page in our catalogue where we allow the publishers to talk about themselves. We sell them as a publisher within a larger context of the consortium of independent presses. They need us to get into those markets. It's a very volatile world out there.

Why do you use commission reps instead of in-house reps? PGW uses in-house reps.

We can't afford to. They're an eighty-million-dollar company, we're a nine-million-dollar company. We couldn't afford to pay the salaries of all those people. I think our commission reps are some of the best in the business. I mean these people amaze me. Most of them have been with us since the company started. When we send them information, they read it. They ask intelligent questions. I mean, think about these poor guys: We give them five hundred titles a season.

Our sales conference lasts two days. We go to New York. Our publishers present their books. It starts at eight o'clock in the morning with a publisher meeting when we talk about what we're doing. Then we turn the room over to them if they want to talk among themselves. We then go into a meeting with our reps where we review the season, and then we have our publishers present their books. They get about two minutes per book. They talk to the reps about things that are not in the catalog, kind of what the passion behind this book is. It goes on all day. Then we have new publishers present on Sunday. But it's two full days. And these reps are sitting there and they've been there for two weeks. I mean they're representing twenty-five publishers. Some of them are representing InBook. They're representing Chronicle. So I'm constantly amazed at the care and the way that they react...people like Bob Harrison. He's a book lover. He's a book reader. He gives us good feedback.

Eventually, would we like to have house people? Yeah, but I kind of enjoy this relationship with the independent reps. I think independent presses and independent reps and independent booksellers are tied together. It's a culture, a thing that's going on.

We had an interesting meeting here last Saturday. There's an independent booksellers consortium. They came into the Twin Cities and had two days of meetings. These are booksellers like the UConn Bookstore, Kepler's, Page One, Harvard Bookstore, Olsson's, Tattered Cover, Prairie Lights, Schwartz, Hungry Mind... These are the key independent booksellers and they got together and talked about things. They originally were doing some remainder buying together, but they were talking about how can they create best-sellers or how can they promote books.

We had the opportunity to take them to dinner, so we hired a bus and we brought them here. We gave them a tour of the warehouse and I gave a little talk about how I view a lot of the problems for independent booksellers and independent publishers as being similar, and how can we work more closely together on co-op advertising, and what works and what doesn't. And I thought it was a great opportunity to meet buyers and also the owners of these stores. I knew a lot of them, but to sit down and talk with them....

That's another major issue. We need to keep the independent booksellers alive. There have been several who have gone out of business. They're going out of business every day, and we need to keep them alive for the diversity of ideas, which is the epitome of what independent small publishers is about. Yeah, we do a lot of business with the chains. Yeah, I appreciate what they do for us. But these people [i.e., independent booksellers] hand-sell books. Hungry Mind has a program—"The Hungry Mind Twenty-five." It's twenty-five books that the staff picks, they give a twenty-five percent discount. I think Prairie Lights has the same kind of deal.

It was a really nice night, to have those people come by to talk with us. And I hope they continue to do more in support of independent publishers. It's hard to get them to take five or ten of a book. But maybe there are certain books that would carry well. These people are interested in the books that we have. These are people that we can send galleys to.

We worked with Curbstone on that book, *Shopping Cart Soldiers*. It's a great story. This guy was Scottish and he came here and he went to Viet Nam. He's an interesting guy. He was homeless for a while. Maxine Hong Kingston is kind of like his mentor, and—you know, how do you make a book these days? How do you get a book out? How do you get people interested? When they send out galleys, they send me twenty galleys. I send them to people—booksellers, friends, other sales reps I know that work for Random House or Farrar—you kind of get a buzz going. You have to do more and more of that kind of hand-selling to make a book.

I think there's a fundamental shift in what makes people buy books. How do they get their information? Reviews that used to work don't necessarily work. What's the role of the internet? I mean now it's kind of a lot of noise about not that much selling, really. People like Amazon.com are losing a tremendous amount of money. Barnes and Noble has their website coming up. Borders has a website coming up. I think what the internet has done—it's the new toy, and people are spending hours doing whatever they're doing. I mean we have a web page and it's linked to our publishers. I'm interested because I don't want to be left behind, and I see a whole generation that may get their information that way. But now I think of it as a distraction. It takes up time that people used to devote to reading a book.

I don't know what the answers are. What funding will help get books sold? How do you get books sold? How do you get them in the stores? How do you get them out of the stores? How does somebody find them? If you send two copies of a book to Barnes and Noble, it's a sixty-thousand-square-foot store, it's somewhere in the back. Unless someone is going in to look for for it, how does that ever work?

If it's not on the shelf, in front, in the middle aisle—right.

Right. Even if you're in the Discover program, the Discover New Writers program, where the brochure is up front—still, the competition. The sell-through on that stuff, for us, is probably about fifty percent.

We had a whole seminar we put together for our publishers to try and make some sense of where we thought all of this stuff was going. It's painful to watch publishers taking forty, fifty, or sixty percent returns. There's a limit, before they start going out of business. I mean Coach House Press, a thirty-year-old publisher, published Michael Ondaatje, Margaret Atwood, and they went belly up. I mean there are all kinds of reasons. But I think it's not inconceivable that you'll see a number of literary publishers not be able to make it.

Well, that depends on what they're willing to do. I mean we all face crises.
Right.

I recall my realization several years ago that it was never going to be profitable. I was never going to break even. And I talked with another publisher who had been at it longer, and he said, "Yeah, you just have to decide whether or not you want to do it. Either you're going to subsidize it or you're not going to publish." And so I did. And that's what I do. Some years I make some money. Most years I don't.

I was trying to come up with some ideas about—you know, the NEA is not sure they're going to fund individual publishers, or what they're going to do with money. I wonder if there could be a way to raise the profile of independent literary publishers in this country. I don't know that it would be possible, but, you know, could you get substantial money to do this, could you put out a series of ads and promos for independents, for chains, that plays up on people's interest in literary publishing. If you buy a Graywolf book, you're special; if you buy a Copper Canyon...you kind of play up—maybe it's elitism, I'm not quite sure about the right way to go with this. You know, like microbreweries—could you...could you...?

What I want to say is, gee, there's this whole segment of book publishers doing really interesting things. But how do you get to the people? How do you tell them about it? Can you promote them as a larger group? The Curbstones, the Graywolfs, the Coffee Houses, the Copper Canyons. Or would you just be banging your head against the wall? Maybe you could get a brief amount of publicity for the attention span of the average American, about fifteen minutes, and then it would go away. But somehow we have to figure out how to reach the audience.

Looking at it on a national level may be okay, but everything is so much more expensive that way. As opposed to looking at it on a regional level, and emphasizing the regional trade shows, and sending people to bookstores regionally. Author tours. Books cost so much money to advertise, and the return on that is zip. For that same amount of money, for less money, you can send authors on tour. And that does sell books.

It does. You know, my wife is a free-lance publicist and so she's constantly setting up tours. But it's really a crap shoot these days, given the number of people that show up and where they're reading and how the bookstore publicizes it. And now the bookstores are asking for money sometimes when people read. It's relatively new, but everybody is trying to become more profitable, and subsidize those things. On a regional basis, certainly, you can do quite a bit.

I don't mean staying within your own region. I mean going to other regions as well. Maybe working out some sort of exchange between publishers. Everybody is facing the same problems. Everybody is concerned especially with shelf space. I would like to see a seminar or a workshop, and not restricted to the nonprofits. My own feeling is that the nonprofits tend to be too insular in their thinking, because they're concerned with getting money from particular sources. But if we assume that the problem is getting money from whatever source, we have an awful lot in common. Milkweed Editions is a nonprofit, yet they remind me a lot more of Seven Stories or Four Walls Eight Windows than they do of Coffee House in what they choose to publish and how Emilie regards what she wants to do, and the purpose it serves.

I think we need—we talked about this when the shit was really hitting the fan. We were trying to think of how we could get some people together to start talking about it, because there are some systemic problems involved in what we're doing. And all these publishers are having these problems. The returns are just—the bookstore feels like, "Look, I took a shot at your book, you didn't promote it, and I need to return it." The publisher goes, "I gotta take the book back regardless of what condition it comes in, and I'm getting screwed." How do you make sense out of that? Who bears the burden of all of this? How do you get people into stores? I mean there's a whole lot of stuff that people really need to start talking about. And the chains need to be involved in this conversation too, because fifty percent of all books sold in this country through bookstores are sold in Barnes and Noble, Books-A-Million, Crown, and Borders. Get the independents in, get the reps, talk about it—just an open dialogue. I'm not sure what's the best way to put that together, but we really have to go into it, and talk.

Charlie Winton
Publishers Group West, Inc.,
Avalon Publishing Group, Inc.

"[T]he wonderful part of the book business is that every day there are new ideas and new things to think about and talk about; there's an intensity that is sometimes a little relentless, but you always have to—you know, it's not like we get to invent something here and then ship it for the next fifteen years. Every six months—four months really, with three seasons—you have to go out and say, you know, this is new and hot."

Forty-five years old when I interviewed him, his shirt hinted at a physique as trim as an adolescent's. His hair, falling to his shoulders, also promoted the idea of adolescence, though adolescence of another era, or perhaps of the artistic outsider. Too, his speech, informal and a little slangy, encouraged in his listener the notion of softness, and maybe vagueness. All of this—the softness and vagueness, the affectedness of a man on the fringe—may be true of Charlie Winton, or may not, but behind the facade is a man who knows very well what he is about.

He was born in Sacramento, California because there was no hospital in Sutter Creek where his parents lived. His father was a lumberman, the third generation of Wintons to make a living in that industry, and after several years in Sutter Creek took his family to Prince George, British Columbia where the company's primary operation was. They returned to California, to Modesto, in 1959. The house there was where Charlie would spend his holidays and summer vacations—he went to boarding school in Pebble Beach, near Monterey—but for all intents and purposes he left home when he was fourteen. He enterered Stanford in 1971, graduating four years later.

I interviewed Charlie Winton, CEO of Publishers Group West and Avalon Publishing Group, at PGW's corporate headquarters in Berkeley on Friday, May 15, 1998. We talked at a table in the outside court early in the afternoon of a brisk but sunny day. Most of the construction of the new offices was complete, but all around us were the sounds of the finishing work. The new offices are very near railroad tracks and Winton warned me that a train would be passing through soon.

I majored in communications, primarily film and broadcasting. I had a notion about going into the film business, but really wasn't terribly well grounded in it. So when I got out of college I moved down to Los Angeles and spent about four, five months sort of flailing around, not really getting anywhere. Of course, I was resistant to any help that anybody might be able to provide me, so I ended up moving back to Palo Alto in the late fall of that year. And, as circumstance would happen, I got engaged to, really, unload a truck. That's the way my career started in publishing.

I'd been unemployed for about six months, and it was like a week-long job where somebody was moving their book warehouse back from John Wiley. The people involved there—Jerry Ficklin was the principal—he had sold his company to Wiley in '74 and then he bought the company back in '76 or right at the end of '75.

You're talking about John Wiley, the publishers?
Yeah. The big guys, yeah.

Why had they been interested in that company?
He [Jerry Ficklin] was connected with New Math. A lot of that came out of Stanford. In fact, his father-in-law was one of the creators of New Math. That's how he got his start in publishing. Page Ficklin was the name of the publishing company. It was a small textbook publisher primarily. Mathematics, some social science, whatever. In any case, they had bought themselves back from Wiley. They were setting up their own warehouse underneath their editorial office. A very small operation in downtown Palo Alto. So, anyway, I just took this on as a week's project and then, once they were set up, they needed to hire somebody to run whatever sort of warehouse it was—it was fairly low-key—and I was the most likely candidate. I needed to have a job and I'd been screwing around for six months and I needed to start doing something. In any case, that's basically how I got into publishing.

447

Within the course of that year, 1976, this was right at the start of '76, the idea of Publishers Group West was born out of afternoon discussions. In the textbook business you have peaks of the year in terms of shipping. Primarily in the late summer, but also for the spring semester. In any case, Jerry had published a couple of titles that had cross-over potential had they been published in a more orthodox environment, in terms of how one would get the books to market by using a sales force. At that point in time, really, the sole vehicle for distributing one's books, if you were a small or independent publisher, was Bookpeople, which was a pretty passive situation. Put the books in a warehouse and try to create some demand. It was basically a demand-driven model, not a sales model. It was a wholesaler model, not a distribution model. By the end of the summer of '76, Jerry was turning forty and I was a youngster then, so we went out on an on-the-road trip around the western states. It was sort of a passage for him, being over forty, and testing the notion that one could have a collection of independent publishers and go into bookstores and actually represent the list in a more traditional model.

Were you going to bookstores and simply asking about it?

No, we were trying to sell stuff. He had a couple of other friends who threw in with us and we were doing some textbook business as well, so we were very much focused on university towns and/or university bookstores. UCLA, the schools in San Diego, schools in and around Tempe, and then Albuquerque, the University of New Mexico, up to Boulder and Salt Lake. It took us the better part of a month to do the whole trip. We were driving around in a VW, we had a VW van, and his family was from northern New Mexico and had a place out in the Red River Valley behind Taos, and I had friends from college in various places, so it was a fun trip and we had a lot of good times as well as just trying to do our best at scoping out whether this would work.

It worked well enough, so in December of 1976 Publishers Group West was incorporated as a subsidiary of Page Ficklin Publications. At that point the business became a little more evolved, although it was still very, very small and funky and, you know, not much of anything. My first three or four months, I moved to Denver and I became the rep for Publishers Group West. I was still supplementing whatever

I was doing at PGW, because there was really not that much to sell; I was getting a small salary doing textbook sales for a consortium of small textbook publishers. Again, I was very focused on university towns. We had whatever we had there that we might be able to sell. It was fairly countercultural, so that was a good sort of synchronized way to go about things. I made a long trip through Chicago and Minneapolis and went to B. Dalton. Didn't really have anything happen there, but made our first presentation at B. Dalton.

By May, it was clear that I wasn't going to keep doing that. I went to the ABA which was held in San Francisco that year, 1977.

[A train's horn sounds, approaching fast. Winton sighs. I stop the tape.]

[As the sound of the train's horn recedes]: We're back on now. You went to the ABA in '77.

Okay. So anyway, it was just more a matter—Page Ficklin moved from Palo Alto to Monterey, which was Jerry's life decision. And what happened was—Jerry had basically had his assistant monitoring whatever activity Publishers Group West had its first four or five months of '77 and she was not going to move down to the Monterey Peninsula, so that created an opportunity for me to become what I would describe as the general manager/sole employee of Publishers Group West. Jerry was running the publishing company, Page Ficklin, and Publishers Group West was sort of this little—you know, it was incorporated for five hundred dollars, so it wasn't like there was a lot of money that was put into it. So I had gone to high school down there and I was familiar with the area and I was not really sales-rep-oriented, as it were. I was twenty-four then. I had just turned twenty-four. So I could run the business. I had enough general skill to run the business. I've always been extremely good with numbers as such. At the same time I could pack all the books, and I wasn't too proud to do everything. I was sort of a one-stop shop in terms of making the little idea keep going.

And then at the end of 1977 it become clear, really, that Jerry was not that interested in Publishers Group West. And I was. So at that point in time I and Steve Mandell brought Bill Hurst in. Steve and Bill were reps in the West Coast area. And, basically, we bought the company. For five thousand dollars. We each put up eighteen hundred bucks. Page Ficklin continued to own a little bit of the company, but that is when we really started on our own. Bill joined us at that point. He was repping for And/Or Press.

I think the first year our sales were thirty thousand dollars and we lost about five grand. We really didn't have any expenses; I wasn't making any sort of salary. There was where we started really, in 1978, as an independent, self-owned company. Sales went up that year to about a hundred and fifty grand.

Then in 1979 I found, just living in Monterey—I was living in Carmel, actually; the business was over by Cannery Row—but it was just a little quiet and out of the way, and if we were really going to happen we needed to be back in the Bay area. So I moved the business back up to the East Bay here in, I think, May of 1979. And at that point in time two people who are still here and are principal partners, Randy Fleming and Mike Winton—Randy I'd gone to Stanford with and Mike is my younger brother, and then, actually, my wife, Barbara—we sort of formed the core of Publishers Group West, and that was in the summer of '79. There were four of us there and, again, it was very home-grown and sort of everybody did everything. We'd do the business part of things in the morning and then go buy a couple of six-packs and turn on the Rolling Stones and go pack some books in the afternoon. And that's what we did.

I think that year, 1979, the ABA was in Los Angeles—it was just before I moved up here—and we had gained some level of consciousness in terms of the world of small presses. When we first started, one of the critical things was we had to charge more because we had sales reps. The previous model was effectively a fifty-percent-discount model, and if we were going to put commission salespeople on the road, we had to raise the discount to fifty-five. Of course, that was—I don't know if it was controversial, but it was not...it was the whole process of, you know, "Why do I need you? I've got good people; you're trying to charge me more," you know, not understanding the service. At that point in time we didn't sell to wholesalers. A lot of things changed over the next five or six years as we got more sophisticated and engaged in the real business of distribution.

450

Where did the sales model come from? Did it come from another business, or another industry?

No, it was just really that Jerry had come through a more orthodox publishing background rather than from John Wiley, [which was] for textbooks. You always had sales reps. That's just the way one got the books into the buyers' hands, through a combination of cataloguing and somebody going in and pitching the books. It wasn't rocket science, it was just sort of an extrapolation of a more orthodox model and pushing it onto the small press, which was starting to blossom in the late '70s. There was a very vibrant community here and by the ABA in Los Angeles we were able to really make some inroads into the small press world that existed primarily in northern California at that time. By the end of 1979 our sales had grown to about half a million dollars and we were starting to become a more real business. We were still selling a lot of, you know, how-to-grow-marijuana books and that sort of thing. And/Or Press was probably twenty-five percent of our billing. But it was working and we were all very young and just having a good time. The notion that we would possibly sell a million dollars' worth of books, it seemed like, you know, boy, we would be really successful then.

When you say you took in five hundred thousand dollars, are you talking about gross or net?

Net. The reality was that our level of sales and distribution was so...so...meager isn't the correct word, but it certainly wasn't the Simon and Schuster model. I'll bet our return rate then was something like five or seven percent. Of course, none of the books had Publishers Group West printed on it anywhere, and everything was nonexclusive, so one could buy a book from us and return it to Bookpeople, or buy it from Bookpeople and return it to us, to the degree that you could figure out where to return it at all, and perhaps you'd end up returning it to the publisher.

That still happens all the time.

Yeah. So it wasn't...you know, it was semi-organized anarchy at that point. But then in 1980 we had the first real sort of new publisher, which was Nolo Press. Bill Hurst had always been Nolo's representa-

451

tive and he decided this company he had invested eighteen hundred dollars in was now stable enough that he could—he used to have a little company called Bill Hurst Books—he would do Nolo on the side. And in 1980 he decided that that was cool; he would throw it into our bag. He was mostly just getting commissions off of it; he wasn't really making any money on it. He was the shipper and biller and it was getting hard for him to do; he would pay somebody to come in and write the invoices and try to collect the money. So it was a perfect opportunity for everybody. So that sort of moved us along.

And then, shortly thereafter, B. Dalton started buying Nolo books from us. That was something that really helped us evolve that account. In those days, B. Dalton, particularly the regional buyers, they treated a lot of the small presses as sort of regional product. But that started to become an active account for us. It had been something that had been left fallow. There hadn't been a formal approach from any of the other people who were doing small presses, Bookpeople and The Distributors and those people, and so we just sort of capitalized on that opportunity and that kicked us up probably—not that account, but the combination of Nolo and then really starting to sell some books to B. Dalton and, you know, just continuing to get better books and getting our name out there. I'm sure it was in 1980 that our sales went over a million dollars.

We were on to something at that point. We were starting to hire other employees. My wife left; she had been there for about six or seven months. You know, the business started to take on a life of its own, so it was less...but it was still very much of a funky, family, wild place to work, for sure.

Probably the next notable thing is that we started working with Carroll and Graf Publishers who were a couple of—Herman Graf and Kent Carroll had worked with Barney Rosset at Grove and they had a parting of the ways there. They started their own company and, through the connection with Bill Hurst, and just opportunity, we were able to start working with them. And that provided really our first exclusive publishing-distribution relationship. And also it was on a discount that was done as a percentage of net billing, which allowed us to sell to wholesalers. That happened in 1983. We had done a few things. We had worked with a division of Knapp called Rosebud Books, I think in '81 and '82—

A division of who?

Knapp. They used to publish *Architectural Digest.* Some people down in Los Angeles. They also did some regional guides. That was really our first exclusive, but it was a much smaller program. We did sell some books to Ingram then, in '81, but Carroll and Graf really kicked things into gear. By '85 we had made a complete evolution of what the business looked like. The contractual relationship between us and the publisher had moved from a flat discount to a percentage of net billing; it had moved into an exclusive model. That exclusivity was something we dealt with probably through '86. When we converted over, we lost some publishers who didn't want to go exclusive, but we were able to sell to wholesalers. The whole concept of having more formal engagements with the publishers and editorial content and sales conferences and all those sorts of things emerged out of our relationship with Carroll and Graf, because, again, they had come from a—certainly Grove was not an orthodox company, as you know from interviewing Barney [Barney Rosset; see the interview with him in this volume], but it was basically running on more of a New York model of how things would work.

When you say "editorial content," what do you mean?

Well, at this point we're highly engaged with each publisher in providing a lot of shaping of how the books are published—whether it's the title, the package, hardcover, paperback, the price, what the package looks like—to the degree that we're engaged early on, whether the book is bought or not, so that we can input to create a better shape. Many publishers talk to us about a book even while the book is in some developmental stage. A lot of times a book is conceptualized in a very general way and we can actually get more out of it by focusing on one part of the whole rather than trying to do a general book. So that's just something that we—you know, it's not every book by any stretch, but we have a lot of back-and-forth with our clients and very much operate in a partnership mode. It's not specifically consulting but it gets into that type of a thing. It's a sounding board in terms of developing—whether it's the book or just the whole notion of what the publishers should be thinking about in developing their own editorial persona, and how we do that together and all of those sorts of things.

So that was just starting to germinate at that point in time. By the late '80s it had gotten a lot more formal, but we were starting to think more about what it was that we were doing and how we would do it, and how the various pieces of our publishing group fit together. I think that really emerged in the early '80s when we tried to look at our list as being a collective group of books that should fit together editorially in a cohesive way, so that we wouldn't be a New Age distributor or a literary distributor or a travel distributor or a computer book distributor. Our desire always was to be able to do everything. So we would try and develop relationships with publishers that would, through maybe a combination of two or three publishers, would give us category strength. That was a philosophy that was unique or different, at least, at that time. I think everybody is pretty generalized now. I think companies like Consortium are still largely literary and there are New Age companies, things like that. We're more, we've always been, generalists. We've had about twenty best-sellers now.

You have in-house reps now, right?

Yeah, we've had in-house reps since 1988. I mean that's when it started. I shouldn't say that quite so precisely. I think by '90 we were all in-house, but we started hiring in-house in '88. So it's been ten years for a number of the reps. And certainly we always sold to the national accounts in-house. Which I did, and Randy did, up until about '85.

Then we hired Julie Bennett. She joined us in '85 and that, again, was sort of an incremental professionalization of certainly our national account selling. We really began to professionalize the business with Julie. Gary Todoroff joined us in '88. Mark Ouimet, Susan Reich also, in terms of professionals. Mark and Susan both joined us in 1990. Those were certainly notable hires. Susan was the associate publisher at Random House. She left them in 1990 to come to work here as marketing director. Mark was the managing director of the Stanford University bookstore.

So over the course of '85 to '90 we really went through a process where, as the business became a fifteen-million-, then a twenty-million-, and then a forty-million-dollar business, we were able to

454

attract a high-caliber professional that had worked in mainstream publishing or bookselling and was able to give us, you know, an enhancement in a way that we would think about what we were doing. Because all of us just grew up—I mean, my whole career in publishing has been at Publishers Group West. I started working, one way or another, effectively just right out of college, so it's all learned, as it were, by doing. To the degree that you can bring in smart people who fit in with your personality mix, which is always important in your corporate culture and all of that, and that they can help you extend whatever your idea is, you can keep evolving and extending what it is that you're doing.

It's not like we can—the wonderful part of the book business is that every day there are new ideas and new things to think about and talk about; there's an intensity that is sometimes a little relentless, but you always have to—you know, it's not like we get to invent something here and then ship it for the next fifteen years. Every six months— four months really, with three seasons—you have to go out and say, you know, this is new and hot. Certainly we're very focused on backlist. About fifty percent of our billing is backlist.

When did Avalon come about? That's your publishing arm, right?

Yeah. Avalon was started, really, in '92. It wasn't called Avalon at that particular point; it was just a—as we got more and more engaged in the process of publishing, and we became in some ways... By 1990, as a distributor, we had become sort of a pseudo-publisher. The marketplace—because of our discount schedule and the way we approached the market, in that we organized everything in a collective way—considered us a publisher. When the vendors talked to the accounts, they would give you the vendor ranking and we were always ranked with the publishers rather than the wholesalers.

At some point we started to have best-sellers. *50 Simple Things You Can Do to Save the Earth* was a big break-out book for us in 1990; it sold about a million and a half copies to the trade. And we needed to engage in the financial support of all that. In other words, we were the ones holding the banking relationships, and at appropriate times we needed to engage in the process of moving the money through the market so that we could keep books being printed, keep people moving along.

So Avalon originally was really just a part of Publishers Group West. It wasn't Avalon; it was the whole sort of financial support of the publishers. We would utilize our banking horsepower and try to direct it at certain programs—people had asked about it and were receptive—where we could, in effect, create a stability of cash flow which would allow companies to grow.

So Avalon would invest in companies that you were already distributing.

Yeah, exactly. I mean, later on. This is sort of pre-Avalon, 1990. What I'm trying to get at here is that Publishers Group West went beyond sales and distribution to editorial consultation, and then it became a financial support. So we could allow an aggressive, newer company to have a steadiness of cash flow because we were sort of publishing-sophisticated, as it were.

Eventually this, of course, drove our bank crazy that we were a little bit wild-West in terms of how everything was done on an intuitive basis rather than with security agreements and all of that. Anyway, by 1992, what ended up happening was we had started thinking that maybe we should convert one of these things into actual capitalization rather than just lending the money.

You were lending money till '92?

Yeah, maybe from '89 through '91. It wasn't an organized thing. It was organized but there wasn't a business plan that we were trying to execute. It was opportunistic and entrepreneurial and, you know, somebody would have a hot book so we would help them reprint the book, and we could just make that decision. You know, *50 Simple Things..*, we were very engaged. At some point in the manufacturing of that book it almost became as though we were the co-publisher or something.

Moon Travel Handbooks was the first publisher to approach us, in 1992. In the late '80s they had taken on an investor, Odyssey, a couple of guys out of Hong Kong. And Odyssey was interested in divesting a portion of their equity, or the whole thing. They were engaged at the time in some sort of negotiation with...I think it was the *Encyclopedia Britannica*. I got a call from Donna Galassi who was

456

marketing director at Moon at the time, and she sort of said, you know, "Odyssey isn't necessarily certain that they want to sell the company, they'd like to sell at least some of it, and we were thinking that you guys might be interested in taking a minority position because that way you get to preserve the distribution relationship. If you don't do that it's fairly likely that they'll have to sell the whole thing, because no big publisher is going to buy a minority share." So that was really our first step. We invested a reasonable amount of money, not a lot of money, but a reasonable amount of money.

Then, by 1994, I'd say about eighteen, twenty months later, Odyssey wanted to sell more of the company, so the next station in life was basically to take a control position. So at the point where we controlled that asset, we created Avalon. We could no longer hold that asset as a sort of sub of Publishers Group West. So in 1994 we reconfigured our corporation to where the corporation is actually Publishers Group, Incorporated with two wholly owned subsidiary corporations, Publishers Group West, which does the distribution activity, and Avalon Publishing Group which does the publishing and investment activity. Over time we've made about ten other investments. Seven Stories, Four Walls [i.e., Four Walls Eight Windows], Berrett-Koehler, Foghorn, Carroll and Graf are all companies we have minority investments in. [In January 1999, Avalon bought controlling interest in Carroll and Graf.]

I suppose if Four Walls or Seven Stories sold their companies, then they would—
It's really giving them the capital to grow their business with the notion that the revenue comes back to us in distribution. It's a fairly conservative investment strategy. We have control positions with Thunder's Mouth Press and Marlowe and Company and now Blue Moon Books. We own a hundred percent of those, so those are companies that we're operating. Susan Reich is now—Susan left the company in 1995 and she rejoined us this February as the COO and publishing director of Avalon. She manages our control positions on the publishing side. I'm CEO of that company as well, but Susan is really the day-to-day operator, although we work very closely together.

That's something where we haven't done an enormous amount

of investing over the last eighteen months because we needed to capitalize, which we've now done, so we'll probably do a little more here in the next year or so. Our orientation is pretty much focused on majority or hundred-percent positions, but that doesn't preclude us from doing another minority position. A minority position is really more of an investment for Publishers Group West. If the property is sold, then Avalon would get its money out, hopefully with a nice return, but the revenue comes from the distribution fee, whereas with the Avalon control positions we can presumably make a profit as a publisher as well. And that's something that we're working on reasonably well at this point. It can get better.

You mentioned backlist earlier.

Yeah. I mean the two things that we have always emphasized aside from trying to have a good time—we've always tried to have some fun—are the diversity of the books that we're representing and building a backlist. To the degree that we build backlist, we have more power in the company in terms of consistency of business, consistency of cash flow, fewer returns—

Can you get the stores to take backlist?

Yeah. Now it's—the computer is your friend or enemy there. I mean certainly it's different than what it was fifteen years ago. You know, we had to diversify. At some point in the late '80s we became typed as a backlist vendor. That proved to be something of an impediment in terms of achieving the kind of advances we wanted on the frontlist, because if it was an independent store they'd say "I'll take a couple and then we'll reorder it," or this chain store: "I'll take five hundred." And so as our clients got more sophisticated and got a little bit more aggressive about wanting to launch books at a higher level, we needed to train the market that we had a frontlist dynamic as well.

At this point I think we have a real good mixed persona. We can have a book like *Cold Mountain* or *Ship of Gold* right now where next week we have our initial lay-down of a hundred thousand copies. So it's just like any major publisher. But, by and large, our advance orders, our lay-down numbers, are a little more conservative than the major publishers because that suits most of our clients' interests in terms of their cash management and risk management. By and large, our clients are predominantly interested in building backlist. Everybody's got a frontlist component now.

You have to marry each publisher's goals to what we're trying to accomplish. We certainly have publishers who are more frontlist oriented. It's really a matter of that whole meeting and partnership that I was speaking about earlier. With each client, you define: What are the goals? What are we trying to accomplish? On an overall editorial basis, how can we enhance that? What can the publisher do to enhance its reputation? Then you take that down to each individual book and you work it book by book, publisher by publisher, and try to sort it out. Some people are doing sixty-five percent frontlist, thirty-five percent backlist, and some people are exactly the opposite.

When you say "doing backlist," what do you mean? Reprinting backlist, or—?

Yeah. Or just trying to generate backlist. If the emphasis of what they're publishing is paperback nonfiction, and they're trying to create books that go out in the five-, six-, seven-thousand-copy range, or four- to eight-thousand-copy range, whatever, the purpose is to get the book into the marketplace in order to generate reorders for several years. It's not that we're going to make the best-seller list; it's going to be a book that generates fifty or eighty or a hundred and eighty thousand dollars every year in revenue. And then there are other books, hardcover fiction, literary books, where your window of opportunity is two to four months after the book ships, and if the book's going to crack, that's when it's going to happen. If it doesn't, then maybe you come back and get it in paperback. You know, developing literary backlist is not a precise science, put it that way.

Certainly Grove, who we've been working with now for five years, where you have the combination of Beckett and Miller.... And then Morgan [Morgan Entrekin, publisher of Grove/Atlantic] is doing a wonderful job of buying—Jerzy Kosinski, Jeanette Winterson—you know, trying to enhance the backlist that Grove has, all within the fit of what Grove is.

How many new titles does Publishers Group West do—?

It would be about twelve hundred a year, maybe thirteen hundred a year. The fall season is a little heavier, winter season is a little lighter.

I interviewed Bob Harrison, a commission sales rep who works mostly for Consortium and The Mountaineers. He says he does about a thousand titles per season.

That's the advantage of having house reps. Twelve hundred books a year is a lot of books, but some commission reps are probably selling two and a half, three times that. Obviously, with a house situation, just like a major company, you can direct your energy towards a title or an opportunity as it arises. That's a tremendous luxury. You try to break a book out, bring everybody's attention to it. With *Montana 1948* we did a hell of a job, sort of running with that book, really making it into something. And I think that that's the advantage of having a dedicated sales force: You can say, "Hey, this is hot right now. Let's go!" As you know as a publisher, you have a window of opportunity in a frontlist situation to make it happen.

If you're publishing more backlist, you can be more patient in allowing the book to come up over time. Something like *Girlfriends* which was on the best-seller list for a year—actually, we didn't break that book out on the best-seller list until fourteen months after it was published. It was paperback, it was always selling very well, it wasn't that it went from minimal to best-seller, but we sort of ramped it up over a period of a year. We went into a sales conference at the end of 1996 and we said, you know, we can make this book a best-seller. We can just do it on distribution. And just as we were about ready to do that, a related title was selected to be featured on Oprah. We knew what would happen: The original title would sort of slipstream. Even though it wasn't really mentioned on the show, it was that last little thing that kicked us up over the top. We had enough books out there that it was just a little bit below the list. Then it was on the list for a year.

I feel like we're at a really good point right now. Things have worked out in a kind of good, wonderful way. I feel like we've always had this knack for finding the book of the moment. In your publishing life you always look to have an impact. We've had now, three times in particular—we've certainly had more best-sellers, but *50 Simple Things*

460

where, at first, for that period of a few months we were, you know, we were right there—Earth Day and ecology consciousness and...whatever.

Another time we had a great run was when the Oliver Stone movie, *JFK*, on the assassination, came out. We had three books on the best-seller lists, and one of the books the movie was based on. We felt like we were hand-to-hand with the CIA and, you know, we were doing.... We since learned that things were not quite so straightforward. Anyway, it was like whatever you were doing captured a larger audience's attention. And that happened with *Cold Mountain* last year. The whole thing of having a literary first novel that goes on to win the National Book Award and sells a million and a half. That's just a rewarding and fun thing.

You look back over the list of Publishers Group West and it really is a publishers' group and a collection of individuals, people that we sort of organized. So it gives us a tremendous amount of opportunity to move from this to that to the next thing. But it's all sort of connected and it all fits together in a way that feels as though it's part of the same general thing.

Considering Cold Mountain, *do you think its success is an anomaly, or do you think the market has changed?*

Partly. Good books are always, you know, in demand. It's a signal to the publishers, big or small, that quality is a really important thing. With *Cold Mountain*—it's kind of funny, it was not dissimilar from what we did with *Montana* [*1948*], it was just on a different scale. Instead of starting with a three-thousand-copy advance, we had a twenty-five-thousand-copy advance, and we had the publicity and marketing—and Grove is significant—and we all just pushed together really hard and we had the support of all the booksellers. It wasn't surprising to me that it was a best-seller. When a quarter of a million copies becomes a million and a half copies, that's something you can't predict. That was just sort of magic, or whatever it is. Good karma.

Eric Kampmann
Midpoint Trade Books

"I failed one time, and to go through all the pain and suffering and loss of money, and then to start again in the same way would be a sign that I am the most tremendous fool that ever was put on the face of the earth. I have to believe that what we're doing today is significantly different from what I did in the '80s, and failed at."

We did the interview in Seattle late on a balmy evening in early August 1996. Eric Kampmann was in western Washington to visit a number of publishers whose books Midpoint distributes, and, incidentally, to reconnoiter Mt. Rainier with the idea of climbing it the following year. Midpoint was new then, had, in fact, begun shipping books only the previous February. We ate at Chinook's, a seafood restaurant at Fisherman's Terminal in the Magnolia district. I had intended to eat, then record the interview at the table, but the level of noise surrounding us prohibited this. We went to a Denny's across the bridge in Ballard where a young man in the waiting area told us that this was the third busiest Denny's in the country after those at Disney World and Disneyland, and an assistant manager told us it was the second busiest after the one in Anaheim. We were seated in a booth against the far wall, as distant from the restaurant's main activity as possible. At the nearest table six high school kids—a boy and five girls—were conversing with enthusiasm. Kampmann said the boy was with so many girls because he was a basketball player.

Kampmann was born in Philadelphia, graduated from Brown University in 1966, got a Master's degree in English literature at SUNY, Stony Brook, and had put in about a year toward a Ph.D. when he left the university. His decision to leave was based on his wanting to get married, to break with university life, and to move to New York. He currently lives in Greenwich, Connecticut with his wife and four children and commutes by train into New York City where Midpoint is located. He says that publishing was an obvious choice of career for him.

Why?

I was familiar with books from my graduate work, and was very interested in the publishing business, as I thought about the '20s and '30s in American publishing, which was somewhat romanticized. There was a romantic charm to it that is somewhat interesting. My father had been in advertising, but he died in 1963 and that avenue really closed down for me at that time. So, really, I was making my own career choices by that time. It ended up being publishing.

Did you write, other than for course work?
Not really. No.

So it was either advertising or publishing. When advertising closed off, that left publishing. Is that what you're saying?
Well, it was the easiest job to get that was appealing that didn't require a law degree or a business degree or something like that. And I wanted to go to work, so...I went to work.

Who did you go to work for?
Viking Press.

As what?
A sales rep in a small territory in the Northeast, working out of New York City. I spent almost five years at Viking. I started out as probably the lowest-ranked rep in terms of territory or anything in 1970. In '73 I became assistant sales manager. In '74 I left Viking to go to St. Martin's Press as the sales manager. I was there for three years, '74 to '77. I became the director of sales at St. Martin's in 1976. Then I was hired by Simon and Schuster in September of '77 to be national sales manager, and two years later became director of sales, and, shortly after that, a vice-president. And that carried through February of '81 when I left that part of my career and started my own company.

I felt I had progressed in terms of the career track I was on very quickly. But I couldn't figure out what the next step was, and I didn't want to become one of these rotating sales managers going from one big company to the next. That was static to me. So I made a dramatic change. It was a little bit more—there was an additional step before I started my own company. I went into partnership in a small company in New York with two women who already had developed a publishing company. I was going to be their partner, but I very quickly saw that that was no work for me. So I worked with them for six months and then started my own distribution company in the fall of '81.

The partnership—was that distribution or publishing?

Publishing. But my role there was more in the sales area. Sales and marketing. But I also brought some books in. So I did some editorial kinds of activities.

Your company was called?

It is called Kampmann and Company. Actually, at the same time I also got a consulting job with Beaufort Books, which was a Canadian-owned, general trade publisher with an office in New York City. And they gave me office space and a consulting fee, and I helped them at the same time I was developing Kampmann and Company.

Kampmann and Company grew from a dead-start zero to something like eight hundred thousand dollars its first year. It grossed up to seven or eight million dollars by '86 or '87.

What kinds of books were you distributing?

General trade, but they ranged from books on rock 'n roll subjects like Michael Jackson or a book on the Beatles to novelty books like *The Shower Song Book* to general trade fiction and nonfiction. The general orientation was what is commonly called the book trade.

How many publishers did you have?

In the neighborhood, after I got it really rolling, of sixty to seventy-five publishers.

Were you organized differently then than now?
Very differently.

Can you tell me how you were organized then?
How I was disorganized then? One of the problems was that the

models I was using to build the distribution company were very expensive. So I hired an outside distribution center, I had an outside computer-service bureau, I hired commission reps, I had a New York office, and when I added up the costs of doing all that stuff, it was as much as or greater than the fees I was getting from the publishers for doing their distribution. So it was marginally profitable to unprofitable, based on the cost-stucture of the company. My problem was that I simply didn't— I used pieces of the distribution sales model that I had known in my previous jobs, and I was not able to put something together that was more cost-efficient. In the beginning it was marginally profitable.

Then there was a second component. My biggest client was Beaufort Books, which became the distributed publisher of Kampman and Company from '83, and I bought that company in '84. I had actually bought the assets of another publishing company in '82 or '83, so I had already done some quasi-publishing activities within Kampmann and Company. And I understood Beaufort well, I thought.

I bought the company in '84, but it was not a good decision. It was a two-million-dollar operation. It was almost all new books and it needed a lot more capital to run. I didn't have enough capital to support it. It quickly became a cash drain for me, as opposed to a cash cow. So that gets us through the '80s.

Didn't you have something to do with National Book Network?

Right. In '88, or late '87, to solve the cost problem, I had to move my warehouse to a new facility in Connecticut at Bridgeport. And they, it turned out, were not very good at doing their job. This was a company called Key Book Service. They were a wholesaler who had distribution facilities. And I thought they would help solve some of the cash-flow problems, but in fact they were a disaster, from an organizational point of view, just waiting to happen. And by the spring of '89 it was not clear they were going to survive. In fact they declared bankruptcy. They went into Chapter Eleven in the spring of '89 and ultimately that forced my company into Chapter Eleven.

It was a very tough period, but in May of '89 I reorganized Kampmann and Company—basically moved out of that facility. And we made an arrangement with National Book Network where they would do all the distribution and my company, Kampmann and Company, would do all the sales. So, essentially, in one very dramatic period, I stopped all my publishing activities, I stopped all my distribution activities, I continued on with about thirty of the sixty publishers I had been working with, and I kept the one thing we were strongest at, which was sales.

National Book Network itself was a small, less-than-one-million-dollars-worth-of-business, distribution/sales company. They let all of their sales people go. We came in to replace them, and through this contract we were able to build NBN up into the second largest sales/distribution company in the business. By the time our contract was up in '94, we were doing about thirteen million dollars worth of business through NBN, working with about eighty publishers.

Why did you want a publishing company?
Uh-h-h-h-m...

Sorry.
Well, because a part of me wanted to be a publisher. I mean that was an opportunity that presented itself, and I grabbed it. I also had had some success in packaging and doing quasi-publishing activities on a somewhat more formal basis.

The problem with Beaufort was more to do with the nature of that company rather than whether I should have been involved with publishing. I bought another publishing company after Beaufort which was very successful for me. Hastings House. But Beaufort was all frontlist, it had an infrastructure that had a significant ongoing-cost basis for running it, and the fact that we always had to go out and replace past books with brand new books, because there was very little backlist to it, was a burden I didn't understand. It would have required a great deal of actual cash in hand to do that. It was just a bad model for me. I had no backlist. The books did not generally sell more than several thousand copies per title. And there were no big winners. So it was a drain rather than an asset.

You talk about models a lot. Were you thinking in terms of models or paradigms at that time in your life?
The only thing I was really aware of—I'm sure I thought about

structures for everything. Some of the things I'm doing today, I did in 1982. For example, national-account selling has always been part of what I personally did. So that is something I'm doing today that I did then.

The other thing that I was aware of—not the extent of it, nor would I have predicted what really happened in the industry—was that there seemed to be a need, a place, for somebody to help the emerging class of smaller independent publishers who seemed to be suddenly appearing on the scene in all parts of the country. And that process seemed to grow. As I was starting my company, it seemed to be happening more in California and other places, not so much in New York where the traditional publishers were housed. But I was aware that there was a need for it. I was not aware of the dimensions of it, nor where it would lead.

Where it led was to a world of many, many more independent publishers coming on line all the time for a whole host of reasons, some having to do with the lower cost it took to get into this business. The low cost, the personal computer, the home office concept, the regionality of a lot of these publishers—the New York crowd that was always publishing higher and higher and higher kinds of media in the cultural stratosphere had neglected the grass roots and suddenly the independent publisher was coming in and finding books and authors who were appealing to perhaps a fairly small audience, but still an audience, in some cases an audience that had a national potential in terms of sales. And that's where these publishers needed somebody or some company to help them get entrée into the trade business—the trade world of selling through the wholesalers and the retailers. And that's what Publishers Group West and Kampmann and Company and National Book Network and these companies—that's what they're there to do.

Where are we now? What years are we talking about?

Well, my life at National Book Network was a five-year agreement between Kampmann and Company and National Book Network that ended the middle of 1994 and, sadly for us, for a variety of reasons that are not important to this discussion, the contract was very, very favorable to Kampmann and Company, and they wanted to change that and we didn't want to change it, and so we went our separate ways.

It was about that same time that I made a decision that if I was going to continue on—I'd been doing this now for fourteen years, being on my own, being an entrepreneur, developing a group of companies, some successful, some not, and I was approaching the age of fifty-one and I said that whatever career choice I make at this point is going to be probably the last important one I make. At least that's the way it looked at the time. So I wanted to make the right type of decision and I wanted to structure the kind of company that not only would last, but would be profitable from almost the first day it did business. It was that and other considerations that we saw in terms of changes in the industry that led to the structure of the company, which we launched in September of last year, and which started actually shipping and billing in February. That company is Midpoint Trade Books, which is basically in the tradition of Publishers Group West.

We think that we have developed a model that focuses its energies very, very accurately on what the market really needs today, both on the publishing side and on the bookselling side. That's what we think.

What changes do you see occurring in the industry today?

[Laughs.] I'm glad you asked. Well, some of the things that I think are...I'm not analyzing these in terms of good or bad, or what's good for the world or bad for the world, but just as changes. The large publishers obviously continue to be what they are, do what they do, and some things they do very well. But, by doing business the way they do, they've actually created an opening in the marketplace for the independent publisher who does what he does somewhat differently. So one of the things I think has happened over the last fifteen years is while the big publishers continue to get bigger, the independent publishers are continuing to get better.

What do you mean by "better"?

Better in terms of the way they're publishing their books. They're competitive in many, many ways. In fact, a sign of this is a book like *The Celestine Prophecy*, which was a self-published book done by a fellow down in Alabama that became one of the biggest best-sellers of the '90s when Warner's came along and took over as publisher. One of the signs that independent publishing is vital and alive is that large publishers have started to see the smaller publishers as an editorial resource, as kind of a farm team. I think that's an arrogant way of looking at it, and I think really what's happening is many, many good books are being published by independent publishers and the large publishers are finding it more and more difficult to find the next celebrity best-seller, blockbuster, General Powell type of book. And they always have to pay more and more money for these things, in terms of author advances and stuff.

The independent publishers are not necessarily seeing cost increases in the way they do business because they have an efficiency in being a sole proprietor or a one- or two-person operation working out of the home or a small office in parts of the country that do not require massive amounts of money to set up a company, whereas the big publishers are saddled with huge, ravenous, leviathan-type infrastructures that need to be fed day after day, week after week. I think it's a losing proposition in the long term, at least in the trade business.

The opportunities for selling books also have broadened, not only because of the advent of the superstores, but also because there are many places that are not really bookstores that are now selling books. Here you're talking about the large merchandisers like the warehouse clubs, or gift shops or airport stores. There are lots of places selling books today that offer the publisher sales opportunities that didn't exist before.

I think, really, the momentous change which is hard to see, in a way, is that the independent publisher has an authentic and important role today in the trade publishing business, much more so than ten years ago. And I think that trend is going to continue, given the economics of the business.

It always has been a bit of a mom-and-pop business. When the conglomerates came in and bought up some of these established publishing companies, that worked for a while, but I'm not sure it's going to work in the long run. In fact, if I could venture a guess, I would think that one of the things you might see in the next five to ten years is some of these larger publishing houses being broken apart and sold off in pieces. Rather than more consolidation going on, you might see more fragmentation.

There's a great deal of capital in America. If somebody wanted to get a piece of Simon and Schuster, and Simon and Schuster didn't see that as a profit center anymore, you might be able to buy it and set up your own thing. Maybe what's not profitable to Simon and Schuster is profitable to somebody else.

What you're really buying is not the people; you're buying the books. You're buying the titles. You might be buying some expertise, but if you could buy a good set of backlist titles from one of these publishers, you might be able to get it pretty cheap and you might be able to set it up and make it profitable.

The profitability of a book has to do with how much overhead in the company is being charged against that book by every sale they make. If you're charging thirty percent of the general cost to run the company so that basically every sale is being forced to carry a thirty percent load beyond everything else, it's going to have a hard time being profitable if it's only selling five or six thousand a year. But if it has a negligible overhead being charged against it, suddenly it's thirty percent more profitable, or twenty percent more profitable.

I think that one of the things my company is involved in sort of ties into the second series of forces going on, which is the growth of the superstores in the bookselling community, which has really taken off in the '90s, fueled primarily by the explosive growth of Barnes and Noble and the significant growth at Borders as well as the Books-A-Million chain, Crown superstores, and others.

Now, the superstore is basically, I think, an evolutionary development from the old mall chain stores, the Waldens and B. Daltons, which were predominant in the mid- to late '70s all the way through the mid- to late '80s. They had about a ten- to twelve-year run and everybody thought that was the wave of the future. But it turned out that the demographics in America ensured that the mall stores, which were based on foot traffic coming through these large, centralized shopping districts, went to a much more complete kind of inventory, and people wanted more rather than less in terms of title selection and atmosphere. And the superstores, by and large, at least so far, have been very, very successful. They're modeled, actually, on places like The Tattered Cover and other very successful independent enterprises that have offered wonderful customer service. Basically, the superstore, in many ways, is as old as the hills. It's just a full-service bookstore, in this case owned by a centralized buying operation.

The other thing that's been going on is that mall store sales have been flat and the independent stores have been put under a great deal of pressure by the opening of the superstores. The independents' growth has been pretty flat, as well.

The most revolutionary change that is changing almost everything in the way books are sold and distributed in the United States is the maturing of certain national and regional wholesalers into very significant and professional one-day delivery systems. So that if one of these wholesalers, like Ingram Book Company, has stock, virtually any store in America can have access to that inventory in a single day.

It's a remarkable change from when I came into the business, which was essentially an East Coast business and the West Coast had to wait anywhere from four to six weeks to get inventory on faster-moving titles. That's not true anymore. The national wholesalers like Ingram and others have made access to fast-moving titles almost immediate. That's changing the way books are sold by publishing sales forces, by just-in-time inventory management control, a whole host of things making bookselling a more rational, more dynamic business, in a way. I think these are very exciting and positive changes.

In addition to that, there's a tie-in to what I said before in that the warehouse clubs and other retail channels are expanding and competing actively for best-sellers. For example, Staples Office Supplies stores have a selection of business-related titles that they buy and sell in fairly significant numbers. So an independent publisher, or a larger publisher who pays attention, will expand its sales base well beyond the sales they might get in the trade into some of these other retail outlets.

That's quite an essay. Do you deliver this...this...?
Well, I have.

For a class? Did you say [in an earlier, untaped, conversation] you teach?
Yeah. For the last twelve years I've taught at the Radcliffe publishing course up at Harvard College where I'm one of the people running a workshop. The workshop takes about a week. It's a wonderful experience. They divide the students into ten publishing houses which have to be developed on a real-world basis, using real titles.

Everything is vetted against real-world numbers, and it's a great experience. It's very dynamic and very, very intensive. So we do that, and I've done a lot of speaking in the past, in various places.

Now your dad was in advertising. Did he have his own company?

Yeah, he had his own small company in Philadelphia. He was building it up. It was a fairly typical advertising firm. Some of the things he was doing in his company I sort of used as a structural concept for my own company. I'm still doing that. He had a small company so he outsourced a lot of the copy-writing and other activities they did. So he didn't have a lot of full-time people working there. I tried to do that myself when I started Kampmann and Company, but I didn't do it as successfully as I would now if I were to do it again. We're not doing that now. Everybody involved in the company is a stockholder and is working in the company.

A lot of the things distributors are doing for smaller or independent presses are things that the larger publishers do themselves.

I think that's true.

I wonder now who is the publisher. It seems to me that what Midpoint is doing, in part, is the publisher's function. Doesn't that make Midpoint the publisher? I'm not trying to single out Midpoint.

No, no. I think that the real point in all of that is to go back to how an independent publisher makes a living, if that's his intention, in the activity of publishing books. If I was to act as a consultant and say "Here's how to structure a company," I would tell them to outsource every activity outside of the book development itself. In other words, the relationship between the publisher and the author should remain the function of the publisher and the author. I define that as an editorial function and it's something that it's not easy to substitute. All of the other activities you can substitute. You can bring in outsiders to do that activity on your behalf. You can hire them. That's what outsourcing is all about.

One of the changes that has occurred is that the outsourcing has not always been all that professional. Now there are a lot of ex-employees from the large publishing houses or large chains who are basically expatriates of these companies, who are available and who are quite good, quite professional about what they're doing, and they have set up their own independent companies to provide services for this publisher.

So what does it take to be a publisher? It takes the ability to conceive and develop the book which may still be only a manuscript or an idea, and then putting together a network, utilizing computer networking and these service operations which are done on a per-job basis, essentially. So you only pay for what they are doing for you, specifically for that project. You hire them to do the various jobs that need to be done, that actually are exactly what the large publishing houses do internally. But you don't have an ongoing overhead. If the book gets delayed, the costs to you also get delayed, so you're not funding something that doesn't exist. If the independent publisher will use that model, and find the people that he can rely on to get the job done when the job must be done, then he's increased his ability to publish, and his power and reach become significantly greater than anything you can imagine for one person with a computer in his home.

Even here in Seattle, which has not been known as a big publishing mecca, there are a lot of people who provide these services in various branches of publishing, not just trade publishing, that a publisher could call upon, and not incur the enormous expense of hiring a salaried employee who may or may not know how to do the job well. It's a superior answer to an eternal problem.

The services you're talking about include cover design, page design, prepress—

There's nothing that you can't buy outside of your home and still call yourself a publisher. Because it still boils down to the editorial function of developing the manuscript, preparing it for publication, preparing it for the printer—in other words, getting it into the production cycle, developing a marketing concept for the book, finding distribution, putting together publicity and advertising, promotion, getting advice on the timing of the book, the pricing, the packaging.

All of these things are available but, like all advice, the publisher, or the person in the center of this wheel, must feel confident of the people he or she is dealing with. If that confidence doesn't exist, then it is not working at its optimal level. And vice versa. The person being hired has to have confidence the publisher will live up to his commitments as well. If he or she says they're going to do this or that, then that in fact is accomplished to the best of their ability.

That, in a way, is the good news and the bad news all wrapped up together, because you can imagine that the structure is a tenuous one. It must always be massaged because these are outsiders, so the relationships need to be nurtured and developed. "Maintained," I think, is a better word. But if that is done, which does take a certain amount of energy, then the plus side of it, I think, is very favorable to the independent publisher.

Does your vision for Midpoint incorporate a mission beyond growth? Or does growth signify something else to you?

Actually, our mission is not growth. I mean it's necessary in all companies to grow for a while, but I personally don't feel that growth is our mission per se. I would think that if you were to walk around our organization and ask why are we doing what we're doing, why did we start this company, what is it we're doing that gets us up in the morning and makes sense to us as individuals, the answer would be a very, very simple word: love.

It's the love of what we do. It's the enjoyment and pleasure in attempting to do something well and actually seeing it accomplished, and then doing something else well the next day. It's the enjoyment of hearing somebody say something nice about us after we've accomplished something, and us saying something nice to somebody else because they also have accomplished something.

We had a few things in mind but they always come back to that love-of-what-you're-doing business. That is, we wanted to say nothing to anybody that was a promise that we didn't think we could live up to. So our promises are modest, by and large, in the way we've presented Midpoint. We're not trying to be a Simon and Schuster or a Random House. I think I had a little bit of that in my mind back in the '80s when I started Kampmann and Company, because I came out of those companies. But at this point, I think we don't have that insecurity.

I think we believe, in starting Midpoint, that there continues to be a significant need for a service company to help the independent

474

publisher organize their activities, optimize their sales, do all the things that will make them better at what they're doing and will make our company better as well.

In addition to that, we thought it was very important to write a contract that was profitable for us, but not on the backs of the publishers. So we had to be very disciplined in our approach to our own cost structure. The framework of the company is very simple so that we don't have a lot of hidden costs that get shifted to the publisher or get reflected in a lack of profitability. It's very important for us to be profitable with a very low level of sales, so that we will have the capital to fuel growth and make improvements as we develop and become something of a bigger presence in the industry. It comes back to if I didn't love what I'm doing, there would have been absolutely no reason to have started Midpoint, because I would have been just grinding my teeth day after day.

I failed one time, and to go through all the pain and suffering and loss of money, and then to start again in the same way would be a sign that I am the most tremendous fool that ever was put on the face of the earth. I have to believe that what we're doing today is significantly different from what I did in the '80s, and failed at. I succeeded in parts of it, but I failed, ultimately, in terms of the bankruptcy. We succeeded greatly at NBN, but even there the model was more or less the same as at Kampmann and Company, and it took NBN four years to become profitable.

I personally learned, and all the people working with me learned a great deal from their past experience, so that when we started Midpoint, we abandoned all of the things that would drag a company like us down, and we put at the core of the company the things that were good about what I did and what the people around me developed in the past. We were very concerned that if we got into this business of serving companies in sales and marketing and distribution activities, that publishers would feel that they were getting every cent of what they were paying for in terms of growth and good relationships.

The book is the commodity. The fact that we are knowledgeable about that book is the method. The fact that there is a system out there that has to be adhered to for the good of the book is really our role.

Which means that we get the publisher, no matter how idiosyncratic they may be as individuals, to conform to the standards of the industry, which none of us have made up. We can only feed off of it, we can't change it. And to the extent that we don't try to change it, but just use it for our purposes, I think the books that we have to sell will do better, by and large, than by a philosophy of total recalcitrance, or a philosophy of—oh, what's the right word? Basically an individualistic point of view of "I don't have to pay attention to any of this stuff out there. The big publishers are a bunch of parasites. The big wholesalers are a bunch of cannibals. And I don't want anything to do with it." I think that that is not a sound business approach.

Now, I think it's fair to say that a small publisher who makes a choice not to deal with this world, and has alternative ways of selling his books, has a perfectly legitimate way of doing business. The only thing I am saying is if that publisher chooses to expand his horizons into the superstores and into other markets, then the role of the publishing services company like National Book Network, or Midpoint, or PGW comes into play. It's our role, as professionals, to help the publisher conform to what he needs to conform to, like having EAN barcodes on their books, bringing them out on time, pricing them correctly, getting them into our catalogue, giving us all the sales information we need. Suddenly, when they do that kind of stuff, they have a very effective sales force working for them, not working against them. Or they're not working against it. So it's a matter of point of view and philosophy as to whether the independent publisher wants to go that route.

What you described just now is a set of procedures. Is that what you mean by "standards of the industry" or do you mean something different?

Well, there are no standards in the industry. It's basically the norms of the industry that have been developed by no one in particular that everybody seems to follow. For example, it's a norm of the industry that books are returnable. Many people believe that that is nonsense and that books shouldn't be returnable and we should stop this craziness now before we all get flooded with returns. That's all probably true. But in the meantime, in order to sell books today, you must sell them on a returnable basis or you're not going to get the sale. So that's what I'm talking about. The norm is that books are returnable. It may be a crazy

476

norm, but that's what it is.

The fact that the large superstores require a three- or four-month lead time to get a book into the stores is a norm. Simon and Schuster follows that. Random House follows that. It's not always been as structured as it is today, but that's what it is. If we want to be contrary and say we'll sell two months or one month in advance or on the day of publication to these people, that may be good for our self-esteem but it's going to be terrible for sales. Because, in ninety-nine cases out of a hundred, sales are not going to happen.

There are exceptions. Books will come along that are very hot, that the stores will want despite the norm, and will actually break procedure in order to get the book in. I've seen that happen many times. It's not a good method to work in general, because they're not going to make that exception in general. They're going to make it in specific, individual cases where there seems to be an overwhelming necessity.

The other thing that is very important for an independent publisher to keep in mind is that none of these stores need them. They could live without them, if that had to happen. On the other hand, the superstores, and almost all the stores, are inviting the independent publishers in through distributors and other methods because they do want them. They may not need them, but they want them. They want a wider range of inventory, they want more diverse books. They're always looking for new opportunities to sell books. So this is a paradox, the necessity for being wanted. I think when the independent publisher knows that and can take advantage of that situation, that will give him wider distribution.

We're miles and miles away from what we could be. We know that. When we started shipping books in February, we were shipping essentially to two or three accounts. We've expanded that to a much wider range of accounts, but it's still a fraction of what we want to do. But, also, we stay within the idea of partnering much more with wholesalers and not trying to become a wholesaler, not competing with the Ingrams, but partnering with the Ingrams. I think that our model of Chris [Bell], Gail [Kump], and Eric doing the selling is a great one, and I think that as we develop that into marketing components with special sales opportunities, all of which have been done so far, but will be expanded upon, we'll become a very powerful sales organization.

BOOKSELLERS

Dee and Chuck Robinson
Village Books

"What's scary is the narrowing of what was once a very diverse marketplace, in terms of where one could buy books. As that narrows, I worry for what will be available. What will be able to be published, you know?"

Chuck Robinson was already talking about his State Department-sponsored trip to the Middle East in the fall of 1997 when I turned on my cassette recorder. His group, which included the poet Colleen McElroy, a literary agent, a representative of New York's publishing scene, and himself as a bookseller, was supposed to go to Jerusalem, Jordan and Morocco, but there was trouble in Jerusalem so they spent all of their time in the other places. Their purpose was to talk about intellectual property rights.

Two years before that, there was a journey to Macedonia funded by the Soros Foundation. Its role was to explore the possibility of setting up a booksellers school. The American Booksellers Association had established several schools in Eastern Europe and wanted to extend them into the Balkan countries. As it happened, it was not set up.

Chuck Robinson has served on the boards of directors of the Pacific Northwest Booksellers Association and the American Booksellers Association, and has been president of the former organization and vice president and president of the ABA. Dee Robinson has been on the board of the PNBA and has chaired its Literacy Committee. She has taught at both the ABA's Prospective and Professional Booksellers schools.

They met as freshman in Sioux Falls College (now the University of Sioux Falls) in South Dakota. Chuck: "We met [during] orientation week and ended up dating when we were freshmen, but not right away. We were engaged when we were sophomores and married when we were juniors, and that was over thirty-one years ago."

They opened Village Books in 1980. At present the store is a two-million-dollar-a-year operation. It has twenty-two employees. There

481

*are ten thousand square feet of bookselling space; the Colophon Cafe
takes up another two thousand square feet. There are about fifty thousand titles in the store itself and seventy thousand in their database. The
store publishes a magazine called* The Chuckanut Reader, *named for
the Chuckanut Mountains south of Bellingham. Dee [laughing]: "It
doesn't mean that Chuck is a nut, although we have—"*

*I talked with the Robinsons early on a sunny evening in mid-
April 1999 in the Colophon in Bellingham, Washington, a little off of
Interstate 5, a half-hour from the Canadian border. My friend Ron
Dakron and I had recently had books published and had come up from
Seattle to read from them; I used the occasion to interview the Robinsons.*

So. How'd you get into books?

Chuck Robinson (laughing): How did this bad accident happen? Is this what you're asking? [All three of us laugh.]

Dee Robinson: Well, we'd been in education.

As teachers, or—?

DR: Well, we had both been teachers at one point. Right when
we left, Chuck was a consultant to a special ed district. Several school
districts.

CR: In Illinois. The Quad-city area. Western Illinois, right along
the Mississippi River. The special education district that I worked for was
sixteen school districts. I was the main consultant for seven of those
districts, and then worked with the people in the other districts also.
Helped set up programs and staffed kids and trained teachers, super-
vised student teachers, helped parents work with school districts. Something I liked doing a lot. I started doing it when Public Law 94142 was
passed in 1976, I think it was. Federal law called the Education For All
Handicapped Children Law. It called for the school districts to provide
education to kids, regardless of their handicap. And I had already been
teaching in special ed, plus Dee was teaching special ed at the time, and
I went to work as a consultant to help the school districts comply with
the law, and help kids get the best possible education under the law that
they could.

DR: We were enjoying what we were doing, but we decided to
take a year off and travel around the country. This was '79. 'Seventy-

482

eight we made the decision, and then we finished the school year and bought a little motor home and fixed it up and sold our house and most of what we owned and packed away the rest.

No kids?

DR: No kids. Took off to travel, thinking that we probably would go back to the jobs. Chuck was on a leave of absence and at that point I could have gotten a job easily—special ed was still a pretty easy market. But we began traveling and started thinking, Do we really want to go back to Illinois? If we don't go back, what would we do? Where would we go? So we started thinking about other things we might want to do. We thought it might be fun to do something together, and we started thinking about retail businesses. The only think that really made sense to us, the only thing we really considered seriously, was a bookstore. I think anybody who goes to college and gets a liberal arts degree probably develops some kind of affinity for bookstores. So we started stopping, talking to booksellers all over the Northwest at that point, and—

CR: This was the area we came to first because we had some friends we'd met in the Midwest who had moved back to the Tacoma area, and we had told them for several years we were going to come out and see them.

DR: And we fell in love with the Northwest. So we started stopping and talking to booksellers, and everybody we talked to was really incredibly open about talking with us about the business. Everybody loved what they were doing. They loved the business. They said it's no way to get rich, but it's a wonderful way to make a living if you can make it work. Someone along the line told us about the American Booksellers Association, and they also said they do these schools where they teach people how to open a bookstore. So we started exploring that and found out there was a school coming up in the spring. This one was in...

CR: It was outside Detroit, I believe.

DR: Yeah. In Michigan.

CR: But by that time, we had already decided we were going to open the store.

DR: Yeah. We made the decision.

CR: We had decided where we were going to be and everything. We had already moved to Bellingham. We moved here in February of 1980.

DR: Cut our trip short, because we knew if we kept traveling we wouldn't have any money left to do the bookstore. We had owned our house the best five years you could own a house back then, so we had this little—very little [Chuck laughs]—pool of money.

CR: Way too small.

DR: We thought it was a fortune, but it was nowhere near enough.

CR: Well, it must have been. Nineteen years later, we're still here.

DR: Well, it was enough. We bought the bookstore with the money from our house, basically. So we started exploring places that we would like to live that we thought could support a bookstore. We looked at the map and picked out some places. I think we actually went to the library and checked in the Yellow Pages to see how many bookstores the towns had, and we picked out some that looked like they were possibles and then visited them. And at that point Bellingham had one good independent bookstore, Fairhaven Books. Which started in Fairhaven [a Bellingham neighborhood], over in the marketplace. They had moved downtown a year and a half or two years before we were looking here. So we decided we were going to come to Bellingham. We went down and talked to them, introduced ourselves and said that we were wanting to start a bookstore and we thought Bellingham could support two. And they said, "I think you're right." They weren't sure Fairhaven was the place to be because they had left Fairhaven. But we looked at Fairhaven and talked to a lot of the business people here. The people who were here seemed to be pretty stable. There were a lot of empty spaces at that point, but it seemed that the neighborhood had kind of bottomed out and was on its way back up. So we found a location. We started upstairs in this next building, which we now own. Wish that we had—

CR: —bought it then.

DR: Of course, we couldn't have started a bookstore. Choice between buying a building and a—

Did you go to the school before you opened the bookstore?

484

DR: Yeah, we got really into it.

CR: We got to the point where we had Bellingham, but then we were looking.

DR: We moved here in February, found that, first, we wanted the bookstore, then we signed the lease—no, we didn't sign the lease, because we didn't know for sure—

CR: We didn't have the place for the bookstore.

DR: —what building we were going to be in when we went back in April to the book school. 'Cause we had an idea of where it was going to be and talked to people there and they talked us out of that location, which was probably the best piece of advice we got.

CR: We actually looked at some train cars that were over here. There was a train car—we even figured out how we could configure the shelves and everything. One of the first things that a couple of people at that book school said was, "What if you're successful? Where are you going to expand?"

DR: And it was right on, because we would have outgrown that in ten minutes. We opened in June of 1980, and I think we projected—

CR: We projected we'd do a hundred thousand dollars worth of business, and we did one-seventy.

That first year?

CR: That first year. So it was about seventy percent more than what we'd projected we could do. We were just sort of guesstimating what we—

DR: Yeah. When you're first opening up—

CR: The numbers all worked well on a pro forma sheet if you did a hundred thousand. Easy to figure the percentages. [He and Dee laugh.] Never was a math whiz.

Did you have to take out a loan?

CR: As Dee said, the amount of money that we had was...we thought that we had enough to get started in the store and have some money to live on for the first year. And actually it wasn't enough money to live on for the first year, but fortunately the store started doing well by the end of the year, and we were able to— we actually did turn a profit, so we were able to start drawing money from the business even in that first year.

That's very unusual.

CR: Very unusual, yeah.

DR: We did it all ourselves for the first few months. We didn't hire anybody, and—

CR: We spent a lot of hours in that store over the first, well, the first *several* years. I mean, it was—

DR: Nineteen years. [She and Chuck laugh.]

CR: The first nineteen years, that's right. And this year is totally different. [They laugh again.]

DR: We were in that space for two years, and then we moved over to just half of the upstairs here. And then three years later we added the cafe and took over the rest of the upstairs here. And then finally cut a hole in the floor and came downstairs, and then a few years later cut a hole in this wall and went in there. So it's been gradual.

You deal in both new and used books, right?

DR: Right.

And you shelve them together, like Powell's does?

CR: Well, we do in the section over here. We call this our bargain book annex. It's a combination of publishers' remaindered books and used books. They are shelved together. The rest of the store is all new books. Well, the rest of the store is primarily new books.

DR: ...the writing section...

CR: The writing section, which is over here, we mix new and used. It's a concept I actually believe in, in mixing up—I think Powell's does it well, and other people are starting to do that. I think in the long run we probably will do that. For us here, in this space, it will mean pretty much reconfiguring the whole store in terms of where we are going to put what. I think we probably will do that at some point.

DR: Maybe refixturing part of the store.

CR: Yeah. It probably would need some refixturing.

Is this a response to Barnes and Noble having moved in?

CR: No, not so much that as it is a response to the way the book

486

business is going in general. Any number of things, I think, has sort of pushed it that way. I mean, Mike Powell has said for years that he couldn't understand why other booksellers weren't selling used books. Of course, that's a store that came from the opposite direction, in starting with used books and moving into new books, from the time his father had the store. But I think it's something that does allow us to offer something that's not as likely to be done by chain stores, whether it's Barnes and Noble or anybody else. Conceptually, it seems to make sense. Somebody once asked, "Why would you let the publisher be the determinant of whether or not you were going to carry a particular book? The publisher decides they're going to let the book go out of print, so you stop carrying the book?" And it makes sense. You know, all books are out there and available, whether they're new or used. You can supply what the reader is looking for if you go to that broader combination of books. So I think we will move in that direction.

DR: And you can also determine your profit margin and your pricing. You can say what you'll pay for it and you can decide what you'll sell it for.

CR: Yeah. And you get some better margin out of that, and you have a little bit more control over the inventory. And the other thing that's happened is, if we were to try to keep the same backlist on our shelves that we had, say, five or six years ago, the cost of doing that is incredible. If you look at Vintage Contempories, as just one example, and the escalation of those prices over the years—Camus' book, *The Stranger*, probably went from six ninety-five to thirteen dollars. I don't know specifically if that's in five years, but in fairly recent memory it was still only six ninety-five.

DR: And so many of the backlist books that were mass marketed now moving to trade [i.e., trade paperback] probably doubles the original price, which means the cost for us to carry the same inventory base has really escalated.

It's interesting. For publishers, the cost of production has not increased.

CR: Right.

What has changed is that there are so many more middlemen,

so many more people for me to go through to get to you.
DR: Uh huh.

So where before I was able to offer a forty-percent discount directly to you, now, after I've expanded nationally, I get only thirty-five percent of the list price, which, after I pay royalties, may be only a few cents profit per unit.
DR: Right.

CR: Right. I've thought for some time that independent publishers' future and the independent bookstores' future were very much tied together. There are a lot of similarities, I think, in terms of the difficulties of the marketplace. I worry a lot for small and medium-size publishers as both publishing and the retail end become more conglomerated.

In Bellingham now, there's Village Books and there's a Barnes and Noble. Is there another bookstore?
CR: There's both a B. Dalton and a Walden in the mall. There's no other—
DR: Well, there's The Textbook Place now.
CR: The Textbook Place, which is fairly recent. They have a trade department that is—they expanded when they expanded their store. So they have—
DR: They're an off-campus textbook—
CR: Yeah. Not owned by the university or run on the university campus. It's actually in an older strip mall area.

The name of it is not "The Textbook Place," is it?
CR: Yeah.

That is the name of it?
CR: Yeah. [He and Dee laugh.]
DR: I think it might be That Textbook Place now, actually. I think the last time I saw an ad, it said That Textbook Place.
CR: Okay. I thought it was The Textbook Place, but—
DR: It's The or That, I'm not sure, but I think it's That.
CR: It's a couple of people who had been buyers for Nebraska Book Company, who used to do the buy-backs and everything. Origi-

nally, they started in a smaller space, selling new and used textbooks, very little in the way of trade books. And they got an opportunity to move into a bigger space, and they put in a fairly good-size trade department which, in fact, is being run by a guy who used to work for us for a couple of years while he was in school. So there's that. And then beyond that there are mostly used-book stores who sell a few new books, but not much. Then, of course, there are all the other kinds of outlets. Fred Meyers has some books, the grocery stores have books, you know, places like that.

Have the on-line bookstores had any effect on your business? Can you tell?

CR: It's hard to measure.

DR: We assume it has.

CR: Yeah. We hear about it from people. I mean, I would guess just from the number of people who get information from Amazon and bring it to us and say "I'd like to get this book" because they aren't in a rush to get it, or for whatever reason, they want to buy it locally— anytime you get in a number of those, you've got to believe that there's a number of people that are going directly to them and ordering the books. I think that anybody out there, they're getting the lion's share of that business.

Do you think you might be getting more business because of Amazon.

DR: People just being more aware of books, or researching, or —?

Well, Ron and I drove in together, and we were talking about that. I, for example, would never buy from Amazon.com unless I'd already seen the book. But what I would do is look for something on Amazon.com and then go to a store and look at it. Touch it. And I'd buy it from the store.

DR: Mm hm.

CR: Right.

And he's the same way. And so we suspect—

CR: Our problem is, none of us are twenty-five.

What do you mean?
CR: We're all of a certain age, that buying something like that—I mean, that's—

Oh, I see.
CR: That may be a thing of the past.

It's possible. There is the aesthetic involved, yeah. But I need to see how the book is written. It may be a subject I'm interested in, but if it's not written well, I probably won't get it.
DR: Right.
CR: You know, more and more, the databases are including sample chapters, they're including— I don't know if on Amazon that's entirely true, but there are other databases out there—I don't know if it's going to be true in MUZE, with the ABA doing the thing for the independent bookstores. Do you know about that? About BookSense.com?

Yes, I do. But maybe you could explain it for the cassette.
CR: Sure. It's scheduled to come on line at the end of this summer. What it is essentially is that the American Booksellers Association is funding the building of the back end of an ordering system that will link in, in any number of different ways, to bookstores' own websites. So you could go from the most fundamental thing of "I'm a small bookstore, I don't have a website, give me a website where I can tell people to go and order"—that costs one amount of money—or "Give me ten books that I can hook into my current website," or "Custom design a website for me." There's all these different ways that one can do it.

And they would be linked?
CR: Yeah. The way it would be is that you would go—I mean we've had a website for probably about four years now. We can take some orders on-line; it's not a full search system like it will be this summer, and consequently we don't get very many orders that way. But

490

people will be able to go to our website in the future; it will look just the way it has always looked except they'll be able to go and search and get books the same way that they would on Amazon, using the MUZE database, which has been a pretty good database.

And then there's the ability for stores to customize with their own pick lists and best-seller lists, and they can put their events list up and that sort of thing. All of this won't happen immediately, but over time there's going to be a way for stores to build their own affiliates program like Amazon has. And I think there will be some value in that, because we know people who tell us, "We'd rather do business with you than with somebody else." Beyond that, one could give somebody some value in return for directing people from their website. If it's some other kind of company, or if it's a therapist who has a list of books and says, "Order this book by punching here," and they come over and order it from our website, I think we'll be able to build those programs locally and at least stem some of that erosion of sales.

It's hard for us to measure it here. You know, the Seattle area has such a high-tech base; I continue to hear that an awful lot of the books that are ordered, people are ordering when they're at work, from the computer at their desk, that sort of thing. In an environment like Seattle, I can't help but believe that there's a lot of business going over to Amazon. I mean they're getting it somewhere, obviously. And readership hasn't grown, so it's dividing up this pie in some different way.

I'm sure that most readers in this country are not reading for the aesthetics or for pleasure; they're reading for information. And if that's the case, then they probably would go directly to Amazon or BarnesandNoble.com, or whoever.

DR: I don't know if the numbers are still true, but it wasn't all that long ago when the number one category of books being sold on Amazon was computer books.

CR: It's changed. That was their first year. They were not doing the millions and millions and millions of dollars of business that they are today.

Village Books sells—
CR: We're pretty much a general bookstore. You know, we feel

we have some strengths. We've always talked about better contemporary fiction. I don't even know how to say it exactly, because it's not necessarily all—it wouldn't all be classified literary fiction, by any means. But we have a good market for well-written contemporary fiction. So the shift into trade books has probably played pretty well for our store. The mass market, grocery-store sort of book doesn't sell all that well for us. There are exceptions. We sell mysteries really well.

I think mass market paperbacks are taking a beating nationally.
CR: Yeah, they are taking a beating, even in the grocery stores.

But trade paperback sales are going up. I would say that the population is getting older and the print is larger and there's more leading between the lines in trade paperbacks. [All three laugh.]
DR: Oh, yeah. Oh, yeah.
CR: I'm sure that's a factor.
DR: And just the ease of handling. You know, when you try to read a mass market book—people share books, and mass markets don't share well. They don't stand up to lots of readings.

Do you or did either of you have literary ambitions?
DR: I don't.
CR: No. I enjoy writing. Well, I haven't really toyed all that much with writing something with, you know, a literary ambition. I write for our store magazine and things here at the store, and there are parts of that that I enjoy doing. I don't really envision myself writing a book. I don't think I have a novel in me, for instance. If you're talking about things I've thought about, I got involved in doing some family history and stumbled across a pretty interesting story about a great great uncle who was murdered. And I thought, you know, this would be an interesting thing to write down, but more like a family history. And then occasionally some books—nonfiction books—that would be interesting to put together. Guide books to the local area. Whatever. I wouldn't describe it as literary ambition at all.

Do you both read?
CR: Quite a bit. Dee more than I do because, for one thing,

she's a faster reader. She goes through probably, oh, I bet you go through three times as many books in a year as I do. We read fairly widely. Dee reads a lot of—

DR: I read a lot more fiction. Mysteries. You probably read more nonfiction than I do.

CR: Yeah, but not more nonfiction than I read fiction.

DR: It's kind of nice to have a job where you can read and have a good excuse for it.

CR: It's research.

DR: Yeah, I have to do this for my job.

CR: Right. We do belong—well, let's see, since '94, we've belonged to a book discussion group that's three other couples and ourselves. Actually got into it in sort of an interesting way, because Dee and I talk to book groups all the time, recommend books to them and talk to them about ways to get book groups started and that sort of thing. And three couples were starting this book discussion group and invited us to talk to them about books and so forth, and in that first year they read a lot of the books we recommended and came back a second year to talk to us and happened to mention in passing that they were interested in adding a fourth couple to the group. And we said, "Well, you don't want to talk about it with us; we might be interested if you're interested in having us join the group." Of course, they were a little intimidated, thinking that booksellers would have all the literary insights, and, of course, over time they found out we don't. Their ideas about these books are just as good as our ideas about the books. But it's been interesting because—one of the values we see in the group is we read some things that none of us would probably pick up on our own.

How do you decide what books you want to read?
CR: Concensus in our group.

I mean personally.
CR: Gee, that's hard. Boy. There're certain authors, of course. People who wrote something that we really liked, or several things, so that we will probably always read the books that they bring out. Other times it can be having met somebody and heard them talk or heard them read, or having a recommendation from another bookseller sometimes,

or one of our customers.

DR: One of our customers, yeah. Or sometimes I see a book up at the register so many times, I think, "I need to take a look at this." I read a lot of recommendations from customers, and other staff members.

CR: Reading copies that come through the store. We get a lot of them, but when we go through the stacks certain ones, the title or something about it, will be catchy, and we'll look at the information. So it's really a variety of things.

What you're describing mostly is varieties of word of mouth.

CR: Exactly. Yeah. You know, Carl Lennertz got famous for all of the recommendations he was making when he was at Random House. He used to send out newsletters to bookstores and he would recommend—of course, his job was marketing Random House books, but in his newsletter there were always two or three titles that were somebody else's books [about which] he said, "It's one of the greatest books I've ever read; you really need to read this book."

He was in the marketing department at Random House for eighteen years, and then he became the associate publisher of Little, Brown. And then after Little, Brown went through all of their stuff with Warner over the last year, or less, actually, Carl just walked away from Little, Brown. He appeared one day and all of the trade stuff that he—he just tendered his resignation and left. Everybody wondered what would happen to him. Well, last week, I guess it was, just over a week ago, ABA announced that he's coming on board to be the marketing person for Booksense. We're excited, because Carl's great. He's really, really good in book marketing. But one of the things he did is he built such credibility out there that when he talked about certain books that were Random House books, you were more inclined to trust his judgement because he was also telling you about, you know, Harper's books. It's sort of the notion, too, that if you get in the habit of promoting good books, you sell more books. He's gotten a reputation over the years; he's referred to, within the business, as Mr. Bookseller. *Publishers Weekly* has referred to him that way, and I think he actually started out as a bookseller, but he's been in sales and marketing for years.

What kind of work did your parents do?

494

DR: My dad was a printer. He started out as a newspaper editor in a little town in Iowa, then went to work for someone else doing fine-quality printing.

At Bumbershoot one year, there was a woman and her adult daughter standing at my table. Suddenly the younger woman passed out. And the mother didn't seem that concerned. I mean she was helping her regain consciousness and all, but she didn't seem that concerned. And I said, "Is there anything I can do? What's going on?" And she said, "Oh, that's okay. Her father was a printer." Does that have any meaning for you? [The Robinsons break out laughing.]

CR: Oh, my God.

It made sense to her. It doesn't mean anything to you, huh?

DR [still laughing]: No. What a reaction!

CR: What a great line.

She meant it. It was a—

DR: That's the point—yeah.

CR: That's funny.

DR: I mean I certainly do recognize the smell of ink. It has lots of memories. Most of mine are pleasant; maybe hers aren't.

CR: Maybe they are. I mean maybe she swooned. [All three of us laugh again.] Maybe it was a swoon, not a— Actually, I have roots in the newspaper business also, but it goes back to my grandfather on my father's side. He was a newspaper person and a printer also. And then my dad was a cement finisher in construction for years. My mom, during my growing-up years, took care of us kids. There were four of us. But by the time I was in junior high, she worked outside the home doing a variety of things. I used to tell my friends in college she was a call girl; she was a telephone operator. [Laughs.] She did that for several years, and then they put in the automated exchanges. But she was a telephone operator when they still plugged the things on the board. My folks were both readers, as was your dad particularly, but both my dad and mom—

DR: My mom, in later years, became a full-time reader.

CR: Well, yeah.

DR: She lost her sight. She spent most of her time listening to books on tape.

CR: Of our four parents, my mom is the only one still living. Dee's mom just passed away this year at ninety, and her dad's been gone for several years. My dad's been gone for a lot of years now. But my mom is still a reader. I guess that's an encouragement for reading. And you read before you went to school.

DR: Yeah. Well, my brother, who was older, could read and I didn't think that was fair that he knew how to read and I didn't, so I made somebody teach me, I don't know who.

Did you grow up with a love for books, or did that—?
DR: Yeah, I did. Yeah.

CR: Yeah, I think an appreciation of—I remember we used the library a lot. I grew up in a small town where there wasn't a bookstore. I don't remember buying—I remember getting books as gifts for Christmas and birthdays and so forth, most often from family that didn't live right there. There was not a bookstore. My first encounter with a bookstore was really when I was in college.

Pearl Kilbride [of Ruminator Books; see interview, this volume] told me—she grew up in North Dakota—there was a mobile library that would come occasionally, and there was a drugstore. Those were the only two places to get books until she went to college in Oregon.

DR: There was a bookstore in my town when I was in high school; I don't think it was open before that. But I remember going in there—it must have been there when I was in junior high too, because it was right down the street from the junior high and I remember going in, and it was a little place, but it had more books per square foot than I've ever seen in any other bookstore. It was amazing. I used to marvel at how they squeezed books into every little nook and cranny.

We went to the library every week. We brought a stack of books home and the next week we brought them back and got another stack.

There was a book that came out in the '70s called Book Traveler. *It was published first in the* New Yorker *and then by Dodd, Mead. It was about George Scheer, a book rep in the Southeast—*
DR: Oh.

CR: I know that name.

He died a year, maybe two years ago.
CR: Yeah.

Bliven, the author, just traveled with him through parts of the southeastern United States, and described what he did, the things he said. This was in the early '70s; there weren't the superstores like there are now, but there was the beginning of the mall stores. Bliven figured out—a book rep goes to a store and there are things he does other than rep his books. Especially if it's a small store, he might even work the cash register. He may spend three hours in the store, and then he's got a certain number of books to show to the buyer. And Bliven figured out that Scheer spent approximately twenty-six seconds repping each book. Twenty-six seconds. Does that sound right? I mean do you think that sounds accurate?
CR: Well, yeah. It probably is. When I think about some of the publishers' reps that are commission sales reps who have a number of lines—I mean it's not uncommon for a book rep to be carrying twenty-some lines and twenty-some catalogues of books, and even for a Random House rep to have a dozen lines—different imprints. So that probably is not—particularly if you're figuring the average. I mean there are certainly some books that a rep would spend more time with, tell you more about it and show you more and that sort of thing, but—
DR: There are some who would tell the buyers, "You don't need this."

It was twenty-six seconds per new book. So if it's something to re-stock, I guess—
DR: Right. Right. Yeah.
CR: But that's [i.e., new books] usually the ones they give—
DR: That's the ones they're talking about. But I guess—
CR: Yeah, that sounds within reason.

I talked with Bob Harrison. Do you know him?
CR: Oh, yeah. Yeah.

I interviewed him for the book [see interview, this volume].
DR: Oh, good.

I mentioned this to him. I think he was a little put off by it. He couldn't see how he could spend so little time per book. [Chuck laughs.]

DR: He's the commission rep who has a lot of lines. I'll bet if he stopped and counted—

CR: Obviously, part of the reason any bookseller wants to continue to see a sales rep is the relationship that grows between the two of them. Part of that relates to the books and how the salesperson represents those books, and what you can learn to trust of what that person tells you about books. But part of it has a lot to do with the personal relationship you develop, and the amount of time you spend talking to each other about other things, too. I'll bet if Bob would seriously think about how much time, you know, you're talking about—this book reminds somebody of some story, you know, and somebody tells that story and then you're off to the next book. I'll bet the time literally spent on a book isn't a lot more than that.

So a sales rep comes into your store—let's say he's presenting a line of fiction. How do you decide what you want? He's screening it, obviously, if he knows your store.

CR: Yeah, to some extent he'd probably screen. Well, first of all, we should say we haven't been buyers for some time. Krista buys an awful lot of the books in the store; Mitchell buys some; Paul buys some. We don't buy at all, actually, anymore, except for wholesale reorders. But the way we always did think about it, and I think probably the buyers do too, is we look for—what we think we know, to some extent, is who our customers are and the kinds of things they buy. So I guess we'd be looking for similarities, not necessarily similarity in story, but what it is about this book that would be likely to strike somebody or some people that buy books from our store.

DR: What is the publisher willing to do to reach the types of people who shop here? What kind of promotion?

CR: Will they know about this book, or how will they know about this book? Of course, that's less true with new fiction, I realize. It's not broadly advertised or anything. So I guess, in that regard, you're looking at, okay, who do they say this person writes like? Is there something about the story that seems particularly compelling?

And this information comes to you from the rep?
CR: From the sales rep. To some extent, from the catalogue.

DR: Probably ninety-plus percent of the new books we buy come because of the sales reps' visits to the store.

CR: That's probably true, yeah. To what extent it comes from their pre-screening, I'm not sure—they would probably have made choices. As they're going down the list they would be saying, you know, "This is probably one you could live without," and "This is one you really ought to take a look at." Fiction, and new fiction particularly, has always been the hardest, just knowing that you're taking a gamble. Obviously it's hard to divorce your own interests. I mean if something piques my personal interest, I am likely going to buy it. I'm also thinking that I would probably read the book and have the opportunity to hand-sell the book.

Was Cold Mountain *a good seller for you?*
CR: It was a great seller. Actually, Alaine, who is our events and marketing coordinator, is one of the people nation-wide who really pushed *Cold Mountain*. She read a reading copy of it in June—it came out in the early fall, I think. She read it when it first came out. Absolutely loved it. Chose it at that point as her book of the year. And she reads a lot. So when it came in we had a big display. There was a sign up that she had written about the book. She talked to virtually everybody, talked other people in the store into reading it. I read it, you read it. I don't know, maybe half a dozen people or more, more probably, had read it and hand-sold it to a lot of people. And then, of course, it just kind of snowballed; once it got the reputation out there it sold like crazy. We sold a lot of copies before it hit the best-seller list. I mean a lot of copies.

DR: And he [Charles Frazier, the author] came to the store.

Was the cover of Cold Mountain *that important, do you think?*
CR: I think the cover's important.

DR: The cover's very important. Even though we don't get a

499

chance to face out as many books as we'd like to, even when somebody pulls a book off the shelf—I think covers can sell books. *Cold Mountain* had a wonderful cover. *Snow Falling on Cedars*, I think, had a wonderful cover.

CR: Very evocative of the Northwest. I think that cover helped a lot to sell that book. But there certainly have been exceptions. I mean there have been some books with some pretty bad covers that have sold in spite of that. And there have been some books with great covers that haven't sold. I certainly think a good cover is better to have than a bad cover. It's hard to describe what a good cover is. I mean, in general, it's certainly good design, but—

DR: You know it when you see it.

CR: Yeah.

Looking back, would you rather have gone into some other business?

CR: No.

DR: No.

CR: I can't really think of anything I would rather have done. I really think we've lived a—

DR: It's been a good life.

CR: —charmed life. It's really been a great nineteen years. It's hard to imagine having done anything for that period of time that we would have enjoyed doing more. I can think of a lot of things where we would have had a lot more money. But it's really hard to think of things that we would have enjoyed any more.

Are there any issues that you want to talk about, or that I should have asked about that I'm not aware of, perhaps?

CR: One of the issues that—I remember one of the first people I ever heard raise this issue—it was probably fifteen years ago now—was David Schwartz from the Schwartz bookstores in Milwaukee, and he said, "Where are the young people in the business?" Meaning in the bookselling end of the business. And it's kind of a troubling thought about where independent bookselling is going. On the one hand, there are the competitive reasons why we may or may not survive and make it out there as independents. But then the other issue is who's going to run this business? It seems like we're a group of people all of a certain age. People I know who are running some of the successful independent stores around the country—we all fall into that fifty- to sixty-year-old group, or a lot of us do. Even in families where—if you look at Kepler's in the Bay Area, that's a case where I don't know if there's a next generation. That was passed father to son and, as it stands right now, whether it goes someplace else, I don't know. We don't have heirs, so for us there's a transition issue for the business. Jim Harris at Prairie Lights, I don't think has heirs. David and Pearl [i.e., David Unowsky and Pearl Kilbride of Ruminator Books in St. Paul, Minnesota] don't have children, I don't think. It's not always true that a store passes to the—but you just wonder what is the next—? You know, in all of those cases, we're talking about people who are damn near the same age.

When I was doing Publishing Lives, *the first volume, I noticed the same thing. Most of the publishers I was interviewing were all around the same age. Of the thirty-six people I interviewed, I think only three were under forty years old.[1] I mean there are some younger people going into publishing.*

CR: Right. Right. Scott's Books in Mount Vernon are real good friends of ours. And they have a daughter, Megan, who is in her...late twenties?—mid- to late twenties, I guess—who is very interested in running the store, and, of course, their concern now is whether this is a viable business: Will there be independent bookstores out there? But even if it is a viable business, there is some question about where all the booksellers will come from. If the stores can manage to survive, where is the next generation of booksellers going to come from? I'm not just talking about people who work in stores; I think they're going to be there. There are people who will have the passion. But are there going to be the people who have the passion for books *and* for running a retail operation like this? I don't know.

So that is, really, a question, particularly [considering] the conglomeration of the publishing end and now with the retail end. What's scary is the narrowing of what was once a very diverse marketplace, in terms of where one could buy books. As that narrows, I worry for what will be available. What will be able to be published, you know?

Already there's a tremendous amount that is not available. A year or two ago, because I'd published an author who had come to their attention, I was interviewed by the South China Morning Post, *the English-language Hong Kong newspaper. The reporter mentioned some English authors, and I said, "We don't get them here." And she said, "Why not?" I said, "Because American publishers don't import them because they're afraid there won't be a big enough market for them. If I want to read them, I have to go up to Vancouver, B.C. to buy their books. I'm not going to find them in the United States." Since then I have found one of Timothy Mo's books, remaindered. She—the reporter—was appalled. And then I became appalled too. I hadn't really thought about it, going to another country to buy books that I can't find in my own country, until I said it. What am I missing out on? I don't know.*

DR: I remember Rick Simonson [buyer for Elliott Bay Book Company in Seattle] coming through and stopping at our store once after he'd been up in Vancouver, and he had a shopping bag full of books that he had bought because of that very thing. I mean these were wonderful books that were up there that he couldn't get here.

Well, that's all I have. Thank you. It was fun.
DR: Yeah.
CR: Yeah.

Notes

1. Actually, two American publishers of twenty-nine interviewed, and three Canadian publishers of seven interviewed were under forty. See Gold 1996: 18.

Glossary

ABA: American Booksellers Association. Also refers to the ABA's annual conference and trade show. The trade show was sold to, and is now operated by, BookExpo America.

ALA: American Library Association. Also refers to the ALA's annual conference and trade show.

AWP: Associated Writing Programs.

Backlist: books published in the past, kept in print and available for sale.

BEA: BookExpo America.

Book distributor: handles book sales and fulfillment to bookstores, libraries, and wholesalers. A major distributor represents the publishers with which it contracts exclusively. An important feature distinguishing distributors from wholesalers is the distributors' employing sales representatives to present titles to buyers.

Book wholesaler: fulfills orders as they come in. Responds to demand but does not try to create demand. Does not employ sales representatives, or employs very few.

Bumbershoot: Seattle, Washington's annual arts festival, held over Labor Day weekend.

CETA: Comprehensive Employment and Training Act.

CLMP: Council of Literary Magazines and Presses.

COSMEP: an international association of independent publishers. The acronym is obsolete.

F-and-G's: "folded and gathered" signatures; i.e., unbound books.

501(c)(3): Internal Revenue Service classification for nonprofit presses and some other types of organization. This classification allows a press to receive donations that the donor can deduct from his or her or, in the case of corporations, its income tax.

Front list: newly published books.

Just-in-time printing: the practice of printing a title "just in time" to meet projected buyer demand.

MLA: Modern Language Association.

NEA: National Endowment for the Arts. A federal funding agency.

NYSCA: New York State Council on the Arts. A New York state funding agency.

Pick and pack: "picking" books out of warehouse bins and "packing" them for shipping.

PGW: Publishers Group West. A major book distributor.

PNBA: Pacific Northwest Booksellers Association. Also refers to the PNBA's semi-annual conference and trade show. A regional version of the ABA.

Shelf life: the length of time a book is available to be purchased in a bookstore.

Signature: a printed sheet of paper folded to page size for binding.

Subco: The Subterranean Company. A major book distributor.

WESTAF: Western States Arts Federation. Awards annual literary prizes.

Bibliography

"Access Publishers Network Bankrupt." *ForeWord Magazine* 3, no. 8 (August 2000): 11-15.

Alexander, Jane. 2000. *Command Performance: An Actress in the Theater of Politics*. New York: Public Affairs.

Angel, Karen. 1997. "The Small Presses: Getting in the Door." *Publishers Weekly* November 17: 32-34.

Auletta, Ken. 1997. "The Impossible Business." *The New Yorker* October 6: 50-63.

Barbato, Joseph. 1997. "The Rise and Rise of the Small Press." *Publishers Weekly* July: 39-48.

Beach, Sylvia. 1980. *Shakespeare and Company*. Lincoln, Nebraska: University of Nebraska Press.

Bliven, Bruce, Jr. 1975. *Book Traveler*. New York: Dodd, Mead.

Bodian, Nat. 1996. *The Joy of Publishing*. Fairfield, Iowa: Open Horzons.

Carvajal, Doreen. 1997. "Book Chains' New Role: Soothsayers for Publishers." *New York Times* August 12: A1, C5.

Cerf, Bennett. 1977. *At Random*. New York: Random House.

Coser, Lewis A., Charles Kadushin, and Walter W. Powell. 1985. *Books: The Culture and Commerce of Publishing*. Chicago: University of Chicago Press.

Covert, Colin. 1994. "Graywolf Split Felt in Pack of Small Presses." *Minneapolis Star Tribune*.

Dardis, Tom. 1995. *Firebrand: The Life of Horace Liveright*. New York: Random House.

Davis, Scott. 1995a. *The Soul of Our Culture*. Seattle: Cune Press.

—. 1995b. *A Writer Called "X"*. Seattle: Cune Press.

Dennison, Sally. 1984. *(Alternative) Literary Publishing: Five Modern Histories*. Iowa City, Iowa: University of Iowa Press.

Ehrenfeld, Tom. 1995. "The New and Improved American Small Business." *Inc.* January: 34-45.

Epstein, Jason. 2001. *Book Business: Publishing Past Present and Future*. New York: W.W. Norton & Company.

Felson, Leonard. 1995. "Where the Poetry's to be Doubly Enjoyed." *New York Times* Connecticut Weekly Section August 27.

Ford, Hugh. 1980. *Published in Paris: American and British Writers,*

Printers, and Publishers in Paris, 1920-1939. Yonkers, New York: Pushcart Press.

Gold, Jerome. 1995. "Final Thoughts on a Finished Book." *Writers Northwest* 10, no. 3 (Fall): 11.

—. 1996. *Publishing Lives: Interviews with Independent Book Publishers in the Pacific Northwest and British Columbia.* Seattle: Black Heron Press.

—. 1997. "A Hunger for Good Writing." *Poets & Writers Magazine* 25, no. 5 (September/October): 7-8.

—. 1998. "My First Frankfurt." *CunePressMagazine.* www.cunepress.com.

Gontarski, S.E. 1995. Introduction to *Eleuthéria*, by Samuel Beckett. New York: Foxrock.

Guinn, Jeff. 1997. "Writing is on the Wall: Book Publishers Scrambling." *Fort Worth Star-Telegram* August 13: E1, E3.

Henderson, Bill, ed. 1987. *The Publish-It-Yourself Handbook: Literary Tradition and How-To*, 3rd edition. Wainscott, New York: Pushcart Press.

Howell, Kevin. 2000. "Hungry Mind Becomes Ruminator Books." *Publishers Weekly* January 31.

Hunt, Richard. 2000. "Commission Impossible." *Publishers Weekly* March 27: 34-37.

Kinsella, Bridget. 2000a. "PGI: Primed for the Future." *Publishers Weekly* February 28.

—. 2000b. "Alone or in Numbers?" *Publishers Weekly* March 27: 41-45.

Kruchkow, Diane and Curt Johnson, eds. 1986. *Green Isle in the Sea: An Informal History of the Alternative Press, 1960-85.* Highland Park, Illinois: December Press.

Lander, Tim. No date. "Self Publishing and the Culture of Poetry." Self-published pamphlet.

Lapham, Lewis H. 2000. "Notebook: School bells." *Harper's Magazine* 301, no. 1803 (August): 7-9.

Marbrook, Del. 1997. "Baltimore: City of Writers." *Potomac Review* 4, no. 1 (Winter): 4-21.

Menteer, Tamara. 1996. *Judith Roche.* Seattle: Black Heron Press.

Miller, Mark Crispin. 1997. "The Crushing Power of Big Publishing." *The Nation* March 17: 11-18.

Milliot, Jim. 1998. "Small Publishers, Big Business." *Publishers Weekly* November 23: 22-25.

506

Moylan, Michele and Lane Stiles, eds. 1997. *Reading Books: Essays on the Material Text and Literature in America.* Amherst: University of Massachusetts Press.

Oakes, John. 1990a. "Barney Rosset and the Art of Combat Publishing: An Interview." *Review of Contemporary Fiction* (Fall): 20-57.

—. 1990b. "The Last Days of Grove." *Review of Contemporary Fiction* (Fall): 175-178.

Peabody, Richard, comp. 1983. *Mavericks: Nine Independent Publishers.* Washington, D.C.: The Paycock Press.

Quinn, Judy. 1997. "UPG Has Cruise, Rosset, More." *Publishers Weekly* May 26: 25.

Reid, Calvin. 1997a. "Barricade, Blue Moon File for Bankruptcy." *Publishers Weekly* October 10: 11

—. 1997b. "Barricade, Blue Moon Titles Frozen by Court Order." *Publishers Weekly* October 13: 12.

—. 1998a. "PGW Acquires Blue Moon; Sets up Barney Rosset at Avalon." *Publishers Weekly* March 16: 11.

—. 1998b. "Rosset Memoir Is on Way." *Publishers Weekly* March 16: 11.

—. 2000. "Avalon, *The Nation* to Launch Nation Books." *Publishers Weekly* March 27: 14.

Schiffrin, André. 2000. *The Business of Books: How International Conglomerates Took Over Publishing and Changed the Way We Read.* New York: Verso.

Shepard, Martin. 1995. "What Defines Success?" *Publishers Weekly* December 18: 16-17.

Spahr, Juliana. 2000. "Metromania: Poetry, Academy, and Anarchy." *Poets & Writers Magazine* 28, no.6 (November/December): 21-25.

Stein, Sol. 1999. "Vital Signs: Midlist and Other Fictions of Publishing." *Poets & Writers Magazine* 27, no. 6 (November/December): 47-51.

Tebbel, John. 1972, 1975, 1978, 1981. *A History of Book Publishing in the United States.* Volumes 1-4. New York: R.R. Bowker.

—. 1987. *Between Covers.* New York: Oxford University Press.

Tillman, Lynne. 1999. *Bookstore: The Life and Times of Jeannette Watson and Books & Co.* New York: Harcourt Brace & Company.

Truesdale, C.W. No date. "New Rivers Press: The New York Years."

Unpublished manuscript.

Whiteside, Thomas. 1981. *The Blockbuster Complex: Conglomerates, Show Business, and Book Publishing*. Middletown, Connecticut: Wesleyan University Press.

Whouley, Kate, ed., with Linda Miller and Rosemary Hawkins. 1996. *Manual on Bookselling: Practical Advice for the Bookstore Professional*. 5th edition. Tarrytown, New York: American Booksellers Association.

Wilhelm, Greg. 1999. "Who is Answering to Readers?" *ForeWord* 2, no. 11 (November): 19.

Wolff, Geoffrey. 1977. *Black Sun: The Brief Transit and Violent Eclipse of Harry Crosby*. New York: Vintage Books.

Wolff, Kurt. 1991. *Kurt Wolff: A Portrait in Essays and Letters*. Chicago: University of Chicago Press.

Index

513

515